My Jerusalem

My Jerusalem

ESSAYS, REMINISCENCES, AND POEMS

edited by Salma Khadra Jayyusi
and Zafar Ishaq Ansari

OLIVE
BRANCH
PRESS

An imprint of Interlink Publishing Group, Inc.
www.interlinkbooks.com

This book is dedicated to Reverend Dr. Michael Prior (1942–2004)

First published in 2005 by

Olive Branch Press
An imprint of Interlink Publishing Group, Inc.
46 Crosby Street, Northampton, Massachusetts 01060
www.interlinkbooks.com

Library of Congress Cataloging-in-Publication Data

My Jerusalem / [compiled by] Salma Khadra Jayyusi—1st American.
p. cm.
Includes bibliographic references.
ISBN 1-56656-549-9
1. Jerusalem—History. 2. Jerusalem—Description and travel.
3. Jerusalem—Ethnic relations. 4. Palestinan Arabs—Jerusalem—History. 5. Arab-Israeli
conflict. 6. Jerusalem in the Bible.
I. Jayyusi, Salma Khadra.
DS109.9.M98 2005
956.94'42—dc22   2005013703

This book is published with the cooperation of PROTA (the Project of Translation from
Arabic); director: Salma Khadra Jayyusi, Cambridge, MA, USA

Printed and bound in Canada by Webcom

To request our complete 40-page full-color catalog, please call us toll
free at **1-800-238-LINK**, visit our website at **www.interlinkbooks.com**
or send us an e-mail: **info@interlinkbooks.com**

CONTENTS

The Classical Scene

Voices of Jerusalem

ACKNOWLEDGMENTS

This large book has been several years in the making, and it was only possible to bring it out at all because a number of factors combined to facilitate its preparation. There was, in the first place, a valiant readiness, on the part of a small number of people, to sponsor the work. I must, in this respect, thank al-Sayyid al-Ustadh Abd al-Aziz Saud al-Babitain for his spontaneous gift to this project in 1997. Mr. Babitain is founder and vigilant propagator of the Kuwaiti-centered Babitain Prize for Poetry, and at the same time a true lover of Arabic literature who has demonstrated, through his pan-Arab literary policy, the indivisibility not just of Arabic culture but of the Arab spirit itself. I owe him many thanks. Gratitude is also due to Mrs. Suad Husseini al-Jufali, a woman of great vision and patriotism, whose Palestinian loyalties have merged with her adopted (through marriage) Saudi loyalties with grace and aplomb. She is the founder and director of a large center for developmentally challenged children in Jeddah and is simultaneously a supporter of numerous Palestinian projects in Jerusalem and elsewhere, while taking care at the same time to strengthen cultural ties with international organizations. Profound thanks go to four other patriots, Dr. Salman Abbasi, Dr. Nabil Qaddumi, Dr. Riyadh Sadiq, and Dr. Marwan al-Sa'ih, Palestinian businessmen based in the Gulf area at the time in question. Their sincere involvement in their country's plight, and their keen interest in disseminating knowledge on the subject, has been exemplary. Their gift to this project, no less generous than the others mentioned, has enabled us to broaden the scope of the work, introducing into it new feature's that have the effect, I hope, of making it more attractive and less gloomy than the subject itself would normally dictate. For to speak of Jerusalem is to speak of constant anxiety and pain, of a deep feeling of loss and anger, of unspeakable distress and alienation from a world order that closes its eyes to a persistent act of vandalism and usurpation, visited on an innocent people through no fault of its own. A time will come—I have no doubts on this score—when the colossal human tragedy now being enacted before an indifferent world will be utterly plain to new generations, and I hope that this book, in which we have striven to mitigate loudly voiced anger with images of authentic human experience, of the quiet suffering of individuals in the face of destitution and banishment, of the artistic reaction to the challenge of evil, will be one source of knowledge.

Many thanks are due to the eminent scholars who have written for this book, thereby demonstrating that a great cause like the Palestinian can truly live only through cumulative cooperation on the part of an international body of lovers of justice and true interpreters of data, events, and facts. Through such writing as this, the world is given an example of courage, integrity, and objective observation that has not, unfortunately, always been in evidence among some other writers when dealing with Palestinian history and the history of Jerusalem.

My affectionate thanks go also to the poets who sent me their poems for this book, and to the many writers of personal accounts, mostly provided on request and with the greatest love and enthusiasm. Profound thanks, too, must go to our editor for style, Christopher Tingley, who has once more used his linguistic alchemy to meet the strict demands of the English language and to produce meticulous results in this area.

—Salma Khadra Jayyusi
Director, East–West Nexus, PROTA

FOREWORD

Jerusalem's significance is self-evident, borne out by the fact that it is held sacred by the adherents of three major religions of the world: Judaism, Christianity, and Islam.

No city other than Jerusalem claims the distinction of having the footprints of so many of God's Prophets and Messengers who, from its hallowed soil, summoned people to worship and obey God and pursue righteousness. It was here that Abraham gave the stirring call to serve the One True God and to hold fast to the universal moral code prescribed by Him. It was here that David and Solomon harnessed their efforts to direct people to a life of piety and righteousness and sought to establish an order that would ensure the ascendancy of rectitude and justice in human affairs. It was here that John the Baptist exhorted people to give up their sinful ways and repent sincerely to God. It was also here that Jesus taught men to love both God and God's creatures; true religious life, he stressed, called for earnestness of purpose and sincere commitment to pursue the substance of righteousness and benevolence and not merely its form. And finally, Jerusalem became the transit point in the Prophet Muhammad's journey to the vast expanse of the Heavens.

For anyone even to visit this city is a spiritually enriching experience: In Jerusalem one breathes in an air of serene holiness and is ever reminded of God's sheer reality and His closeness to His creatures.

Jerusalem's history and civilization, especially since the advent of the Prophet Muhammad (peace be on him), is a rich and challenging subject for study and research. The book before you is an attempt to bring together, within the span of a few hundred pages, the work of a select group of writers and scholars on Jerusalem.

There are, however, several reasons that bestow a unique significance on this enterprise. For Jerusalem is not just another city among a host of Arab and Muslim cities of historic fame. There is no city besides Makkah and Madinah that the Muslims cherish as much and for which they have the same degree of devotional reverence as Jerusalem.

Contrary to what might be presumed, Muslims do not believe that Islam was "born" in the 7th century CE or that Muhammad (peace be on him) was its "founder." Instead, they believe that Islam began with the very emergence of humanity on earth. Islam's distinctive characteristic is not its exclusive affirmation of the Message of Muhammad (peace be on him); it is rather its insistence on the affirmation of the Message of all the Prophets and Messengers of God—in fact, Muslims make no distinction between them (Qur'an 2: 295). For, according to the Islamic view of things, all of them brought a Message from God that, in its essentials, was the same; God "sent down upon you [i.e., Muhammad] the Book with the truth, confirming what was before it, and He sent down the Torah and the Gospel aforetime as a guidance to people..." (Qur'an 3:3–4). Likewise, the Qur'an does not look upon the previous scriptures as its rivals, but as its worthy precursors. Thus Muhammad's prophethood is perceived by Muslims as an extension of the prophethood of the earlier Prophets and Messengers of God.

Abraham and Jacob and Moses and Jesus, are not, therefore, primarily considered as the Prophets of Jews and Christians whom Muslims also revere in some secondary sense. On the contrary, they are their own revered Prophets. To illustrate: when a Muslim reads the Qur'anic account of the conflict between Moses and Pharaoh, he does not look upon it as a conflict between the Jews led by Moses and the Copts led by Pharaoh. He rather looks upon that conflict as one between Islam and disbelief; between Muslims and unbelievers. Unless one grasps this characteristic concept of Islam, one will be unable to appreciate Islam's essential catholicity, its inclusive attitude, and its spiritual kinship with the "People of the Book."

The fact that a whole succession of Prophets carried out their mission in Jerusalem, and that the city remained the foremost center and radiating point of monotheism, endears it to Muslims. Islam's jealous maintenance of the Jerusalem connection reflects its strong sense of being rooted in the long tradition of Revelation and Prophethood in history.

Jerusalem became a part of the Islamic state in 15/638. This happened during the first wave of Islamic expansion, which began during the last part of Abu Bakr's caliphate (11–13/632–634), but assumed extraordinary momentum during the caliphate of 'Umar (13–23/634–644). Jerusalem's capitulation took place when, as the historical record shows, the Caliph 'Umar himself came to Jerusalem to preside over the event. On that occasion, 'Umar made a Covenant with the people of Jerusalem that mirrors the early Muslims' vision of how the non-Muslims who are willing to live in the Domain of Islam should be treated.[1] The text of the covenant, which has been preserved by history, is not substantially different from the agreements made by the Muslims with the other cities such as Damascus that were conquered around the same period. In all these agreements the non-Muslims were assured security of their lives and properties, and above all, the right to freely profess and practice their faith.[2] If anything, the Covenant of Jerusalem is even more emphatic in spelling out these assurances. The Covenant does not simply reflect an attitude of "tolerance" towards non-Muslims; it is deeply imbued with goodwill, benevolence, and magnanimity towards them. It gives due recognition to their human dignity and to the right of all human beings, regardless of their religious affinities, to live in peace and honor and according to the requirements of their religious faith.

Since Jerusalem's conquest, the city has mostly been administered by Muslims. Given Man's imperfection, Muslims have no immunity from occasional lapses, from failures to live up to the ideals laid down by their religion and to rise to the high standards set by their forefathers. In treating the non-Muslims living in Pax Islamica, however, their overall record is fairly good. This holds true also of their performance in Jerusalem and the Holy Land, despite the periods of turbulence and upheaval, especially during the Crusades, through which the Holy Land passed. All in all, under the aegis of Muslim rule, Jews and Christians had security of life and property, enjoyed religious freedom, and lived with dignity. This was thanks to the early example of the Prophet (peace be on him) and the principles enshrined in the Covenant of 'Umar, which, in the course of time, led to the development in Muslim countries of an institutional framework that provided the non-Muslim communities religious freedom as well as a fair degree of internal autonomy. In sum, the dominant climate of opinion and the Muslim administrative practices encouraged an acceptance of religio-cultural diversity. Also, amity and good neighborliness generally obtained in the relations among the different religious communities. The Holy Land witnessed all this no less than other parts of the Muslim world.

Today Jerusalem, this citadel of peace and devotion to God, is on fire, quite literally. Flushed by a sense of unlimited power stemming from the West's unconditional support, Israel's attitude over the years has become increasingly provocative and belligerent. To the utter disappointment of the moderate people of the world, the Israelis, as an act of enhanced provocation as well as blind faith in the ability of power to solve all problems, have at the dawn of the new century and millenium elected a leadership with a track record of carnage and crimes against humanity. Thanks to this, Israel is set on a course that will presumably lead to ever more bloodshed, suffering, and agony for a period of time known only to God.

Against this dismal background, we are coming forth with this special collection on Jerusalem, holding out an olive branch to all despite the gloom of the current circumstance. We are trying to hold aloft Jerusalem's torch with the insistence that piety, justice, benevolence, compassion, and concern for all humanity should prevail in the Holy Land.

—Zafar Ishaq Ansari

INTRODUCTION

Salma Khaḍra Jayyusi

The situation in present-day Jerusalem needs to be made clear not only to those directly concerned with the holy city's plight at this time, but to every person of conscience: Muslim, Christian, Jew, and others. While the issue of Jerusalem does indeed reach to the core of the three monotheistic religions, and is therefore an unavoidably religious issue, it also involves a major human confrontation, one created not by facts of history but by an insistence on an exclusive possession. This is not to say that a people exposed, as the Jews have been, to centuries of oppression and humiliation, to lengthy episodes of exclusion, and periodic gross usurpation of rights and life, should not dream of a place able to afford them power and dignity. No person of conscience can or should forget for a moment the long-term predicament that colored Jewish life through so many centuries. But the answer to this cannot and should not be sought through an imbalance of perception, a shortness of perspective, an utter lack of sensitivity towards other, innocent people, and a total deafness to human rights and historical logic.

The story of contemporary Jerusalem is the story of major dispossession; it represents a serious historical uprooting, the obliteration of an intimate relationship that had lasted for so long and testified to so much authentic human experience. The worst aspects of this lie hidden in the folds of future history. What is happening in Jerusalem now, through sheer military force, will never stand the test of time. As in all its past experiences, Jerusalem—citadel of the three monotheistic religions—will be born once more and will re-assume its identity. This is where the responsibility for future generations lies. The aggression—conducted with much haughty misconception of human nature, of the cycles of strength and weakness in nations, of the fatigue that will eventually afflict the powerful—gives neither present nor future generations of newcomers on the scene a freehold covenant. This city can have no exclusivity. It is a place hallowed by so many, desired by so many, loved and honored by so many, bound to countless millions by centuries of spiritual affinity and authentic history.

This book is devoted to a description, in so far as space allows, of Jerusalem, past and present. I have arranged the various entries— papers, essays, personal narratives, and poems—into three major sections, devoting the first, for its immediacy and crucial importance, to the contemporary scene. The second section is on the classical scene, that long history of Jerusalem, which still holds its crucial memories carved in the city's present signature. Probably no other city on earth clings to its long past history, which it constantly evokes and holds as proof of its modern identity, as does Jerusalem. The third section is devoted to selections of creative expressions about the city, its exclusive place in people's hearts and its contemporary, unrelenting plight. The poets represented here have either lived in Jerusalem, or have felt the injustice of the planned usurpation of the holy city and been inspired to express their feelings in poetry. Both write with love and sorrow, and sometimes with anger. There are also personal accounts of the individual experience of Jerusalemites. The writers speak of Jerusalem's modern relationship with its indigenous people, and the way the latter have either been forced to leave during or immediately after one of the bloody conflicts that the city has suffered, or are forced to leave it now by present-day Israeli contrivance. These accounts are an impassioned expression of the longing of Jerusalem's Arab people and the memories they hold even in their forced exile.

In the first section, on contemporary Jerusalem, I wanted the reader to be able to gaze on what is happening to Jerusalem now, the plight is suffering as it undergoes gradual attrition in its physical aspects, and, step by step, loses its identity. It reflects how Jerusalem, through a clever but obvious design that turns itself, in self-defensive delusion, into law, is being gradually deprived of its indigenous citizens. These laws, in fact, tear at the roots of the city, at its 2,000-year-old genealogies, at its natural rights as a city inhabited by civilians who had inherited it from so many generations of a population that built and rebuilt it, century after century. These laws are now implemented against a helpless original population. Some of the entries have described, dramatically, this willful, heart-rending dispossession, the sly programmed theft that hides behind a law of its own creation. Anthony Coon provides an accurate study of the transformation of the holy city. Yasser al-Rajjal, an engineering specialist on Jerusalem, has noted in objective detail the assault on Jerusalem's architectural heritage over recent decades, and the serious disturbance of its skyline by the massive high-rise apartment buildings erected for Jewish settlers from abroad. Bayan Nuweihet al-Hut gives a concise overview of Jerusalem's history in modern times, concentrating on modern events—over the course, that is, of the 20th century—that have contrived to make Jerusalem the primary issue in the intricate and highly painful political history of modern Palestine.

On the question of law, we have three narratives. Adnan al-Sayyid Husain, a specialist on the subject, gives a description of the fate of the city in Arab–Israeli negotiations, negotiations always tilting against its Arab identity; Muhammad al-Farra, formerly Jordan's representative to the UN, gives an eye-witness report of what went on in the United Nations regarding Jerusalem. The third piece, by Judge Eugene Cotran, reflects the legal disaster into which Jerusalem has sunk vis-à-vis international law. Michael Prior's paper could belong equally to the contemporary and to the classical sections. I have constantly wondered how the Christian world has failed to see how the Judaization of Jerusalem means the cleansing not just of its Muslim but also of its Christian population—both indigenous to the city and both accustomed to coexistence, side by side, over centuries. The Christians are the one religious entity to have lived almost constantly in the city. I was very pleased when the late Father Prior agreed to concentrate on the Christian aspect of Jerusalem, on which he was a foremost authority. His paper examines the New Testament and establishes the Christian attachment to the city within the wider context of religious attachment to certain specific places. Taking a most interesting approach, Dr. Prior describes the attitude of the Crusaders, which was a remarkable mixture of pious devotion to the holy places together with barbarism and a spirit of overbearing, bellicose colonialism. Spanning the centuries from medieval to modern times, Dr. Prior speaks of the Christian pilgrimage to the Holy Land. In dealing with modern times, he describes how the Christian Church had to deal with Zionist aspirations to establish a Jewish state around Zion.

The second section of the book deals with ancient and medieval Jerusalem. The relationship of the city to the three monotheistic religions is here described. I would like to dwell more on this section, because of the general confusion about Jerusalem's multiple identity and the disproportionate knowledge of basic facts about its history. The chapter on Christians in pre-modern times considers aspects of the historical Jewish connection with Jerusalem, and, most importantly, describes the peaceful entry into the city, in 637 CE, of the Muslim army. The city bore the name Aelia Capitolina at the time— or Ilya' as the Muslims by then called it—given it by the emperor Hadrian (Aelia being part of his family name). The paper here reflects the civilized essence of the Islamic spirit and way of life, still unappreciated by the modern world: its humanity, together with a tolerance conspicuously absent in so many other faiths and cultures towards those of a different faith—and all this made manifest so early in the history of human rights in the world. The impeccable justice of 'Umar ibn al-Khattab, the second Orthodox Caliph (d. 644 CE), is here demonstrated in the famous covenant (*al-'uhdah al-'Umariyyah*) that he gave to the Christians of Ilya', granting them full freedom of worship. This is well exemplifed in the chapter written by Abd al-Fattah al-Awaisi on the covenant. It is also interesting to read of the alienation of Orthodox Arab Christians from the Latin Crusaders, and of the help they gave to Saladin in his re-conquest of the city in 1187 CE. There were, indeed, during the long periods of Islamic control in Jerusalem instances of intolerance, when prejudices intrinsic to uncultivated individuals came into play; but this was always in violation of the protective shield provided by genuine Islam for "the People of the Book," beginning with 'Umar ibn al-Khattab in the first half of the 7th century CE and reinforced by many other rulers, including the great Saladin himself.

The piece by Thomas Thompson is a revelation of a system of thought that, harking back to ancient times, now tries to subjugate a modern world to an impossible, nightmarish fantasy. It lays bare an ancient scene of religious concepts whose affinities are shared by the religions, including Judaism, that sprang up in the ancient Middle East from Mesopotamia, to Palestine, to Egypt. It also demonstrates the presence of a pervasive concept within ancient Near Eastern political thought in many texts from at least the 15th century BCE: The divine is the sole creator of the world and the king, who is given a lofty place and function, is his son. Through the king's rule, the whole of creation consolidates its goal in a universal and everlasting happiness. The figure of David in the Psalms is a Hebrew version of the role of the king in the ancient Near Eastern mythology. The covenant of the king with God includes, among other notions, holy war, banishment and deportation, and the destruction of peoples who do not accept that God as their king. The intrinsic association of the use of military force to destroy the powers of evil and to create eternal peace for the nation is the key thematic element of royal ideology throughout ancient literature. In the Bible, these tropes are reiterated in literary terms and are centered on the relationship of "royal ideology of holy war and the creation of an eternal peace." This is the role that Jerusalem plays in Biblical tradition. This essay is essential for an understanding of the mentality of the Jewish settlers in present-day Palestine, and explains to a great degree the acquiescence of the West, which believes in the "misread" Biblical traditions, leading to the deportation and uprooting of the indigenous population of Palestine and the attempt to destroy those who remain. For, according to the adopted Biblical traditions, these people are the forces of chaos, which the king must hold in chains in order to usher in bliss and happiness for his people. It is wrath and destruction of the other that will prepare for a transcendent happy time of peace with God. The goal of military campaign is to "bind and chain" the enemy to his new role as client, answering to a new patron. "For those who resist the claims of patronage there are corresponding curses," and deportation of the rebellious is a typical aspect of the divine patron's control over destiny.

In the Hebrew Bible, Jewish history presents Jerusalem's superiority as a capital of Israel in the 10th century BCE, as a capital of the Davidic-Solomonic Empire. However this was very short-lived, and it was only at the transformation of the kingdom of historical Israel (bit Humri) into an Assyriac province after the Assyrian conquest of Samaria in 722 BCE that Jerusalem became the only religious and political capital of the remaining population of what was believed to have been originally twelve tribes, the sons of Jacob. The fall of Samaria is put in contrast to the salvation of Jerusalem at another Assyrian campaign, that of Sennacherib's against Judah and Jerusalem in 701 BCE. In the Biblical discourse, Jerusalem was spared because of its faithfulness, its loyalty to a true patron, god Yahweh. It is this salvation that served as a foundation myth for the Biblical Zion ideology's election of Jerusalem as the true place for Yahweh's dwelling. Anchored in history, but interpreted theologically, the Hebrew Bible offers its own version of a failed revolt. This has been admirably shown in Ingrid Hjelm's meticulously researched paper.

André Raymond's historical account of the links between Jerusalem, the Arabs, and Islam combines balanced overview with original quotations, judiciously selected and spanning the whole period, that bring these links vibrantly to life.

Keith Whitelam discusses the much advertised recent finding of an archeological inscription, purportedly found by an undeclared person in the Haram al-Sharif grounds. The inscription is described as dating back to the Jewish King Jehoash, who ruled Jerusalem at the end of the 9th century BCE, and it has aroused great commotion and come to be regarded as having "global repercussions effectively vindicating the Jewish claims to the Temple Mount." Whitelam argues the validity of such claims, and reminds us how the past of Jerusalem and ancient Palestine has been constructed and how its present situation is being deliberately crafted.

It is this consistent invention of a different past and present of Jerusalem that has prompted me to seek the personal accounts in this book. These accounts were solicited out of a love of Jerusalem and a dedication to recording its "lived" history, as narrated through the personal testimonies of its authentic children, now mostly uprooted and driven by the winds of politics into exile all over the world. However, they, through their impassioned accounts, give back to Jerusalem its true color and authentic modern history.

Michel Eddeh writes, from his personal viewpoint, an essay dealing with Jewish claims on the Aqsa Mosque and the Haram al-Sharif compound. Mr. Eddeh is the former Lebanese minister of education, who has made a thorough study of Jewish claims to this area, studded with historic Muslim and Christian shrines and revered by Muslims and Christians throughout the world.

The paper by Oleg Grabar speaks of the three systems of religious beliefs Jerusalem has known since the end of the pagan period in the 4th century CE: the Christian, the Muslim, and the Jewish faiths. He points to the fact that throughout history one of the first two has dominated: the Christian one from the time of Constantine (d. 337 CE) to the early 7th century, when the Muslims took over the city, and also during most of the 12th century, when the Crusaders dominated, and the Muslim one for the rest of the time. The infrastructure of the monuments, whether the Holy Sepulcher or the Haram al-Sharif, expressed religious and ideological values characteristic of the predominant system. He observes, however, that the overwhelming picture offered of medieval Jerusalem is that "of separate religious communities" not merging together, but all maintaining "the indivisible uniqueness of each faith and people." This paradox is deeply embedded "in the very fabric of Jerusalem, medieval and probably modern." However, the physical space of the city and the monuments symbolizing its holiness, which are constant features, are partly independent of the faiths to which they belong, and it was they that defined the city more than "the changing mosaic of men and women, of authority and religion." Here lies the "originality" of Jerusalem: the fact that, among all the holy cities of the world which he knows, Jerusalem is a city of holiness for three religions and can even accommodate an unusual variety of sub-denominations of these three faiths. The rest of the paper concentrates on a history of the development of al-Haram al-Sharif as a religious space within Islam in medieval times.

The essay by Ra'if Najm, an engineer and a prominent specialist on Jerusalem's architecture and structural history, vividly depicts the

Old City: its monuments, its streets and quarters, and especially the Aqsa Mosque and the Dome of the Rock.

Ten personal testimonies are provided in the the third section, which is composed of creative expression dedicated to Jerusalem. These accounts are the testimonies of Palestinians, mainly Jerusalemites, for whom Jerusalem remains a living entity and an ever warm and precious presence in their hearts and minds. Personal account literature is both warming to the heart and gripping to the imagination, richly evoking universal experience, here of the forced exile to which so many of the world's victims have been exposed: the experience of homelessness and loss, of seeing, with shock and bitter chagrin, their own rights denied, their own homes usurped by strangers, their own city mutilated and swallowed up.

Many of the poems offered here are written by Arab Americans, for whom the issue of Jerusalem implies not only a human predicament but a contradiction vis-à-vis the human rights so insistently preached by America to the world. It is a contradiction to which they react with outrage, as do all other Arab Americans, myself included, who are aware of the stark violations of human rights in Jerusalem and the whole of Palestine. One day, surely, America will recognize the contradictions implicit in its stance. No wrong can live forever; no injustice can forever prevail.

Two creative essays give this section of the description of Jerusalem's aesthetic aspects a unique significance. Both were undertaken in the 1920s and both were written by great writers who were then acting as journalists for one or another European periodical. The essay by Muhammad Asad, the Muslim name of Leopold Weiss, was written by him when he was still a Jew, but one can immediately notice his interest in the general holiness of the place and in its people, Arabs and Jews alike. He speaks of both Arabs and Jews in the Jerusalem of the twenties in a style that is moving in the extreme, with an intimacy and a human recognition of familiarity and kinship. It humanizes the relations between Muslims and Jews, which are at the moment not just strained but completely antagonistic. Perhaps the greatest salvation for existing problems can be induced by the aesthetics of a situation, by the imaginative writings of great essayists and poets.

The piece by Kazantzakis is equally heart-warming. He too finds in the Mosque of Omar an affinity only those endowed with a sense of the human oneness of experience can savor.

When, recently, I was laying the groundwork for a project on "The Medieval World Through Muslim Eyes," which aims to bring out in English a body of accounts by medieval Muslim travelers, I was deeply moved to note the terms in which these travelers referred to the numerous Jewish and Christian shrines in Palestine. Three examples may suffice here. First, we find the 11th-century CE Persian Muslim traveler Nassir Khosrow describing, in his famous *Safarnamah*, how he prayed at many Jewish and Christian shrines when he visited Palestine. Second, we have the 14th-century Afghani Muslim traveler, 'Ali al-Harawi, author of the book *al-Isharat li Ma'rifat al-Ziyarat*. He too, when visiting Palestine, prayed at many Jewish and Christian shrines. Third, we have *al-Hadrah al-Unsiyyah fi al-Rihlah al-Qudsiyyah*, by the 18th-century Damascene 'Abd al-Ghani al-Nabulsi, where the same cycle of visits is repeated. It hardly matters whether the grave of Lazarus visited by these Muslim travelers was the true one. We are dealing here not with historical geography, but with the issue of faith; with the tender relationship of Islam to Christianity and Judaism, as decreed by the Muslim faith itself.

The issue of Jerusalem is real and many-sided. Yet, when I think of Jerusalem, I think not only of the wider metropolitan city of modern times, outside the walls where I have lived, studied, and loved; I think, first and foremost, of the Old City, the essence of Jerusalem's being and history: of a walled city, elegantly fortified with stately, well-balanced ramparts, opening on to the world through its famous seven gates. Yet these walls have never stood in defiance of the city's holiness and religious centrality. The Dome of the Rock, the Holy Sepulcher, the minarets and steeples, rise proudly yet humbly before the eye. To the beholder scanning the Old City from any of the surrounding hills that have afforded it shelter over the centuries, Jerusalem's monuments stand higher than the walls erected to protect them. But now there have arisen, around much of the historic area, vast, overwhelming rows of solid concrete structures, laying siege to the skyline around the city and choking its very soul. These speak a different tongue.

Jerusalem's many builders over the centuries could never have envisaged the massiveness, the monolithic solidity, the impermeability of these endless high-rise apartment buildings, ring upon ring of them, entrenched there at the dictate of a crazed scheme that speaks of aggression and fear, defying the air of beauty and elegance that had always characterized Jerusalem. When I was growing up, it was an aesthetic experience, constantly renewed, to come upon the Old City from any of Jerusalem's metropolitan entrances, east and west, to be struck time and again by the peaceful walled citadel, with the Dome of the Rock perched majestically at the center of its heart. Ah! City of cities! When will you know peace? This is not your old age. You can never grow old. This is your time of trial, your time of solicitude, yours and that of a great portion of humanity: Muslims and Christians of the world, but also those others, equally perturbed, who are heartfelt lovers of beauty, and who revere the heritage of man and his creative bequest.

Love is not a universally similar experience. It can create miracles, but also tragedies; it can build and beautify, but can also destroy and disfigure. In its present ordeal, Jerusalem demonstrates this only too well. If science could gather back voices from past and forgotten centuries, the chants of Muslim Sufis and the hallelujahs of devout priests would forever fill the air around Jerusalem. How many times has the name of God echoed above its minarets and steeples, reverberated in the *adhan* and the chime of church bells, so much a part of Jerusalem and of our vibrant memory of it. The longing of the Diaspora Jews to its eternal spirit has been a painful experience, nurtured by centuries of alienation and persecution. But the longing that brought generation after generation of Christians and Muslims to pray at its founts of bliss and holiness is no myth. Century upon century of prayer and devotion, century upon century of love, of familiarity, of the humanizing ardor of the soul, of the wondrous entry into regions of exaltation and beatitude to which only faith can usher—has all this been mere meaningless sounds in the void, unheard by God and man? Has it all been a lie, assembled and contrived? Two millenia of hailing the name of Jesus and the Christian saints, 1,400 of Islamic supplication and trust in God, of pious entreaty and devotional rapport—has none of this ever existed? Has all this not left its mark on the city's heart and soul?

The story celebrates itself; there has never been any need for invention. History affirms it all. The monuments, the traditions, the family sanjaqs, the elegant minarets and spires, the stately domes, the winding stairways, polished and smoothed with the myriad steps of men, women, and children of multiple creeds, but predominantly Muslim and Christian—they are all there. The atmosphere throbs with memories. How can the hand of man ever destroy what all these centuries have so splendidly created and preserved? What kind of fury, what obsession, drives the hand of man, armed now with an arsenal of the most deadly weaponry, to pour out its design of destruction on the city's helplessness, mutilating its lineaments, tearing asunder its humanity, ripping its inner being out?

JERUSALEM

Naomi Shihab Nye

Let's be the same wound if we must bleed,
Let's fight side by side even if the enemy
is ourselves; and I am yours, you are mine.
                    —Tommy Olofsson, Sweden

I'm not interested in
Who suffered the most.
I'm interested in
People getting over it.

Once when my father was a boy
A stone hit him on the head.
Hair would never grow there.
Our fingers found the tender spot
And its riddle: the boy who has fallen
Stands up. A bucket of pears
In his mother's doorway welcomes him home.
The pears are not crying.
Lately his friend who threw the stone
Says he was aiming at a bird.
And my father starts growing wings.

Each carries a tender spot:
Something our lives forgot to give us.
A man builds a house and says,
"I am native now."
A woman speaks to a tree in place
Of her son. And olives come.
A child's poem says,
"I don't like wars,
they end up with monuments."
He's painting a bird with wings

Wide enough to cover two roofs at once.

Why are we so monumentally slow?
Soldiers stalk a pharmacy:
Big guns, little pills.
If you tilt your head just slightly
It's ridiculous.

There's a place in this brain
Where hate won't grow.
I touch its riddles: wind and seeds.
Something pokes us as we sleep.

It's late but everything comes next.

The Contemporary Scene

THE ARABS, ISLAM, AND JERUSALEM

André Raymond[1]

The links between Jerusalem, the Arabs, and Islam predate even the conquest of Palestine by the Muslims. Jerusalem holds a privileged place in the context of the Prophet Muhammad's proclamation and propagation of his religion; a place that is hardly astonishing if we consider the influence of the Old Testament and the Gospels on the nature and development of Islam. In Muslim tradition, the founding event of Islam, commemorated each year by the sacrifice of a sheep on the occasion of the Great Feast (*'id al-kabir*), is the act of submission (*islam*) on the part of Abraham (called Ibrahim in the Qur'an); this occurred on Mount Moriah, in a place that would become the site of Jerusalem. The Qur'an alludes to the destruction of the Temple (Sura 17:4–7). It was, according to the earliest traditions, from Jerusalem that the Prophet's night journey and ascension to Heaven (*mi'raj*) took place, as related in the Qur'an (Sura 17:1); the "Farthest Mosque" (*masjid al-Aqsa*) being situated on the holy mount of Jerusalem. It is not surprising therefore that, at the time the community was being initially established in Makkah, Muslims' prayers should have been directed towards Jerusalem; the city remained the direction (*qibla*) in which believers turned up until the second year of Muhammad's stay in Madinah, when prayer came to be directed, instead, towards the Ka'ba in Makkah. There still exists, in the Banu Salama quarter of Madinah, a mosque known as "the two qiblas" (*qiblatayn*) where a *mihrab* set to the north, towards Jerusalem, recalls this original orientation. Jerusalem is thus one of the holy cities of Islam, and a visit to its mosque forms part of the major religious journeys. In this connection the celebrated Damascene jurist Ibn Taymiyya (d. 1328) recalled the Prophetic tradition (hadith): "Do not set out on a journey except to one of the three mosques: the Holy Mosque [in Makkah], the al-Aqsa Mosque [in Jerusalem] or my Mosque [in Madinah]."

The importance accorded to Jerualem was naturally reinforced by the Arab–Muslim conquest that unfolded after the Prophet's death in 631. In 638 the Christian Patriarch Sophronius offered to surrender the city to the Commander of the Faithful, 'Umar, who entered without violence; according to tradition, the Caliph visited the city escorted by the Patriarch and, thanks to indications in the Qur'an, had no difficulty in finding the Temple Mount (Haram), by then fallen into neglect. He thereupon had it cleared and cleaned. It was 'Umar who, five centuries after their expulsion under Hadrian (135), permitted the Jews to return to Jerusalem; he bestowed on Jews and Christians the status of "protected people" (*dhimmi*), which gave them freedom to practice their religion. The local population, which remained there and was, over the centuries, supplemented by people come from Arabia, who had adopted the Arabic language, but were only partially converted to Islam, a substantial part of the original population of Palestine and Jerusalem remaining Christian. Even after the Crusades, and the extraordinary violence that accompanied the capture of Jerusalem in 1099, there were no reprisals against the Christian population when Saladin recaptured the city (1187), and a strong Christian presence remained in the Holy City. At the beginning of the 19th century, Christians still made up a third of the population of Jerusalem. This Arab connection with Jerusalem, established in 638, was maintained uninterrupted over thirteen centuries—a period longer, of course, than that of Roman and Byzantine domination (six and a half centuries) and even that of the Jewish presence there (eleven centuries between the Kingdom of David and the expulsion). The city's eminent status in the Muslim world was underlined by the building of two of the oldest and most prestigious sanctuaries of Islam. In a place totally neglected by the Christians throughout six centuries, the Muslims erected first the Dome of the Rock (*qubbat al-Sakhra*), on the spot hallowed by tradition as that of Abraham's sacrifice and as that from which the Prophet made his night ascension (leaving the mark of his foot in the rock). The Umayyad caliph 'Abd al-Malik was responsible for this monument (691), whose cupola and mosaic decorations, with their ancient and Byzantine elements, are among the most remarkable examples of Muslim art. The al-Aqsa Mosque, built in 717 by 'Abd al-Malik's successor al-Walid, in the southern part of the Haram opposite the Dome, is also closely bound to Qur'anic tradition: "Glory be to Him who caused His servant to travel by night from the Sacred Mosque [in Makkah] to the Farthest Mosque [masjid al-Aqsa], whose precincts We have blessed." (Sura 17:1)

These two monuments have, over thirteen centuries, symbolized Muslims' unbroken attachment to Jerusalem. In 1326 the Moroccan traveler Ibn Battuta wrote as follows:

> We reached Bayt al-Muqaddis [the "House of the
> Sanctuary," i.e., Jerusalem], may God glorify it. This it is
> which comes, for illustrious character, immediately after
> the two noble temples [of Makkah and Madinah]... The
> city is large, illustrious and built out of hewn stone... The
> holy Mosque of Jerusalem is wondrous, marvellous and of
> truly great beauty; and it is said that there is not, on the
> whole face of the earth, a temple greater than this
> Mosque... The Dome of the Rock... is one of the most
> wondrous of edifices, and one of the most solidly built, and
> one of the most extraordinary in its form. It has, in
> abundance, its portion of beauties, and has received its
> ample part of all wondrous things.

A city open to pilgrimage from the three great monotheistic religions, Jerusalem knew only one truly dark period. At the beginning of the 11th century, the immoderate Egyptian caliph al-Hakim persecuted the Christians and Jews and, in 1009, had the Holy Sepulcher destroyed, and the conquest of Palestine by the Seljuq Turks brought Atsiz's savage reprisals on the inhabitants of the city, who vainly sought refuge in the Mosque and the Dome. The Crusaders, after capturing Jerusalem in 1099, massacred Muslims and Jews and turned Jerusalem into a Christian city where non-Christians were not permitted to live. It was Saladin who, in 1187, restored Jerusalem's true role; he left the Holy Sepulcher open to the Christians, and in 1192 pilgrimage began once more. After one last tumultuous episode—when, following the ceding of Jerusalem to Frederick II in 1229, the city was forbidden to Muslims and Jews—the city, and Palestine, in 1244 came under the sway of the rulers of Egypt.

Under the Mamluks, who governed it from Cairo (1260–1516), then under the Ottomans who reigned in Istanbul (1516–1918), Jerusalem was a city of middling importance, a center for the region, but it was its great religious prestige that underlay the interest shown in it by rulers: major architectural works shaped the old city and gave it the form it has preserved to this day. The Mamluks endowed the interior of the historic city with splendid religious monuments, schools (*madrasa*) and foundations (*khanqa*) for the teaching of Islam that affirmed the city's Muslim character. At the end of the 15th century, the chronicler Mujir al-Din (1456–1522) noted as follows:

> From a distance, the sight of Jerusalem, filled with lustre
> and beauty, is one of the celebrated wonders... When God,
> by His grace, permits the pilgrim to reach the sanctuary of

al-Aqsa and the place of prayer revered by Abraham, he
feels an indescribable sense of joy and happiness, and
forgets the pains and hardships he has endured.

Equally extensive were the works initiated by the Ottomans, above all
by Sulayman the Magnificent, who transformed the city's exterior
aspect (1537–1541) through the construction of the walls and gates
still virtually intact to this day, and through renovation of the Dome
of the Rock, for which he provided the ornamentation that continues
to arouse the admiration of visitors. Around 1540 an anonymous Jew
and Joseph ha-Kohen, who lived in Jerusalem at the time of Sultan
Sulayman, gave a sense of the ongoing work:

> Jerusalem, the Holy City, was destroyed through our sins.
> Now they have begun to build the walls around the city by
> order of the King, the Sultan Suleyman... The reputation
> [of the Sultan] has spread throughout the land, for he has
> undertaken much work.

Under the Ottomans the city experienced a certain renaissance;
and, above all, it became a place where the communities coexisted in
peace (the main difficulties were to be found between the Christian
denominations), and where the various types of pilgrimage could be
performed without hindrance: by Christians, coming in ever greater
numbers from the west or from Middle Eastern cities (such as Aleppo)
with Christian communities; by Jews, whose numbers multiplied in
the course of the nineteenth century. Around the year 1800, Jerusalem
had 6,750 Arabs (4,000 Muslim, 2,750 Christian) and 2,000 Jews.

Jerusalem's prominent place in the Muslim scheme of things is
reflected in the extensive literature about the "merits" (*fada'il al-Quds*)
with which it is endowed, in common with other great cities of the
Muslim world. The authors of these treatises highlighted the city's
sacred character, and its outstanding worth as attested by the presence
of its two great mosques, by the memory of the prophets and saints,
by the night journey of the Prophet of Islam, by its role as the first
qibla, and by the part it would be called upon to play at the moment
of the Resurrection and Judgment, "when the narrow bridge
over which the whole of Creation will pass will be thrown from the
Mount of Olives to the Temple Mount." The highest Christian
authority has, in its turn, noted the strength of this bond between the
Muslim community and Jerusalem. In his speech delivered on June 21,

1980, Pope John Paul II said:

> We cannot ignore the profound attachment of Muslims to Jerusalem... This attachment was already explicit in the life and thought of the founder of Islam; and it has been strengthened by an Islamic presence in Jerusalem, almost uninterrupted since 638 AD and attested by certain monuments of signal distinction, such as the al-Aqsa Mosque and the Mosque of 'Umar.

This veneration is shared by the millions of Arab Christians living today in the various countries of the Near East. For every Arab, Muslim or Christian, it is "the Holy" (*al-Quds*).

JERUSALEM AS THE KEY ISSUE

Bayan Nuwaihed al-Hut

Grief-stricken Jerusalem
Walks the Via Dolorosa
And the world?
A cold heart!
—Fadwa Tuqan

Introduction

Since the First World War, no issue has had the full attention of the Arab world and of the wider Islamic world like the question of Palestine. To the Arabs, it has become the primary issue, and its central question has been the city of al-Quds al-Sharif, variously called Bayt al-Maqdis and Jerusalem, the city that is the focal frame of reference for Judaism, Christianity, and Islam. But which Jerusalem are we talking about? The truth is that each group sees what it wants to see in the city, rather than what the city is truly about. Each nation, each group, when talking about the present and future of Jerusalem, talks about a Jerusalem different from the others. At the beginning of the third millennium, which Jerusalem are the Arabs—the inhabitants and main builders of the city, and, apart from the interim period of the Crusader rule, its residents since the 7th century—talking about: the Islamic, the religious, the historical, the Arab, the symbolic, or the ancient Jerusalem? Or is it 20th century Jerusalem, the pre-1948 city, the Greater Metropolitan Jerusalem; or the post-1948 smaller Arab section of the city? Or is it the contemporary Jerusalem, which has been expanding ceaselessly since 1993?

The tragedy of Jerusalem lies precisely in this maze of infinite directions. The Arab–Israeli conflict over Palestine in general and over Jerusalem in particular combines religious, historical, legal, and political aspects—all of which make for a unique type of confrontation. The conflict over the city is perhaps the longest in history. Aside from its position as the focus of conflict since ancient times, it has sustained a central confrontation throughout the 20th century and into the 21st.

The purpose of this short study, however, is to survey the developments in this ancient and glorious city, and to identify what has been left of the modern Jerusalem that we knew before its first catastrophe in 1948.

Jerusalem in the Zionist Mind

One of the salient features of Zionist literature is the unquestioning and indiscriminate merger of religion and history. A "chosen history" is written and re-written for the "chosen people." The religious and historical significance of Jerusalem to both Christians and Muslims is constantly downsized and depreciated. According to Zionist writings, Christians have other significant holy places elsewhere in Palestine: in Bethlehem, where Jesus was born; in Nazareth, where, according to Christian belief, he was raised; by the side of the River Jordan, where he was baptized; and in the Galilee, where he preached and performed his miracles. For Muslims, the Zionist literature argues, Jerusalem is not the first or the only holy city. The holy city to which they make pilgrimage is Makkah. Besides, as one Jewish historian claims, Jerusalem is mentioned 656 times in the Old Testament, just a few times in the New Testament in relation to certain events relevant to the Christian faith, but never in the Book of Islam.[1]

It is not my intention here to discuss these Zionist claims at any length. It is sufficient, in this respect, to refer to a report presented by an Israeli team of archaeologists in July 1998, after a two-year excavation in East Jerusalem. Their report states that "Jerusalem was an important and developed city long before the time of King David. It had an elaborate and sophisticated system of water distribution and distillation which was the most advanced and protected in the Middle East. The system was constructed about 1800 years before Christ, i.e., eight centuries before King David, which means that it was built during the Canaanite era."[2]

The Legal Status of Jerusalem since 1948

Following the end of the British mandate on May 15, 1948, United Nations General Assembly Resolution No. 181, known as the Partition Resolution, became the legal umbrella for the future of Palestine. On the basis of the Partition Resolution, Palestine was to be divided into three parts: a Palestinian state, a Jewish state, and a third part to be administered by the United Nations under special international arrangements. This last part included what was then the municipality of Jerusalem and the adjacent villages and towns extending, in the farthest east to the town of Abu Dis, in the south to the city of Bethlehem, and in the farthest west to the town of Ain Karem, which included the developed portion of the Kalonia area.[3]

The Partition Resolution was never implemented with relation to the partition plan, including the issue of Jerusalem. Only the item relating to the establishment of the Jewish state was executed after Israel occupied the western and larger part of Jerusalem. The Palestinian state was not established, and the remaining Palestinian territories were divided between Jordan (which annexed the West Bank and eastern, i.e., historical, Jerusalem where the Old City lies), Egypt (which became responsible for the administration of the Gaza Strip) and Syria (which took charge of the Himma area).

On January 23, 1950, Israel declared Jerusalem its political capital. A new de facto position was thus developed in Jerusalem between the two wars of 1948 and 1967. This led to a de jure status. Sovereignty over the city was, therefore, divided between Israel and Jordan. Following the June 1967 war, the city was confiscated by the Israelis, and several parts of the Old City were emptied by force of their inhabitants and either demolished or inhabited by Jewish families. Israel began a series of arrangements and legislative measures to serve its own interests, with no regard whatsoever to international law.[4] In 1980, the Knesset passed a law declaring that an entire, unified Jerusalem was the capital of Israel.[5]

The Israeli decision was not recognized by all states, and even the countries that had initially sympathized with it withdrew their diplomatic missions from Jerusalem in compliance with the Security Council Resolution No. 478, which denied the Israeli law announcing Jerusalem as the capital of Israel, and declared it invalid according to international law. Over time, however, certain embassies and diplomatic missions started moving from Tel Aviv to Jerusalem, despite successive US assurances that the Israeli actions and plans to change the position and status of Jerusalem were not recognized. Such verbal American assurances were eventually torn to pieces by the decision of the United States Senate that formally recognized Jerusalem as the capital of Israel and called upon the administration to transfer the US embassy to Jerusalem by May 1999.

On the other hand, the Oslo Agreement, signed on September 13, 1993, by Palestinian President Yasser Arafat, failed to resolve the legal controversy over Jerusalem; rather, it confused the issue further by making only a casual reference to Jerusalem in Item (3) of Article (5), which noted that there would be a permanent status of negotiation on such issues as Jerusalem, the refugees, settlements, security arrangements, borders, and relations and co-operation with other neighbors.[6] Discussion of the issue of Jerusalem was thus deferred for another three years, which were then extended for a further three years. In the meantime, Israel managed to issue and implement another series of legislative measures intended to complete the Judaization of Jerusalem, and followed a parallel course of action aimed at curtailing, as far as possible, the number of Arab Jerusalemites.

Land Confiscation Laws

1. The Refugees' Estates Law
This was the famous law dealing with lands owned by absent Palestinians (refugees).

2. The Prescription Lapse of Time Law
This obliges Arab property owners to produce a certificate to prove that they have been using the land for fifty years. Since Ottoman documents were inaccurate, and because most of the lands were not topographically classified, this law resulted in confiscation of large amounts of land long owned by Palestinians, as the owners, lacking such required documents, faced an impossible situation.

3. The Dispensation Law
This allowed the Israeli government to confiscate land without going back to the courts, by declaring the land in question to be a military area.

4. The Uncultivated Land Law
This stipulated that, if land was not cultivated, it would be confiscated.

5. The Land Cultivation Law
This aimed at dividing cultivated lands into smaller portions, in order to put an end to large estates.

6. The Land Concentration Law
This allowed the Minister of Agriculture to declare any heavily cultivated land to be "intensive land," and hence confiscate it.

7. The Property Tax Amended Law
This involved levying high taxes on developed areas. Many Arab developers failed to pay such taxes and left for other areas in the region such as the West Bank, and finally lost their rights as Jerusalemites.

8. The Green Zones
This law prevented the construction of any buildings on areas classified as "green." Some of these areas were developed as public parks, but most were earmarked for the development of buildings for settlers, and for other Israeli projects.

9. The Forestry Law
This law allowed the Israeli forces to own and control all forests as "no-man's-land."

10. The Land Confiscation Emergency Law
This law allowed the Israelis to enter any area to protect and secure the safety of immigrant Jews. This law paved the way, in 1948, for confiscating the lands of 35 villages in the Jerusalem area, forcing their inhabitants out. However, the twelve Israeli settlements established in 1948 had increased to 64 by 1967.[7]

Laws and Restrictions Aimed at Reducing the Arab Population

Since 1995, Israel has been imposing legal restrictions on Arab Jerusalemites. Those who wish, for instance, to apply to the Ministry of the Interior for renewal of an identification card, or to register the birth of a child, must prove they have lived in Jerusalem for seven years. They must produce such supporting documents as lease agreements, water and electricity bills, school certificates, tax receipts, etc. Should the Ministry, for one reason or the other, decide that a Jerusalemite has not resided in Jerusalem for the required period of time, this person will lose the right to residence and must leave the city by a certain deadline.[8] Jewish Israeli lawyer Lea Tsemel has argued that "If Benyamin Netanyahu were a Palestinian, he would have lost his right to stay in Jerusalem because of the 12 years he had spent in the United States."[9]

Attempts at Judaizing Jerusalem during the Mandate

In the Zionist scheme of things, the term Judaization meant much more than turning Jerusalem into a city with a predominantly Jewish stamp on its buildings, streets, names, institutions, and language. Until 1870, Jerusalem was surrounded by a historical wall built by the Ottoman Sultan Sulayman the Magnificent during the 16th century. The wall encircling the Old City had a number of main gates that opened out to the different corners of Palestine. Inside the wall, there are many highly visible and holy sites of Islam and Christianity: such magnificent sites as the Dome of the Rock (the jewel of Jerusalem) and the blessed al-Aqsa Mosque, both constructed in the 1st century AH/7th century CE, the Church of the Holy Sepulcher, built in the 4th century CE and the Roman Byzantine Church of the 5th century CE. A great number of religious sites and landmarks in old Jerusalem were in the custody of the Arabs until 1967. There were 199 Islamic sites from the days of the Umayyads, the 'Abbasids, the Fatimids, the Ayyubids, the Mamluks, and the Ottomans. There were also 60 Christian sites, including churches, monasteries, and schools from the Byzantine era up to the beginning of the 20th century. In addition there were fifteen Jewish sites, such as synagogues and schools—all built in the 19th or early 20th century or established in leased buildings.[10]

After 1870, a large number of affluent Arab Jerusalemites moved out of the Old City and developed residential quarters in the city's northern, eastern, and western environs, and a number of Jerusalemite families built their houses on some *waqf* (religious endowment) lands they had owned. These quarters were later named after the families that built them.[11] Toward the end of World War I, the Arabs constituted the majority of the inhabitants of Jerusalem within and outside the walls. The Judaization of Jerusalem started during the Mandate period after the entry of General Allenby into the city in December 1917. The grounds were then laid by the British for developing the Jewish quarters while imposing restrictions on the expansion of the Arab quarters. Allenby's engineers started this by dividing Jerusalem into the four sections that provided the blueprints for all subsequent plans. These were: the Old City and its walls, the places surrounding the Old City, western Jerusalem, and East Jerusalem.[12]

The first manifestations of actual Judaization took place at the beginning of the term (1920–1925) of Herbert Samuel, the first British High Commissioner who was Jewish. This started with the construction of the first Israeli colony of Romina in 1921. The colonies—which were later called settlements—had reached sixteen by 1948.[13] The city was randomly re-planned in 1921 by adding to it a number of Arab quarters and suburbs, and, in 1946, the city borders included all the Jewish congregations. The Judaization plans during the Mandate were not confined only to building residential Jewish quarters but included also the construction of huge institutions such as the Hebrew University in 1925, and, later on, the buildings of the executive committee of the Zionist movement and the Jewish Agency, as well as the Hadassah Hospital, which were all built on Mount Scopus on the northeastern side of Jerusalem, thus enabling the Jews to expand their colonies and settlements around the city. In contrast, there were no similar institutions for the Arabs, who were deprived of any political representation, with the possible exception of the High Islamic Shari'ah Council, which was, in fact, not only a religious institution but the national headquarters in which Muslim and Christian Arabs met.

The greatest danger, then, experienced by Jerusalemites was the growing influx into their city of waves of immigrant Jews from Germany and other parts of Europe in the 1930s and early 1940s. Of the total population of 164,400 people in 1948, there were, in Jerusalem, 99,320 Jews and 65,010 Muslim and Christian Arabs: i.e., 60% Jews against 40% Arabs.[14]

On the other hand, outside the municipal limits, i.e., in the villages and populated areas around Jerusalem, the ratio was exactly the opposite: 60% Arab and 40% Jewish of a total population of 274,950 people.[15]

Attempts at Judaizing Jerusalem (1948–1967)

By the time the armistice agreement was signed by Israel and Jordan in 1949, Jerusalem had been divided into three areas;[16] one under Jordanian rule, comprising an area of 2,220 dunums[17] (11.48%); a second under Israeli rule, covering an area of 16,261 dunums (84.13%);[18] and the third under the administration of the United Nations, made up of an area of 850 dunums (4.39%).[19] The Israeli government soon started constructing new settlements in the Jerusalem area on confiscated Arab lands. In the period between the two wars of 1948 and 1967, the number of settlements increased from 12 to 64, and the boundaries of the municipality of Jerusalem tripled by incorporating Arab towns and villages such as Dir Yasin, al-Malha, 'Ain Karem, and Beit Safafa. In the meantime, the area of Jerusalem under Israeli rule doubled from 19,331 dunums in 1948 to 38,600 dunums just before the 1967 war.[20]

Further Attempts at Judaizing Jerusalem (1967–1993)

Immediately after the fall of Arab Old Jerusalem to the Israeli army on

June 5 and 6, 1967, and following the withdrawal of the Jordanian army from the eastern part of the city, Israeli bulldozers started demolishing the Magarbeh Quarter opposite the Wailing Wall.[21] Destruction was meted out to 135 houses occupied by families of Moroccan, Algerian, Tunisian, and Libyan descent; about 650 people were given only two or three hours to vacate their homes.[22] Israel thus put into practice a new principle of Judaization that gave it the right to destroy entire residential quarters to establish its own authority over occupied areas. The work of destruction included, in all, two mosques, about 700 buildings occupied by over 6,000 Arabs, and 437 stores supporting about 700 families. On the ruins of these buildings rose compounds of houses and buildings that were later called the Jewish Quarter.[23] In 1987, the then Minister of Defense Ariel Sharon took up residence at the heart of the Islamic area in Old Jerusalem. This move signaled a new era of Judaization, and the beginning of more Israeli penetration into Arab quarters.[24]

Thirteen years after Ariel Sharon had had a house of his own in the heart of the Islamic area, he was once more in power and made that "storming visit" to al-Aqsa Mosque on September 28, 2000, accompanied by hundreds of fully equipped soldiers. There were hundreds of Palestinians surrounding the mosque and waiting to pelt them with stones. Sharon and his soldiers were finally forced to leave, and a second wave of the intifada had begun. In an attempt to isolate Jerusalem from the West Bank, the Israelis divided the city into three wide circles. The first turns around the Old City and connects it to the western section as well as the Jewish suburbs. The second circle moves around the Arab suburbs outside the Old City in order to separate Jerusalem from the Arab areas. This circle includes eleven settlements. The third circle surrounds Metropolitan Jerusalem with a range of housing projects designed to isolate the city from the West Bank. This circle includes Jabal Abu Ghneim and a residential project in Ras al-'Amoud.[25]

In the period between 1991 and 1993—that is to say, between the Madrid Conference and the Oslo Agreement—the Israeli government laid down plans for further Judaization of Jerusalem. These included, among other things, confiscating more lands from al-Malha village west of Jerusalem, building many more settlements in the area, constructing a highway between Ramallah and Bethlehem through Jerusalem, and undertaking huge constructions in eastern Jerusalem covering an area of 250,000 dunums, thus turning Jerusalem into a totally different city.[26]

Further Attempts at Judaizing Jerusalem (1993–2000)

The signing of the Oslo Agreement did not result in freezing or harnessing settlement projects or the plans to fragment and dissect territorial space, nor did it change the features and configuration of Jerusalem; on the contrary, the plans for Judaizing Jerusalem became more severe.

Since 1995 there has been a mushrooming expansion of settlements in terms of both numbers and size, and at least 50,000 houses have been built. On June 21, 1998, the Israeli government endorsed a plan for a Metropolitan Jerusalem. Former Israeli Prime Minister Benyamin Natanyahu declared publicly that the aim of the new plan was to maintain the size of the Arab community in Jerusalem as a minority that, in his view, must not go beyond 30% of the population.[27] The most significant element in the Greater Jerusalem project is to achieve a 70% Jewish majority of the total population of the city and separate Arab Jerusalem from the cities of Ramallah and Bethlehem, merging it completely with the Israeli-controlled Metropolitan Jerusalem.[28] By the year 1993 the number of Jews inside the Old City and in the Arab suburbs surrounding exceeded, for the first time, the number of Arabs: the number of Jews was 160,000, while that of the Arabs was only 155,000.[29] Some sources did not expect much further increase in the number of the Jews in the near future.[30] According to Professor Khalidi, who uses the term "Eastern Jerusalem," the number of Jews would be in the region of 180,000, i.e., the size of the Muslim and Christian Arab population combined.[31] Metropolitan Jerusalem will eventually stretch from the village of Beit Shams in the west, half way to Tel Aviv, down to Hebron in the south and then beyond Ramallah in the north, and including a few kilometers from Jericho in the east. It will cover an area of 1,250 square kilometers.[32]

The Situation of the Arab Population

Perhaps the most cogent expression of the situation of Arabs in Jerusalem is what anyone can see on television screens and in the newspapers: a Palestinian family stands in shock and horror at the sight of their house being demolished by Israeli bulldozers. These images and media presentations are substantiated by figures and statistics. Since 1967, somewhere between 85% and 90% of the lands of Palestinians in East Jerusalem have been confiscated, leaving only about 13.5 percent left for them to build on and dwell in. The Israeli state has adopted a series of procedures to cut down the number of Jerusalemites, such as imposing spiraling taxes that range between US$25,000 and US$30,000. Jerusalemites who cannot pay such exorbitant taxes are forced out of the city. The military siege and the six police checkpoints that control movement into and out of Jerusalem have dealt a severe blow to the economic and educational status of Jerusalem as well as the other parts of Palestine.[33] Subsequently, and in less than five years, 2,817 Arab citizens have lost their right of residence in Jerusalem.[34] Other more comprehensive estimates indicate that 11,000 identity cards have been withdrawn.[35] According to Shaikh ʿAkramah Sabri, the Mufti of al-Quds and Palestine, about 220,000 Jerusalemites do not live inside the city, and as such are threatened with losing their identity cards. Indeed, they may have lost them without being notified.[36] Similarly, and since the signing of the Oslo Agreement, the number of Arab houses demolished for lack of a license was 671, of which 102 were in the city of Jerusalem and were wiped out under the auspices of both the Labor and Likud parties: there were 71 houses demolished during Labor party government rule, and 31 during that of the Likud government.[37]

In the meantime, Israel has imposed a series of restrictions on any form of representation by the Palestinian Authority in Jerusalem. Israeli security forces have already taken action against a number of Palestinian institutions working in Jerusalem, and thirteen such organizations have been included in the Palestinian Authority "list," such as the Orient House, al-Quds University, the Ministry of Awqaf and Holy Places, the Land and Water Institution, etc. The policy of siege and enclosure has continued.[38] Nathan Sharansky, minister of interior affairs, announced on October 17, 1999, that there would be a lifting of such policies (which had been going on since 1995),[39] but the siege never stopped completely, and the policy of demolishing houses was maintained in East Jerusalem and its vicinity.[40]

It became obvious that Jerusalemites were not to be allowed to live in Jerusalem as citizens with rights and dignity, but rather permitted to remain there, alive but no more. Very often, and only after their houses had been demolished inside Jerusalem, they would be allowed to look for new houses to live in outside Jerusalem.

Attempts at Destroying al-Aqsa Mosque

The Israelis are continuing their plans for turning Jerusalem from an Islamic city into a completely Jewish city. Paramount among their projects is the destruction of al-Masjid al-Aqsa (that is to say the entire al-Haram al-Sharif) and the rebuilding, on its ruins, of the Temple of

Solomon. Similarly, there have been assaults on the properties of Christian churches and monasteries. The most serious attack took place in April 1990 in the heart of the Christian area, when 150 armed Israelis occupied the Saint John Hospital, which was under the Orthodox Patriarchate. For the first time in 800 years, the Church of the Holy Sepulcher and other Christian sites closed their doors in protest. In sympathy and solidarity, the Higher Islamic Shari'ah Council closed the doors of al-Haram al-Sharif to foreign visitors on Friday, April 27, 1990.[41] Israeli attacks against Christian properties continued, but the main interest of the Israelis has been centered on the destruction of al-Aqsa. According to the Jewish architect David Crolinker, Prime Minister Ben Gurion was planning to erase the city completely after the 1967 June war. Another option was to destroy the entire city wall and all Arab buildings, declare Jerusalem a unified city, then, on the site of the al-Buraq Wall, build the Temple on the ruins of al-Aqsa, by erecting ten pillars symbolizing the Ten Commandments.[42]

In the turmoil of the occupation of 1967, the chief army rabbi, Shlomo Goren, urged the military commander of Jerusalem to seize the opportunity of the chaotic war situation and destroy al-Aqsa Mosque. Such plans were manifested immediately by the demolition, in June 1967, of the Magharbeh Quarter near the Wailing Wall. The first outright attack on al-Aqsa, however, took place in 1968, when an Australian Christian called Michael Dennis Rohan tried to burn it. The occupation authorities hastily announced that he was a lunatic. Several such attempts were made in the 1980s; in 1983, for example, 46 Israelis placed explosives under the Mosque. The Israeli authorities claimed to have discovered this, but could hardly claim all 46 were insane! Many such attempts were also made by the so-called Custodians of the Temple, with a view to laying the cornerstone for the third Temple. A similar assault in 1990 resulted in the massacre of eighteen Palestinians and injury to a hundred others. There are now many fanatical societies and non-government institutions in Israel, such as the Gosh Emunin, the Custodians of the Temple, the Movement for the Reconstruction of the Temple, and the Movement for Preparing for the Temple. All these and similar organizations have the single purpose of destroying al-Aqsa Mosque. Rabbi Yousef al-Baum, founder of the Movement for Preparing for the Temple, once said: "Until we perform our prayers and rituals in the Temple, we shall be only half Jews."[43] On the legal and practical levels, one may refer to two documents. The first is what was described as the Yerushlaym

Covenant, which was signed officially at the end of May 1992 by the then head of state, Chaim Hertzog, and a number of Israeli leaders.[44] This covenant expresses the determination to turn Jerusalem into a Jewish city.[45] The other is the Knesset resolution of May 1994, which stipulates that the status and unity of Jerusalem and its suburbs is not a political or a security issue, but rather a manifestation of the spirit of the Jewish people.[46] The Israeli authorities try to give the impression that they are against any terrorist attempt to destroy al-Masjid al-Aqsa and al-Haram al-Sharif. They have even asked for provision of further protection for al-Aqsa.[47]

However, these announcements are mere symbolic and hollow manifestations; the underlying aim is constantly and implicitly endorsed and supported. The long-term plan, to be implemented over time, is to get the whole world accustomed to a Jerusalem without an al-Aqsa Mosque, as a necessary prerequisite for building the Jewish Temple.[48]

Resisting Judaization

Jerusalemites have stood up bravely against attempts at Judaization and defended the integrity and status of their city. They have courageously defied the Israeli plans for appropriating more Arab land and property and for reducing the Arab population, and have opposed the growing threats against al-Haram al-Sharif. One of the most important steps was the decision of Dar al-Fatwa in Jerusalem, issued in 1996, which prohibited the sale of land and property to both Arabs and non-Arabs, except by a decree given by Dar al-Fatwa.[49]

As for the continued Israeli attempts to cut down the Arab population, the only alternative Jerusalemites had was to go back to their city after an enforced temporary exile outside. Consequently, the Israeli authorities were surprised to see an increase rather than a decrease in the number of Arab Jerusalemites. On the other hand, the mufti of al-Quds and Palestine, Shaikh 'Akramah Sabri, declared that al-Aqsa Mosque has not received sufficient attention up till now. There is, it is true, a committee for the development of al-Aqsa with remote Jordanian supervision, but al-Haram al-Sharif still needs tremendous material support. It was surprising that, at a recent conference in Doha for the protection and maintenance of Islamic sites, al-Aqsa was not covered by the campaign for collecting donations and assistance.[50] These pursuits are in direct contrast to what the Zionists and the Israelis are now doing to exercise control and appropriation of the Islamic holy sites in the city.[51]

A Beginning Rather than an End

My brief exposition of the focal points of the attempts at Judaization, and the dangers facing Jerusalem at the beginning of the third millennium, leads to a number of major problems and paradoxes that must be addressed in order to liberate the city and alleviate the grievance and injustice to which Jerusalemites are subjected.

These include: delineating Arab and Muslim responsibility for Jerusalem; determining the borders of the city; establishing the frame of reference for defending and protecting the Islamic holy sites; forcing Israel to comply with international law and resolutions; drawing a distinction between the *mujahid* and the terrorist in the face of the forces that have been mobilized in the last quarter of the 20th century identifying Muslims and Islamists as terrorists.

Many people like to believe that peace can be achieved simply by signing an agreement, any agreement. Peace between unequal partners, however, is outright capitulation that must not be accepted. Otherwise the tragedies of 1948 and 1967 will recur. The road ahead is thorny, but with firmness of resolve all obstacles can be overcome, and hopefully one day the people of the region will enjoy a stable peace based on justice and fair play. Jerusalem, however, is likely to remain for at least some time the major issue; without addressing it, progress will hardly be possible.

JERUSALEM: OCCUPATION AND CHALLENGES TO URBAN IDENTITY

Yasser Ibrahim Rajjal

Introduction

Jerusalem has witnessed a number of changes as a result of Israeli occupation practices, and these changes have affected the urban environment of the city in several ways, leading to an evident alteration in the city's urban identity. Aspects of this alteration include:

1. Morphology of the city: the distinctive urban form, tissue, and pattern of the city and landform, and the relation of these to the built and natural environments.
2. Behavioral aspects: these involve the human relations generated by the urban environment, along with the activities produced and assimilated by the city.
3. Spiritual and symbolic meanings linked to the urban environment of the city of Jerusalem.

Israeli occupation has played a major role in creating these aspects of change, leading to transformation of the city's urban identity into a model of repression and authoritarianism as opposed to a model of a spiritual city.

This study proposes that these changes be dealt with through the establishment of standards or criteria designed to ensure an ongoing and authentic identity, characterized by organic growth and a respect for historical continuity.

With the spiritual and human features it embodies, the city of Jerusalem may be regarded as an outstanding urban site with a unique cultural identity acquired through the city's historical development. This cultural identity springs from the interplay of the city's morphology with the various behavioral aspects and patterns of human activity generated by the city and from the spiritual and symbolic connotations of the locale.[1]

As such Jerusalem represents a peerless model of the spiritual and human city. However, over the last five decades of the 20th century, Jerusalem was subjected to a series of measures and practices that have adversely affected these aspects of its urban identity, causing the city to lose much of its spiritual and human character and to take on a western flavor, but marked by repression and authoritarianism. This study demonstrates the relevant aspects of change from three viewpoints: first, the city's morphology; second, behavioral aspects; and third, spiritual and symbolic connotations.

I

THE CITY'S MORPHOLOGY

The city's morphology involves interaction of the built environment with structural and spatial elements on the one hand, and with the natural environment on the other.[2] These interactions produce the land form and urban form and tissue. The city constitutes, in fact, an example of organic growth extending from bottom to top, within a general framework that highlights the pre-eminence over the city of the Holy Haram of Jerusalem and the Dome of the Rock. The Holy Haram constitutes a podium linked to the ground. It encompasses the city and emphasizes the Dome of the Rock as an element of major importance in the formation of the skyline; for it is possible to see it from all directions except the north, and in a manner that highlights a large part of the city, distinguishing it from other parts. Furthermore, the simplicity and purity of the Dome's formation and its perfectly engineered shape has supplied an image that can be easily remembered and retrieved. This has, naturally, enhanced the emphasis of the city's cosmic order.[3]

The other buildings of Jerusalem comprise an overlapping residential entity whereby buildings are linked to the ground and to one another, so forming a compact tissue broadly characterized by solidity and by vertical apertures often constructed in pairs. The slight differentiation in the height of buildings—which, with very few exceptions, do not exceed three stories—has made it possible to link the roofs of buildings with the city roads, and to gain easy access to these roofs from street level. A number of vertical structures permeate this urban tissue, such as church towers, mosque minarets, and cedar and evergreen cypress trees, which act as distinctive landmarks. These landmarks have created a system of spatial orientation, endowing the city with a high degree of clarity in the eyes of its inhabitants. Moreover, the hierarchy of the city roads, in terms of width, importance, and degree of privacy, has contributed to a bolstering and consolidation of this spatial system. In addition, the spatial diversities and the interlocked character of light, shade, and structural density induce a sense of warmth and longing positively reflected in the city's inhabitants and their attachment to the city.

The Old City of Jerusalem grew to encompass a number of new sectors outside the walls. The last quarter of the 19th century, it should be noted, witnessed the rise of Arab quarters interspersed with constructions belonging to the Christian Church of Jerusalem, which passed into the Church's hands by purchase or through Ottoman Turkish gifts of state land. The period in question also witnessed the rise of Jewish quarters outside the walls to the west.[4] Until the Israeli occupation of the western sector of Jerusalem in 1948, the city's growth suggested gradual and sustained development, in harmony with the city's form, tissue, and urban pattern[5]—although this growth did not, it must be said, lack a touch of modernity.

Distortion of this harmony began, in actual fact, a few years before the occupation of the city's modern sector, in that Jewish control of the city required the forced evacuation of the Arab inhabitants by means of psychological warfare and through destruction of the city infrastructures. This coincided with the demolition of a number of buildings in New Jerusalem, including governmental, commercial, and touristic public buildings, as well as residential ones. This forced many of the Arab inhabitants of the city's modern sectors to leave their homes; and, as a result, these sectors were reduced to scattered ruins and deserted quarters and houses separated by thick meshes of barbed wire. The morphological harmony of these modern sectors, of which Arabs had once owned about 80 percent, then vanished completely after the Israeli troops seized most of them in 1948. They were converted, within just a few months, from mixed population sectors into purely Jewish populated ones, while the Old City (inside the walls) and some parts of the new sectors outside the walls remained under Arab control. In the meantime a dividing wall was set up all along the armistice line between the Arab and Israeli sides.

The subsequent aggression of 1967 caused the rest of Palestine to fall into Israeli hands, and the whole of Jerusalem became subject to Israeli law. The dividing wall between the two parts of the city was then removed. Jerusalem became more or less directly linked to "Eretz Israel," and the official annexation of the city was proclaimed on July 31, 1980, when united Jerusalem was declared to be the capital of

Israel and the official center for the head of the state and the high court of justice.[6] Meanwhile Jerusalem, with its various old and modern sectors, was subjected to a series of measures that have led to major alterations in the city's morphology. These are as follows:

Isolation of the City from its Natural Surroundings

The western sector of the city was proclaimed the capital of Israel on December 1, 1949, and as such fell under the Israeli legal jurisdiction.[7] The measures imposed included the Absentee Property Law, which permitted confiscation of vast areas of city lands and the lands of surrounding villages—such as Shaykh Badr village, which was totally obliterated so that various governmental buildings, like the Knesset and the Ministry of Foreign Affairs, could be established on its site.[8] This was accompanied by huge construction activity: the new sectors were emptied of most of their Arab inhabitants, both Muslim and Christian, and new settlement complexes and blocks were built to accommodate Jewish immigrants.

These settlement centers were planned with a view to the strategic requirements of fortifying the Israeli occupying state against popular movements, commando operations, and any future wars. As such, the buildings have a military character: the high stone walls, solid and closed, smack of a continuing persecution complex, and are generally indicative of encroachment, aggression, and hegemony.

These centers, moreover, surround the city from all directions, in a series of successive cordons that serve to isolate the city from its Arab environment and shut it off visually from most directions. The result has been an altered skyline in the west. The settlement centers can be classified under three main headings: locational settlement centers; functional settlement centers providing employment opportunities for settlers in the tourist, agricultural, industrial, and military fields; and ideological settlement centers, which are probably the most dangerous, in that they target old Arab quarters. In fact the last two decades have witnessed the intensive presence of extremist religious groups, which aim to settle in Muslim and Christian Arab quarters inside the walls and to replace Islamic monuments by modern Jewish ones.

Ethnic Considerations in Urban Growth

It must be added that the Jewish quarters built outside the city walls at the end of the 19th and beginning of the 20th centuries had a strategic dimension, aimed at creating a later Jewish majority. Thus, in 1921, the borders of the Jerusalem Municipality under the British mandate were demarcated to encompass these quarters,[9] which were annexed to the city despite their relative distance (about 7 km) from the city walls, while the Arab population concentrations and residential quarters from the east and the south of the city were kept outside municipal borders.[10]

The occupation of the city in 1948 was accompanied by the extension of the municipal borders pursuant on ethnographic considerations, expansion being linked to Jewish presence in a bid to achieve an absolute demographic majority for the Jews, and reduce the Arabs to a minority not exceeding 24 percent of the city's overall population. Jewish population concentrations were, therefore, annexed to the Jerusalem Municipality. Lands belonging to Arab villages were also annexed, while Arab population concentrations were excluded. The aim of these measures was to acquire the largest possible land area with the minimum number of Arab residents.

Expansion was marked by conflicting criteria in pursuit of this aim: sometimes the location's topography was the criterion adopted; at other times existing streets were adopted as a frame of reference for defining expansion. This has brought the present area of Metropolitan Jerusalem to 840 sq km[11] i.e., 15 percent of the entire West Bank area. On the Arab side, and before the whole city came under Israeli occupation in 1967, expansion of the municipal borders outside the city walls was limited. The Arab municipal area did not exceed 5.6 sq km.[12] The structural plan recommending that the Arab Municipality should encompass an area of 135 sq km was approved in 1957.[13] However, various circumstances prevented implementation, and this had contradictory positive and adverse effects on the city. On the positive side, the city's general image from the east was maintained. No large constructions were undertaken that might screen the Holy Haram and the Holy Dome of the Rock. The adverse impact was that the city was later to lose its Arab demographic majority.

Perpetuation of the City's Partition

After the Israeli occupation of the whole city in 1967, a new plan was drawn up for Jerusalem and adopted as a model. It was, for security purposes, to start from the hilltops surrounding the city, in order to block off the Old City.[14] However, the plan ran counter to all normal and accepted concepts of urban planning in mountainous sites, leading to a change in the landform and the inherited spatial extension. Although the plan aimed, in appearance, at the unification of the city, in practice it perpetuated partition, through the establishment of a green belt surrounding the Old City—thereby replacing the partitioning wall disposed of in 1967 and shutting the city off from its natural extension. This required that all the historic quarters and cemeteries surrounding the Old City walls be removed, and replaced with what is known as "Wolfson Park."[15]

The plan also included the removal of blocks from the old quarters inside the walls and the establishment of new settlement centers in their place. This made the entire Old City (within the walls) a target for settlement projects involving the planting of 26 Jewish units inside Arab high density population concentrations, with the underlying objective of strangling the city and progressively driving out its Arab inhabitants. This has, needless to say, produced a demographic imbalance, whereby Arab quarters have been turned into small pockets amid large, overwhelming Jewish quarters. Thus a new element, negative and strange, has been added to these settlement centers, distorting the general features of the city, in that the buildings of these centers differ from those predominating in the Old City in terms of form, tissue, and pattern.

Dictating a New Geopolitical fait accompli

The Israeli occupation authorities have given much attention to security control over entry points, outlets, and roads leading to Jerusalem. They have embarked on the construction of a network of tunnels under the Old City, so as to link settlements in the east of the city with those lying in the west; one of these tunnels was completed by the end of the year 2000. In addition to this, many large tracts of Arab lands and many Arab villages have been confiscated to construct detours, not to mention the obliteration of many historical sites for organizational purposes. Special care has been taken to change the urban identity of the Old City and its surroundings, the relevant planning proposals providing for complete removal and replacement by new interlaced quarters via a network of roads below ground level. This will accelerate the forced emigration of the indigenous population, dictating a new geographical fait accompli with political implications and connecting the settlement pockets inside the walls, thereby achieving security control.

II

BEHAVIORAL ASPECTS

Behavioral aspects constitute a major factor in the formation of the city's urban identity, representing as they do the human relations generated by the urban environment, and the activities produced and assimilated by the city. In this respect, Jerusalem might be described as a large theater on the urban spaces of which various human activities are played out, performed by the common people. This is carried out in a manner reflecting the patterns of daily life and its concomitant social and cultural growth and change. As such, Jerusalem has been a crucible of different civilizations throughout history, and this has been manifested in its diverse types of architecture, the languages, appearance, and dress of its residents, and the contents of its commercial stores. More recently, though, the level of activity in Jerusalem's urban spaces has, as a result of social segregation and acute change in the demographic pattern, declined sharply, and the nature of activity there has also changed. These changes may be attributed to the following aspects.

Change in the City's Demographic Reality

Driving the Palestinians to emigrate from Jerusalem was not something phased and linked to the 1948 and 1967 wars. The occupation authorities have actually deprived refugees of the right to return, in breach of Resolution 194 adopted by the United Nations General Assembly on December 11, 1948,[16] while the door was opened wide for Jewish immigration and the settlement of new immigrants inside and outside the walls of the Old City. These newcomers have brought with them new socio-cultural values, mostly of western origin—values conflicting with the prevalent eastern ones and not easily and smoothly adaptable to coexistence with the latter.

The outcome has been daily clashes between indigenous and newly arriving residents, along with provocation of Arab inhabitants through encroachment on their sacrosanct mores, in an attempt to uproot them and drive them to emigrate, with loss of their lands and property through confiscation or forgery of their title deeds and documents—something that has contributed substantially to the city being emptied of many of its Arab inhabitants. All this was clearly demonstrated after Sharon contrived to occupy one of the Arab houses on al-Wadi Road inside the walls. The result was an increase in the aggressive acts perpetrated by such extremist Jewish religious sects as "Atairet Kohanim," "Torah Kohanim," the "Young Israel Movement," "Shovabanim," and others.[17] In order to secure a majority Jewish population, the 1974 "Entry to Israel" law was linked to a package of by-laws and regulations setting conditions under which permanent residence in the city could be terminated. This caused thousands of Jerusalemites to forfeit their right of residence, because they happened to be outside the city for work or study. In addition, the annexation of lands in Eastern Jerusalem was not accompanied by demographic annexation, so that Arab Jerusalemites became mere residents rather than full citizens, something undoubtedly contrary to the rights they were entitled to expect from the occupation government.

This provided the Israeli authorities with an opportunity to cancel the residence of many inhabitants for unexpected reasons. Next came the promulgation, in 1998, of the "Establishment of Living Centers Law,"[18] which linked Arab residence in Jerusalem to the place of habitation and work. By virtue of this, right of residence was accorded only to those living within the municipal borders; the Jerusalemite citizen working outside Jerusalem was reduced to a mere visitor to his own city. Consequently, about 40 percent of Jerusalemites were threatened with loss of permanent residence in the city, in that they were regarded as visitors rather than residents. To this should be added the application of the Absentee Property Law to the city of Jerusalem, which has, in its turn, led to the confiscation of the land and real estate of those who happened, for one reason or another, not to be in the city when it was occupied.

Complication of Building and Development Procedures

The occupation government has failed to recognize the Palestinian right of ownership to numerous lands and real estates, on grounds that these are in fact common property (shared by more than one proprietor), or, in certain areas, on account of faulty records.[19] This has led to the withholding of licences for building or carrying out repairs, and, in consequence, to the demolition of any building built or worked on without such licenses, in addition to the destruction of any building whose owners or inhabitants are accused of security violations. Obtaining a building license requires about nine years of exhausting follow-up procedures, along with costs amounting, more often than not, to US$20,000. This, it goes without saying, obstructs Arab urban development within the city.

In addition to all this, the maximum number of stories in Arab quarters is three, while restrictions in Jewish ones are minimal.[20] A further result has, therefore, been a rise in land prices in the city and the need for those wishing to expand their living quarters to move outside the city.

Decline of Commercial and Social Activities

A new plan has been adopted for the Old City's commercial center, leading to a restriction of traditional commercial and handicraft activities. As a result most of Jerusalem's ancient markets have lost their specialized virtues and their ability to absorb a variety of activities, and this, in turn, has been instrumental in changing the city's urban identity and in the decline of its distinctive business activities.

III

SPIRITUAL AND SYMBOLIC MEANINGS

The spiritual and symbolic meanings linked to the city of Jerusalem and its urban spaces have had a special and important place in shaping the city's architectural identity. As a cradle of the monotheistic religions, Jerusalem had become a shining light for the peaceful coexistence of religions, denominations, races, languages, and customs, within a general Arab framework. Israeli occupation, in contrast, has made for a distortion of the spiritual and symbolic meanings embodied in such civilizational coexistence. The following examples will illustrate it.

Distortion of Christian Religious Symbols

This distortion includes frequent encroachments on Christian holy places and symbols, such as the razing to the ground of a number of quarters on the two sides of the Via Dolorosa where Christian Arabs stage their annual Easter procession, leading to loss of clear boundaries for some parts of the road. Those taking part in this event have been forced to set up chains of human rows to identify the relevant features in the parts razed.

Israel has, moreover, exploited large tracts of Christian religious endowment land for the construction of housing complexes. One reason for this is that Israel regards the Orthodox Church as a mere sect or denomination, not as an independent church. The 1997 agreement between the Vatican and the occupation government perpetuated this situation, placing the Orthodox Church under Israeli legal jurisdiction and granting Israel the right to intervene vis-à-vis Christian endowments, especially with regard to building on lands.[21]

Encroachment on Islamic Religious Symbols

Numerous acts of aggression against Muslim sacred places and religious symbols have been committed in an attempt to seize the Holy Haram of Jerusalem and establish the so-called "Third Temple" on the site of the Holy Dome of the Rock.[22] Recommendations for the realization of such designs have been made plain. The arson attack on the al-Aqsa Mosque on August 21, 1969, by an Australian Christian extremist (with possible Israeli complicity) had this aim. The fire damaged or destroyed a third of the Mosque area,[23] including Saladin's pulpit, with its symbolic implications for the liberation of Jerusalem from the Crusaders, as well as the prayer niche, the wooden dome, the gypsum decorations and other parts of the Mosque.

Many archeological excavations have also been carried out in accordance with a methodical scheme that gives due attention to the endorsement of a Jewish presence in Jerusalem, but distorts and diminishes the notion of a continuous Arab presence in the holy city. Excavations have been made under the Aqsa Mosque to unearth the so-called Wailing Wall. The foundations of the Aqsa Mosque have suffered from this treatment, so that the Mosque is now liable to cracking and collapse should such works be continued and intensified. Many Muslim religious monuments have also been seized, including seizure of the Tankiziyyah School close by the western wall of the Holy Haram for use as a Jewish synagogue. This has coincided with the cutting of a ditch under this wall (which, according to Jewish claims, comprises the western wall of the Temple) and the erection of another Jewish synagogue inside it. This has jeopardized the safety of a large number of adjacent buildings, thereby providing an excuse for their elimination. Many historic buildings have been demolished and destroyed for this reason, including institutes, schools, mosques, markets, and churches.

Restricting access to the Aqsa Mosque courtyards is, it must be added, one of the major aims of the occupation authorities. This is being effected by closing the city and preventing worshippers from entering it on several occasions, not to mention attacking worshippers and pricking them with bayonets.

Changing the Historical Memory

The names of numerous Arab monuments, streets and squares in the city of Jerusalem have been changed, with a view to effecting a corresponding change vis-à-vis the historical memory of these places and imposing a new environmental and cultural identity commensurate with Jewish religious concepts. Significant examples are the name "Temple Mount" given to the Holy Haram, calling the Holy Buraq Wall the "Wailing Wall" and giving new names to many other monuments, including the city gates.

The following table shows some Arab sites in Jerusalem and their Jewish names:

Arab Names	Jewish Names
al-Haram al-Sharif	Temple Mount
Ha'it al-Buraq (al-Buraq Wall)	Wailing/Western Wall
Harat al-Shurafa' (Shurafa' Quarter)	Jewish Quarter
Bab 'Abd al-Hamid ('Abd al-Hamid Gate)	New Gate
Bab al-Zahirah	Herod's Gate
Bab al-Asbat (Tribe's Gate)	Lion's Gate
Bab al-Rahmah (Mercy Gate)	Golden Gate
Bab al-Nabi Dawud (Prophet David Gate)	Zion Gate
Bab Muhammad, Huttah, Magarbeh	Dung Gate
Tariq al-Wadi (Valley Road)	Hibai Road
'Aqabat al-Khalidiyyah	Hishmonim Road
Dir Mar Yuhanna (St. John's Monastery)	Noab David
Hawsh al-Shawish (Shawish Courtyard)	Beit Ruth

IV

CONCLUSION

It is evident from the above account that the city of Jerusalem is presently facing many dangers to its identity as a spiritual and humane city and to its character, which is threatened both by westernization and by aspects of tyranny and repression in its midst. It is utterly impossible to attribute these transformations to simple factors of urban growth. It is rather a matter of Israeli occupation practices and the role these play in consolidating such transformation through the following measures:

1. Building and organizational laws currently in effect in the city.
2. Confiscation of lands and the refusal to recognize the rights of disposal of property.

3. Israeli settler practices designed to provoke and intimidate Arab residents.
4. Israeli settlement projects inside and outside the walls, and the adverse and distorting impact of these on urban form, tissue, pattern, and skyline.
5. Judaization of the city, the capture of the Holy Haram of Jerusalem, and the building of the Third Temple.

Hence it is essential to establish viable criteria in the light of the present situation of the city, with a view to ensuring continuity and authentication of identity through organic growth with due observance of historical identity. There is an urgent need, with regard to the city's morphology, for alternative structural plans to be prepared and counter-measures to be imposed, and also for dealing with the present political, ideological, geographical, economic, and demographic aspects. This includes:

1. Proposals for achieving demographic balance in the city and assimilating the Jewish minority through the development of contact areas with the new sectors in the city.
2. Protection of the Old City, including the Holy Haram of Jerusalem, in a bid to prevent changes to the urban, social, and economic reality of the city.

With regard to behavioral aspects, the present study calls for measures designed to prevent the city being emptied of its inhabitants. Other measures would include a review of the Ottoman property registers and the issuing of title deeds for all the real estate for which Israel does not recognize Palestinian ownership, in addition to the protection of property from settlers' threats.

As for safeguarding the spiritual and historic symbols linked to the city, the study calls for the setting up of architectural, historical, legal, and social field studies with a view to identifying the endangered sites and buildings and establishing comprehensive means of preserving this human civilizational heritage through emergency repairs to endangered buildings, wholesale urban revival of the city, setting an order of priorities for work and linking this to the preservation of human factors and defense of the rights of individuals to their property in the city. This includes encouragement and backing for researchers and scientific bodies[24] working on the registration, documentation, and restoration of buildings in the Old City.

THE URBAN TRANSFORMATION OF
JERUSALEM AFTER 1967

Anthony Coon

Jerusalem in 1967

At the time of the 1967 war the armistice ("green") line dating from the 1948 cease fire divided the city into West Jerusalem, which contained the central government institutions of the state of Israel, and East Jerusalem, which included the old walled city and the religious sites, and which had been designated as the "second capital" of Jordan following the annexation of the West Bank to Jordan.

In 1967 the population was about 200,000 in West Jerusalem and 70,000 in East Jerusalem, and the municipal areas were 38 and 6.5 sq km respectively. Thus, the west side had a population nearly three times as great, and a municipal area nearly six times as great, as that of the east side.

The era of Jordanian administration witnessed the emergence of a modern commercial area to the north of the Old City in the Shaykh Jarrah neighborhood, and extensive residential development along the Ramallah road—also to the north of the Old City, and outside the then municipal area.

This period began with a substantial influx of Palestinian refugees from West Jerusalem after 1948 (and the departure of a smaller number of Jews from the old city), while the occupation of East Jerusalem in 1967 appears to have resulted in the loss of some 23,000 Palestinians.[1] Immediately after the 1967 occupation Israel annexed some 70 sq km of the West Bank. This annexation has not been internationally recognized. The area includes the Jordanian municipal area of East Jerusalem, an airport, and most of the land and some of the population of 28 villages. This area was included with West Jerusalem and is administered by the (Israeli) Municipality of Jerusalem. It is referred to in this paper as "annexed East Jerusalem."

Palestinians from outside the boundary of annexed East Jerusalem are not allowed to live in East Jerusalem, and are normally prevented by the Israelis from entering it. Many localities (such as Abu Dis) outside the boundary of annexed East Jerusalem are considered by Palestinians to be part of Jerusalem; these localities come under the control of the "civil administration" of the military government, with (since 1995) most civil affairs in most of the urban locations ("Area B")[2] being the responsibility of the Palestine National Authority.

Plans in 1967

There are few cities with as long a planning history as Jerusalem. A series of plans commissioned by the Mandate authorities from 1918 to 1944 urged that development in the Old City should be strictly regulated and that urban development should take place to the west, northwest, and southwest. The area of the "Holy Basin" between the Old City and the Mount of Olives–Mount Scopus (Jabal at Tur–Al Masharef) should remain undeveloped in order to conserve the views from and to the Old City, to retain the setting of the holy sites, and to provide areas of "public open space" for quiet enjoyment of the population.[3]

At the time of the Israeli occupation of East Jerusalem in 1967 the official development plan was an "outline" (master) plan prepared in 1963 under the 1955 Jordanian planning law.[4] The area falling under Jordanian administration in 1948 included very few of the areas designated for urban development by the Mandate plans, and this new plan remedied that situation.

It covered not only the (Jordanian) municipal area, but also an area some ten times as large surrounding it to north, south, and east, which was at that time being considered for incorporation within the municipality. This plan was prepared for the Jordanian government by Henry Kendall, who had previously drawn up for the Mandate authorities the 1944 Jerusalem plan, and the regional plans covering each administrative district of Palestine (referred to below). The 1963 plan—i.e., the plan legally in force when the Israelis occupied East Jerusalem and the West Bank—provided very extensive opportunity for new residential development north of the Old City, as well as to the east (at Abu Dis), and in the south (at Beit Safafa and Sur Bahir); several new industrial areas were also proposed. The Holy Basin was to be kept open.[5]

It is interesting to speculate how the development of East Jerusalem would have progressed since the 1967 occupation if the provisions of the 1963 plan had been respected by the occupying power as is required under international law.[6]

The 50 sq km of residential land would have provided ample

opportunity for Palestinian urban expansion to the present day, including opportunity for the expected rural–urban migration from the West Bank. Work places and industrial opportunities could have been provided in the proposed industrial areas, with consequent benefits to the environment (by relocation of the unsatisfactory workshop area of Wadi Joz) and to the Palestinian economy. Furthermore, the plan provided no sanction for any of the Jewish settlements which subsequently took place, and indeed the plan, if it had been retained, would have precluded construction of most of these settlements because of the specific zoning for agriculture and forestry in most of the subsequent settlement areas.

The plan was therefore incompatible with Israel's development policies. These were never formally set out in any plan or policy statement, nor have they been to the present day—either in annexed East Jerusalem (falling under the responsibility of the Israeli municipality of Jerusalem) or in the rest of the West Bank (administered by the military commander through the Civil Administration). According to Israeli and Jordanian law, development can only be controlled if there is an approved outline plan for the city. No such plan has been approved for annexed East Jerusalem, though the Jerusalem Municipality prepared a plan in 1968 that, though never approved, guided the initial land confiscation for Jewish settlement through the policies it implied.

These policies, which have only become apparent from observation of what is actually happening on the ground, include land confiscation, settlement construction, and strict control and demolition of Palestinian development, as discussed later in this paper. In retrospect it is interesting to note that these mechanisms are little different from those used within Israel itself after 1948 and even in the pre-state period. Throughout all these periods the policies have been formalized behind closed doors by Jewish para-statal organizations, especially the Jewish National Fund, and then implemented by reference to the law—i.e., Israeli law within annexed East Jerusalem and Jordanian law elsewhere.

The Israeli government ignored and then in 1974 formally canceled the 1963 plan.[7] This meant that there was no plan for the area that had been annexed to Israel seven years previously. It is likely that few Palestinians (or even Israelis) had previously been aware of this plan. In terms of the plans "inherited" by the Israelis on occupation of the West Bank in 1967, there is an interesting and instructive contrast between the fate of the (1963) plan for Jerusalem and the plans elsewhere in the West Bank. The plan for Jerusalem provided extensive scope for Palestinian development and was relatively up to date; the Israelis canceled it. The rest of the West Bank was covered by two regional plans prepared in the early 1940s (by Kendall under the Mandate) which neither expected, nor provided for, any significant development to take place; the Israelis have used these regional plans as pretext for the demolition of thousands of Palestinian homes.[8]

These regional plans had no doubt lain (like the 1963 plan) forgotten on an administrator's shelves: the regional plans were only "discovered" by the Israelis in 1980 and 1985.[9] Since then they have been used to prevent Palestinian development taking place (and to justify the demolition of houses built without a permit) almost everywhere that was not developed in the 1940s—when the population was six times smaller than at present. These policies apply now in "Area C,"[10] which includes some land within 4 km of the Old City and which most Palestinians would consider to be part of Jerusalem, though beyond the boundary of annexed East Jerusalem.

Changing East Jerusalem from a Palestinian to a Jewish City

In many ways the Israeli government policy of "demographic balance" enunciated in 1973 may be considered to be the cornerstone of Israeli policy in Jerusalem. The policy, suggested by the Gafni committee, was that "a demographic balance between Jews and Arabs must be maintained as it was at the end of 1972."[11]

As with so many of the policies followed under the occupation, it has a superficial reasonableness (who could object to "balance"?); its meaning and operational significance were never spelled out, and it remained little noticed or commented upon for several years, especially by the Palestinian community. In practice, and with the benefit of hindsight, what the policy meant was that there would be a maximum level of Palestinian housing allowed permitted, such that the number of Palestinians in the Jerusalem Municipality (i.e., the Palestinian population of the Palestinian areas that had been annexed six years previously) should not be allowed to exceed 26.5% of the total population of Jerusalem. This was despite (or rather because of) the fact that the Palestinian rate of natural increase was half as much again as the Jewish rate, as it still is, and there were even then few opportunities for development within West Jerusalem. In direct consequence of this policy it was going to be necessary over a ten-year period from 1972 to transfer more Jews into Palestinian East Jerusalem than the number of Palestinians living there at the time.[12] The number of Jewish settlers would have to be even higher to compensate for the net outward movement of Jews from West Jerusalem, mainly to the West Bank settlements, the population of which was a concurrent Israeli government policy. If such a rapid rate of colonization could not be achieved, then the only way of keeping to the target would be by restrictive means, including expulsion of Palestinians from the city, refusing permission for Palestinian housing, and actually demolishing houses built by Palestinians.

The only Palestinians allowed by the Israeli government to live in Jerusalem are those who were living within the area annexed in 1967 and their descendants. These people are issued with "blue cards." At least 6,257 of these cards had been confiscated by 1998.[13] This resulted in the expulsion from the city of most of these people and their families.

Land Confiscation

In 1967 most Palestinian land was in small private ownership parcels; some was state owned, though very little of this was in Jerusalem. Confiscation of private land (also termed "land seizure" by both Palestinians and Israelis) has been an essential prerequisite to Jewish settlement both in annexed East Jerusalem and in the rest of the West Bank. There are however important differences both in timing and in procedures. The city's draft 1968 master plan noted that "effective development of [East Jerusalem] will require the expropriation of substantial areas." As usual, the policy needs to be de-coded: what it meant and what actually happened was that land should be seized from private (Palestinian) owners and vested in the Israel Land Authority, which is controlled by the Jewish National Fund and then leased (as noted below) only to Jews. Hence, "effective development" meant development exclusively for Jews in an area that, at the time of the 1967 occupation, was populated entirely by Palestinians. By 1970 a quarter of annexed East Jerusalem had been confiscated—a far more rapid rate of confiscation than was achieved in the rest of the West Bank. By 2001 about 35 percent has been confiscated.[14]

Most of this land (including almost all of the earlier expropriations) was confiscated by using a 1943 Mandate emergency regulation[15] (against which no appeal is effectively possible) authorizing expropriation when there is "public need" for such action.

The then deputy mayor of Jerusalem has since commented:

> This was an extraordinary interpretation of the word public: the only legitimate public was Jewish, and therefore only Jews were entitled to benefit from the expropriation. The Arabs, a "haphazard collection of individuals" were to have their private property confiscated so that Jews could settle in Jerusalem and create geopolitical "facts" there.[16]

Different procedures have been used outside annexed East Jerusalem. The main methods have been to requisition the land for "military" purposes and, since 1980, to seize land on the grounds that it was not properly registered (the process of registration was stopped by the Israelis in 1968) or not in continuous agricultural use; in either case the land is transferred to the Israel Lands Authority (ILA).[17]

Both within and outside annexed East Jerusalem land confiscation has, with rather few exceptions, not included the actual houses of Palestinians. Thus the Israeli government claims that settlements themselves are not intended to displace Arab inhabitants, nor do they do so in practice.[18]

However, recent land confiscations have come ever closer to Palestinian homes—in some cases completely surrounding them, with intense physical and psychological pressures to move. One example of such pressure, which has not so far been successful, is the case of the Aqel family, whose home is just 1.5 km north of the old city. In 1950 they fled to land they owned here from just across the border in Israel. In 1967 they found themselves again under Israeli rule, and the following year notice of expropriation was served on all of their land, including their home, under the 1943 regulation. The Hebrew University, whose buildings now surround the 150-square-meter plot containing the Aqel home, then developed the land mainly for housing. At the prompting of the university (who wish to use the land for parking) the family have been issued with numerous orders to quit as well as curfew orders, and have been refused permission to enlarge or even maintain their now dilapidated home. On May 11, 2000 they received a demolition order because they had undertaken unpermitted renovations and the land was ILA-owned. As of now, this order has not been carried out.[19]

Settlement Construction

The Jewish population of annexed East Jerusalem has risen from zero

in 1967 to 168,000 in 2001. All except 3,000 in the expanded Jewish
Quarter of the Old City live in new settlements, which have been built
by the Israeli government on confiscated land.[20] These include the
largest settlements in the occupied territories (Ramot and Pisgat Ze'ev,
each with nearly 40,000 people), which form part of an almost
continuous link between West Jerusalem and the settlements beyond
annexed East Jerusalem, and, in so doing, fragment the Palestinian
neighborhoods within occupied East Jerusalem into two sectors.

The settlement population within annexed East Jerusalem is
similar in size to that elsewhere in the West Bank; the bulk of current
(and future) settlement activity is taking place outside the annexed
area. The last major settlement in annexed East Jerusalem is that at
Jabal Abu Ghneim; this settlement, named Har Homa, was started in
1997. Har Homa and Gilo together form another major Jewish
development continuity, dividing Palestinians in Jerusalem from the
Bethlehem area to the south. The settlements have a physical,
environmental, demographic, and strategic reality, and much has been
written about these aspects. However, perhaps the most fundamental
factor to their character is the legal/administrative mechanism used by
the Israeli government to ensure that the settlements remain Jewish—
not just in the immediate future, but for all time. Settlements built for
an incoming group would normally be infiltrated by the local
(Palestinian) population, but this has not happened: for example, it is
understood that not a single inhabitant of Ramot is Palestinian. How
has this been achieved, even under the watchful eye of an international
community supposedly alert to overtly discriminatory practices? The
mechanisms used by the Israelis are all indirect, heavily disguised, and
controlled essentially by the Jewish para-statal organizations rather
than being the subject of debate in Israeli political institutions. Hence,
the procedure is very different from discrimination under the
apartheid system in South Africa, when the rules on where the subject
people could live were rather clear. The methods used by the Israelis to
ensure the Jewish character of settlements include the following:

Choice of implementing agency. The lack of any approved plan for the
municipality means that overall targets and mechanisms can be kept
obscure. The key to ensuring the Jewish identity of a new settlement
is the choice of implementing agency. In many cases this is the
Ministry of Housing (who have never built housing for Palestinians in
Jerusalem); in other cases the agency may be the Jewish National Fund

or related body (who are precluded by their constitution from providing for non-Jews). The process of selecting the agency is covert. In two cases (Reches Shuafat and Har Homa), Palestinians whose land has been confiscated have attempted to apply, but with no success. The instructions issued by the municipality to the firms designing each new settlement are prepared at the political level, not by the municipality planners, and it is these instructions that specify the client group and the ethnic character of the settlement.

Exclusion of non-Jews from renting. All land for settlements is vested in the Israel Lands Authority.[21] The ILA does not sell land—it rents it for periods of 49 years. The rental contracts specify that the lease for the land is invalid if the holder of the lease is an "alien person." An alien person is defined (on the lease, which of course no Palestinian is ever likely to see) as one who is not "...entitled to the status of immigrant under the Law of Return." That law specifies that such a person must be a Jew.[22] Hence, all Palestinians are considered "alien" and thus unable to lease a home in a settlement, even if a Jew wished to sub-lease to them.

Exclusion of non-Jews from entering settlements. Palestinians are prevented by military order from entering any settlement without the prior permission of the military commander. As with the leases above, the words "Palestinian" or "Jew" are not mentioned: the order allows entry only to Israeli citizens and holders of foreign passports. This order does not apply in annexed East Jerusalem.

Expulsion from the Old City. In an unusually frank decision, the High Court of Israel ruled in 1975 that the Burqan family should be expelled from the house the court agreed was his undoubted property, on grounds of "public utility," because the area of the expanded Jewish quarter was to be confiscated in order to restore its "natural ethnic" quality.[23]

Restriction and Demolition of Palestinian Housing
Both Palestinian neighborhoods and Jewish settlements are planned under the same procedures: an outline plan under the 1965 (Israeli) planning law is prepared; applications for building permits that accord with the plan are granted; unpermitted development may be demolished. The procedure is frequently claimed by the Israeli government to be even-handed. In practice things are very different.

On the one hand, plans for the Jewish areas are prepared rapidly, the infrastructure and housing are massively subsidized, facilities are provided, and the individual plots are defined ready for construction. In the Palestinian areas, on the other hand,

◄ After cancellation of the 1963 plan, all work on new outline plans was frozen until the late 1970s; the first plan was approved in 1984, and several neighborhoods still have no plan. Legal development is impossible where there is no plan.

◄ The cost of permits (which includes an infrastructure levy) is extremely high.

◄ The plans designate no significant areas for new development— only for "infilling" between existing development. The designated development areas (including areas already developed) constitute only 9 percent[24] (7 sq km) of the area of annexed East Jerusalem.

◄ Land outside the designated development areas is zoned as *shetah nof patuah* (open landscape area), where no Palestinian development is allowed. Such areas have frequently been rezoned for Jewish development in the past—as at Reches Shuafat, Har Homa, Beit Safafa, and even French Hill, which had been so designated in the 1968 plan.[25]

◄ Permitted densities and building heights in Jewish areas are between two and three times as much as allowed in Palestinian areas.[26]

◄ Permits are not granted for new development until new plots are established in a "detailed plan." Very few such detailed plans have yet been approved. Nor are permits granted on land within annexed East Jerusalem owned (as much of it is) by residents outside.

Consequently, few building permits are issued to Palestinians; only about 3,000 have been issued since 1967.[27] This has undoubtedly contributed to the bad housing conditions and level of overcrowding,[28] as well as the deplorable quality of infrastructure and poor standards of urban design. The number of houses built by Palestinians under the occupation appears, however, to have kept pace with the rapid pace of population increase. Much of this development takes place at night or during the Jewish holidays. Obviously the great majority of this construction is conducted without permits and consequently liable to be demolished. Since 1987 at least 284 Palestinian homes in East Jerusalem have been demolished for lack of a building permit,[29] leaving nearly 2,000 people homeless. The Israeli government claims that the policy applies equally to Jews and that similar numbers of Jewish homes have been demolished.[30] Action has indeed been taken against Jewish homes, but mainly for minor infringements, such as removal of a porch or garden wall; not a single inhabited home of a Jew has in fact been demolished. The number of homes under demolition order is far higher than the number so far demolished, and the inhabitants of these threatened houses live in constant fear of arrival of the bulldozers, which come at short notice accompanied by hundreds of armed police, who order a local curfew to reduce international publicity. Most of the recent demolitions have been on the pretext that the house is in *shetah nof patuah*. Demolitions take place in all neighborhoods, and it appears that houses rebuilt after previous demolition and houses near projected Jewish development are particularly at risk. In the latter category are

⇥   Al-'Isawiya, which stands in the way of the Jewish development linking West Jerusalem and the West Bank, and where a protesting neighbor was shot dead by police during a demolition in 1998, and
⇥   the village of al-Walaja, where a new Jewish settlement is planned and where 45 of the 60 homes are under demolition order, as also is the mosque and the only access road to the village.

Conclusion

This paper has examined some aspects of the way Palestinian development in Jerusalem has been administered under the occupation, rather than the conduct of the occupation per se. Most of the conclusions apply also to the other Palestinian areas under occupation—the West Bank and the Gaza Strip—but Jerusalem is of particular concern because it has the planning problems of almost any major city, and because its history, its sites, and its panorama are so precious to the followers of Judaism, Christianity, and Islam the world over. Palestinians might—even under occupation—have looked forward to an orderly environment, adequate facilities and housing, and a modest prosperity, if the occupying power had, as required under international law, implemented the plan in force at the time of the occupation in 1967. Instead, the Israeli government has successfully restricted Palestinian development largely to the same areas covered in 1967; instituted a massive and costly program of construction of new neighborhoods for the Israeli Jewish population; and has been successful in ensuring the exclusion of Palestinians from these new neighborhoods.

Meanwhile the standards of housing, local environment, infrastructure, and facilities available to Palestinians have suffered. There can be few places on earth where the environmental and living standards of two sectors of the population are in such marked contrast. There is surely nowhere else where this has been achieved over 30 years so consistently, with so little change in policy, by a succession of governments, and with such sharp discrimination between a favored population and an exploited population. The urban transformation that has been wrought by the Israelis in Jerusalem has certainly been astonishing. No wonder that, as they search for ways to end the occupation, Palestinians are now giving thought to how the wrongs of this transformation can be put right.

THE JERUSALEM QUESTION IN
INTERNATIONAL LAW:
THE WAY TO A SOLUTION

Eugene Cotran

Status of Jerusalem in International Law

The legal right to ownership of Jerusalem—what lawyers call sovereignty—has been claimed by many peoples over the ages. Historians have devoted time and energy to stressing that Jerusalem has been occupied respectively by the Canaanites, the Philistines, the Israelites or Hebrews, the Greeks, the Romans and Byzantines, the Arabs and the Ottoman Turks.

Jews, Christians, and Muslims, each in their turn and with equal vigor and fervor, have emphasized that Jerusalem (in particular the Old City and Holy Places) has a special meaning and significance for them, so that it has rightly been said that Jerusalem belongs to the "whole world."

I do not intend in this paper to delve into historical or religious rights. In the first place, these have been amply documented elsewhere by historians and others more qualified than I. Secondly, I do not consider that such a historical survey will help in any way towards a practical solution to the problems that exist now between Israel and the Palestinians.

The way to a solution to the present impasse lies not in ancient history, nor in using the argument of who got there first or who has the better historical or religious right. The starting point, it seems to me, is modern rather than ancient history, and a recognition by Israel of three basic principles:

1. The truly international character of Jerusalem;
2. That might is not right; and
3. That the only possible solution to Jerusalem (and indeed to the whole of the Palestine problem) will necessarily be based not on exclusive ownership or sovereignty, but on a sharing arrangement with the Palestinians, by whatever name that is called.

My starting point, therefore, will only go back to 1922, when a British Mandate was created by the League of Nations over Palestine. There is no dispute that at that time the vast majority of the population of Palestine consisted of Arab Palestinians and that there was only a very small minority of Jews (some 10 percent). As we all know, Jewish immigration increased considerably during the Mandate, and more so in the aftermath of the Second World War, the Zionist movement being in earnest then; aided and abetted by the British government and the Balfour Declaration, the Jewish population had increased, by the end of the Mandate in 1948, to some 25 percent in Palestine, and to some 48 percent in Jerusalem. However, the Palestinian Arabs continued to own the majority of the land in Palestine, including Jerusalem.

The next point in time was of course the Partition Plan of 1947, and it is no coincidence that the Plan truly recognized the international character of Jerusalem by its recommendation that neither the Jewish state nor the Arab Palestinian state should have sovereignty over Jerusalem, but that Jerusalem should be a *corpus separatum* with an international special regime administered by the UN.[1]

It was of course not to be—hostilities broke out, resulting in the creation of the State of Israel, which was larger than what was allotted to it under the Partition Plan; thousands of Palestinians were expelled from their homes, creating a tragic refugee problem, and the whole of West Jerusalem was incorporated as part of Israel, the eastern sector, including the Old City, uniting with Jordan.

Again, I need not delve into the policy of what has been termed "legalized theft" of the land by legislation that virtually deprived West Jerusalemites, and indeed the whole of the Arab Palestinians, of their land in all parts of what became Israel.

The Palestinians became "absentees," and are still absentees 50 years on.[2] In brief, history repeated itself some twenty years later, when, following the Six Day War in 1967, Israel forcibly occupied the whole of the West Bank and East Jerusalem, including the Old City. This time they were even more daring and brutal than in 1948. Not content with the same policy of "stealing the land" from the so-called absentees of Arab East Jerusalem (whom they had expelled), they extended the area of Arab East Jerusalem, and declared the whole— West, the extended East, including the Old City—to be the "eternal undivided Capital of Israel."[3]

Again, as though that were not enough, Israel, having "stolen" the land, pursued a policy of replacing the Arab Palestinians by Jewish settlers and settlements in and around Arab East Jerusalem. This continues up till today, despite the Oslo Accords—a case in point being the debacle at Jabal Abu Ghneim (Har Homa), where building began in 1997.

Although the title of my paper suggests that I am going to give a learned analysis on the position of Jerusalem in international law today, I am in fact going to be very brief on this topic. Another Palestinian, the late Henry Cattan, the best known writer and authority on the Palestine question, has written extensively on the subject, and has shown beyond any shadow of doubt that by any standards of civilized behavior, fairness, justice of international law, Israel's actions over Jerusalem are illegal, null, and void.

In his last book, *The Palestine Question*,[4] the late Henry Cattan dealt with the problem of Jerusalem in Part III (chapters 20, 29, and 30, p. 247–260). In chapter 29, entitled "Israel's Illicit Actions in Jerusalem since 1948," he refers to the unlawful usurpation of Jerusalem (West, East, and the Old City), the eviction of the Palestinian inhabitants therefrom in 1948 and 1967, the plunder of Arab Refugee Property, movable and immovable, the Judaization of the population, the colonization of the city and its environs, the demolitions, in the Old City, of the Magarbeh Quarter, the Mamillah cemetery and other Arab-owned buildings, and the extensive excavations in the vicinity of and underneath al-Haram al-Sharif. He concludes the chapter as follows:

> Since 1967 UN resolutions have dealt specifically with the Old City. The UN has:
>
> 1. affirmed the "legal status" of Jerusalem;
> 2. condemned or censured Israel's actions in Jerusalem and proclaimed the nullity of all legislative and administrative measures taken to change the status and historic character of the city, including expropriations of land and properties and transfer of populations;
> 3. called upon Israel:
>> (One) to withdraw from the territories occupied in 1967 which include the Old City of Jerusalem;
>> (Two) to rescind all measures taken to change the legal status, geography and demographic composition of Jerusalem;
>> (Three) to permit the return of the Palestine

refugees displaced in 1967;
(Four) to dismantle and cease the establishment of
settlements in the occupied territories, including
Jerusalem.

Although UN resolutions have since 1967 emphasized the illegality and nullity of Israeli actions in the Old City of Jerusalem, this does not mean that similar Israeli acts in modern Jerusalem are any less tainted. Whether it be the usurpation of modern Jerusalem, or the expulsion of its inhabitants, or the confiscation of Arab property, or the transfer of Jews to the city, all those acts are illegal and null and void both under international law and UN resolutions."[5]

The Way to a Solution

The starting point of any solution must be Oslo and the Declaration of Principles (DOP) of September 1993. The opposers of Oslo have maintained that Oslo and the famous White House handshake between Arafat and Rabin has solved nothing and intensified the problems. Jerusalem, refugees, and settlers (the three most difficult problems) were left to the final status talks, which have not even started; settlements are continuing in and around Jerusalem; the Israelis cannot be trusted; and the Palestinians gained nothing out of Oslo.

For my part I have never accepted this argument. When I studied the Declaration of Principles, I wrote enthusiastically, suggesting that the DOP from a legal point of view can lead ultimately to a solution acceptable to Palestinians, that is, an independent State of Palestine in the West Bank and Gaza, with East Jerusalem as its capital. I felt at least relieved that Jerusalem was put on the agenda for the final status talks, and that there was provision for participation in the elections by Palestinian residents of East Jerusalem.

While acknowledging misgivings and problems, I argued that Israel made various legal and political concessions in DOP,[6] viz:

1. First and foremost the Palestinians had recognition from Israel that they are a "people." Formerly Palestinians were referred to in Israeli legislation as inhabitants of Judea, Samaria, and Gaza. The recognition of a "people" in international law carries with it the right to self-determination.

2. They explicitly recognized UNSC Resolution 242 and a settlement based on it.

3. They explicitly recognized the PLO and its Provisional

Government by dealing with it and signing an international treaty with it.

4. They implicitly recognized the State of Palestine declared in 1988, already recognized by some 120 states.

5. They agreed to treat the West Bank and Gaza as a single territorial unit, again implicitly recognizing the unity of the State of Palestine and the approximate borders of the state. The use of the word "borders," left to the final status talks, was significant.

6. They agreed to, and did in fact give, control leading to full self-government of parts of Palestine, to be extended to the whole at the end of the interim period of five years.

7. They have withdrawn their military and civil administration from Gaza, Jericho, and other cities of the West Bank, and will eventually withdraw from the whole of the West Bank and thus end 27 years of tyranny and brutality.

When the DOP was signed in September 1993, opposers of Oslo said that the Israelis would not fulfill their part of the bargain. They were not right, at least until the May 1996 elections, when the Labor government was still in power. Although the timetable was delayed, withdrawal did take place under Phase 1: Gaza and Jericho. The PNA arrived in Gaza in May 1994, and the five-year period—the interim phase—started then. Further prolonged negotiations for Phase II, i.e., elections and redeployment, were finally agreed at Taba, and the Interim Agreement for the West Bank and Gaza, signed in Washington on September 28, 1995.

Elections for president (*Ra'is*) and a Legislative Council of 88 members took place in January 1996. As already mentioned, Arab residents of Jerusalem participated. The elections were free and democratic and so certified by international observers. Withdrawal took place from all the cities under the first phase of redeployment (except for the small pocket of Hebron) and was on schedule until the Israeli elections in May 1996, when the whole process became stalled by Mr. Netanyahu's election as prime minister and the advent of the new Likud government.

It is therefore clear that the criticisms of the Oslo peace process should not lie with the provisions of the agreements per se, but with

1. The failure of the Netanyahu government to carry out Israel's obligations under them, and indeed the flouting of them day by day.

2. The lack of an effective mechanism for enforcing its provisions.

I say "effective," because, although there is a provision for settling disputes by conciliation and arbitration, it is drafted in the vaguest of terms and has not been used. It says that: (1) disputes as to the interpretation of the Agreement shall be settled by the Joint Liaison Committee; (2) disputes that cannot be settled by negotiations "may be settled by a mechanism of conciliation to be agreed by the parties"; and (3) the parties "may agree to submit to arbitration disputes relating to the interim period which cannot be settled through conciliation. To this end, upon the agreement of both parties, the parties will establish an Arbitration Committee."[7]

Following the Jerusalem al-Aqsa mosque outrage on September 22, 1996, followed by the killing of some 75 Palestinians and the wounding of some 1,000, the Netanyahu government continued and persisted in its provocations and deliberate breaches of the Oslo Agreement, viz:

1. by saying that there would be no further redeployment "until Arafat stops the Hamas suicide bombers";
2. by the closure of the Palestinian self-rule areas;
3. by the closure of East Jerusalem and denying the right of residence to Palestinians in the City;[8]
4. by the confiscation of large areas of land from Jenin in the north to Hebron in the south;
5. by announcing and commencing the building and enlargement of settlements in the West Bank and in and around Jerusalem;
6. by refusing to commence the final status negotiations on Jerusalem, settlements, and refugees;
7. by withholding tax revenues to be paid to the PNA, and by general economic starvation.

But that is not all. There is a dangerous trend of condoning extremist actions and violations of human rights and devaluing of Palestinian life by the extremist element in Israeli public opinion, and even by the courts.

Haim Baram, in his column in *Middle East International* under the heading "A Society Gone Mad," says that "there is a growing murderous insanity unleashing itself on the Palestinian population and manifesting itself everywhere."[9]

On October 27, 1996 an Israeli settler, Nahum Korman, entered the West Bank village of Husan and kicked to death a ten-year-old Palestinian boy, Hilmi Shawasha. Korman was not indicted for murder, but for manslaughter. In November, an Israeli court imposed a fine of less than one penny on four soldiers found guilty of fatally shooting a Palestinian at a road block.

Worse still, and contrary to the UN Torture Convention,[10] the Israeli High Court of Justice on November 14, 1996 condoned, indeed allowed, the use of force and torture on a Palestinian prisoner Mohamed Hamdan by the Israeli General Security Service (Shein Beit) during his interrogation for alleged involvement with Islamic Jihad. Other decisions of a similar nature followed.[11]

1997 started with a glimmer of hope, in that the Protocol Concerning Redeployment in Hebron was signed on January 15, 1997 in the presence of the US Special Middle East Coordinator. Both sides reaffirmed their commitment to the Oslo Peace Process and the Interim Agreement. But, although the Israeli military forces did redeploy within ten days as provided in the Protocol (except for area H2, where they stayed for the "security" of the 400 or so Israeli settlers in the city), hope thereafter was short lived: in March the further redeployment that took place was only from some ten percent of the areas agreed in the Interim Agreement and Protocol. Further, the Netanyahu government reneged on negotiating on the outstanding issues in the Interim Agreement, and also on the obligation to commence the all-important final status negotiations within two months of the Hebron Protocol.

The last straw, however, came in April, when Israel announced its decision (and indeed started implementing it by sending in the bulldozers) to build housing units on Arab land in East Jerusalem at Jabal Abu Ghneim, creating what would be the settlement Har Homa.

Worldwide condemnation, two UN Security Council Resolutions (vetoed by the US) and two General Assembly Resolutions[12] (with only Israel, the US, and Micronesia voting against) fell on deaf ears— the building at Jabal Abu Ghneim went ahead, with a further housing settlement at Ras El Amoud threatened.

The subsequent visit by US Secretary of State Madeleine Albright did not shift Mr. Netanyahu. He repeated that he would not budge on the Jabal Abu Ghneim settlement, and only partially returned to the PNA the withheld tax revenues. It was later learned that Arab houses at Ras El Amoud had been occupied by militant Israeli settlers (though these were replaced a few days later by religious students, said to be a "compromise"), and the Israeli Defense Force began training for full scale guerilla warfare in the PNA-controlled Palestinian areas.

In these circumstances, what hope is there for the final status talks and for Jerusalem?

It is clear that reliance on the United States either to be an "honest broker" or to put any pressure on Israel is simply not realistic. The way ahead it seems to me is procedural, in two ways:

1. The parties cannot be left to negotiate the final status talks alone; a real mediator is required and should be agreed or imposed. There has been a lot of talk of a European Union initiative. Why not Norway, who succeeded before? There is no reason why the mechanism for conciliation cited above should not be used (see note 7).

2. The status of Jerusalem cannot be left to the "parties" alone, simply because it is in fact an international problem and specifically a UN problem, since Palestine was a Mandate and the UN Partition Resolution provided that Jerusalem be a *corpus separatum* to be administered by the UN.

Indeed the key to a solution may well be in the resolution adopted by the General Assembly following Abu Ghneim, which I would like to cite in full:[13]

> The General Assembly aware of the commencement, after the adoption of General Assembly resolution 51/223 of 13 March 1997, of construction by Israel, the occupying Power, of a new settlement in Jebel Abu Ghneim to the south of East Jerusalem on 18 March 1997, and of other illegal Israeli actions in Jerusalem and the rest of the Occupied Palestinian Territory,
> Noting with regret that the Security Council, at its 3747th meeting, on 7 March 1997, and at its 3756th meeting, on 21 March 1997, twice failed to adopt a resolution on the actions referred to above, as a result of the negative vote of a permanent member of the Council,
> Reaffirming the permanent responsibility of the United Nations with regard to the question of Palestine until it is solved in all its aspects,
> Reaffirming also the principle of the inadmissibility of the acquisition of territory by force,
> Having considered the serious deterioration of the situation in the Occupied Palestinian Territory, including

Jerusalem, and in the Middle East in general, including the serious difficulties facing the Middle East peace process, as a result of recent Israeli actions and measures,

Affirming its support for the Middle East peace process, started at Madrid in 1991, on the basis of Security Council resolutions 242 (1967) of 22 November 1967, 338 (1973) of 22 October 1973 and 425 (1978) of 19 March 1978, for the principle of land for peace and for the full and timely implementation of the agreements reached between the Government of Israel and the Palestine Liberation Organization, the representative of the Palestinian people, and of all commitments reached between the parties,

Recalling its relevant resolutions, including resolutions 181 (11) of 29 November 1947 and 51/223, and the relevant resolutions of the Security Council, in particular those on Jerusalem and Israeli settlements in the occupied territories, including resolutions 252 (1968) of 21 May 1968, 446 (1979) of 22 March 1979, 452 (1979) of 20 July 1979, 465 (1980) of 1 March 1980, 476 (1980) of 30 June 1980, 478 (1980) of 20 August 1980, 672 (1990) of 12 October 1990 and 1073 (1996) of 28 September 1996,

Reaffirming that the international community, through the United Nations, has a legitimate interest in the question of the City of Jerusalem and the protection of the unique spiritual and religious dimension of the City, as foreseen in relevant United Nations resolutions on this matter,

Reaffirming also the applicability of the Geneva Convention relative to the Protection of Civilian Persons in Time of War, of 12 August 1949,[14] and the regulations annexed to the Hague Convention IV of 1907[15] to the Occupied Palestinian Territory, including Jerusalem, and all other Arab territories occupied by Israel since 1967,

Recalling the obligation of the High Contracting Parties to the Geneva Convention relative to the Protection of Civilian Persons in Time of War to respect and ensure respect for the Convention in all circumstances, in accordance with article I of the Convention,

Conscious of the serious dangers from persistent violation and grave breaches of the Convention and the responsibilities arising therefrom,

Convinced that ensuring respect for treaties and other sources of international law is essential for the maintenance of international peace and security, and determined, in accordance with the preamble to the Charter of the United

Nations, to establish conditions under which justice and respect for the obligations arising from treaties and other sources of international law can be maintained,

Also convinced, in this context, that the repeated violation by Israel, the occupying Power, of international law and its failure to comply with relevant Security Council and General Assembly resolutions and the agreements reached between the parties undermine the Middle East peace process and constitute a threat to international peace and security, Increasingly concerned about the actions of armed Israeli settlers in the Occupied Palestine Territory, including Jerusalem,

Aware that, in the circumstances, it should consider the situation with a view to making appropriate recommendations to the States Members of the United Nations, in accordance with General Assembly resolution 377A (V) of 3 November 1950:

1. condemns the construction by Israel, the occupying Power, of a new settlement in Jebel Abu Ghneim to the south of occupied East Jerusalem and all other illegal Israeli actions in all the occupied territories;

2. reaffirms that all legislative and administrative measures and actions taken by Israel, the occupying Power, that have altered or purported to alter the character, legal status and demographic composition of Jerusalem are null and void and have no validity whatsoever;

3. reaffirms also that Israeli settlements in all the territories occupied by Israel since 1967 are illegal and an obstacle to peace;

4. demands immediate and full cessation of the construction in Jebel Abu Ghneim and of all other Israeli settlement activities, as well as of all illegal measures and actions in Jerusalem;

5. demands also that Israel accept the *de jure* applicability of the Geneva Convention relative to the Protection of Civilian Persons in Time of War, of 12 August 1949, to all the territories occupied since 1967, and that it comply with relevant Security Council resolutions, in accordance with the Charter of the United Nations;

6. stresses the need to preserve the territorial integrity of all the Occupied Palestinian Territory and to guarantee the freedom of movement of persons and

goods in the territory, including the removal of restrictions into and from East Jerusalem, and the freedom of movement to and from the outside world;

7. calls for the cessation of all forms of assistance and support for illegal Israeli activities in the Occupied Palestinian Territory, including Jerusalem, in particular settlement activities;

8. recommends to the States that are High Contracting Parties to the Geneva Convention relative to the Protection of Civilian Persons in Time of War to take measures, on a national or regional level, in fulfillment of their obligations under article 1 of the Convention, to ensure respect by Israel, the occupying Power, of the Convention;

9. requests the Secretary-General to monitor the situation and to submit a report on the implementation of the present resolution, within two months of its adoption, in particular on the cessation of the construction of the new settlement in Jebel Abu Ghneim and of all other illegal Israeli actions in occupied East Jerusalem and the rest of the Occupied Palestinian Territory;

10. expresses the need for scrupulous implementation of the agreements reached between the parties, and urges the sponsors of the peace process, the interested parties and the entire international community to exert all the necessary efforts to revive the peace process and to ensure its success;

11. recommends that a comprehensive, just and lasting solution to the question of the City of Jerusalem, which should be reached in permanent status negotiations between the parties, should include internationally guaranteed provisions to ensure the freedom of religion and of conscience of its inhabitants, as well as permanent, free and unhindered access to the Holy Places by the faithful of all religions and nationalities;

12. rejects terrorism in all its forms and manifestations, in accordance with all relevant United Nations resolutions and declarations;

13. decides to adjourn the tenth emergency special session of the General Assembly temporarily and to authorize the President of the General Assembly to resume its meetings upon request from Member States. *3rd plenary meeting 25 April 1997*

This resolution, comprehensive on Jerusalem as it is, is only deficient in calling in paragraph 11 for "a comprehensive, just and lasting solution to the question of the city of Jerusalem, which should be reached in permanent status negotiations between the parties." Since the UN has a permanent responsibility for the question of Palestine and the city of Jerusalem as reaffirmed and repeated in the resolution, it seems to me that the responsibility must extend to the procedure of negotiating; which, as I have said before, needs to be internationalized by mediation and participation of the UN or through an international conference.

Going from procedure to substance, many solutions have been suggested, viz:

1. The Arab optimists have said that, since Israel has usurped the whole of Jerusalem—the West in 1948 and the East, including the Old City, in 1967—the whole of Jerusalem should go back to Arab control in the context of a Palestinian state. This of course is a dream and will not happen; so it is really a non-starter.

2. The next dream—equally absurd—is that Israel should keep the whole of Jerusalem, as their undivided and eternal capital. This is not a solution and equally a non-starter.

3. The third, which appears to be the PLO position accepted in the proclamation of the State of Palestine in 1988 and officially maintained since then, is to return to the position prior to 1967: i.e., East Jerusalem going to the Palestinian state (as Jordan has ceded any right to it to the Palestinians), to be the capital of Palestine; and West Jerusalem to be the capital of Israel. Under this proposal sovereignty over the East (including the walled Old City with its religious sites) would lie with the Palestinian state, and sovereignty over West Jerusalem with the Israelis.

4. A variant of solution (3) is that put forward by Dr Adnan Abu Odeh, viz "two capitals—(Palestine in the East... and Israel in the West)" with sovereignty in the East to Palestine (al-Quds), in the West to Israel (Yerushalaim), with no one having sovereignty over the walled Old City containing the Holy Places (to be called Jerusalem), which will be governed by the highest Muslim, Christian, and Jewish religious authorities. The conceptual framework for addressing the national aspirations of both the Palestinians and Israelis in Jerusalem is premised on the following considerations. Firstly, the Walled City, the truly Holy Jerusalem, would belong to no single nation or religion, and no state would have political sovereignty over it. It would be called

"Jerusalem" and would be governed by a council representing the highest Muslim, Christian, and Jewish religious authorities. Next, the Palestinian part of the city (the urban areas that stretch beyond the ancient walls to the east, northeast, and southeast) would be known as al-Quds, over which the Palestinian flag would fly. The Arab inhabitants would be Palestinian nationals, and would vote for their own national institutions. On the other hand, the urban areas to the west, northwest, and southwest of Jerusalem would be know as Yerushalaim, over which the Israeli flag would fly. The Jews residing in the Walled City would be Israelis and would vote, as they do now, in their national elections. The Arabs in the Walled City would be Palestinian citizens and vote in their national elections. As for the Holy Places, the following basic conditions would be essential. The Old City is the truly holy part of Jerusalem and as such, should be separated administratively from the rest of the city; it would be a spiritual basin for Judaism, Islam and Christianity. No national flag would fly over the Walled City, which would be open for all, for it belongs only to the One God, and the sacred shrines would be the symbol of the city's God-given holiness and spiritual significance. Each religious authority would be responsible for running and maintaining the holy sites of its faith.[16]

5. The "condominium" solution, that is, joint sovereignty over an undivided city, akin to the idea of co-ownership of property. This idea has been proposed by various international law authorities, including John V. Whitbeck, who says: Only one solution is conceivable—joint sovereignty over an undivided city. In the context of a two-state solution, Jerusalem could form an undivided part of both states, constitute the capital of both states and be administered by an umbrella municipal council and local district councils. In the proper terminology of international law, Jerusalem would be a "condominium" of Israel and Palestine.[17]

6. The idea of "scattered sovereignty," put forward by the Israel Palestine Center for Research and Information (IPCRI), whereby every piece of land in Jerusalem is clearly delineated on lines of sovereignty, but the two sovereigns—Israel and Palestine—will be limited in their sovereignty by adhering to a Jerusalem Charter and a Jerusalem Court of Justice. There would either be two municipalities, an Israeli and a Palestinian, or one overall municipality jointly controlled by Israelis and Palestinians.[18]

It seems to me all solutions have merits and demerits. The common denominators seem to be that:

1. Jerusalem should remain one undivided city with no borders or physical barriers;
2. Sovereignty should somehow be shared between Israel and Palestine;
3. There is no reason why it cannot be the capital of both states;
4. Functional jurisdiction should be given to one overall municipality consisting of Palestinians and Israelis, or two municipalities, one Arab and one Israeli;
5. A special regime should apply to the Old City and Holy Places.

I feel that, in addition to these common denominators, there should be provision for an international UN presence by means, for example, of a UN Secretary for Palestine:

(a)   to keep an eye, from an international point of view, on the administration of the Old City and Holy Places;

(b)   to have overall supervision of whatever settlement is reached and deal with any problems which may arise. The ideas of IPCRI relating to a Jerusalem Charter are in my view good, though I do not like their idea of a "scattered sovereignty."

What is more important now is to rescue the Oslo process, which began by the DOP in 1993. The solution to Jerusalem must necessarily be part and parcel of an overall settlement culminating in an independent State of Palestine. But the parties are unable to start the last phase of the process, which includes Jerusalem. The UN must intervene not simply by calling on the parties to talk as they have done in the latest and other UN Resolutions, but to help them along the road to peace by: (1) fulfilling those parts of Oslo and the Interim Agreement which remain unfulfilled by Israel by conciliation and arbitration; and (2) calling and convening an international conference for the final status talks on Jerusalem, refugees, settlements, and borders.

One hopes that such re-internationalization of the talks will yield better results than leaving it to the parties to agree. If one is to avoid more suicide bombs, or another intifada, or more militant Israeli settler activities, or the threatened guerrilla warfare by the IDF, the international community must act now.

Postscript

Things have of course got much worse since writing the above in 1997–1998. Although hopes were revived for the final status talks with the defeat of Mr. Netanyahu and the election of Mr. Barak in May 1999, these hopes were misplaced, since the envisaged Framework Agreement finally failed at Camp David in August 2000. Ariel Sharon then made his inflammatory tour of the Haram al-Sharif in Jerusalem's Old City on September 28, 2000, which resulted in the al-Aqsa intifada. This was followed by Barak's brutal response, now continuing and intensified under Sharon as prime minister, against the civilian population of Palestine, their homes, towns, and villages, and with the killing and murder of Palestinian men, women, and children, contrary to all norms of civilized behavior, human rights, and international law. The recent "cease-fire" is clearly not working and the need for international protection and internationalization of the conflict resolution process, which I prayed for in 1997–1998, is now more pressing than ever before. As far as Jerusalem is concerned, it is clear that the so-called "concessions" made by Barak at Camp David were no more than a variant of the "Abu Mazen/Belin plan" and did not go anywhere near enough to satisfying the minimum Palestinian position of Palestinian sovereignty in East Jerusalem, including the Old City.

HOLY PLACES, UNHOLY DOMINATION:
THE SCRAMBLE FOR JERUSALEM

Michael Prior

Introduction

Much of the discussion about Palestine revolves around the city of Jerusalem. Different religious and national groups—Jewish, Christian, and Muslim on the religious side, and Palestinian and Israeli on the national—express their attachment to the city through distinctive narratives. When diverse narratives are allowed their place, there is, of course, no occasion for disharmony. Conflict arises, however, when the narrative of one group seeks to silence or displace those of the others, and when one group seeks to impose hegemony over the others.

No physical factor can account for the significance of Jerusalem: it does not lie on any major trade-route; it is not blessed with proximity to any mineral resources, nor with soil that is suitable for large-scale agricultural development; its water supply is not abundant. Its importance, then, is best accounted for in terms of its religious significance.

Jerusalem and its Three Religions

For Jews Jerusalem is primarily the city of David, which became the centralized location of worship in the First and Second Temple periods, centered on the divine presence of the Ark of the Covenant in the Holy of Holies in the Temple. For Christians Jerusalem has some of the resonances it has for Jews. But what evokes the strongest sentiment in the Christian heart is the fact that Jerusalem is the place of the death, resurrection, and ascension of Jesus, and where the Holy Spirit descended on the early Church. Its significance for Muslims is reflected in its normal Arab name, al-Quds (the Holy), or the more elegant al-Quds al-Sharif (the Noble Holy Place), and in one of the oldest Islamic names for the city, al-Bayt al-Muqaddas (the Holy House). It is one of the three holiest places in Islam, the destination of the Prophet Muhammad's nocturnal journey to the Far Distant Place of Worship (Qur'an 17:1), and the place from where the Prophet ascended into heaven.

Away from the city, synagogues and churches throughout the world were oriented in the direction of Jerusalem, and before fixing on Makkah, Muslims, too, faced Jerusalem as they prayed. However, while devotees of each of the three religions share an intense attachment to the city, it is different for each religion. The differences are fundamental, and derive from quite distinctive theologies. The Jewish Law demanded that every male should make pilgrimage to Jerusalem three times a year at Passover, Feast of Weeks, and Tabernacles (Exodus 23:7; Deuteronomy 16:16). During the Second Temple period even diaspora Jews sought to observe it (Mishnah Aboth 5:4; Mishnah Tannit 1:3; Josephus Wars 6:9, etc.).

In the rhetoric of some of the more Orthodox strands of Judaism, many of the commandments of the Jewish Law can be performed only in Eretz Yisrael (the land of Israel), often in connection with worship in the Jerusalem Temple. While in Islam Jerusalem yields in priority only to Makkah and Madinah, there is no Qur'anic requirement demanding of all Muslims some religious activity in Jerusalem—pilgrimage to Makkah is required of everyone who is able to make the journey. Similarly, even though Christianity's attachment to the Holy City is unmistakeable, there never has been a requirement of Christians outside to visit it, not to mention to live there. The physicality of Jerusalem, then, has significance for a particular kind of Judaism, in a way that only its sacred shrines have for international Christianity and Islam.

With such interest shown by each of the three religions, one might expect Jerusalem to be an ideal location for inter-religious dialogue and sharing. Whatever the potential for such concord, both history and the events unfolding in our own generation reveal serious obstacles to progress. Since religious significance is scarcely ever isolated from more general cultural and, especially, political factors, any discussion of theological considerations ought to be carried out in the wider context of national, and, in the case of Jerusalem in particular, international politics. Moreover, at different periods in the history of the city the adherents of each of the three religions have striven to convert into political hegemony its sacred associations with their own religion. History confirms also that the most spiritual realities can be manipulated to further the political interests of groups near to hand, as well as the foreign policy interests of great powers. Throughout its long history Jerusalem has consistently interested foreign powers.

The Western Scramble for Jerusalem

In the 19th century alone, England, Russia, Germany, and France were engaged in "a scramble for Palestine," which invariably took the form of establishing Christian institutions in the land, thereby uniting Christian missionary endeavor with imperialist interest. In the 20th century, after the long period of Ottoman hegemony (1517–1917), Britain ruled the region from 1917–1948, and, since the creation of the State of Israel in 1948, the US has increased its interests in the area, while the former USSR also maintained strategic interests in the region. Since the establishment of the State of Israel and the conquest of West Jerusalem in 1948, and the conquest of East Jerusalem in 1967, the Israeli government has stridently attempted to "Israelize" (a more apposite neologism than "Judaize") the city further and reduce its non-Jewish character. With victory in the June 1967 war, political Zionism finally had achieved its goal of controlling the whole of Palestine west of the Jordan.

The speed with which Israel proceeded to benefit from its victory suggests that "the territorial fulfillment of the Land of Israel," only partly achieved in 1948, and frustrated by Israel's requirement to withdraw after the Suez War of 1956, was one of the central aims of its aggression.[1] Its long-term territorial intentions were signaled by evicting the some 1,000 residents of the ancient Moroccan Quarter of Jerusalem (Hrat al-Magarbeh), and destroying some 135 houses and four Muslim religious sites, just two days after the capture of East Jerusalem, to make way for a plaza in front of the Western (Wailing) Wall. A further 4,000 Arabs were expelled from Jerusalem's Jewish Quarter and its surroundings in order to enlarge and "purify" it. Moreover, within days of the occupation the Knesset passed the law extending the boundaries of East Jerusalem to include villages close to Bethlehem in the south and Ramallah in the north. This action, judged by the UN and almost all states as illegal, was confirmed in 1980 when the Knesset declared "Jerusalem in its entirety" (i.e., West and East) to be its "eternal capital."

In celebrating "Jerusalem 3000" in 1996 the Israeli government and Jerusalem municipality took David's capture of the city as its starting point, thereby ignoring its previous 2,000 years of existence, and emphasising Israeli-Jewish hegemony over the city. If "Jerusalem, the eternal, undivided capital of Israel," however replete with unhistorical assertions, has been a mantra in Israeli discourse, particularly since 1980, it has not always been so. Indeed, even Palestine itself was not the sole goal of political Zionism at the beginning.[2]

Christians and Jerusalem

Of course, there has always been intense religious interest in Jerusalem on the part of Christians. But firstly, one asks, who speaks for "Christianity," and who speaks for "Jerusalem"? Within the Church in Jerusalem itself tradition has established a hierarchy, with the three patriarchal Churches (Greek Orthodox, Armenian Orthodox, and Latin Catholic) enjoying special authority. Then, on the outside, there are the Holy See (the Vatican),[3] the World Council of Churches, the Middle East Council of Churches, and other national or regional ecumenical bodies that express concern for Jerusalem. No one body arrogates to itself the right to speak in the name of all Christian bodies on this subject of universal interest. In addition to that shown by the different branches of the worldwide Christian Church, the concerns of the indigenous Arab Christian community of Palestine are paramount to this day. All Christian Churches hold the Bible in veneration. It witnesses to the fact that the Holy Land and Jerusalem mark the locus of God's dealings with the Israelites, and of His intervention in human history in the person of Jesus Christ. When one talks of a sacred place within Christianity, then, invariably, one associates it with the manifestation of some aspect of the divinity within history, be it the history of Jews and/or of Christians.

The Holy Land has a person-sacredness, prior to Jesus, one very much enhanced through his ministry. It is not surprising, then, that from a very early period Christians from abroad went on pilgrimage to the Holy City and surrounding areas, for the sake of the Holy Places, and in particular, to trace the footsteps of Jesus. However, as we shall see, it was those residing in the land, rather than pilgrims from outside, who were the architects of a Christian Holy Land.[4]

Nevertheless, despite the prominence of pilgrimage within its tradition, Christianity has always maintained a certain ambivalence about the significance of place. The reasons are theological, and in the course of such disputation recourse is made to certain texts within the New Testament. I confine myself here to the particular perspective of one New Testament author, Luke.[5] Jerusalem features prominently in Luke's two-volume work, the Gospel of Luke–the Acts of the Apostles. The scene opens in the Temple (Luke 1:5–25), and ends with Paul in (open) prison in Rome (Acts 28:16–31). The events concerning the Good News of Jesus Christ, then, begin in the capital of Jewish faith and tradition, and end in the capital of the Roman Empire. Jesus' Ascension into heaven, recorded both at the end of the Gospel and at the beginning of the Acts, serves as a hinge for the two-volume work, as the following arrangement of the text suggests:

Ascension
Luke 24
Acts 1

Mission in Jerusalem Luke 19:41–24:49	Mission in Jerusalem Acts 1:12–8:1a
Mission in Samaria and Judea Luke 9:51–19:40	Mission in Judea and Samaria Acts 8:1b–11:18
Mission in Galilee Luke 4:14–9:50	Mission to the "ends of earth" Acts 11:19–28:31

Reading from the left, Luke's Gospel moves from Galilee (preceded by some scenes in Jerusalem before and after Jesus' birth in Bethlehem, Luke 1:1–4:13) through Samaria and Judea, to the ministry in Jerusalem. This has its climax in the Ascension, recorded in both volumes (Luke 24, Acts 1), as a hinge joining them. The second volume (Acts) begins its account of the Church's ministry in Jerusalem, moves through Judea and Samaria, and ends in Rome, with the mission to the "ends of earth." There is, then, a parallel structure to the Luke's two-volume account of Jesus' ministry (Gospel of Luke) and that of the community of his disciples (Acts of the Apostles).

The Gospel of Luke (24:44–49) and its echo in the Acts of the Apostles (1:3–8) synthesize Luke's account of the ministry of Jesus, and propel his readers forward into the continuation of that mission in the Church, a mission beginning in Jerusalem, but destined for the ends of the earth. The text stresses that the universal mission was inaugurated by the risen Jesus; the mission of Jesus and of the Church is in fulfillment of the Scriptures; and suffering and rising from the dead will befall the prophet Jesus. But above all, for our purposes, the Gospel is to be proclaimed to all nations, beginning from Jerusalem. Here Luke reveals the dynamic movement from Jerusalem, the place where his Gospel begins and ends, to the capital of the empire, at which point he closes his Acts. If Luke propels the Gospel to the mainly gentile city of Rome, he recognizes the seminal function of Jerusalem, the capital of the Jewish faith.

The link between the mission to the gentiles and that to the Jews is intimate. In both Luke (24:47–48) and in Acts (1:8) the witness to Jesus will begin in Jerusalem, and be carried forward into all Judea and Samaria, and finally to the end of the earth: "Stay in the city, until you are clothed with power from on high" (Luke 24:48), and, "But you shall receive power when the Holy Spirit has come upon you" (Acts 1:8).[6] It would, of course, be ludicrous to conclude that Luke's perspective denies the legitimacy of Christians living in Jerusalem. However, the question of the link between Christian communities around the world and the birthplace of the religion remains. The significance of Jerusalem for Christians lies not only in the fact that Christianity was born there, but more fundamentally that in that location the saving activity of God was accomplished. Jerusalem highlights for Christians that their religion is not a matter of mere ideas and ideals, but derives from the intervention of God in history in that place and its surroundings.

Jerusalem is the city in which the Church was born, and for that reason the Church of Jerusalem can lay claim to being the Mother Church of the entire Christian world. Indeed, throughout the world, Christian church buildings face Jerusalem, and the altar in each church binds the community with the Church of the Resurrection in Jerusalem.

Jerusalem as a Sacred Place for Christians

According to Mircea Eliade, who surveyed the occurrence of the symbolism of the center of the world in diverse regions: "To Christians, Golgotha [the place of Jesus' crucifixion] was the center of the world; it was both the topmost point of the cosmic mountain."[7] The ancient map, Mappa Mundi of Hereford Cathedral, places Jerusalem, and the Crucifixion, at the very center of the world. Eliade argues that humankind cannot live without a sacred place, and he names this universal condition the nostalgia for Paradise: "The desire to be always, effortlessly, at the heart of the world, of reality, of the sacred, and, briefly, to transcend, by natural means, the human condition and regain a divine state of affairs: what a Christian would call the state of man before the Fall."[8] Nevertheless, St. John's Gospel, chapter four, is presented frequently as raising the question of the significance of place in the Christian dispensation, since Christ spoke of worship neither on Mount Gerizim, nor Mount Zion, but in spirit and in truth. Furthermore, St. Gregory of Nyssa's (d. 394 CE) famous letter of 379 CE is considered to be an embarrassment to supporters of pilgrimage, since he claims that Christianity has no thoughts on places. Instead it stresses that the core of religion relates to closeness to God and neighbor. Going to places brings people no closer to God, he claims, and hence Christians should stay at home. Contrary to popular opinion, however, Gregory was no doctrinaire critic of the tactile spirituality one associates with places sanctified by Christ. He recognized that in a profound sense the Holy Land was especially holy for Christians because of the fact that Jesus traversed it. The terrain itself, he says, has "signs of the Lord's sojourn in the flesh."[9]

The notion of a sacred place is fundamental to pilgrimage, and no pilgrimage site matches Jerusalem.[10] Unlike most pilgrimage termini, it is the goal for three religions, and for the different groupings within each. While the origins of Christian pilgrimage to the Holy Land are obscure, the practice certainly predates the conscious efforts of the emperor Constantine (r. 306–337 CE) to provide a physical anchorage for the Bible.[11] The province of Palestine harbored the Christian origins of the pilgrims. Immediately after his victory at Chrysopolis in 324, Constantine ordered the restoration of the Church's property in the eastern part of the empire. Presumably, the news that the Holy Sepulcher had been discovered and that the site had been converted into a Christian basilica increased the number of pilgrims to the region. We have accounts of pilgrimages by the Bordeaux Pilgrim (333 CE) and Egeria (381–384 CE) illustrating their desire to visit the Holy Places. Egeria's Bible was her constant traveling companion. According to the account of St. Jerome (d. 419 CE), veneration of the sacred sites, and especially that of the Cross and the Tomb of the Resurrection, was high on the priorities of two Roman noblewomen, Paula and her daughter (Letter to Eustochium 9:1).

It is clear from a survey of early Christian pilgrimage that a major concern was to visit the places associated with the Bible, and especially with the ministry of Jesus in Jerusalem. So widespread was the practice of pilgrimage to Jerusalem by the end of the 4th century that Bishop Gregory of Nyssa felt obliged to remind Christians that, whereas the Lord in the Beatitudes called the blessed to possess the kingdom of heaven (Matthew 5:1–12), he did not include going up to Jerusalem on pilgrimage among their good deeds; and where he spoke of blessedness he did not include that kind of devotion (Epistolae 2).

However, while pilgrimage played a major role in the formation of a Christian idea of a holy land, it was the Christians who were born in the land itself, or came to live there, who were the architects of the notion, not the pilgrims from abroad, who came and went back home.

The indigenous Christian community included Eusebius of Caesarea (d. 340 CE), Cyril of Jerusalem (d. 387 CE), Jerome, Paula (d. after 386), Melania, Hesychius, the monks who lived in the Judean desert, Cyril of Scythopolis, Sophronius, and John of Damascus (d. 749 CE). Indeed, "Almost every Christian thinker who contributed significantly to the Christian understanding of the holy land lived, at least for part of his or her life, in the land."[12]

From Religious Attachment to Political Hegemony

Granted the significance of the Holy Places within Christianity, one may question whether, and if so to what extent, Christians ought to interest themselves in political control over the terrain of the Holy Places. The question arose in a particular way in the 11th century. The Crusades represent a particular expression of Christian attachment to Jerusalem and the Holy Land. But, as always, religious and theological factors find their place within a matrix of wider political, social, and ideological factors. The Crusades were a series of expeditions from Western Europe ostensibly designed to wrest the Holy Land from Islam, and retain it in Christian hands. However, purely political factors also influenced the movement: the east offered the prospect of land for an expanding population in Europe. The Crusades were marked by extreme brutality. It is sufficient for our purposes to indicate the kind of religious and theological thinking that was presented as justifying the barbaric behavior associated with them. As a holy war authorized by the Pope, it was an attempt to recover Christian territories lost to the infidels.[13] The papal justification of recourse to violence can be traced back to the views of St. Augustine (d. 430 CE), who, appealing to Abraham's preparedness to sacrifice even his son, and to the killings by Moses and Elijah, argued that God could directly command violence, and that to obey the command was an admirable example of faithful obedience.

When war was waged in the name of God, then, it was a just war par excellence. Collections of Augustine's views were compiled just before the First Crusade (c. 1083 by St Anselm of Lucca; c. 1094 by Ivo of Chartres). In the 1070s and 1080s Pope Gregory VII (d. 1085) introduced the idea of a knighthood; the groups of knights, called into being by the Pope, and scattered in Germany, France, and Italy, marked a step towards the Crusades. When Pope Urban II (d. 1099) proclaimed the First Crusade at the Council of Clermont in 1095, he called out soldiers "for Christ's war." The aim of the Crusade was the liberation of the Patriarchate of Jerusalem.

In terms of the prevailing theology, the sins of an individual Christian merited temporal punishment, and could be atoned for only by the confession of sins, and by undertaking the acceptable discipline of penance. The journey to Jerusalem to liberate the Church could function as the penance. Indeed, by the decree of Urban II Crusaders were granted a Plenary Indulgence, i.e., all the temporal punishment their sins had merited would be remitted. Moreover, in the event of dying in the course of the Crusade, they would be granted the status of martyr. Thus, in December 1095, Urban II wrote to the faithful in Flanders, appealing for volunteers "to liberate the eastern churches," guaranteeing that the military enterprise would serve for the remission of all their sins. Fulcher of Chartres (written 1100–6) records the words of the Pope's sermon at the Council of Clermont (November 27, 1095): "Oh how shameful if a race so spurned and degenerate, the handmaid of devils, should conquer a race endowed with the faith of almighty God and resplendent with the name of Christ!" The Pope appealed to the greatness of King Charlemagne and Louis: "May you be especially moved by the Holy Sepulchre of Our Lord and Saviour, which is in the hands of unclean races, and by the Holy Places, which are now treated dishonourably and are polluted irreverently by their unclean practices... Take the road to the Holy Sepulchre, rescue that land from a dreadful race and rule over it yourselves."[14] The urgency of the task is emphasized by the Pope, in a passage that unites Christian piety, xenophobia, and ignorance:

> Jerusalem is the navel of the world, a land fruitful above all others, like a second paradise of delights. The Redeemer of the human race made it famous by his birth, embellished it by his life, sanctified it by his passion, redeemed it by his death, left his seal on it by his burial. This royal city, placed at the centre of the world, is now held captive by her enemies and is enslaved to pagan rites by a people which does not acknowledge God.[15]

The audience, we are told, shouted in unison: "God wills it! God wills it!" The Pope referred to the Crusade as "a holy pilgrimage." The pilgrims must carry the cross on their front or breast, in compliance with the Gospel exhortation, "Whosoever does not carry his cross and come after me is not worthy of me." A series of Crusades followed the First Crusade (1096–1099): Second (1145–1153); Third

(1189–1193); Fourth (1202–1204); Fifth (1217); Sixth (1228); Seventh (1248); Eighth (1270), but when the Mamelukes conquered Acre in 1291, Christian rule in the East ended. The devastation caused by these foreign incursions is inscribed deeply in the collective memory of the peoples of the Middle East.

The next significant interference from a "Christian" power in the political life of Palestine came with Britain's General Allenby's capture of Jerusalem on December 9, 1917, preceded by His Majesty's government's declaration of sympathy for Zionist aspirations (the Balfour Declaration of November 2, 1917). Soon after (July 24, 1922), the League of Nations entrusted to Britain the responsibility to establish the Jewish national home (the Mandate for Palestine, Article 2), with the Mandate incorporating the terms of the Balfour Declaration (Preamble; Articles 2, 4, 6, 7, 15, 22, and 23). Clearly the intentions of the British government and the League of Nations to further the interests of the Zionists would have immediate implications for the indigenous Arab Christian community of Palestine. This new development sounded alarm bells for Christian bodies from the outside also, which feared for the security of their interests in Jerusalem and the Holy Land. Because of its centralized organization and the extent of its constituency, the Holy See was to be at the forefront of opposition to Zionism. Let us trace its evolving stance to developments in the Holy Land and Jerusalem since then.

Jewry, Zionism, the Holy See, and the Holy Land

In line with the growth of western interest in the region during the period of decline of the Ottoman Empire, the Holy See expanded its interest in the Christian Holy Places.[16] Prior to the Balfour Declaration its major concern focused on their likely fate "in the custody of the synagogue." Secretary of State Cardinal Gasparri remarked: "It is hard to take back that part of our heart which has been given over to the Turks in order to give it to the Zionists."[17] On March 6, 1922, Gasparri severely criticized the draft of British Mandate for Palestine, which Lord Balfour (d. 1930) had presented to the League of Nations on December 7, 1920, as being incompatible with the Covenant of the League of Nations. The British plan would establish "an absolute economic, administrative, and political preponderance of Jews," and would act as "the instrument for subordinating native populations."[18]

One detects here the emergence of a concern for the rights of the Palestinians in the land, whose Christians were among the staunchest

Arab opponents of Zionism and supporters of nascent Arab nationalism. It is equally clear, however, that the Holy See had little enthusiasm for an Arab government in the area, which it predicted would be unreliable and weak. The Holy See, at that period, was happy to support the social and economic interests of the Palestinians, but not the implications of Palestinian self-determination. Indeed, as late as January 1948, Mgr. G. Montini (d. 1978; the future Pope Paul VI, then the under-secretary for ordinary affairs) told the British minister to the Vatican that the Holy See preferred that "a third power, neither Jew nor Arab... have control of the Holy Land."[19] Reflecting the new order in the aftermath of the First World War, the Holy See, ever attentive to the needs of the Church universal, began to pay more attention to the interests of the Christian community in the Holy Land, which, of course, was overwhelmingly Arab (80 percent in 1931, according to the British census of Palestine). Interest in the affairs of Arab Christians inevitably led to concern for the wider Arab nationalist community. However, after the Second World War, such was the international support for Zionism in the wake of the virtual annihilation of mainland European Jewry that it was virtually impossible for the Holy See to challenge Zionism publicly.

The establishment of the State of Israel on 79 percent of British mandated Palestine, and the expulsion and displacement of some 750,000 Palestinian Arabs,[20] including some 50,000 Christians—35 percent of all Christians who lived in Palestine prior to May 15, 1948—while acknowledged to be a disaster, did not induce the Holy See to make any diplomatic representations. In his Encyclical Letter, *In Multiplicibus* of October 1948, Pope Pius XII (d. 1958) expressed his anguish at only the general conditions of refugees, and in that which followed it six months later, *Redemptoris Nostri*, he was no more specific. These two encyclicals do not go beyond the expression of predictable, broad moral and religious principles, with no explicit political implications. The Palestinian issue was scarcely mentioned publicly for the next twenty years. The Declaration on Religious Freedom (*Nostra Aetate*) of the Second Vatican Council (1962–65) provided a stimulus to better relations between Christianity and other religions, including Judaism.

Parallel with this was the growing sense of the essential link between the Gospel and issues of justice and peace.[21] Translated to the Middle East, there were then two somewhat competing tendencies developing a greater respect for the Jews, and a growing sympathy for the plight of the Palestinians. A number of significant factors influenced future developments. The victory of Israel in the war of June 1967 imposed a new sense of the reality and power of the Jewish state. Contacts between Jews and Catholics increased. Pope Paul VI (d. 1978) stated his concern at the decrease in the numbers of Christians in the Holy Land. If their presence were to cease, "the shrines would be without the warmth of the living witness of the Holy Places of Jerusalem, and the Holy Land would become like a museum."[22] In addressing Israeli Jews on December 22, 1975, he said:

> Although we are conscious of the still very recent tragedies which led the Jewish people to search for safe protection in a state of its own, sovereign and independent, and in fact precisely because we are aware of this, we would like to ask the sons of this people to recognize the rights and legitimate aspirations of another people, which have also suffered for a long time, the Palestinian people.[23]

This was the first time that any Pope had recognized the rights and legitimate aspirations of Jews to a sovereign and independent state of its own. The other side of the coin lay in his appeal to the victors to recognize the corresponding rights of the vanquished. By 1983 Mgr. W. Murphy, under-secretary of the Pontifical Commission for Justice and Peace, acknowledged that the Holy See "recognizes the factual existence of Israel, its right to exist, its right to secure borders, and other rights that a sovereign nation possesses." Pope John Paul II welcomed Shimon Peres, the Israeli prime minister, to the Vatican on February 19, 1985. The Pope's visit to the Roman synagogue on June 25, 1986 marked another stage in the growing cordiality between the two bodies. After Peres' visit, the Holy See spokesman referred to differences on essential problems, which included the status of Jerusalem, the sovereignty of Lebanon over all its territory, and the lot of the Palestinian people.[24]

The appeal for recognition of the rights of both peoples has been a constant call of Pope John Paul II. Its most comprehensive expression is contained in his communiqué released to the press after Yasser Arafat's visit to the Pope (September 15, 1982).[25] Moreover, in his Apostolic Letter, *Redemptionis Anno* of April 1984, he said:

> The Palestinian people who find their historical roots in that land and who for decades have been dispersed, have

the natural right in justice to find once more a homeland
and to be able to live in peace and tranquillity with the
other peoples of the area.[26]

During his visit to Austria in June 1988, the Pope called again for
equality for Israeli Jews and Palestinians, and pointed out that full
diplomatic relations between the Holy See and Israel are "dependent
on a solution to the Palestinian Question and the international status
of Jerusalem." The Palestinians, he went on, have a right to a
homeland, "like every other nation, according to international law." In
his Easter Message of 1991 John Paul II said:

> Lend an ear, humanity of our time, to the long ignored
> aspirations of oppressed peoples such as the Palestinians,
> the Lebanese, the Kurds, who claim the right to exist with
> dignity, justice and freedom.

The signing of the Fundamental Agreement between the Holy See
and the State of Israel on December 30, 1993 marked a new phase in
their relationship. Like many agreed statements before it, it is viewed
very differently by the two signatories. While supporters of Israel see
in it approval of the state by a major moral authority, the most the
Holy See can point to are statements about general principles of
religious freedom to which the State of Israel commits itself. The
absence of any reference to Palestinian Arabs, or to the injustice done
to them on the establishment of the State of Israel and since, is
striking. The only reference to overtly political matters is in Article 11,
wherein both parties commit themselves to the promotion of peaceful
resolution of conflicts (paragraph one), and the Holy See solemnly
commits itself "to remaining a stranger to all merely temporal
conflicts, which principle applies specifically to disputed territories and
unsettled borders" (paragraph two). In the course of the 20th century,
then, the attitude of the Holy See to the Holy Land has changed, in
line with the momentous changes that have taken place in the Middle
East and in its own perception of its role in the world, and in its desire
to exercise its mission to be the Church of the poor. Contemporary
Catholic theology, with its recovery of the sense of the Church as the
people of God, could not allow its interests in the region to be
exhausted by a parochial interest in the religious monuments of the
past.

Concern from Within

Since Jerusalem is primarily the domain of those who live there, one must pay particular attention to its inhabitants. There are 114,000 Palestinian Christians in Israel, and 50,352 in the Occupied Territories, giving a total of 165,000 Christians in Israel-Palestine, or 41.3 percent of all Palestinian Christians worldwide.[27] For the Christians of the Holy Land, who refer to themselves as the "Living Stones," Jerusalem is a spiritual center and a place of frequent pilgrimage, and for those who live in the Holy City itself, it is also their physical home. However, the very survival of these Christians is under threat. After he had visited the Holy Land and Jordan (1992), Archbishop George Carey of Canterbury expressed his fear that "In fifteen years' time Jerusalem and Bethlehem, once centers of strong Christian presence, might become a kind of Walt Disney theme park."[28]

In addition to the devastation of the 1948, the Israeli occupation of the West Bank and Gaza has resulted in massive emigration of Christians from the region, to the extent that the Christian population of Jerusalem has fallen from some 40,000 in the 1940s to some 10,000 today. When one takes account of patterns of natural growth, the gap between the present Christian population and that which it would have been, had it been allowed to develop, is all the greater. Emigration surveys show that Palestinian Christians leave both the Occupied Territories and Israel for identifiable economic and social reasons, reflecting the dire political situation: they lack the opportunity of earning their living, and ensuring some stability and future for their children.

The situation has become even more acute since the onset of the second intifada in September 2000. The claim that the growth of Islamic fundamentalism (the less tolerant and inclusive strands of Islamic revivalism) has added to Christian emigration is not supported by the findings of any of the emigration surveys.[29]

One of the results of the first intifada was the increased politicization of the Christian Churches in the Holy Land. Moreover, a new awareness of the situation of the Palestinians was developing in the Churches in the west. The British Council of Churches sent a ten-member delegation to Israel and the Occupied Territories (March 1989),[30] and the Middle East Council of Churches reciprocated, with a delegation to Britain in November-December 1989, which left British Christians in no doubt that Palestinian Christians shared in the aspiration for an independent Palestinian state.

Parallel to the mass movement of opposition to the occupation,

Palestinian Christians were developing an indigenous liberation theology. This continues to have a significant effect on opinion within the Churches abroad. Organizations promoting links between Christians abroad and those in the Holy Land were founded (for example, *Living Stones* in Britain), and in Palestine itself *Sabeel,* the Palestinian Liberation Center, was established.

The new climate resulted in the production of significant studies by both Palestinian[31] and international scholars,[32] and the convening of international conferences, both at home[33] and abroad,[34] which have exposed the human cost to the Palestinian community of the Zionist enterprise. In addition, I commissioned and edited a collection of essays, giving personal impressions and analyses, by nineteen prominent scholars/church leaders and human rights advocates, Catholic, Anglican-Episcopalian, Presbyterian, Methodist, and Mennonite, from seven different countries, who witness how encountering the Holy Land inevitably stimulates the most profound soul searching.[35]

Another noteworthy feature of the activities of the Christian Churches in Jerusalem is the unity they manifest in their present crisis. The leadership has issued common statements, including "The Significance of Jerusalem for Christians" (November 14, 1994).[36] This statement summarizes the theology of Jerusalem agreed by all Christians, and situates the discussion within the current political climate in which the members of the indigenous Christian Church in Jerusalem live their daily lives.

The document stresses the holiness of Jerusalem for Judaism, Christianity, and Islam, and appeals for reconciliation and harmony among people, whether citizens, pilgrims, or visitors. Because of its centrality and the postponement of its final status in the current Arab-Israeli peace process, it is important to reflect on Jerusalem. The statement records that Jerusalem has been destroyed time and again, only to be reborn anew and rise from its ashes. Religious motivation has often played a preponderant role, leading to the supremacy of one people over the others. Yet its universal vocation and appeal is to be a city of peace and harmony among all its inhabitants. The lesson of history is that it cannot belong exclusively to one people or to only one religion. Jerusalem should be open to all, shared by all. Those who govern the city should make it "the capital of humankind."

The statement reiterates the Christian vision of Jerusalem, deriving from the Old Testament and the ministry of Jesus. It summarizes the contribution Christian theology and the practice of pilgrimage make to the Christian estimation of the city. It describes the place of the continuing presence of a living Christian community in the land, the "Living Stones" who enliven the holy archeological sites. For these local Christians, as well as for local Jews and Muslims, Jerusalem is not only a Holy City, but their native city, where they live with the right to continue to live there freely, and with full freedom of access to its holy places for those who live outside the city. Its special status presupposes a special judicial and political statute for Jerusalem that reflects its universal importance and significance for the three religions, locally and internationally. The representatives of the Jerusalem Church concluded:

> Jerusalem is a symbol and a promise of the presence of God, of fraternity and peace for humankind, in particular the children of Abraham: Jews, Christians and Muslims. We call upon all parties concerned to comprehend and accept the nature and deep significance of Jerusalem, City of God. None can appropriate it in exclusivist ways. We invite each party to go beyond all exclusivist visions or actions, and without discrimination, to consider the religious and national aspirations of others, in order to give back to Jerusalem its true universal character and to make of the city a holy place of reconciliation for humankind.

Internationalizing the Christian Concern

On October 27–28, 1998, at the invitation of the Latin Patriarchate of Jerusalem, delegates from several Roman Catholic bishops' conferences in Europe, the Americas, Africa, and Asia, together with the members of the Assembly of Catholic Ordinaries of the Holy Land, assembled in Jerusalem to reflect on the question of Jerusalem. Archbishop Jean-Louis Tauran, secretary for the Holy See's Relations with States, presented a paper outlining the Holy See's position on Jerusalem. Metropolitan Timotheos read a paper outlining the Greek Orthodox position, and Latin Patriarch Michel Sabbah presented the 1994 Memorandum.[37]

Archbishop Tauran insisted that

> the distinction often made between "the question of the Holy Places and the question of Jerusalem" is unacceptable to the Holy See. It is obvious that the Holy Places derive their meaning and their cultic and cultural uses from their intimate connection with the surrounding environment, to

be understood not merely in terms of geography but also and most especially in its urban, architectural and above all human community and institutional dimensions.

The situation in Jerusalem today, he insisted, has been brought about and is maintained by force, and the 1967 military occupation and subsequent annexation of East Jerusalem is illegal. Unilateral action or an arrangement imposed by force, he insisted, "cannot be a solution."

The Holy See, rejecting every exclusive claim to Jerusalem, insists that the city is sacred to Jews, Christians, and Muslims, and is the cultural heritage of everybody:

> Jerusalem is an unparalleled reality: it is part of the patrimony of the whole world... The Holy See continues to ask that it be protected by "a special internationally guaranteed Statute." The historical and material characteristics of the City must be preserved; there must be equality of rights and treatment for those belonging to the communities of the three religions found in the City; and the rights of access to the Holy Places must be safeguarded.

He adds that "The sacred character involves Jerusalem in its entirety, its holy places and its communities with their schools, hospitals, cultural, social and economic activities." Any solution must have the support of the three monotheistic religions, both at the local and international level, and he proposes representation not only for the contending parties, the Israelis and Palestinians, and the sponsors of the peace process, but wider representation to guarantee that no aspect of the problem is overlooked—a clear bid for the participation of the Holy See itself.[38]

The final communiqué of the meeting reiterated the unique value of the city for the three religions, the region and the whole world, expressing the hope that Jerusalem would be a universal symbol of fraternity and peace. It should be a place of encounter and reconciliation among religions and peoples. While being viewed as "the Mother Church" for Christians down the centuries, it is a city of three religions and two peoples, for whom it embodies "the heartland of their respective national aspirations." In working towards an ultimate solution political leaders ought to take account of the concerns and hopes of believers. In a context of the ongoing closure of the city to Palestinians who live outside, it reiterated that "Free access to Jerusalem should be guaranteed to all, local people and pilgrims, friends and opponents. There should be a special statute for Jerusalem's most sacred parts, and that statute should be supported by international guarantee."[39]

One detects in the World Council of Churches (WCC), which reflects the views mainly of the Protestant churches, a remarkable unanimity with the concerns of the Holy See, which, of course, presents the perspective only of all Christians in communion with Rome. In addition, national or regional Protestant churches have issued statements relevant to Jerusalem.[40] The eighth assembly of the WCC, meeting in Harare (December 3–14, 1998), issued a comprehensive statement on the status of Jerusalem. It reiterates the significance and importance of the Christian communities in the city, condemning once again the violations of the fundamental rights of Palestinians in Jerusalem, which force many to leave. It considers that negotiations concerning the future status of the city should take place without delay, and should be a product of a comprehensive settlement for the region. It recalls the framework established in international law related to the status of Jerusalem. The statement notes that the United Nations retains authority and responsibility for Jerusalem, and that "no unilateral action nor final legal status agreed by the parties can have the force of law until such consent is given." The statement recognizes that the solution to the question of Jerusalem is in the first place the responsibility of the parties directly involved, but that the three religious communities have a central role to play in the negotiations.

The assembly adopted the principles that must be taken into account in any final agreement: the peaceful settlement of the territorial claims of Palestinians and Israelis should respect the holiness and wholeness of the city; access to the Holy Places should be free; the rights of all communities of Jerusalem to carry out their own religious, educational, and social activities must be guaranteed; free access to Jerusalem must be assured and protected for the Palestinian people; Jerusalem must remain an open and inclusive city; Jerusalem must be a shared city in terms of sovereignty and citizenship; the provisions of the Fourth Geneva Convention must be honored with respect to the rights of Palestinians to property, building, and residency; the prohibition of effecting changes in population in occupied territories; and the prohibition of changes in geographical boundaries, annexation of territory, or settlements that would change the religious, cultural, or historical character of Jerusalem without the agreement of the parties concerned and the approval of the international community.

Conclusion

It is clear that Christians have a special reverence for Jerusalem, mainly as a city associated with the climax of the ministry of Jesus and the birthplace of the Church. While it would prefer to have its religious interests guaranteed by authorities favorable to its perspectives, the Church has endeavored to protect them by various agreements with the successive rulers.

The Christian attitude to Jerusalem in the 20th century has been dominated by the challenge of Zionism and its determination to create a state for Jews from around the world, at the cost of depriving the indigenous population of its homeland. The attitude of the Holy See to the Holy Land has changed, in line with the momentous changes that Zionism introduced into the Middle East, and in its own perception of its role in the world, and in its desire to exercise its mission to be the Church of the poor. While it has never diluted its interests in the Holy Places, various developments within Christian theology, not least those concerning the disadvantaged, have made it increasingly sensitive to the population of the region.

We have noted the similarity in the various pronouncements of the Holy See and the WCC, and a sharing of perspectives with the leadership of the Jerusalem Church. In addition to concern about specifically religious issues, there is widespread anxiety for the human and national rights of the people of Jerusalem and its surrounding areas. These cluster around concern for equality for the three religions in the city and for the two nations. The fact of Israel's existence and its hitherto unchallengeable power is rather taken for granted, and the religious leadership by and large has settled for an approximate justice for the Palestinians, without demanding the rolling back of the Zionist aggression and the full compensation that a full justice requires.

Yet, given the "international community's" general disdain for ethnic cleansing, it is surprising that Christian reflection on the Holy Land has not gone much further than reflect predictable conformity with political realities as they develop. At best, one detects in the attitudes within the churches an adherence to "the fallacy of balance," the assumption that in this unique situation of conflict there is an equality of rights, an equality of pain, an equality of sacrifice, etc., as if "the rights of the rapist and the victim" were finely balanced.

It is disappointing that the Holy See, as a major moral authority, has not, since the establishment of the State of Israel at least, offered a more fundamental moral critique of Zionism. If religious bodies do not offer a critique of the axiom of "rule by force," who will?

There is abundant evidence to demonstrate that political Zionism, from its inception, was a colonialist ideology, which, while proffering its exclusivist nationalist solution to the problems of Jews worldwide, was fully intent on expelling the indigenous non-Jewish population of Palestine. It is also widely known that that ideology was detested by virtually the whole Jewish religious establishment, albeit for reasons internal to understandings of the Jewish faith. Concern for the higher values of justice has to yield to the imperatives of diplomacy and the ideals of inter-religious dialogue. It appears that the Christian conscience of the west has been anaesthetized by the constancy with which it is reminded to recall Christian barbarisms against Jews in the past, in particular, of course, the horrors of the Shoah (Holocaust).[41]

The Holy See and other major Christian bodies have shown little inclination to examine the issues from the perspectives of fundamental justice. Eight years after the Holy See's historic recognition of the State of Israel, there is little evidence to suggest that its abandonment of its hitherto moral critique of the State of Israel will contribute towards some form of restitution for the injustices done to the Palestinians, and towards a sensible peace in the region. This despite even the visit to the Holy Land undertaken by Pope John Paul II in February–March 2000. As if to reflect the relative impotence of religious idealism versus the rule of force, within thirty minutes of the end of the Pope's visit to Dheisheh refugee camp (March 22, 2000) a riot erupted in the camp. And not long afterwards, the second intifada exploded, for which Ariel Sharon's gesture emphasizing Israeli political hegemony over Haram al-Sharif, a complex sacred to Muslims, was the immediate catalyst.

JERUSALEM AND THE FORGOTTEN
DOCUMENTS

Muhammad Husain al-Farra

I

Jerusalem was and still is the pivot and the key factor of the Palestine question. It will perhaps be best to begin this study by setting out what took place before, during and after the June war of 1967, then move on to the forgotten documents relating to Jerusalem.

Discussion of the Holy City at the international level necessarily involves addressing the Palestine question as a whole. Let us, therefore, begin with an account of what happened when the Israeli army waged the 1967 war, for which it was well prepared in the military, political and media spheres. The material set down here was not made public in the earlier writings on this war, and people may or may not know how the war began. What is almost totally unknown is how, when hostilities broke out, communication was severed between the governments of the Arab countries directly involved and their embassies at the United Nations; how we were unable to make contact with our respective capitals and receive information and instructions from them; and how we became, so to speak, the defendant party in the Security Council, as Israel pre-emptively took the role of plaintiff by filing a complaint against us in the Council.

Israel was ready for war, while we Arabs, unusually, were not represented in the Council that year—because we could not agree on a delegate to represent the Arab states! Two Arab countries ran for a single seat, which led to a split in the votes and to India taking the Arab seat. When Israel triggered the war, therefore, we had no notion of what was going on in the closed Security Council chamber. All we knew was what was passed on to us by the Arab and American news agencies and radio stations, all of which spoke of Arab victories in the battlefield. This was splendid news for us, news made still more comforting and reassuring by repetition. It was, however, totally untrue.

The first resolution adopted by the Security Council, on June 6,

1967, was for an immediate cease-fire, to take effect as an initial step. The next step, we presumed, would be withdrawal by Israel from the territories occupied by them; but this did not materialize. Israel was careful, in this context, not to offend the United States, lest they provide opposition in the Security Council. Israel was also careful not to make the same mistake as it had made during the Tripartite Aggression against Egypt in 1956, when President Eisenhower ordered Israel to withdraw. Israel, the president had said, as a state occupying the territory of another state, could not dictate terms and conditions of withdrawal, nor could military conquest be the framework for discussing peace terms. The US stance in 1956, during Eisenhower's presidency, was not, therefore, the same as that taken in 1967 by Lyndon Johnson and by those presidents succeeding him in office.

During the six days of the war, all our allies were happy at the news coming in: of our success and the advances of our troops on the ground. The head of the USSR delegation, Ambassador Federenko, came to me smiling and congratulating us, believing that our armies had proved their combat capabilities, and that Soviet weapons—i.e., those being used by Egypt and Syria—were proving superior in performance to the American weapons with which Israel was fighting. Some hours later contact was resumed between the UN and the Arab capitals. The first telephone call I received came from H. E. Ahmad Touqan, the Jordanian foreign minister, requesting me to accept the cease-fire. When I received these instructions, I assumed the news we had had through the news agencies and other media had all been concocted by Israel and certain foreign powers to enable Israel to win the diplomatic round at the United Nations, just as it had won in the battlefield.

The impact of these instructions, both on us and on friendly countries, was painful in the extreme. I passed the instructions on to the Egyptian ambassador, Muhammad 'Awad al-Quni, with whom I maintained a diplomatic coordination akin to military coordination in the field. A few hours later a phone call came to Ambassador al-Quni from Cairo, and he asked me to accompany him, so as to keep me informed. As al-Quni listened, he could not believe what he was hearing. "What are you saying, Sami?" he asked. The caller, I knew, was Sami Sharaf, head of President Jamal 'Abd al-Nasir's office, and he was telling al-Quni to accept the cease-fire. "Thank you," was all al-Quni said, before ending the call. Then he looked at me and said: "The call's a hoax. It's quite impossible. I'm going to contact the President at once." The speaker, he added, could not possibly have been Sami Sharaf. He took from his pocket a small notebook containing the direct phone number of President 'Abd al-Nasir. As soon as al-Quni began speaking, President 'Abd al-Nasir recognized his ambassador's voice. "Yes, Muhammad," he said, "accept the cease-fire immediately. It really was Sami Sharaf speaking to you just now." The conversation ended; whereupon al-Quni wrote a message of no more than two lines to the president of the Security Council, to the effect that Egypt accepted the cease-fire except in case of self-defense. He handed the message to his deputy Dr. 'Abd Allah al-'Aryan to be passed, in turn, to the president of the Security Council. Then he went home.

This account is illustrative of some of the things happening at the United Nations during the 1967 war. Let us now move on to three documents related to Jerusalem, which will, I hope, hold a special significance for the current negotiations. The first is the document in connection with the al-Aqsa Mosque's western wall in Jerusalem, issued by the Shaw Commission in December, 1930;[1] the second is Resolution No. 242, issued by the Security Council in the aftermath of the 1967 War; and the third is Resolution No. 252 on Jerusalem, submitted by Jordan and approved by the Security Council in 1968.

II

DOCUMENT ONE: THE BURAQ WALL DOCUMENT

The Buraq Wall is the western wall of the Aqsa Mosque; and the Buraq Document is an international document meriting attention; we should insist on its validity throughout the coming negotiations, as something binding on Israel and on the world Jewish community. No members of the Zionist movement or the world Jewish community can disavow commitment to this document, issued in December 1930, in connection with what Muslims call the "Buraq Wall" and Jews "the Wailing Wall."

The document was prepared by a commission set up by Britain, with the approval of the League of Nations, to arbitrate Muslim and Jewish claims on the Western Wall.[2] Leaders of the Zionist movement had repeatedly claimed ownership of the wall and the courtyard adjacent to it, the issue being definitively and explicitly decided by the Shaw Judicial Commission at the end of 1930. As such, the claims of Israeli leaders, immediately after the 1967 War, as to Jewish ownership of the wall were in contravention of the decision of this international commission set up by the British Mandate and approved by the

League of Nations.

The commission was appointed following the Buraq uprising in 1928–1929, when the Jews attempted to bring seats and benches and place them alongside the western wall of the Aqsa Mosque. Muslims from Jerusalem, Hebron, and neighboring villages thereupon revolted, breaking up the seats and driving the Jews off. Disturbances developed into full-scale fighting, in which Muslims from Hebron and towns and villages surrounding Jerusalem took part. This led Britain, with the approval of the League of Nations, to form an investigative Royal Commission to examine the question of ownership of the wall.

The commission was made up of three jurists, one Swiss, one Swedish and one Dutch: Eliel Löfgren, Charles Barde, and C. J. Van Kempen. At the first meeting the commission and the parties agreed to follow the conventional procedures of British courts, which gave the parties the right to summon and question witnesses.

The defense on the Muslim side was headed by 'Awni 'Abd al-Hadi for Palestine, and Ahmad Zaki Pasha and Muhammad 'Ali Pasha for Egypt. The Jewish side was represented by Dr. M. Elishea, David Yelen, and Rabbi M. Blua. The Commission heard the pleas of both sides. In addition to the lawyers mentioned above, eleven further lawyers attended on behalf of the Muslims. They came from India, Morocco, Algeria, Libya, Egypt, Syria, Transjordan, Iraq, the Dutch East Indies (Indonesia), and Muslim regions of Africa that had not yet attained independence.[3]

In the course of these hearings 61 documents were submitted by the lawyers, comprising 35 from the Jewish side and 26 from the Muslim side. The Commission held 23 sessions, during which it heard 52 witnesses: 21 from the Jewish side, 30 from the Muslim side, and one British official.

The judicial commission reached a verdict embodied in a decision of 75 pages. The Commission's conclusions are summed up as follows: The Commission has been duly convinced that ownership of the Wailing Wall and the right to dispose thereof belongs to Moslems, that the Wall itself as a part of the holy Haram also belongs to Muslims, and that the Jewish party has not claimed any ownership at any stage of investigation carried out by the Royal Commission, neither in the Magarbeh Quarter nor in any part in the neighborhood;[4] and that the Jewish party in its pleading explicitly said that it does not claim or ask for any part of the Wall and it did not go further than asking for permission to visit the Wall.[5]

Israel's present-day claim therefore conflicts with the admission of former Jewish leaders and the decision of the specialized and competent international commission.

III

DOCUMENT TWO: RESOLUTION 242

Document Two, which merits mention and provision of background detail both on account of its intrinsic significance and because it was and still is a major document vis-à-vis negotiations, is Security Council Resolution No. 242, dated November 22, 1967. The Resolution reads as follows:

> The Security Council,
> Expressing its continuing concern with the grave situation in the Middle East,
> Emphasizing the inadmissibility of the acquisition of territory by war and the need to work for a just and lasting peace, in which every state in the area can live in security,
> Emphasizing further that all member states in their acceptance of the Charter of the United Nations have undertaken a commitment to act in accordance with Article 2 of the Charter,
>
> 1. Affirms that the fulfillment of the Charter principles requires the establishment of a just and lasting peace in the Middle East which should include the application of both the following principles: One. Withdrawal of Israeli armed forces from territories occupied in the recent conflict; Two. Termination of all claims or states of belligerency and respect for and acknowledgement of the sovereignty, territorial integrity and political independence of every state in the area and their right to live in peace within secure and recognized boundaries free from threats or acts of force.
>
> 2. Affirms further the necessity: One.* For guaranteeing freedom of navigation through international waterways in the area; Two. For achieving a just settlement of the refugee problem; Three. For guaranteeing the territorial inviolability and political independence of every state in the

area, through measures including establishment of
demilitarized zones.

3.   Requests the Secretary General to designate a
Special Representative to proceed to the Middle
East to establish and maintain contacts with the
States concerned in order to promote agreement
and assist efforts to achieve a peaceful and accepted
settlement in accordance with the provisions and
principles of these resolutions.

4.   Requests the Secretary General to report to the
Security Council on the progress of the efforts of
the Special Representative as soon as possible.[6]

This resolution emerged as a result of contacts and discussions
lasting six months, after the Arab side had refused to accept the draft
resolution submitted by the United States. It was rejected by Mahmud
Riyad, foreign minister of Egypt; also by 'Abd al-Mun'im al-Rifa'i,
foreign minister of Jordan and by Dr. George Tumeh, ambassador and
permanent delegate of Syria at the United Nations, upon instructions
from his government. At one stage of the negotiations concerning the
new draft resolution, Mahmud Riyad and 'Abd al-Mun'im al-Rifa'i
came to my office accompanied by British ambassador Lord Caradon,
who submitted the draft of Resolution 242. There was controversy
over whether withdrawal should be from "occupied territories" or "the
occupied territories"—an ambiguity that did not occur in the other
four official languages of the Security Council, namely, French,
Russian, Chinese, and Spanish. Lord Caradon said the meaning was
the same, adding: "After all the amendments accepted by the US, it is
not in a position to accept any further amendments."

In another meeting attended by George Brown, the British foreign
secretary, Mahmud Riyad and 'Abd al-Mun'im al-Rifa'i George Brown
said: "Whether you add 'the' to 'territories' or not, the meaning is the
same." He went on to say: "This is my own wording, and I advise you
to accept the draft as amended, because to come out without a
resolution will not be in your interest." This being the case, we could
not but accept the draft resolution. The only alternative was to leave
without a resolution; and, had this happened, it would have been
interpreted in the interest of Israel, which could later have alleged that
its occupation of Arab territories was legitimate because it was not
opposed by the Security Council.

Egypt, Jordan, and five other Arab states accepted the draft resolution, which was, however, rejected by Syria and six other Arab states. Thus the Arabs were divided into seven Arab states for and seven against. At our request the US committed itself, before the Security Council, to use all its moral and political influence for implementation of the resolution. Throughout all these stages the US was keen that it, and none of the other great powers, should be the political gainer within the Security Council. After voting, the United States formally declared, in the Council, that it would use all its political and legal weight to ensure implementation of the resolution. The brief speech by Lord Caradon conformed to what Foreign Secretary George Brown had said.

With the passage of time, because of changes in the international environment and because of Arabs' weakness and internal differences, Israel seized the opportunity to begin laying down its own conditions and to insist that Resolution 242 did not cover the city of Jerusalem. By this means Israel gave the resolution a new interpretation based on Israeli claims; and Israel's insistence on this led me to suggest to Their Excellencies 'Abd al-Mun'im al-Rifa'i and the prime minister of Jordan, Bahjat al-Talhuni, that a new draft resolution be submitted with respect to Jerusalem. This is Document Three in this paper, namely Resolution 252.

IV

DOCUMENT THREE: RESOLUTION 252

I suggested to the foreign minister of Jordan that we should return to the Security Council with a view to obtaining a resolution that would demonstrate, explicitly, the position of Jerusalem. The proposal was put before Prime Minister Bahjat al-Talhuni, who supported the idea and submitted the matter to His Late Majesty King Husayn. The king approved the proposal provided the success of an appropriate resolution could be guaranteed. He pointed out how the American veto could be used to nullify the resolution even if it gained the requisite number of votes for passage.

In fact the Jordanian government was afraid that the necessary resolution would fail, and approval was not, in consequence, easy to obtain. I was of the opinion, however, that if we secured the participation of Muslim, Arab, and non-aligned countries, over and above the Socialist Bloc countries in the Security Council, in discussing the matter and expressing their personal views—even though they had no right to vote—then it would be difficult for the United States to defy the world opinion and use the veto—even though it had threatened to do so and had officially communicated this intention to me.

I submitted the draft resolution, which had already been approved by Jordan. The United States strongly opposed it, submitting its own draft resolution asking that we withdraw our resolution. To the surprise of the US delegation, however, when it came to the vote, we did not withdraw our draft resolution, rather requesting that it be given priority. The US did not use its veto, and the resolution was passed with a majority of thirteen states, the US and Canada abstaining.

Our resolution became Resolution No. 252, and read as follows:

> The Security Council,
> Recalling General Assembly resolutions 2253 (ES-V) and 2254 (ES-V) of 4 and 14 July 1967,
> Having considered the letter of the Permanent Representative of Jordan on the situation of Jerusalem (S/8560) and the Report of the Secretary General (S/8146),
> Having heard the statements made before Council,
> Noting that since the adoption of the above-mentioned resolutions, Israel has taken further measures and actions in contravention of those resolutions,
> Bearing in mind the need to work for a just and lasting peace,
> Reaffirming that acquisition of territory by military conquest is inadmissible,
>
> 1. Deplores the failure of Israel to comply with the General Assembly resolution mentioned above;
> 2. Considers that all legislative and administrative measures and actions taken by Israel, including expropriation of land and properties thereon, which tend to change the legal status of Jerusalem are invalid and cannot change that status;
> 3. Urgently calls upon Israel to rescind all such measures already taken and to desist forthwith from taking any further action which tends to change the status of Jerusalem;
> 4. Requests the Secretary General to report to the

Security Council on the implementation of the present resolution.

In favor of the resolution: 13
Against the resolution: —
Abstained: 2 [7]

Time passed, and Israel continued its endless evasive tactics. On July 7, 1968, at 10 AM, George Bull, the American Minister, told H.E. Minister 'Abd al-Mun'im al-Rifa'i in my presence that he had placed pressure on the Israelis to tell him how they viewed future Jordanian–Israeli relations. Abba Eban, the Israeli foreign minister at that time, replied as follows: "Israel has no territorial ambitions except Israel's security and safe boundaries and Jerusalem comes within this conception." Eban went on to say: "If we enter into serious discussion Jordan will get a very large area of what it has lost: not the June 4 line, but there will be a Jordan on both sides of their river. Jerusalem will come within this conception. Jordan will be able to have access to the Mediterranean ports. The Jordanians will not have territorial gains but they will get access to the ports." Eban added that he recognized the importance of Jerusalem for the Muslim world and for Israel, and that his state would broaden its vision to work out a solution within the framework of the unity of Jerusalem. It was Eban, incidentally, who provided the introduction to Weizmann's memoirs, writing as follows: "All the pacts, conventions and resolutions are mere opportunities which we seize until we have fulfilled our aims from them, and which we will then discard, proceeding in accordance with our pre-planned policy." A statement made by Israel Galilee, a member of the Israeli Knesset, before that assembly on May 8, 1967, when the decision was taken to ban the military parade in the Holy City and prevent the ambassadors of other countries taking part in the parade, reads as follows: "We will be judges of the military parade on the day celebrating independence in Jerusalem. The number of ambassadors taking part is not the crux of the problem. It is our own stand, the strength of the Israeli army, and that Jerusalem will remain our capital." He added: "No country will escape its responsibility for not sending its representative to the parade." He went on to say: "Israel has not asked for permission from anyone to stage the parade in its capital and to transfer the Knesset there. The day will come when all the world will realize that Jerusalem is the capital of Israel as a result of the political fait accompli which we, and no one else, will create." Israel has in fact succeeded in this and proclaimed Jerusalem its capital, so confronting the whole world with a new attempt at a fait accompli— and, by this means, disavowing even the Balfour Declaration, which states as follows:

> His Majesty's Government views with favor the establishment in Palestine of a national home for the Jewish people and will use their best endeavors to facilitate the achievement of this object, it being clearly understood that nothing shall be done which may prejudice the civil and religious rights of existing non-Jewish communities in Palestine or the rights and political status enjoyed by the Jews in any other country.

It should be recalled here that participants in recent negotiations have failed to reach any agreement because one of the parties, namely Israel, reverts to endless and labyrinthine maneuvers. An expansionist policy, the construction of settlements, disavowal of the Buraq decision and violation of Security Council Resolutions 242 and 252 concerning Jerusalem—all these herald no promise of peace but rather remind one of Israel's past record and indicate how things are going to be in the future. The question posing itself here is whether it is possible for Arabs, for the sake of Jerusalem, to close ranks, address Israel in the language it understands and strive to foster relations with Muslim and other friendly countries—exactly as was the case when such countries rose on all sides to save the Buraq Wall.

JERUSALEM IN ARAB—ISRAELI
NEGOTIATIONS

Adnan Al-Sayyid Hussein

From the Palestine Partition Resolution of 1947 up to Camp David II's American-sponsored negotiations of 2000, the final status of Jerusalem remained subject to discussion at both regional and international level. Between these two dates, however, material and political alterations changed the city's individuality and all but transformed its character and destiny.

It is no accident that negotiations about Jerusalem's status have been left to a subsequent stage or to final negotiations. All parties, whether directly or indirectly concerned with the Palestine question, prefer to leave the issue hanging.

Why, we may ask, should this be? Is there not a fine thread linking Camp David I (1978) with Camp David II (2000)? And how can the current arrangements be viewed without regard to the details and complications of Arab–Israeli negotiations? Nearly a quarter of a century of negotiation has passed in relation to Jerusalem, with all the multiple secrets, consequences, and lessons involved.

UN General Assembly Resolution 181 of November 29, 1947 had provided for the creation of Jerusalem as a special entity subject to special international arrangement. The resolution provided for the partition of Palestine into two states: one Palestinian Arab, the other Jewish. This conflicted with the British Mandate document on Palestine and with the classification of Palestine within Category A of countries eligible for total independence.

The resolution defined the city of Jerusalem as comprising the Jerusalem municipal area and neighboring villages and towns. It was bounded by Abu Dis in the east, Ain Karem in the west, and Bethlehem in the south, while the northern boundaries were set by the General Assembly at Shu'fat. In other words, this regional entity covered the eastern and western parts of Jerusalem, with the proviso that the entity would be subject to internationalization.

What exactly did this internationalization entail? The city of Jerusalem was to be placed under actual UN supervision and accorded a treatment different from that in force in other parts of Palestine. The Trusteeship Council, a UN organ, was to be charged with administrative control over the city. All residents were to be de facto Jerusalem citizens unless they specifically chose nationality within either the Arab or the Jewish state; in point of fact, the Jerusalem arrangement had brought a new nationality into being.

All this meant that, contrary to a widespread misconception that the western part of the city was under Israeli sovereignty, there was no actual Israeli sovereignty over any part of the city. This is confirmed by the Lausanne Treaty of May 12, 1949, by which Israel had agreed to abide and which emphasised the internationalization of Jerusalem within the framework of the Partition Resolution referred to above.

It is true that economic, social, and cultural relations remain between both the Arab and Jewish states on the one side and the city of Jerusalem on the other. Nevertheless, such relations do not imply Israeli sovereignty over the city or any part of it, given that all international documents show Jerusalem to have been part of a Mandated Palestinian entity. It was lamentable that, in the aftermath of the 1948 catastrophe, Israel should have captured the western part of Jerusalem, with the eastern part falling under Jordanian control. As such, Israel captured over 84 percent of the total area of Jerusalem, and this new fait accompli was confirmed in the armistice concluded between Jordan and Israel on April 3, 1949. However, the terms of the armistice specified explicitly that the division was a matter not of political boundaries but of military lines of demarcation, which would not prejudice any subsequent final settlement of the Palestine issue.

The Israelis launched an immediate campaign to efface the Arab character of West Jerusalem. This began with an absentees' property law, whereby Israel seized the possessions of Palestinian refugees forced to leave the city, then moved on to seizure of the property of those Arab residents remaining under Israeli authority. In sum, Israel confiscated 80 percent of the area of West Jerusalem owned by Arabs; and, according to a carefully designed and calculated Israeli plan, the number of Arabs in West Jerusalem was reduced from 105,540 to none!

In the course of the June 1967 war, Israel occupied East Jerusalem, along with the West Bank; the Holy City came under total occupation. The annexation and Judaization went on amid fruitless Arab and international protest, leading to radical changes in the city's character and identity.

Between 1968 and 1990 the UN Security Council passed eleven resolutions calling for the rescinding of all Israeli measures liable to change the status of Jerusalem, and urging the Israeli occupation authorities to halt settlement activities in the Occupied Territories, including Jerusalem, to dismantle existing settlements, and to recognize basic Israeli law with respect to Jerusalem. They also requested that foreign governments withdraw their diplomatic missions from the city and condemned the violence committed by Israeli security forces within the Holy Haram (mosque) of Jerusalem. It is noteworthy that five UN Security Council resolutions were passed with the assent of all members, including the United States. In the six other resolutions the United States abstained from voting—i.e., did not use its power of veto. All this, it should be noted, took place during the cold war period.

In addition, successive Arab and Muslim resolutions were tabled, alongside others tabled by the Non-Aligned Movement, stressing the Arab character of Jerusalem, emphasizing the invalid nature of Israeli measures, and calling for the withdrawal of the occupation forces from East Jerusalem, including the Old City. These resolutions also repeatedly urged the necessity of an independent Palestinian state with Jerusalem as its capital. It is sufficient to point out here that the 1969 al-Aqsa Mosque fire, set by an Australian Christian, was a major factor underlying the establishment of the Organization of the Islamic Conference (OIC), which now has 54 member states from Indonesia in the east to Senegal in the west.

Nevertheless, though the Egyptian–Israeli negotiations at Camp David in September 1978 contrived to establish a general outline for peace—including, for the first time, a formula for Palestinian autonomy—they made no specific reference to Jerusalem. In fact the correspondence exchanged between Menachem Begin and Anwar Sadat preferred to postpone any decision on the fate of Jerusalem for later negotiations, to be conducted after conclusions concerning a future autonomy.

Why should this be? Because Jerusalem represents the core of conflict, and because it is the natural as well as the strategic capital of Palestine. In addition, Jerusalem, by virtue of its symbolic religious and civilizational status, virtually epitomizes the entire Palestinian question.

Another reason for the postponement was that involvement in detailed negotiation over the city would obstruct the course of negotiation in other areas. This is hardly surprising, given that the Camp David formula referred to above was rejected by the Palestinians on grounds that it failed to specify their right to self-determination, including the establishment of a Palestinian state with Jerusalem as its capital.

The Egyptians and Israelis agreed, then, that settlement of the Jerusalem issue should be deferred, to obviate obstruction to negotiations for a Middle East settlement and to await the start of negotiations with Syria, Jordan, Lebanon, and the Palestine Liberation Organization. During this deferral period Israel was moving on apace with the Judaization of East Jerusalem and cordoning the city off with belts of settlements that virtually obliterated its Arab character—in fact Jewish settlers in the eastern part of Jerusalem came to outnumber the Arab Jerusalemites originally resident there. All this was, of course, quite apart from the seizure of Arab lands and water resources.

The first Palestinian–Israeli Oslo agreement likewise failed to address the fate of Jerusalem, preferring to follow the same line as Camp David in deferring this pending permanent status negotiations. The same applied to the issues of refugees, settlements, borders, security, and relations and cooperation with neighbors. Appendix No. 1 of the aforementioned Oslo agreement permitted Jerusalemite Palestinians, and specifically those residing in the city, to take part in elections for the Palestinian Legislative Council; such participation being subject to a Palestinian–Israeli agreement.

While the United Nations General Assembly continued to refer to previous decisions regarding the internationalization of Jerusalem, including rejection of Israeli measures taken outside Israeli borders as defined by Resolution 181, both Palestinians and Israelis rushed to negotiate not about the fate of Jerusalem as a whole—again as defined by Resolution 181—but about that of East Jerusalem alone. Deferral of the Jerusalem issue was part, in any case, of a bid to secure success for some aspects of Palestinian autonomy and to prepare public opinion to accept a settlement. A further reason for deferral was the wish to avoid a possible permanent deadlock in the settlement negotiations, given the centrality of Jerusalem's location and its role vis-à-vis Arab–Israeli relations in general.

At "Camp David II" (as the media dubbed it), where former President Bill Clinton joined with Yasser Arafat and Ehud Barak in weeks of negotiation during July 2000, no real progress was achieved. The underlying cause of this failure was a fundamental difference over Jerusalem.

The Americans wanted a pragmatic solution based on a specific settlement regardless of the rules of international legitimacy—a settlement that guaranteed Israel's security first and foremost, even at the expense of Palestinians and other Arabs; one that would not truly address basic difficulties but virtually gloss over them. To this end the

American administration exerted heavy pressure on the Palestinian National Authority to relinquish parts of East Jerusalem, to waive sovereignty over the lower level of the Jerusalem Haram, and to accept the presence of Jewish settlers within Jerusalem and its perimeter—even to compromise on the issue of refugees and, in the teeth of international resolutions, deprive them of their right to return.

The Israelis, for their part, resorted to calculated blackmail, without offering any written commitment on Jerusalem, on withdrawal from the West Bank, on the rights of Palestinian refugees, or on the future of settlements. They simply propagated unsubstantiated stories in the media about a settlement that would be forged linking the issues of Jerusalem and refugees. In other words, the former was to be bartered for the latter. In actual fact, the Israelis were largely unwilling either to restore East Jerusalem to the Palestinians or to recognize the rights of Palestinian refugees. They were disinclined to accept a just peace in accordance with the rules of international legitimacy, one that would safeguard peace or maintain stability in the Middle East.

It is evident, then, from all these international and regional landmarks and stances, how Jerusalem constitutes to be a fundamental issue and an unrelenting source of pressure on the parties to the conflict. It is also a matter of considerable sensitivity with regard to international law and politics. But have Arabs truly dealt with this issue? Are they dealing with it in a duly responsible fashion? Or do they content themselves with the mere reiteration of slogans from time to time, failing to exert sufficient pressure, at the international level, to save their first *qiblah* and the third holiest mosque in Islam? Where are the Arab diplomatic efforts geared to obtaining absolute priority for the Jerusalem issue, in accordance with resolutions of international legitimacy?

The Classical Scene

'UMAR'S ASSURANCE OF SAFETY TO THE PEOPLE OF AELIA (ISLAMIC JERUSALEM): A CRITICAL ANALYTICAL STUDY OF THE HISTORICAL SOURCES

Abd al-Fattah el-Awaisi

The first Muslim conquest of Islamic Jerusalem on Jumada 1/11, 16 AH (March/April, 637 CE) was an event both remarkable and long-lasting in its effects. It may be viewed as a fundamental landmark, not merely in the history of the region, nor even in Islamic history, but also as an event that reshaped relations between the people of diverse faiths who inhabited the region. Moreover, its consequences contrasted significantly with the destruction, killing, and displacement that had characterized the region's history until then. The arrival of 'Umar Ibn al-Khattab in Aelia marked the beginning of a new and distinguished phase in the relations between followers of Judaism, Christianity, and Islam. Indeed, the foundations for future relations between the three faiths were laid down during that historical visit in the form of what is known in history as Al-'Uhda al-'Umariyya or 'Umar's Assurance of Safety to the people of Aelia.

In the few academic studies on the first Muslim conquest of Islamic Jerusalem, 'Umar's Assurance is regarded as a major turning point in both historic and juristic terms. Nevertheless, historians, both past and present, have debated its authenticity and interpretation, while some of its versions have been used to support particular religious or political standpoints in the current struggle to gain control of Islamic Jerusalem.

The challenge is to adopt a neutral approach in the case of a holy region such as Islamic Jerusalem, where the competing claims of the adherents of three world religions as well as international interests have met and clashed. In addition, a host of problems relating to historical facts about the first Islamic conquest have to be clarified and resolved. Far from being a study of the first Muslim conquest of Islamic Jerusalem, this is a critical, analytical study of the assurance that 'Umar Ibn al-Khattab gave to the people of the Aelia. It aims to examine and compare most of the available versions of 'Umar's Assurance, while focusing on the longest and most famous ones, namely the text given by al-Tabari and that published by the Orthodox Patriarchate in Jerusalem in 1953. In my efforts to ascertain the authenticity of these two texts, I have examined the historical sources.

I do not intend to discuss what are known as Al-Shurut al-'Umariyya or 'Umar's Conditions, by Ibn al-Qayyim al-Jawziyya, which are rejected by some researchers[1] and supported by others.[2] Nevertheless, I will attempt to find some explanation and interpretation of the questions and doubts that have arisen concerning certain versions of 'Umar's Assurance that contain exceptions, restrictions, or conditions, in particular the exclusion of the Jews from residing in Aelia. Moreover, the study will discuss the reasons behind the appearance of various versions of 'Umar's Assurance. The whole study will respond to Daniel J. Sahas's claim that the first Muslim conquest led to the "emergence of an opportunity for the Christians of Jerusalem to contain the Jews, with the help of the Muslim Arabs, through the concessions granted to them in 'Umar's Assurance."[3]

Early Accounts

The early accounts of 'Umar's Assurance, which were relatively close to the period of the first Muslim conquest of Islamic Jerusalem, are general in nature, whereas subsequent accounts that have come down to us contain actual texts, both long and short. Among the earliest historians to report the content of 'Umar's Assurance without any text are Muhammad Ibn 'Umar al-Waqidi,[4] a native of Madinah who joined the Abbasid court, became a judge under the Caliph Ma'mun, and died in 207 AH/822 CE, and al-Baladhuri (died 279 AH/892 CE),[5] who reported it from Abu Hafs al-Dimashqi.

Among the early historians who gave abbreviated versions of 'Umar's Assurance, but without al-Tabari's exceptions, are al-Ya'qubi, the explorer, historian, and geographer, who died in 284 AH/897 CE; and the Patriarch of Alexandria, Eutychius (Ibn al-Batriq), who died in 328 AH/940 CE. Al-'Uhda al-'Umariyya reads: "This is a document from 'Umar Ibn al-Khattab to the people of Aelia. They are given safety of persons, children (sons and daughters), and churches which will not be destroyed or inhabited (taken over)."[6] Although both historians give abbreviated versions, al-Ya'qubi was the first to give the text, which reads "You are given safety of your persons, properties and churches which will not be inhabited (taken over) or destroyed unless you cause some public harm."[7] A similar text was given by Eutychius, guaranteeing safety and full religious rights, although it differs in style and expression. The part about the people of Aelia in al-Ya'qubi's version is in the second person, whereas the third person is used in Eutychius's version. I would argue that if al-Tabari's exceptions were authentic, which we shall discuss below, particularly that concerning the exclusion of Jews from residing in Islamic Jerusalem, Eutychius would have mentioned them. He was a Christian in doctrinal disagreement with the Patriarch of Aelia, Sophronius, who followed the Chalcedonian theology. Eutychius believed in the unity of Christ, whereas Sophronius believed in the Chalcedonian principle relating to the dual nature (God and man) of Christ.[8]

While the best-known Muslim historian, al-Tabari (died 310 AH/922 CE),[9] provides a version quoted from Sayf Ibn 'Umar al-Kufi al-Asadi al-Tamimi (died 170 AH/786 CE), Ibn al-Jawzi (died 597 AH/1200 CE),[10] who seems to give the same account produced by Sayf Ibn 'Umar via al-Tabari, provides a text that appears to be summarized from al-Tabari's version, but without the latter's expansion and exceptions—in particular the exclusion of the Jews from living in Aelia. It may be noted in Ibn al-Jawzi's narration that he substituted 'Ali Ibn Abi Talib as a witness to 'Umar's Assurance for Amru Ibn al-Aas, who was mentioned in al-Tabari's version. This may be due to a mistake, intentional or unintentional, committed by the person who copied the manuscript we have of Ibn al-Jawzi's book.[11] Nevertheless, the historical accounts indicate that 'Ali Ibn Abi Talib was not present at the first Muslim conquest of Islamic Jerusalem, but was deputizing for 'Umar Ibn al-Khattab in Madinah.[12]

The fame of al-Tabari's version of 'Umar's Assurance as quoted from Sayf Ibn 'Umar does not rule out the need to investigate its chain of transmitters. Fame in itself is no proof of authenticity, especially when acquired a long time after the event. Before starting to discuss the narration of Sayf Ibn 'Umar, which al-Tabari quotes, it is important to know that al-Tabari was born at the end of 224 AH/839 CE, and he began writing his history after 290 AH/902 CE and finished it in 303 AH/915 CE. Moreover, the first edition of al-Tabari's history was published between 1831 and 1853.[13] It would seem that al-Tabari was one of a handful of historians who mentioned the version of 'Umar's Assurance together with its chain of transmitters. Nevertheless, he gave "a broken chain of transmitters which is without basis in the study of narration lines."[14]

In short, historical sources reflect, according to their narrators and authors, the general circumstances and socio-political developments prevailing at the time they were written. The sources are colored by the personality of their author, the recording's time, and by the local, political, and religious interests.

Early accounts, which related the content of 'Umar's Assurance without citing any specific version come from Hijaz, such as al-Waqidi's account, which is characterized by moderate Shi'ism, or Syrian accounts such as that of Abu Hafs al-Dimashqi in al-Baladhuri. The accounts that provide versions, whether they be short or long, are mostly Kufic in origin, such as the narration of al-Ya'qubi, who had obvious Shi'ite tendencies, or that of Sayf Ibn 'Umar, who was known for his strong bias towards his tribe of Bani Tamim. It may be that he tried to give his tribe some prominence in his accounts of Muslim conquests. This in turn may be what prompted Wellhausen to accuse Sayf Ibn 'Umar somewhat hastily of tilting many historical events in favor of his school of thought and his theories of history.[15] Shlomo D. Goitein's hasty accusation of Sayf as having little authenticity, and irresponsibility toward Palestinian issues and ignorance of them, based on the latter's account of the Muslim conquest of Ramla,[16] is undoubtedly a trumped-up distortion displaying a shameful bias. Such bias is not based on any rational academic analysis or objective criticism of the historical sources, but rather, at the very least, on religious and political reasons linked to the struggle of the political institution currently ruling in Israel to gain control of Islamic Jerusalem. The attempt of some Israeli academics and orientalists to play down the importance of Islamic sources relating to the period of the first Muslim conquest of Islamic Jerusalem and in particular to undermine the significance of Islamic Jerusalem to Islam, seeks to eliminate other viewpoints and to rewrite the Islamic history of Jerusalem from a single biased point of view. One example of such bias is Goitein's assertion that the Arab conquest is embellished with imaginary myths and legends, and that consequently there remain only a very few authentic accounts of the stages of Muslim conquest and the early centuries of Islamic Jerusalem's life under Islamic rule.[17]

I am inclined to accept the account of Abu Hafs al-Dimashqi as quoted by al-Baladhuri, because it is the most accurate account of 'Umar's Assurance. Compared with the accounts emanating from Hijaz and Kufa, the Syrian accounts of the Muslim conquests in Greater Syria are, generally speaking, outstanding narrations from the most reliable sources. Apart from containing rare and detailed information, they are closer to the places where the events occurred, so the authors had precise knowledge of the Muslim conquests and their secrets. Husain 'Atwan argues that the Syrian accounts are unusually long and detailed and that "they differ from the Hijazi and Iraqi accounts in some aspects of time and place." Nevertheless, the Syrian accounts "concur a little with the Hijazi and Iraqi accounts in their historical framework and internal content, but differ widely with them on other points."[18] If the Syrian and Hijazi accounts of 'Umar's Assurance are brief and general, the Kufic accounts are longer and more detailed, for reasons we shall discuss below.

Al-Tabari's Version

In the name of God, the most Merciful, the most Compassionate. This is the assurance of safety *Aman* that the servant of God (the second Caliph) 'Umar (Ibn al-Khattab), the Commander of the Faithful, has granted to the people of Aelia (Capitolina). He has granted them an assurance of safety for their lives and possessions, their churches and crosses; the sick and the healthy (to everyone without exceptions); and for the rest of its religious community. Their churches will not be inhabited (taken over) nor destroyed (by Muslims). Neither they, nor the land on which they stand, nor their cross, nor their possession will be encroached upon or partly seized. The people will not be compelled *Yukrahuna* in religion, nor anyone of them be maltreated *Yudarruna*. No Jews should reside with them in Aelia.

The people of Aelia must pay the *Jizia* tax like the people of the [other] cities, and they must expel the Byzantines and the robbers. As for those who will leave (Aelia), their lives and possessions shall be safeguarded until they reach their place of safety, and as for those who remain, they will be safe. They will have to pay the tax like the people of Aelia. Those of people of Aelia who would like to leave with the Byzantines, take their possessions, and abandon their churches and crosses will be safe until they reach their place of safety; and whosoever was in Aelia of local people *Ahl al-Ard* (villagers, refugees from the villages who sought refuge in the Aelia) before the murder of *fulan* so-and-so may remain in Aelia if they wish, but they must pay the tax like the people of Aelia. Those who wish may go with the Byzantines, and those who wish may return to their families. Nothing will be taken from them until their harvest has been reaped.

The contents of this assurance of safety are under the covenant of God, are the responsibilities of His Prophet, of the Caliphs, and of the Faithful if (the people of Aelia) pay the tax according to their obligations. The persons who attest to it are: Khalid Ibn al-Walid, 'Amr Ibn al-'Aas, 'Abd al-Rahman Ibn 'Awf, and Mu'awiya Ibn Abi Sufyan. This assurance of safety was written and prepared in the year 15 (AH).

The version given by al-Tabari, dated 15 AH, was until 1953 regarded as the longest and most explicit text, containing the greatest degree of detail and restrictions. I will discuss al-Tabari's version critically and analyze the new restrictions, which are at variance with the conquest and its general trends, and which prompt me to have, at the very least, doubts about them. The versions preceding al-Tabari's neither mention nor support these reservations. The major restrictions mentioned in al-Tabari's version are described below.

I. Exclusion of the Jews from Residing in Aelia

The condition placed on 'Umar Ibn al-Khattab by the inhabitants of Aelia, in particular the Patriarch Sophronius, was that "No Jew should reside with them in Aelia." This restriction or exception is not supported or even mentioned in any of the accounts preceding al-Tabari's. Moreover, it would seem to conflict with the historical events known about the Muslim conquest of Islamic Jerusalem. The researcher has found no Arab historical sources that confirm that 'Umar Ibn al-Khattab forbade the Jews to reside in Islamic Jerusalem. If made during the rule of 'Umar Ibn al-Khattab, such a condition would have been implemented.

Karen Armstrong, in her balanced discussion of this article, argues that "it was the practice of the Rashidun, when conquering a city, simply to endorse already existing arrangements and not to introduce major changes. It has been suggested that the supposed exclusion of the Jews may simply have been an initial step: the Byzantines had banned Jews from Aelia... 'Umar could simply have confirmed the status quo and, later, decided that it was not rational or just to exclude Jews from Islamic Jerusalem." On the other hand, Daniel J. Sahas argues that perhaps the Islamic sources "confused" Heraclius' expulsion of Jews from Aelia in 629 CE, when he conquered the

Persians, with the version of 'Umar's Assurance.[19] There is another possibility. Perhaps the Muslims had nothing to do with this exclusion and it was an invention of Christian authors or probably added by a Christian source,[20] such as the Syriac chronicler Michael the Syrian, and the Christian chronicler Agapius (Mahboub) of Manbij,[21] within the context of the traditional conflict between Jews and Christians. A late source, al-Himyari in al-Rawd al-Mi'tar, stated that "the Christians made it a condition that Jews are not to be allowed to live with them."[22] Greek sources indicate that the Christians wanted Aelia to remain a Christian city and this culminated in a clear sign to exclude Jews from there.[23]

Jewish sources show that the Jews of Syria were "patiently awaiting" the arrival of the Muslim armies because they were groaning under the rule of the tyrannical Byzantines and suffering their cruel oppression in the 5th, 6th, and early 7th centuries CE.[24] While the Jewish response to the first Muslim conquest of Islamic Jerusalem was positive, because it terminated the Byzantines' rule, some Jewish sources go even further. They not only state that the Jews welcomed and assisted the Muslim armies during the conquest of Syria, but also claim that a group of Jews joined the Muslim armies, particularly during the siege of Islamic Jerusalem.[25]

Moshe Gil, however, argues that "one cannot conclude from these sources that there were Jews in the ranks of the Muslim army."[26] He also rejects the claim of Patricia Crone and Michael Cook[27] and makes the accusation that they "exaggerate in seeing here proof of general Muslim–Jewish collaboration."

Despite his doubts about the authenticity of the Muslim sources, Goitein describes the report of 'Umar Ibn al-Khattab as being accompanied by "Jewish wise men... as quite feasible." He justifies his claim by saying that it was a Jewish city before the Romans destroyed it, so it was "natural" for 'Umar to seek the guidance of the Jews.[28] But how could the Jews, who had been absent for 500 years, guide 'Umar Ibn al-Khattab around a city that had been flattened and had its landmarks, elevations, and undulations altered on more than one occasion? History confirms that the Jews, like other groups and peoples, entered Islamic Jerusalem for a period of time and then left it. Their city disappeared conclusively, having been destroyed at least three times since the Prophet Solomon. Nebuchadnezzar destroyed the city and the Temple around 586 BCE. The Romans destroyed the city twice and effaced even its name. The arrival of Pompey in 63 BCE, according to John Wilkinson, was the "beginning of a Roman effort to control the Jews, and ended two centuries later in the expulsion of the Jews from Jerusalem."[29] Titus destroyed the city and burned the Temple around 70 CE, as did Hadrian in 135 CE. After the expulsion of the Jews from Aelia, Emperor Hadrian proceeded with his plan and issued his decision in 139 CE, which stated that "no Jews should be allowed within the district of Aelia Capitolina,"[30] Jerusalem's new name.[31] From a religious point of view, Karen Armstrong argues that "Jerusalem is not mentioned explicitly in the Torah, the first five most sacred books of the Hebrew Bible, and it is associated with none of the events of the Exodus from Egypt. Why should Mount Zion in Jerusalem be the holiest place in the Jewish world and not Mount Sinai, where God gave Moses the Law and bound himself to his chosen people?"[32]

A Jewish manuscript, preserved in Cairo Geniza and dating from the 11th century CE, claims that 'Umar Ibn al- Khattab played the role of arbitrator or forceful mediator between the Christians and Jews in Islamic Jerusalem. According to this document, 'Umar Ibn al-Khattab invited the Patriarch Sophronius and representatives of the Jews to a meeting he attended in person, so as to resolve the issue of Jews residing in Islamic Jerusalem. After a long and contentious debate about the number of Jewish families who would be allowed to reside in Islamic Jerusalem, ranging from 70 on Sophronius's side to 200 on the Jewish side, 'Umar decided to allow 70 Jewish families from Tiberias to settle in the south of the walled city.[33] It would seem that this document was written during the reign of the Fatimid Caliph al-Hakim Bi-Amr Allah, who made life difficult for the Christians.[34] It would seem, then, that the document seeks to remind the Muslims of the justice brought by the Muslim conquerors to Islamic Jerusalem and how they ended the oppression that the Jews had suffered prior to the first Muslim conquest of Jerusalem. Fred McGraw Donner quotes some accounts that say that 'Umar Ibn al-Khattab negotiated sympathetically about Jewish interests. Other accounts quoted by Donner say that Sophronius imposed a condition on 'Umar that Jews should not live with them in Aelia.[35]

Furthermore, a letter by Solomon Ibn Broham al-Qara'i, who lived in the first half of the 10th century CE in Islamic Jerusalem, states that the Jews were allowed to enter and reside in Aelia from "the beginning of Isma'il's dominion," meaning from the first Muslim conquest of Islamic Jerusalem.[36] Jewish sources also claim that the Jews were allowed to pray in Islamic Jerusalem after the Muslim conquest.[37]

Christian sources claim that Jews resided in Islamic Jerusalem immediately after the first Muslim conquest. For example, Theophanes Confessor, who lived at the end of the 8th and the beginning of the 9th century, claimed that the Jews indicated to 'Umar Ibn al-Khattab that the crosses should be removed from the major churches on the Mount of Olives.[38] Moreover, the traveler Bishop Arculf, who visited Islamic Jerusalem as a pilgrim in 670 CE during the Caliphate of Mu'awiya Ibn Abi Sufyan, recounts that he found two groups of Jews in Islamic Jerusalem: the first had converted to Christianity and the second remained Jewish.[39]

Michael Asif claims that small groups of Jews were already living in Islamic Jerusalem and that they increased with time. By the end of the 1st century AH, according to his claims, there was a large Jewish community in Islamic Jerusalem divided into two groups, each with their own synagogues and schools.[40] In contrast Shafiq Jasir argues that no Jews lived in Islamic Jerusalem for the remainder of the rule of the four orthodox Caliphs. He quotes from a modern source, namely Ibrahim al-Shiriqi in his book Jerusalem and the Land of Canaan, that the number of Jews during the Umayyad Caliphate (41–132 AH/661–750 CE) was about twenty males "who used to work as servants in the precincts of al-Aqsa Mosque."[41]

"It should also be noted that by the time of the Crusades", Karen Armstrong argues, that "al-Quds was known as a city of Dhimmis, because Jews and Christians were so populous and successful there. So certainly there was a strong Jewish presence in Aelia, even though most Jews preferred to live in Ramleh." In addition, I would ask, if it is true that 'Umar excluded the Jews from living in Aelia, how could Saladin and other Muslim leaders allow them back? After the re-conquest of Islamic Jerusalem by Saladin in 1187, two new quarters were created within the walls of the old City: the Magarbeh Quarter and the Jewish Quarter, with the Sharaf Quarter in between.[42] According to Donald P. Little, the small Jewish community in Islamic Jerusalem during the Mamluk period "seems to have enjoyed the status of Dhimmis granted to them in Islamic Law."[43] Joseph Drory argues that the Jews "posed no threat to the Muslim character of the town and lived peacefully with the neighbors."[44] Donald P. Little argues that from al-Aqsa Mosque's documents "we learn that the Jews were able to own property in the City and to conduct business; on at least one occasion, moreover, the Shaikh of Magarbeh community intervened on their behalf against governmental abuse."[45]

Not only is the exclusion of Jews from residence in Islamic Jerusalem during the first Muslim conquest not historically proven, but it is also unacceptable to Islamic law. It contravenes the most basic Islamic principles concerning treatment of the People of the Book. Indeed, the reference to the Jews is out of step with and even seems to clash with the main Islamic teachings, based on the Qur'an and Sunna. For example, the Qur'an says

> God forbids you not, with regard to those who fight you for your faith nor drive you out of your homes, from dealing kindly and justly with them. For God loveth who are just. God only forbids you, with regard to those who fight you for your faith, and drive you out of your homes, and support others in driving you out, from turning to them for friendship and protection. It is such as turn to them in these circumstances that do wrong. (Qur'an, 60:8–9)

The Jews were not at that time at any stage of war with the Muslims in Islamic Jerusalem or in any part of the world. As such, how could 'Umar exclude them from living in Islamic Jerusalem? Although at the dawn of Islam, Muslims conflicted with the Jewish tribes in and around Madinah and later in Khaibar, they got along well afterwards, and especially in Islamic Jerusalem. In his attempt to discuss the reasons behind the contemporary conflict between Muslims and Jews, the well-known leading Muslim jurist Yusuf al-Qaradaw argues that "Muslims do not fight Jews because they are Jews, but because they occupied the Islamic land in Palestine."[46]

Islamic teachings reject the philosophy of a conflict based on eliminating the other party so that the victor can have everything for himself. This would mean in effect annulling the principle of plurality. On the contrary, Islam considers that plurality is vital, the nature of everything apart from God. Indeed plurality in nations, religions, and religious laws is part of the design of the universe: "O mankind! We created you from a single pair of a male and a female, and made you into nations and tribes, that you may know each other (not that you may despise each other)" (Qur'an, 49:13); "If God had so willed, He would have made you a single community" (Qur'an, 5:48). As confirmation of this idea, Islam favored another method, namely *tadafu'*, or counterbalance, as a means of adjusting positions using movement instead of conflict: "Counterbalance the evil deed with one which is better" (Qur'an, 41:34).

This conflict-free method is what Islamic teachings see as a means of preserving a non-Islamic presence in this life. *Tadafu'* is not only to preserve Islam's sacred places, but to preserve others' sacred places, as is mentioned in the following Qur'anic verse about the chronology of religions: "...and if God had not counterbalanced [*daf'u*] some people's deeds by others, there would surely have been pulled down monasteries, churches, synagogues, and mosques, in which the name of God is commemorated in abundant measure" (Qur'an, 22:40). This means that from an Islamic point of view *tadafu'* is the means of preserving a plurality of sacred places or the plurality of religions. Perhaps this is what prompted Saladin's letter of reply to Richard the Lion Heart in 589 AH/1193 CE. Richard had demanded that Islamic Jerusalem be surrendered to him and divided between Christians and Muslims, and ruled jointly by Saladin's brother, al-'Adil and Richard's sister, Queen Joanna of Sicily. Saladin replied that Islamic Jerusalem was the sacred legacy of the followers of all beliefs: "Islamic Jerusalem is to us as it is to you. It is even more important for us, since it is the site of our Prophet's nocturnal Journey and the place where the people will assemble on the Day of Judgment. Do not imagine, therefore, that we can waver in this regard."[47]

This methodology is linked to a concept of justice that encompasses all without discrimination between Muslim and non-Muslim: "... and let not the enmity and hatred of others make you avoid justice. Be just, that is nearer to piety" (Qur'an, 5:8). The command to be just in this Qur'anic verse is general and doesn't prefer any one race or group to another. The other teachings of Islam conform to this methodology and concept, in terms of acknowledging other parties and determining their rights, duties, and means of coexistence. In this way, Ahmad al-Sharif argues, the Muslim community is "an open community, where all human beings could live together on the basis of equality and justice."[48] Muhammad Said al-Buti, a leading Muslim jurist, argues that

> The Islamic state is not a monopoly of the Muslims alone... The Islamic system of statehood has a religious concept with which the Muslims have to deal and implement, just as it has an organisational legal concept which encompasses Muslims and non-Muslims. Each group interacts with it according to its status, either from a religious basis stemming from belief in Islam and its tenets, or from a social, legal standpoint based on law and order.[49]

The first Islamic state implemented this concept clearly in its domestic and foreign dealings with non-Muslims. On the domestic front, for example, Prophet Muhammad wrote a document known as "The Madinah Constitution," in which he laid down the basis of relations with the Jews who lived in the bosom of the Islamic state. On the foreign front, we find examples in the contract he concluded with the Magian people of Bahrain and the contract with the Christian inhabitants of Najran. What some early Muslim jurists subsequently wrote about dealing with the People of the Book has been strictly rejected by others, in particular, al-Nawawi in his book *Rawdat al-Talibin* (126–215/10), Ibn Qudama in his book *Al-Mughni* (358–357/9), and Abu 'Ubayd in his book *Al-Amwal,* who warned against adopting such writings. Al-Buti is among the contemporary leading Muslim jurists who have written on the subject; he also agrees that the early rejected Muslim jurists' view "conflicts vehemently with the guidance of the Messenger of God in his words and deeds, just as it conflicts with what the righteous followers did, and with the piety with which God ordered the Muslims to behave towards the People of the Book in the Qur'an."[50] It seems to me that the contraventions, additions, or interpretations invented by some Muslim jurists were produced to please the rulers or match the general circumstances and socio-political developments that affected the position of the People of the Book during certain periods of history, especially the Abbasid state.

II. Arrangements for Residing in or Leaving Aelia

Al-Tabari's version lays down the conditions by which either the residence or exile of people from Aelia should be organized after the first Muslim conquest. They are as follows:

1. The condition that the inhabitants of Aelia should expel Byzantines and robbers from it. The common factor that prompted 'Umar Ibn al-Khattab to put the Byzantines and robbers in the same category is that they were all thieves. The Byzantines had occupied and stolen the land and its resources, while robbers had stolen the people's possessions. It is contained in an expression the end of which almost contradicts the beginning. The beginning affirms that the Byzantines must be expelled, while further on the text gives the Byzantines the choice of whether to leave or stay and pay the tax.

2. If the inhabitants of Aelia are given the freedom to either remain or leave with the Byzantines and robbers, the others in Aelia at the time of the conquest (possibly visitors or villagers who were

refugees from the villages who sought refuge in Aelia) are given the freedom to either remain or leave. This is, one could argue, contained in an expression that cannot be implemented, because it says, "and whosoever was in Aelia of local people *Ahl al-Ard* (villagers) before the murder of *fulan* so-and-so." Zakariyya al-Quda comments on this phrase, saying: "without mentioning the name of *fulan* so-and-so, or giving any clue to his identity or date of his murder. Obviously it is impossible to determine to whom this description applies, so it is impossible to implement. It is impossible that this would be the text of a binding treaty."[51] This term, though, is inaccurate: 'Umar Ibn al-Khattab did not sign a treaty between two parties, rather he gave the people of Aelia an assurance of safety or pledge.

Perhaps the expression "before the murder of *fulan* so-and-so" does not refer to an unknown person, but to a very well-known person at the time of the Muslim conquest. The name of the victim may have been transcribed incorrectly from al-Tabari's original manuscript. It could be "falak" or "falaj" or "falah" and not "fulan." Therefore the matter should be investigated using al-Tabari's original manuscript (which I have not seen) before reaching any conclusion. Undoubtedly, the people of Aelia and the Muslim conquerors knew that person very well, and this prompted 'Umar Ibn al-Khattab to mention his death as an important event that occurred during the conquest and was familiar to the people at that time. It is well known that in those days the Arabs used famous events as landmarks in their calendar. Moreover, it would seem that this victim was neither an inhabitant of Aelia nor a Byzantine nor a robber, but a distinguished visitor to Aelia or someone who was a refugee during the Muslim conquest. The clue to this is that his name appeared after the expression "and whosoever was in Aelia of local people [villagers] before the murder of *fulan* so-and-so." This means that the murder frightened the local people (villagers) and drove many of them to seek refuge in Aelia. Although I cannot categorically make a statement without examining al-Tabari's original manuscript, Mujir al-Din al-Alimi (d. 928 AH/1521 CE) in his version of 'Umar's Assurance does not mention this phrase of al-Tabari's.[52]

III. Date of the Version

The date appearing at the end of 'Umar's Assurance, the year 15, has undoubtedly been added to the version and is not originally part of it. It is well known that the Muslims did not start using the Hijri calendar until the fourth year of the Caliphate of 'Umar Ibn al-Khattab, which was seventeen years after the Hijra. It is inconceivable, as Zakariyya al-Quda argues, "that a document before this date should be dated with the Hijri date."[53]

Discussion of the Orthodox Patriarchate's Version

One of the most significant versions of 'Umar's Assurance in which there are clear appendices and additions is the text registered under no. 552 in the library of the Greek Orthodox Patriarchate in Jerusalem. On January 1, 1953 the Patriarchate published a new version of 'Umar's Assurance, claiming it to be a literal translation of the original Greek text, which is kept in the Greek Orthodox library in the Phanar Quarter of Istanbul in Turkey. In order to ascertain the authenticity of this version, which is the longest and most recent, I examined historical sources, as did Asad Rustum in his book *Historical Terminology*, to ascertain the authenticity of a document that surfaced supporting the Muslim cause in a conflict over the western wall of al-Aqsa Mosque. Rustum submitted this document, which was by al-Duzdar, the commander of the Citadel, to a technical, historical examination.[54]

Using methods of both external and internal criticism that are well known in scrutinizing historical sources, I examined the Orthodox Patriarchate's document and found certain facts that prompted me to doubt the authenticity of the document.

External Criticism

The document is written on relatively modern paper, dating perhaps to the late Ottoman or early Turkish era. Although I was unable to examine its chemical composition, fiber distribution, and water stamp, I found the document had been written in different colored inks, including black, red, and gold. Moreover, some lines were illustrated with various types of flowers. Such artistic decoration was unknown in the early centuries of Islam, especially in the first century after the Hijra, during the second decade of which the Muslim conquest took place.

The document's foreword, body, and ending all contain vocabulary, expressions, and constructions not known at the time of the conquest. Rather they date from the era of Ottoman rule. For example, the document begins: "To the honoured and revered Patriarch, namely Sophronius, Patriarch of the Royal sect on the Mount of Olives in Honourable Jerusalem." In the body of the text it says: "According to the obedience and submission shown by them (the

Dhimmis or non-Muslims)"; and, "because they gave from the dear, venerable, and noble Prophet who was sent by God..." In conclusion it says: "Whosoever reads (*kulluman qara'a*) this decree of ours," as though it is intended to say: "*kullu man qara'a.*" These phrases do not conform to the style of writing prevalent at the time of 'Umar Ibn al-Khattab. Moreover, the document contains some terms that definitely date to the Ottoman period. In the opening of the document the term *Ahd Nama* appears. *Nama* is a Turkish word of Persian origin meaning "deed" or "covenant." Also in the body of the text we find: "O Lord, facilitate the affairs of Hussain," and at the end, the term "this decree of ours" is repeated. All these examples confirm that the document was written or invented during the Ottoman era, perhaps in the second half of the 19th century, or at least was translated from Greek to Arabic during the Ottoman period.

It is important here to explain that regardless of whether this version was written originally in Greek or translated into Arabic, it was undoubtedly written during the period of Ottoman rule, not during or immediately after the Muslim conquest of Islamic Jerusalem. Even if it were proven that there is a Greek text of 'Umar's Assurance, it would certainly not be the original version. This text was written in a very late period in an obvious ecclesiastical style, for religious and political reasons that we shall discuss in another part of this article. Moreover, I have found no historical account indicating that 'Umar Ibn al-Khattab wrote any text or document in any language other than Arabic, nor has any historian made such a claim. Consequently, we cannot depend on this document or rely on it as an original version because it was written in Greek.

Another reason for doubting the authenticity of this document is that the researcher finds its author does not adhere to the Arabic language and uses foreign expressions. The document is written in poor Arabic, using a style that was not familiar in the first century of the Hijra. The Arabs at that time wrote the word "*milia*" with *taa marbuta* at the end, but in this document it appears with *taa maftuha*. The same applies to the following words in the document: *al-Dhimmat, kafat, hadrat,* and *li-ta'at.* The use of *taa maftuha* instead of *taa marbuta* was common during the Ottoman rule of the Arab region. In addition, the document contains many grammatical mistakes. For example, "*al-Maghara dhi al-Thalathat Abwab*" should be "*dhat al-Thalathat Abwab*," and "*wa yu 'addi al-Nasraniyyu ila al-Batrak Dirham,*" should read, "*Dirhaman.*"

Internal Criticism

At the time of the Muslim conquest Aelia was not known as al-Quds al-Sharif or "Honorable Jerusalem" as it is referred to in the document. The name al-Quds was not known at that time. Its name was Aelia, the term applied to it by Hadrian in 135 CE. It would be logical for 'Umar Ibn al-Khattab to address the inhabitants using the name to which they were accustomed. Even if some traditions attributed to Prophet Muhammad are correct, the name used was Bayt al-Maqdis and not al-Quds or al-Quds al-Sharif, terms used in subsequent Islamic eras. In fact the name Aelia continued to be used long after the Muslim conquest, as demonstrated by the poetry of Farazdaq.[55] It is strange that the document exempts the Christians of Islamic Jerusalem from paying the tax. I have found no historical account or juristic formula that supports this exemption from the requirement applied by the Muslims after other conquests. The other unusual matter is that at the end of the document it states that the assurance was given in the presence of a number of "*al-Ikhwa al-Sahaba*," or brother companions, including 'Uthman Ibn 'Affan. It is historically proven that the latter did not attend the conquest of Islamic Jerusalem and that he had indicated to 'Umar Ibn al-Khattab that he should not go in person to receive Aelia.[56]

I also found that the document states the names of some Christian sects, such as the Copts, the East Syrians, the Armenians, the Nestorians, the Jacobites, and the Maronites. It is known that at the time of the conquest the only Christian sect in Aelia was the Greek Orthodox. At the time of Heraclius, which immediately preceded the Muslim conquest, Aelia was part of the Byzantine state, where the teachings of the Eastern Church prevailed. Moreover, in the other versions of 'Umar's Assurance there is no mention of Christian sects in Islamic Jerusalem. Early versions of 'Umar's Assurance focus on the general, without specifying one sect or another. This conforms to the method that prevailed at the time of Muslim conquests. As for the mention of "Franks" among the sects, it raises yet more doubts about the authenticity of the document, because the term was not known until the time of Crusaders.

Not only does this late version mention the names of Christian sects that did not exist in Islamic Jerusalem at the time of 'Umar Ibn al-Khattab, but it also claims that these sects fell under the Greek Orthodox Patriarch. It states that they "are subject to the aforementioned Patriarch and that he has authority over them." Not content with putting the Patriarch Sophronius in charge of all other Christian sects and making them subservient to him, the document goes on to give him and successive leaders of his sect the right to collect one and a third dirhams of silver from every Christian visitor to the Church of the Holy Sepulcher. This places the document in a new light. It would seem to have been invented some time after the Muslim conquest to counter sectarian dissent against the spiritual leadership of the Church of the Holy Sepulcher. As for its attribution to 'Umar Ibn al-Khattab and its additions to the text of 'Umar's Assurance, they are designed to give the document extra weight in support of the Orthodox sect's leadership over other Christian sects.

I must conclude that the document is either forged or at least concocted. Moreover, my analysis of the document makes me suspect that the Greek Orthodox Church published it with these additions in 1953 as part of an inter-Christian struggle for control of the Christian holy places in Islamic Jerusalem. Throughout the Ottoman period, especially in the 17th century and after, relations between Christian communities were marked by "antagonism and dissension" over their respective rights in the Holy places, which several times developed into "bloody clashes."[57] This was an attempt to give the Greek Orthodox Church priority and even leadership over the other Christian sects currently present in Islamic Jerusalem. After the end of the British mandate and the war of 1948, when Jordan took control of East Jerusalem, it could be argued that the Greek Orthodox Church in Jerusalem, which represented the majority of the Christians in the city, felt by 1953 that it was the right time to issue a new version of 'Umar's Assurance, which would give them the upper hand over the other Christian communities in Jerusalem. As Jordan was the first Arab Muslim political regime after four centuries of non-Arab rule, the Orthodox Arabs expected the ruling Hashemite family of Jordan to show sympathy toward their position in Jerusalem.

Conclusion

All these versions of 'Umar's Assurance, especially Sayf Ibn 'Umar's account in al-Tabari and subsequent quotations from it, demonstrate discrepancies and additions. It is not possible to say with any confidence which is the original text that 'Umar wrote and witnessed. Despite this major reservation, I tend to agree with Moshe Gil, who argues that "we cannot disregard him altogether. The version itself (of Sayf Ibn 'Umar's account in al-Tabari) seems to be reliable."[58] I do not agree with Philip Hitti[59] and Tritton[60] in their total denial of 'Umar's Assurance because of disparities between some accounts of the actual text. Nor do I agree with Shlomo D. Goitein, who considers that 'Umar's Assurance is a fabrication without any basis in reality because al-Baladhuri does not mention any text for it.[61] Indeed, it would seem to me that Goitein is contradictory in his analyses of 'Umar's Assurance. He considers al-Baladhuri's account to be the most reliable, but does not accept the accounts of al-Ya'qubi and Eutychius (Ibn al-Batriq), both of whom, he says, provide "general, brief texts not significantly different from al-Baladhuri's account."[62]

Undoubtedly the versions of 'Umar's Assurance have been expanded and embellished with the passing of time. The development would seem to have begun with al-Tabari's version, which he transmitted from Sayf Ibn 'Umar, and continued with the versions quoted by Ibn Asakir,[63] through to that of Mujir al-Din al-Alimi,[64] and concluding with the Greek Orthodox version. The variations are probably related to Jewish–Christian relations, the development of Muslim–Christian relations, and Christian–Christian relations. A consideration of these versions within the framework of the developments of the social and political circumstances of the People of the Book from the time of 'Umar Ibn 'Abd al-'Aziz to Haroun al-Rashid,[65] the resolutions of al-Mutawakkil, and the historical events that followed, shows that the discrepancies, detailed additions, and conditions have, without the slightest doubt, nothing to do with the period of the Muslim conquest of Islamic Jerusalem, nor do they address the situation at that time. Rather they are part of the general conditions and the socio-political web that emerged there, which affected the position of the People of the Book and their treatment within the Abbasid state, to which we have referred above. New juristic ideas and formulae were drafted in response to the new developments that occurred in Islamic periods following the first Muslim conquest of Islamic Jerusalem. 'Abdul 'Aziz Duri argues that the different versions of the text dealt with matters that surfaced later. This led him to conclude that the text of 'Umar's Assurance "was developed to include conditions which have no relevance to the period of the conquest, and that it received juridical formulation capable of meeting new developments."[66]

In conclusion, I am inclined to believe that 'Umar Ibn al-Khattab granted the people of Aelia an assurance of safety for themselves, their property, their churches, and their religion, in return for their paying tax. This was in line with the general trend of Muslim pacts and treaties that were granted to other cities in Syria or concluded with the People of the Book during the period of Muslim conquests. As for additions and conditions attributed to 'Umar Ibn al-Khattab, they are the product of later historical periods, resulting from socio-political circumstances that differed greatly from the time of the first Muslim conquest of Islamic Jerusalem.

This study totally rejects the claim made by Daniel Sahas that the first Muslim conquest led to the "emergence of an opportunity for the Christians of Islamic Jerusalem to contain the Jews, with the help of the Muslim Arabs, through the concessions granted to them in 'Umar's Assurance."[67] What grounds would the Christians of Islamic Jerusalem have for containing the Jews, when they themselves had forbidden them residence in Aelia for several centuries and expelled them from it? If this assertion were true, why did the Patriarch Sophronius ask 'Umar Ibn al-Khattab to renew Hadrian's law and forbid the Jews residence in Aelia? His request was rejected by 'Umar Ibn al-Khattab. The concessions that the conquering Muslims granted the inhabitants of Aelia were not requested by the Christians of Islamic Jerusalem, but were a gift from the Caliph of the Muslims to the people of that region, based on the principles laid down by Islam for dealing with non-Muslims, particularly the People of the Book. If there had been Jews living in Aelia at the time of the conquest, they would have been granted the same concessions as the Christians, which may be summarized as giving them safety for themselves, their property, synagogues, and religion, in exchange for paying the tax. Sahas made his claim based on a text translated from the Greek that closely resembles the Orthodox Patriarchate's text of 'Umar's Assurance, which was certainly fabricated or concocted to serve the political and religious aim of the Greek Orthodox sect in Jerusalem.

Even if other religions regarded the acquisition of Jerusalem as "an aim which threatened other People of the Book and competed with them,"[68] Islamic Jerusalem was not an exclusive region under the Muslim rule. The arrival of 'Umar in Islamic Jerusalem marked the start of a golden age and the beginning of a new era in which the region became an open one for all the nations. Karen Armstrong argues that 'Umar was "faithful to the Islamic inclusive vision. Unlike the Jews and Christians, Muslims did not attempt to exclude others from Jerusalem's holiness"; and instead of excluding these religions in Islamic Jerusalem, "Muslims were being taught to venerate them." In addition, Armstrong argues that

> from the first, Muslims showed that the veneration of
> sacred space did not have to mean conflict, enmity,
> killing... and exclusion of others... From the start, the
> Muslims developed an inclusive vision of Jerusalem which
> did not deny the presence and devotion of others, but
> respected their rights and celebrated plurality and
> coexistence. This inclusive vision of holiness is sorely
> needed by the people of Jerusalem today.[69]

In short, the attitude of conquest, or what I shall term at the end of
this article as "the first Muslim liberation of Islamic Jerusalem," was
contrary to that of both Jews and Christians towards Aelia. The
Muslims liberated the Christians from the Byzantine occupiers of
Aelia, rid the Jews of oppression at the hands of the Byzantines, and
restored their presence in that region after an absence of 500 years.[70]
These events were in keeping with the teachings of Islam based on the
methodology of *tadafu'*, or counterbalance, the concept of justice
based not only on plurality and recognition of others, but on
determining their rights, duties, treatment, and means of coexistence.

JERUSALEM AS THE CITY OF GOD'S KINGDOM: COMMON TROPES IN THE BIBLE AND THE ANCIENT NEAR EAST

Thomas L. Thompson

> *When we speak about God, we speak about what we*
> *hardly understand.*
> *We pass on what we ourselves have heard: merely a*
> *rumor about God.[1]*

Monotheism is neither a unique nor a revolutionary contribution of the Bible to ancient thought. Nor is it intrinsically opposed to the polytheism of ancient Near Eastern mythology. Both belong to the same spectrum of ideas and literature that evoke the transcendent as determining human destiny. The Bible's recurrent discussions of false or empty gods, gods made by the hands of clever men, and the self-ironic description of men as "gods with clay feet," all belong to this critical ancient Near Eastern discussion of transcendence, which insisted upon the division between the human and the divine, and limits of the former in the face of the latter. A coherent, universal understanding of the divine is a pervasive concept within ancient Near Eastern political thought in many texts from at least the 15th century BCE, and is particularly marked in imperial texts. The divine is portrayed as sole creator of the world and the king as his son. Through the king's rule, the whole of creation finds its goal in a worldwide, eternal peace and happiness.

The purpose of kingship in the worldview of the ancient Near East is utopian. Even the purpose of war is to establish peace. This peace is cosmic, for it is the original chaos, from which creation came, subdued by the king. As servant of the gods, he brings foreign nations back to their destined role as clients of the universal divine patron. Through empire the world is united, aligned once again in the proper order intended at creation. The peace that such conquest brings is interpreted theologically. Those enemies once conquered are no longer foreigners, but have become the great king's own people, subjects of divine blessing. Wrong turns to right; violence to peace; injustice and suffering to eternal justice and well-being. The king saves and recreates the world that God created as good. The epitome of the ruler is as son of God, divine servant, the good shepherd of his people: a savior.

Patronage and the Maintenance of Creation

The religious and historical issue of a covenant of the king with his divine patron, implied or expressed, including such personal terms as loyalty and grace, as well as of holy war, banishment, and deportation, and involving the literary or historical destruction of peoples, are well-known aspects of ancient Near Eastern texts.[2] The Bible's theological re-use of such literary trope and rhetoric requires both comparison and contrast. The biblical reiteration of ancient Near Eastern literary tropes is centered in the relationship of creation and royal ideology, of holy war and an eternal peace, with a utopian goal of establishing a place for the divine on earth. This is the role that Jerusalem ideally plays in biblical tradition, and it is the hope of this paper to give expression to something of the literary resonance of this complex motif.

In the development of the extensive leitmotif of a covenant between Israel and its God, the Bible adopts the mythology of this universal, even imperialistic, worldview in its theology; yet its anthropology is ever expressed from the perspective of a subject people. In trying to understand the symbol-system of a particular literature of antiquity, good reading cannot confine itself to any one genre or even a single language, anymore than it can be satisfied with a single text or author. No text is limited by what an author intended to say, not even by the understanding of his colleagues; for those who write use a language that their intellectual world has given them.[3] Without in any way wishing to be systematic or complete, I would like to identify a central cluster of elements involved with the theme of holy war, reflecting the much larger political system of patronage as it is expressed in ancient Near Eastern "royal ideology."

One of the clearest and best known expressions of God as patron and the king as his servant is the carving on the Hammurabi stele, in which the God Shamash hands the king his laws. In the prologue, Hammurabi (18th century BCE) describes himself as having been ordained by the gods from the beginning of creation to promote the people's welfare, to make justice prevail, to destroy the evil and wicked, and to light up the land as the sun.[4] He is the shepherd appointed by the high god Enlil, responsible for his people's prosperity. That the king is divinely chosen by the gods for his role is comparable to the biblical understanding of the messiah as the chosen one and—in the extension of this larger discourse—of Israel as the chosen people. Similarly, Egyptian imperial texts speak of the king as the son of Re, as begotten, raised, or even born from the body of Re. Comparable biblical expressions range from Psalm 2's heavenly messiah or savior, to whom Yahweh has given birth,[5] to an understanding of the entire people, Israel, as Yahweh's first-born.[6]

The Role of the Divine on Earth

The first function of the thematic element of divine patronage is to present the king as representative of divine presence on earth, while maintaining an understanding of the divine as transcendent and universal.[7] In Egyptian hymns, especially of the 18th and 19th dynasties, the pharaoh serves as just such a divine hypostasis. As son of the sun God, his primary role is divine warrior. He is God's presence on earth and carries out the rule of the gods in Egypt. In the Bible, such a role belongs not to the king, but to Yahweh as God's name and presence in Israel. Yahweh—much like the Assyrian God Assur—is alone true king. However, there are other "sons of god"—not strangers to the Bible—who are clients of the divine and yet still indicate that the king himself has a divine role. The particular role of Yahweh's son and divine warrior-king or "messiah" is quite emphatic in such songs as Psalms 2 and 110, as in Isaiah 7, and is directly derivative of Egyptian royal ideology.[8]

War in the Bible, as in the ancient Near East, is always holy war. Through war, the divine reasserts a creative role over the world, by bringing all nations under a single imperial rule of the gods. Imperialism is the specific expression of the divine and universal right to rule the earth. As in the narrative of Marduk's[9] war against Tiamat[10] within the Akitu festival, and in the biblical story of creation out of tohu wa-bohu's chaos and the darkness of tehom, the king maintains creation by enforcing the rule of the divine patron through war.[11] In the legend of Sargon, the king fulfills a three-fold role of government, fertility, and creation. As ruler, he governs his people; as gardener and lover of Ishtar,[12] he produces fertility for the land; and, as conqueror, carves out the mountains and levels the valleys and encircles the sea.[13] In Isaiah, Yahweh similarly levels mountains and straightens valleys to demonstrate his creative "glory" and the presence of his kingdom on earth.[14] The king's roles of creation, government, and fertility are mediated through a series of representatives of his patronage, from the humanity, "created male and female," of Genesis 1:26 to the transcendent king enthroned in heaven that we find in the Psalter.[15]

Tears and Humanity

In Genesis's creation story, mankind, reflecting God's image, is created to rule over the earth like a king. This role is also reflected in the Psalter: "The heavens belong to Yahweh, but he gave the earth to the sons of man."[16] Although in Hammurabi's Code the role of intermediary for the divine, of rising like the sun and bringing justice to the world, belongs to the king, in the Bible the king's role is more complex; one of the Bible's purposes is to reflect on the past as full of illustration of vice and virtue. In the Bible, the role of human kings is ever cast in doubt and serves the purposes of tragedy. Yahweh alone is king,[17] while Israel and its kings "go the way of all flesh" because of their hubris. In its long chain of narrative, the Bible develops a progressive leitmotif in which successive characters assume the role of God's servant. Whether kings, prophets, or priests, they are tested and judged, expected to maintain the humility of small children. Success is rare and fragile in the Bible, whose story is aimed at Israel's failure and destruction. Tears, and especially tears of repentance, are the only mark of virtue proper to men. In the ancient epic of Gilgamesh,[18] Utnapishtim's[19] tears are evoked by the sun with irony to predict the end of the flood.[20] In the Babylonian Akitu festival, tears are a sign of compassion; a king could be denied the throne if he is unable to cry, since this would mean he lacks the compassion necessary to rule.[21] In Egyptian myth, a pun on the words *romet* ("mankind") and *remit* ("tears") defines the essence of humanity, which is created as a tear from the eye of Re.[22] In the Bible, tears are the prelude to a happy reversal of fortune.[23] It is suffering, deportation, and the tears of repentance that bring virtue, understanding, and a pure heart.[24]

War and the Maintenance of Creation

Kingship, empire building, and the pre-industrial social system of patronage are at the heart of the ancient politics of religion. The most central motivating function of religious metaphor in ancient texts is their use in the support of political and especially royal ideology as the means by which creation is maintained over time. The implication is always that all are dependent on the ruler for their existence. The world of the gods is both implicitly and explicitly a metaphorical world: a mirror held up to support and control the values of the king and the ideal peace of good government. The Mesopotamian world's Anu, Egypt's Ptah and Ammon-Re, the Semitic world's El, and the Bible's El Olam all share the role of the eternally divine father of the gods. They epitomize the role of the divine at the head of a pantheon of deities, each of which rule over all the primary functions that determine this world. The function of the king as servant of the gods and shepherd of his people is fundamental throughout the entire ancient world, expressed respectively in the divine roles of Marduk, Horus, Ba'al, and Yahweh as perfect sons of their father. Their subordination to the transcendent mirrors the people's support of the king, and thus forms a link in a mythic chain, the reiterative logic of which presents the king in his role as a son of god and savior of the people, engaged in a cosmic war against false and foreign gods and nations.

The king stands as representative of mankind, legitimately ruling the earth.[25] The first duty of a king as patron is to provide protection for his clients. His patronage depends on his ability as a military man to provide security to the state. In literature, this first duty of the king is expressed in an extension of creation stories. Through the king, the divine is present and functional in the world of men. The king holds chaos bound in chains; he is God's warrior. He maintains creation and brings about the happy destiny for his people that God himself had originally determined at the creation. Destroying and consuming enemies in war leads to life and prosperity for those who submit to the king's patronage. The intrinsic association of the use of military force to destroy the powers of evil and to create eternal peace for the nation are the key thematic elements of royal ideology throughout ancient literature.

Nations in Uproar

One of the elements supporting an understanding of the king as universal are the stereotypical expressions to describe the "nations in uproar" against the divine,[26] in need of subjection under royal patronage. In Egyptian texts, the stereotypical "nine bows" define the pharaoh as universal patron. In inscriptions of both Merneptah and Haremheb, the patronage over the nine bows is a symbol of world peace.[27] In cuneiform literature, Marduk's struggle in the Enuma Elish[28] against Tiamat and the eleven monsters seems capable of supporting a transcendent interpretation of the rebellious twelve Kings of Hatti in Assyrian campaign inscriptions as these same forces of chaos.[29] Such a list of nations, peoples fated for destruction, provokes the theme of holy war in the Bible. Israel's failure to rid the land of such mythic aboriginal peoples of chaos centers on the theme of Yahweh as patron. Israel's role as Yahweh's client demands of it an obedience that an all-too-human Israel is incapable of realizing.[30]

The principle of reciprocity, implicit in the blessings and curses of patronage that drive the story, inexorably brings Yahweh's wrath against his own people, as Samaria and Jerusalem are condemned to destruction. A comparably complex narrative context is found in the Iron Age Moabite inscription of Mesha, which has much in common with the discourse of biblical narrative. This inscription understands Moab's god Chemosh as the king's refuge and the cause of victory over his enemies.[31] Similar to the biblical understanding of defeat and destruction, caused by Yahweh's anger against his people, an earlier subjugation of Moab to Israel is seen as having been the direct result of the god's anger at his own people. In his anger, Chemosh had abandoned his land. He now returns during the reign of Mesha (c 858 BCE). In capturing Israel's town of Ataroth, Mesha tells a story of having killed the entire population so that Chemosh might be intoxicated—a motif that occurs in both Egyptian and Ugaritic myths of war and destruction, in which gods become drunk by drinking men's blood. In Mesha's story, the blood of Moab's enemies is poured out as an offering to the god, while their chieftain, Arel, is dedicated to Chemosh in Kerioth.[32] Mesha also captured Nebo, and, in an expression of piety, kills everyone: "7,000 men, boys, women, girls and maid-servants." He "dedicated them to destruction for (the god) Ashtar-Chemosh." Throughout this short but intensely provocative narrative, it is ever the divine patron, Chemosh, who fights for Mesha, drives the enemy out and instructs the king when to go into battle. Mesha closes his story in peace over the "hundred towns" he has added to his land because his god, Chemosh, "lived there in his time."

Blessings and Curses

As in the Mesha stele from Iron Age Jordan, the typical role of the king in an ancient Near Eastern story is defined as principal warrior in a divine struggle against chaos. Victory in battle is of cosmic proportions and significance. Victory establishes a universal, utopian peace. The pharaoh Merneptah's (r. c. 1213–1203 BCE) peace is described in idyllic terms: a calm comes over the land and fear disappears; fortresses are ignored and people sleep outside at night; cattle do not need shepherds and everyone comes and goes with singing.[33] Not a single enemy is left; the whole world falls under the king's patronage. In Thutmosis III's (r. 1479–1425 BCE) victory song, this world is described as the "great ones of Djahi" in the south and the "Amu of Retenu" in Asia, God's land in the east, the western lands and "the islands of the great green sea." "The great ones of all foreign countries" are bound under the king's patronage.[34] As with David's rule in the biblical stories, Thutmosis' rule is eternal: his "throne of Horus" is established "for a million years" and his house is the work of eternity. All blessing flows from his kingdom. His blessing, like the blessing to Abraham to all nations, is universal: "to lead the living for eternity."[35]

The divine patron's grace and mercy is also universal and includes the people's traditional enemies.[36] The goal of military campaigns is to "bind" and "chain" the enemy to his new role as client. Patronage frees and brings peace to every new subject. For those who resist the claims of patronage, there are corresponding curses. The deportation of the rebellious and the granting of a new land are also typical aspects of the patron's control over destiny.[37] Like the prophet Jeremiah's Yahweh, who makes a cosmic desert out of the faithless Jerusalem,[38] sending wolves and bears to ravage the "empty" city, Merneptah turns the land of Tehenu into a desert and the town of Yenoam into a wilderness. The pharaoh gives fertility to the lands and breath to the nostrils of his people.[39] His patronage is life and it is death, famine and prosperity, desert emptiness and boundless fertility.[40]

This double-edged sword of blessings and curses has its clearest expression in the blessings and curses of vassal treaties[41] and of monumental inscriptions.[42] The client is bound to his patron. He can be either obedient or rebellious, but his choice must be resolute— either/or.[43] The king of justice will determine his fate accordingly.

In celebrating his control over Palestine, Merneptah expresses the dualism of patronage well. The stele uses a story metaphor of marriage and patronage. Israel, whose "seed is no more"—and whose name is possibly originally derived from the linguistically hardly distinguishable name for the Jezreel valley, north of Nablus— personifies Palestine's former husband, lost in the war, and Hurru, the geographic name of the land itself, is portrayed as a fertile widow awaiting the pharaoh as her new husband. Both play roles in an implied story. We are given a negative image of an enemy annihilated: "Israel has become a desert"; and a positive image: of the pharaoh's grace and patronage: "Hurru is a widow for Egypt." As the pharaoh takes his new wife, a new destiny is created: "All lands are united, they

are in peace."[44] The peace and prosperity of divine patronage in the
ancient Near East is classically expressed in the reversal of fortune of
what I have called "the poor-man's song." This is the single most
effective symbol of divine rule and justice, and is commonplace in
ancient Near Eastern texts since the Bronze Age.[45] In biblical texts, it
is a messianic and utopian sign of God's kingdom.

The Kingdom of God and "the poor-man's song"

> Oh Happy Day! Heaven and Earth are in joy . . .
> They who were fled have come back to their towns; they
> who were hidden have come forth again.
> They who were hungry are sated and gay; they who were
> thirsty are drunken.
> They who were naked are clothed in fine linen; they who
> were dirty are clad in white.
> They who were in prison are set free; they who were
> fettered are in joy.
> But troublemakers have become peaceful.[46]

> The bows of heroes are broken; but the weak are strapped
> in strength.
> Those who were filled sell themselves for bread; but the
> hungry are no longer in need.
> The barren bear seven; but the mother of many is left alone.
> Yahweh kills and he brings to life; he sends down to She'ol;
> and he brings back.
> Yahweh makes poor and he makes rich; he humiliates and
> gives pride.
> He raises the poor from the dust and lifts the needy from
> the dunghill;
> he sets them among nobility and gives them seats of honor.
> The pillars of the earth belong to Yahweh; he has set the
> world on them.
> He protects the steps of the pious; but the godless die in
> darkness.
> For it is not by strength that men prevail.[47]

> The blind receive their sight and the lame walk;
> Lepers are cleansed and the deaf hear;
> The dead are raised up and the poor have the good news
> preached to them.
> Blessed is he who takes no offence in me.[48]

This "poor man's song," announcing the good news of a savior ascending the throne of his kingdom, finds an echo throughout ancient literature. It captures the essence of a world at peace. Such royal propaganda develops a critical political philosophy in which justice and compassion take dominant roles. It is reiterated in the writings of the sages, in collections of law, in songs and laments, and in personal and individual prayers. In biblical literature, Hanna's song sings these same cadences to announce an end to Israel's suffering in the birth of a child. With a reversal of the fortunes of the downtrodden, 1 Samuel's "poor-man's song" opens the tragic narrative about Israel's kings. It is a constant of David's songs in the Psalter, and its dark contrasting shadow is found in the prophets' threat of a coming "Day of Wrath" that marks the stories of Samaria's and Jerusalem's destruction.

In the New Testament, the song's "Happy Day" is announced at the opening of Mark's Gospel, and identifies that book as the "good news." It is re-used at the birth of a savior with considerable success in the songs of Mary and Zachariyah in the opening chapters of Luke. As in the story of Samuel—and, for that matter, of Marduk in the Babylonian creation myth ("born in the heart of Apsu: son of the sun god; indeed sun of the gods")—the story of a child's birth is given its classic function of evoking an eternal peace inaugurated by an heroic savior. This song is given to John the Baptist to sing to identify Jesus as "the one who is to come." It becomes the centerpiece of Jesus's Sermon on the Mount and shapes the vision of the "kingdom of God" that closes the Book of Revelations.

The Bible, whose earliest writings are in Hebrew and centered in Palestine, comes late to this idealistic and utopian tradition. It interprets the mythology of the king from the perspective of one of the empire's subject peoples. Its goal is not only to identify Palestine's traditional deity Yahweh with the imperial and transcendent God of heaven, but also to present Judaism's story of its past with a story of an ancient Israel that had been destroyed and rejected by its God. This "Day of Wrath" and this destruction of the past prepares the reader for a transcendent "Happy Day" of peace with God. This story gave the many philosophical and religious communities of early Judaism an identity centered in the metaphors of "first born," "suffering servant of God," and "repentant remnant." Seeing themselves as representative of all who understand, they submit themselves to the divine will to bring a world lost in ignorance back to the eternal peace and happiness that had been intended at the creation.

The worldviews implied in ancient Near Eastern texts and in the Bible have more in common than in conflict. They are closely related in theme, in their literary and mythic expressions in story and form, and historically. They are not opposed to each other in substance. A common system of symbols about reality is used that contrasts divine transcendence and unity with transient humanity's fragmented experience. Such theology belongs to a world that knew that men did not know the gods they wrote about. This literature bridges the intellectual fault that lies between a transcendent and unknown divine world and the transient and tragic world we live in and know too well as false.

The purpose of such royal ideology in ancient literature is educational: to set limits on human ambition, to civilize and make compassionate the violence that our authors find in the human heart. The Old Testament figure of the king as the son of God, enthroned in heaven at the right hand of the father, is used as thematic introduction to the Book of Psalms in Psalm 2. The function of this figure, as it is developed in the Psalter, is to reiterate the theological myth of the king as servant of God and representative of his people's suffering.

The royal propaganda that is part of the ancient Near Eastern tradition is also transposed to fit a Jewish world that did not have its own king, but was part of the greater empire. Already in the Hellenistic period, this myth of a transcendent heavenly king, representing Israel before God, is itself re-used to transform the story legend of a human King David, who had been given and who had foolishly lost his kingdom in this world's Jerusalem.[49] David's story is a reiteration of Israel's: a story of human hubris and a story about the loss of paradise.[50]

In the Psalms, David—like Job in his book—sang his songs with the voice of his audience: the people of Israel. He is threatened by "the nations in uproar" against their true king, who is God. He suffers and cries to God for help. Like the emperors before him, he fights with God's army against the nations of this world. And like these same emperors, his victory, wrought from humility, is a lasting one. Like all the defeated enemies of Sargon (r. 722–705 BCE) and Sennacherib (r. 705–681 BCE), of Thutmosis and Merneptah, all enemies of the good are cast into chains, bound under the patronage of the transcendent. Both as the voice of Israel, and giving a song for the reader to sing, David plays the role of the righteous who seek refuge only in God. He represents the poor man and the helpless widow. In his suffering and tears, he reverses the fate of his people. It is not through the power and violence of a real war—or within the world of politics, that ancient world in which the Bible's literary metaphor had its roots—but through an intellectual struggle in a secondary world of prayer, study, and understanding that the poor man's destiny is reversed.

The Bible's world is a world of story, and its literary aim was ever to create Judaism as a people of piety, impatiently awaiting the kingdom of God in a future, perfect and heavenly Jerusalem. Such an ideal and utopian Israel is not intended as a nation like other nations, ruled by men. Israel is the representative of humanity, as in creation: a people of God. The goal uses the past as foil: for the future of Judaism, not a nation, but a religion. The figure of a suffering messiah and transcendent, savior king does not provide the theme for just a single story in the Bible. The Hebrew Bible presents many roles and characters similar to David's. The theme of divine presence in the world dominates most of biblical literature. Although only the Pentateuch's Moses comes close to sharing the importance of David in reflecting the divine to his people, Abraham and Solomon, Hezekiah and Jonah, as well as other prophets, kings, priests, and teachers, perform this same function in their stories and traditions: bringing the divine into the world.

A single example, taken from the tradition of a priestly messiah in the Pentateuch, illustrates some aspects of this intellectual common ground. Thematically echoing the messiah in Daniel 9, who brings mercy at the appointed time, Numbers (35:25) uses the logic of retribution to bind such mercy to the death of Yahweh's anointed. One who has fled to a town of refuge because of an unintentional manslaughter is to remain there "until the death of the high priest who has been anointed with oil." That is to say, the messiah functions as his protector, a stereotypical role that the anointed of the Psalter plays for the "new Israel." In the past-oriented narrative discourse of Numbers, however, the messiah—unlike David of the Psalter—is a living high priest, who, being human, must die. It is only his office that is eternal and transcendent. In ending the exile of one responsible for such a crime through the death of the anointed one, the text draws on a logic that is explicitly connected with expiation in Isaiah, addressing the "new Israel" in exile: "Speak tenderly to Jerusalem, and declare to her that her term of service is over; her crime is expiated."[51] That Isaiah introduces a utopian fullness of time, in which the messiah reigns in peace, is very clear from the description of a new creation that prepares for the return from exile by a Sargon-like leveling of mountains and straightening of valleys.[52] This trope offers a variant on the "poor-man's song" and links the role of the priestly messiah of the Pentateuch to motifs of the end of exile and the creation of the new Israel.[53] Psalm 11:16's declaration, "The Heavens of heaven belong to Yahweh, but the earth he has given to the sons of Adam," asserts an order in the world that is most uncertain. From an ideal perspective, the creation story presents humanity in Genesis 1 to rule over what God created. This God saw such a world as excellent. However, Genesis 1's story of the creation of mankind in the image of God has an ironic flaw implicit. God did not consider a humanity who, like him, would want to do what it saw to be good. Already by Genesis 9:2 the nature of such a "kingship" in the world is epitomized as bringing "fear and terror" to God's creation.

In these opening chapters of the Bible, the relationship between the divine and human shows itself to be problematic. God rules in His heaven, but all is not right with the world. For the Bible, the "problem of God" has nothing to do with heaven's inadequacies. It is the violence and injustice of our own experience as men that is God's problem. The society men created is incomprehensibly at odds with all that is good. It is a literary and intellectual problem of first importance: one in which the ideal role of the king as inclusive representative of the people is used throughout ancient literature to criticize and challenge the integrity of the values by which we choose to live. The metaphor of the transcendent is used in ancient texts to measure man. In these texts, God ever remains in his heaven; and is known only in the rumors of which Job spoke.

The Messiah as Son of God

The Psalter's reiteration of ancient Near Eastern royal ideology transforms the god Yahweh—the regional storm god of Iron Age Palestine—into the transcendent universal ruler we know from Psalm 104's revision of ancient Egypt's hymn to the sun god.[54] This interpretive reiteration of royal ideology in the Psalter takes its starting point in a single dramatic, but nonetheless puzzling, element of Psalm 2. The messiah king has Yahweh announce the good news of the day: "You are my son. I have given birth to you today."[55]

The scholarly reading of this passage had long viewed this astonishing metaphor—not unreasonably—as part of a festival celebrating the king of Jerusalem's enthronement. As ascending to royal power does not deal really with a birth, the phrase must imply—so it was argued—that Yahweh accepts or recognizes the king as his son. The phrase was even described as a "typical" adoption formula, an interpretation that has particularly marked the understanding of the New Testament's re-use of this verse when Jesus is with John in the Jordan. Dissatisfaction, however, nags the explanation. The Hebrew word "to give birth" is too clear and straightforward to "explain away" —especially in a text that (taking place in heaven as it does) should not be expected to play by the normal rules of men. Somewhat tongue in cheek, I played with the problem by asking: In the ancient Near East, is it women or gods who give birth to children when they are kings? The question was not easily put aside. Kings in ancient Near Eastern texts live in a world somewhere between gods and men. My question about the birth of kings was finally answered two years ago, when, visiting a special exhibit on "The Sun King" at the Museum of Fine Arts in Boston, I found a small wall-relief representing the eighteenth dynasty pharaoh Akhenaten (r. 1353–1337 BCE) in a narrative drawing, or "diptych." In the first scene, he is praying to the sun-god at a royal festival. The purpose of the feast was to renew the strength and effectiveness of the king's administration. The second scene shows him leaving in procession—his prayers obviously answered as rays of the sun cover him. His attendants bow down in prayer, worshipping him. And more—he is drawn magnificently pregnant, ready to give birth. The following months took me into an expansive search for thematic elements of songs and stories related to kingship. Not only are kings in the ancient Near East not always born of women, but often rather of gods, but the interactive echoes of Mesopotamian, Egyptian, and Hebrew myth-making literature, dealing with the king and his ties in the divine world, are many and detailed. So striking are parallels of language and metaphor, I have since come to think of the earliest "Psalm of David" in the form of a victory hymn of Thutmosis III from the 15th century BCE.[56]

One might just as well think of the song of Marduk's accession to the throne in the Babylonian creation story some three or four hundred years later. The figure of David in the Psalms is a Hebrew version of the role of the king in ancient Near Eastern mythology. The connection between the divine messiah in heaven and the human king of stories had deep roots in creation and royal ideology. This seemed worth exploring. The role of the king as son of God is basic to the ancient world's understanding of good governance.

The King as Suffering Servant

The king functions as the epitome of humanity: both as hero and as servant. The central theme of hubris creates the bridge between these two motifs in stories from Gilgamesh on. The issues at stake are the ideal of kingship and the necessity of humility for a just king. God alone is true king. The Babylonian Akitu festival, at which the Babylonian creation story was recited, presents a scene in which the king's claim to the throne can be confirmed or denied on the basis of his compassion and ability to cry, reiterating the Egyptian creation etiology of humanity with its metaphor of the mankind-generating tears of Ammon-Re. After the cleaning of the temple in the Akitu festival, as the king is led into the temple Esangil, the high priest first removes the king's scepter, ring, and mace. He removes the royal crown from the king and lays them on a chair before Marduk. He then goes back to the king and, striking him on the cheek, leads him before Marduk. Pulling him by the ear he makes him kneel on the floor. The king then recites a prayer of humility, declaring his innocence of crime and his constant commitment to good government (including not hitting or humiliating his ministers).[57] When the king's prayer is completed, the priest tells him: "Do not fear . . . the Lord has heard your prayer." Marduk will establish the king's rule "for ever; he will scatter the king's enemies; destroy those who hate him."[58] The priest then restores the king's role and returns to him the scepter, ring, and mace. He brings out the crown and, giving them to the king, slaps his face once again. The text of the ritual comments upon itself: "When the king is struck, if his tears flow, the Lord will be merciful.[59] If, however, his tears do not flow, the Lord will be angry with him, his enemy will attack him and bring him down."[60]

While the remainder of our text is missing, it is particularly clear that a central purpose of the Akitu festival is to re-establish the king's rule in humility. The New Year festival establishes a new creation, and the central battle against the chaos-dragon holds the kingdom in existence in the context of a divinely given eternal covenant with a king, who is himself capable of repentance and mercy. For the king to rule justly, he must also be human. He must learn to weep, for tears are the essence of humanity. That out of suffering comes wisdom is a principle of ancient Near Eastern ethical literature from songs of lament in ancient Sumer to the Book of Job.

In expanding understanding of royal ideology, this motif illustrates the central role of the king in his search for wisdom and piety. Since the king should not merely be wise and just like a Hammurabi or a Solomon, creating a divine justice, but also should be a model of human wisdom, he must come to wisdom the hard way: through suffering. If the king is unable to weep, he is not fit to be king. The king's role is to teach his people how to be human "sons of god." King Solomon, in his role as author of Ecclesiastes, is one who suffers doubt, a role given in the New Testament to Jesus in Gethsemane—a role that finds a minor reiteration in the doubting of the apostle Thomas. It is Job, mirroring the suffering servant of Isaiah and the figure of the divinely betrayed and abandoned David of Psalm 89, who act out the primary representative role of Israel with its God, which draws out the full role of humility as epitomizing the essence of being human. In the language of myth, I would link the metaphor of king as suffering servant with a thematic element of the creation stories: the "cosmic desert" of Genesis 1. The "cosmic desert," out of which an ever new beginning springs, forms the surface narrative of the Bible's segmented story from Genesis to the end of 2 Kings. It is the formlessness and emptiness of exile,[61] not of the creation story, that is the true point of departure for biblical story. Out of a desert of exilic suffering comes new life and resurrection, creating a myth of hope and expectation.

Promises of the Eternal Zion

In closing, I would like to return to the element of peace and to the understanding of the city of God as a city of eternal peace, with which so many expressions of royal ideology find closure. It is the peace of understanding that closes the epic of Gilgamesh, when our hero, now older and wiser, returns to dedicate his life to the building of Uruk and its walls. Only then is he fit to rule and to create a name for himself in a manner fit for a king: that is—like Solomon in Jerusalem—through great building projects. The restless theme of wandering that dominates the Gilgamesh story is expressed in the Bible through the exile motif, where Israel's humanity is scattered over the face of the earth to search for the way back to an eternal Jerusalem to find the tree of life. This restless search has serenity as its goal. The story of Sargon as that of Oedipus, the stories of the wandering Idrimi and a Cinderella-David-mirroring Esarhaddon (r. 681–669 BCE), all give us stories of the king, epitomizing humanity's search for wisdom. These stories all give us the great man teaching us how to be human. This philosopher's serenity has the same literary function of closure as is found in the peace of the warrior-king with its eternal, glad shouts of "shalom" in victory. Like David's last song after the defeat of all his enemies,[62] the theme evokes images of paradise. It inaugurates the million-year reign of the Egyptian pharaohs and the millennium of the apocalypse. This peace—the eternal reign of the king—is ever linked to the creation of the temple and the king's birth from the beginning of time.

This is the significance of a heavenly, transcendent Jerusalem in the biblical tradition. Creation is the origin of its promise. Examples of the foundation of the sacred mound (Jerusalem's Zion) of Egyptian's temple at Heliopolis, of Mesopotamia's Esangila, the birthplace of Marduk, and of the Ugaritic story of Ba'al's long quest for a home, all—much like the story of Yahweh's search for a home—link the king with the temple. Much like Mount Olympus of Greek legend, the understanding of Jerusalem as Zion provides a place for the divine to enter this world. In doing so, it transforms a historical city of the past into a utopian city of peace.

REPORTING THE JEHOASH INSCRIPTION: AN EXCLUSIVIST CLAIM TO JERUSALEM

Keith W. Whitelam

The News Breaks

The announcement in mid-January 2003 of the "discovery" of a stone inscription somewhere in Jerusalem, dated to the 9th century BCE, was soon headline news across the world. What has gradually emerged following an initial media frenzy is a tale of intrigue that would grace the script of an Indiana Jones film or the plot of an Agatha Christie novel. Yet far from being a harmless story of shadowy figures and the discovery of priceless archeological treasures confined to the big screen or the pages of a best-selling novel, this is a story of how the past of Jerusalem and ancient Palestine is constructed and how its present is being determined. The reporting of this story provides an instructive lesson in the manipulation of historical memory.

The many twists in this tale of secrecy and subterfuge could not have been predicted from the initial report, "Sensation or Forgery? Researchers Hail Dramatic First Temple Period Finding," when *Ha'aretz* broke the news on January 13, 2003 of the "discovery" of a broken stone inscription from the reign of King Jehoash of Judah. Significantly, the text of the inscription was very close to a passage in 2 Kings 12 that details how King Jehoash organized temple repairs during his reign. Even if the many twists in the plot, a plot which is still unfolding, could not have been foreseen at the time, what was already apparent was the way in which the report appealed to a dominant historical memory, one deeply embedded in western memory and now in Israeli society, which claims wide-ranging implications for the contemporary struggle over Jerusalem.

The twists and turns in the plot have multiplied, deepening the sense of intrigue and the anticipation that the final scene has yet to be played out. Now we know that the opening scene reveals a hotel room in Jerusalem with a mysterious figure, reluctant to give his name or how he came by the rare artifact, accompanied by a silent companion, possibly a Palestinian, talking with one of the world's leading experts on ancient epigraphy. The scholar, having cast doubt on the authenticity of the inscription, was warned to remain silent about the meeting and the existence of the inscription, since the life of the person who had discovered it was at stake.

It would be over a year later before *Ha'aretz* broke the news of the find to the rest of the world. The initial report claimed that an inscription attributed to King Jehoash had been authenticated by experts from the National Infrastructure Ministry's Geological Survey of Israel following months of examination. At the very opening of the article, the reader is left in no doubt that scientific tests had corroborated the authenticity of the object. The battery of tests are described as so extensive that it is inconceivable that they would not detect a forgery. The views of experts at the Israel Museum, who had been offered the inscription and raised doubts as to its authenticity, are thereby firmly refuted by seemingly objective scientific testing. Yet more significantly, the experts at the Geological Survey are reported as claiming that, if authentic, the inscription could have global repercussions effectively vindicating the Jewish claim to the Temple Mount. This astounding assertion, based on the possible existence of a short inscription, is not questioned in the report but presented almost as though it is self-evident fact.

The mystery deepens when it is revealed that the details of the discovery are rather sketchy: It is reported that unnamed "sources" have indicated that it was found on the Haram al-Sharif, known in the Jewish tradition as the Temple Mount, during recent excavation work, and that it had been sold to an antiquities collector in Jerusalem. The mysterious collector is said to represented by the attorney Isaac Herzog, the former cabinet secretary to Prime Minister Barak.

Reporting the Story

Not surprisingly, the news of the "sensational" discovery of the first royal inscription from one of the kings of ancient Judah was immediately picked up by the world's media. The mystery surrounding its discovery and the identity of the owner added to the drama of the reports. Yet, invariably, it was the claim by Shimon Ilani, Amnon Rosenfeld, and Michael Dvorchik of the Geological Survey of Israel of its significance for the contemporary struggle of Jerusalem that was given most prominence. This was reinforced by the repetition, from the original article, of the view of the Israeli archaeologist Gabriel Barkay that if the inscription were authentic, it would be "a 'sensation' of the greatest import," perhaps "the most significant archaeological finding yet in Jerusalem and the Land of

Israel, because it would be the first inscription that describes events in a manner that adheres to the narrative in the Bible." Questions of its authenticity, which surfaced very early, tended to be downplayed in most early reports, in favor of a series of interrelated claims that suggested that, given the inscription's close resemblance to 2 Kings 12:1–6, 11–7, it provided evidence for the historicity of the biblical texts, thereby undermining the claims of skeptics who questioned standard reconstructions of the period of the Israelite monarchy based on the biblical traditions. Most importantly of all, it was claimed to provide evidence of Israel's claim to the Temple Mount. Subsequent reports illustrated further the way in which the past is used to shape and claim the present. Very quickly, the inscription changed from ancient artifact to a modern "title deed" for the Haram al-Sharif and Jerusalem as a whole. Its symbolic significance could not have been greater.

Typically, an article by Richard N. Ostling of the Associated Press entitled "Authenticity of Purported Jerusalem 'Temple Tablet' Remains Mystery" claimed that

> if authentic and truly thousands of years old, the words on the "Temple Tablet" would undergird Israel's present-day claim to Jerusalem's Temple Mount. This would also buttress traditional Jewish and Christian belief in the reliability of Old Testament history, against liberal scholars who treat the accounts of King Solomon and his Temple as fiction.

Similarly, the BBC News carried a report on January 14, 2003 entitled "'Biblical Temple' Tablet Found" with the claim that "if officially authenticated, the find would be the first piece of physical evidence backing up biblical texts. It could also intensify competing claims to the site in Jerusalem's Old City, where the stone is said to have been found, which go to the heart of the Arab–Israeli conflict." Significantly, a prominent inset on the page display the words of Shimon Ilani of "the Israeli Geological Institute" in bold: "Our findings show that it is authentic." The bold headings within the article also added to the sense of authenticity and significance: "Biblical instructions" and "Sensational find."

Not surprisingly, various conservative Christian websites were keen to report a find they believed offered a powerful endorsement for the historicity of the biblical narratives. So, for example, the Bible Network News, the Canadian Bible Society's News Site, carried the bold headline, "2,800-year-old Stone Tablet Discovery Supports

Jewish Claims to the Temple Mount." Although the article reports doubts over the authenticity of the find, it quotes Simon Ilani and Ammon Rosenfeld of the Geological Survey of Israel as saying that "following months of examination" the inscription is authentic and that "the finding is an archaeological sensation that could have global repercussions and that effectively vindicates Jewish claims to the Temple Mount." The quotation is placed in an inset that, along with the bold headline, underlines the claim to the present. In addition, Gabriel Barkay is reported as saying that given its resemblance to biblical passages, the inscription "has far-reaching implications of the historical importance of the biblical text."

The International Christian Embassy Jerusalem's web page claimed that the tablet belonged to an "Arab antiquities dealer" who is now represented by Isaac Herzog, former cabinet secretary to Ehud Barak. This is followed by the stinging condemnation that

> [t]he ironies in this discovery could not be more dramatic. In its frantic bid to wipe away any trace of the Jewish temples, the Waqf may have unearthed compelling proof of their existence. The Barak government turned a blind eye to charges of "archaeological crimes" on the Temple Mount and then proposed at the failed Camp David summit in July 2000 to resolve the dispute over the site by leaving any antiquities located there permanently buried in the ground. Barak's cabinet secretary is now trying to profit from an inadvertent find on the Mount that only bolsters the demands of many Jews and Christians that the entire compound be thoroughly excavated by trained archaeologists.

The transformation of the inscription from ancient artifact to modern "title deed," which was evident in virtually all the early reports on the "discovery" of the tablet, was made complete on the website of the Temple Mount and Land of Israel Faithful Movement. The inscription, with its call to repair the temple and its pronouncement of a blessing on those who carry out such work, naturally drew the attention of radical Jewish, as well as conservative Christian, groups. It became a rallying cry for the physical and spiritual possession of the Haram. For the followers of the Temple Mount Faithful, there was no doubt as to its authenticity or its implications:

> The most important and exciting archaeological discovery in the history of the land of Israel and Jerusalem was

recently made on the Temple Mount. It was an inscription written on a black stone by the descendant of David, King Jehoash of Judah, who ruled in Jerusalem at the end of the ninth century BCE.[1]

Its political and religious significance was spelled out unequivocally:

> It was only G-d Who closed an historical circle between one of the righteous kings of Judah and his people, Israel, in our endtime generation. It is no accident that this dramatic discovery was made at this time so close to the climax of the godly redemptional process of Israel when the Third Temple is soon to be built. This is a message from the G-d of Israel to the people of Israel to do what King Jehoash did and to repair and rebuild the Temple. This is the most important and exciting point of this discovery. We pray and will do everything possible to ensure that the Israeli Government and people will understand and accept this godly message and will do what G-d expects—immediately build the Third Temple.[2]

Interestingly, although appeal was made to Jehoash's attempts to repair the temple as a modern injunction on observant Jews, the final verses, in which Jehoash uses the temple treasure to pay tribute to King Hazael of Damascus in order to persuade him not to attack Jerusalem, were overlooked (2 Kings 12:17–18). The contemporary significance of the biblical passage and the inscription were expounded further:

> I feel and know that this exciting godly message of King Jehoash was found and directed to our generation. It is so real and these holy words speak to everyone of us. The call of King Jehoash—"Why do you not repair the breaches of the house?"—is a call to our generation.[3]

A further report on the site, "The Yehoash Tablet 2," began by stating that the Israeli Geological Society had confirmed that the inscription was "completely authentic based on very strong evidence" and that "famous experts from various areas of expertise (archaeology, history, linguistics, Biblical linguistics and an expert on the history of the inscription) who checked the inscription confirmed its authenticity." Noticeably, none of the experts were named, except for Gabriel Barkay, who appeared in most early reports. Neither, it should be noted, were any of the experts mentioned who questioned its authenticity. The report then went on:

> The discovery of the inscription caused great excitement in Israel. Many people were moved by the fact that it was discovered on the Temple Mount and was part of the First Temple and of the unique time at which it was found which is the end-time of redemption of Israel and the Temple itself. People feel that the timing is no accident and that it is a clear message from the G-d of Israel Himself that the time is short, the Temple should immediately be rebuilt and Maschiach ben David is soon to come.

The supposed circumstances of its discovery were then used to develop its significance:

> As we wrote in the previous article, the stone with the inscription was found by the Arabs during their excavations on the Temple Mount when their goal was to destroy the evidence of the Jewish identity of the Temple Mount so that they started to claim that the Temple Mount is not a Jewish site and not the location of the Temple and that it is only an Islamic site. However, G-d did to them what He did to Balaam who came to curse Israel and ended up blessing Israel. The same happened here with the inscription of King Jehoash. They wanted to curse Israel by the diggings and the destruction of the Jewish identity on the Temple Mount but G-d handled it so specially when He caused them to find this holy stone and inscription which is such an exciting and clear evidence that the Temple Mount is the location of the Temple and a very Jewish site.

The fact that the inscription should be understood and utilized in such a way by radical and conservative Jewish and Christian groups is no surprise. However, the immediate transformation of the inscription from ancient artifact to modern title deed by reputable news organizations and reporters reveals just how deeply ingrained this historical memory is in western imagination. Despite words of caution from experts at the very outset, and before the inscription had been examined carefully by those with the relevant expertise, the understanding of the inscription and its implications for the modern day were presented as self-evident. The uninformed reporting of the object is a striking example of the construction and manipulation of historical memory that has had such profound influence on the understanding of the history of Jerusalem and ancient Palestine.

The Story Unfolds

The early reports, highlighting their sensational claims for the significance of the inscription, tended to relegate more cautious views to the margins. However, the excitement generated by the announcement brought to light more sober assessments by leading epigraphers, archeologists, and biblical scholars, such as Joseph Naveh, Naadav Naaman, Frank Cross, Kyle McCarter, and others. Yet at the same time as many began to cast doubt on the authenticity of the inscription, the intrigue surrounding its discovery began to deepen. The stone was reported to have been taken from the Geology Institute, and disappeared. The circumstances of its supposed discovery by Palestinians working on the Haram were strenuously denied. Then rumors began to appear concerning the identity of the mysterious antiquities dealer. Eventually, *Ha'aretz* reported that the inscription had been handed over to the police by Oded Golan, who had gained notoriety as the owner of the so-called James Ossuary, a bone box that carried the inscription "James, son of Joseph, brother of Jesus." Golan had recently attended a major international conference of biblical scholars in Toronto where leading scholars had disagreed over its authenticity. The story took a further dramatic twist when is was reported that:

> At night, the Israeli Antiquities Authority and the police searched other storehouses that Golan had not mentioned, revealing hundreds of archaeological finds suspected as being looted, boxes with earth from various locations in the country, chemicals, engraving tools, dental equipment and other suspicious items of this kind.[4]

Although the final scenes of this tale of intrigue remain to be written, and no doubt there are other twists to come, the plot is sufficiently developed for us to analyze its structure and implications.

Stealing History and the Manipulation of the Past

Three months after *Ha'aretz* broke the news of this "sensational" find, increasing numbers of scholars are convinced that the inscription is a forgery. Yet even if it were an authentic royal inscription dating to the

9th century BCE, the fact that the details of its discovery are not known means that it is a looted artifact. It is a piece of stolen history that was being offered for sale on the antiquities market. This fact was never addressed explicitly in the reports. The looting of artifacts is going on across the world on an unprecedented scale. The purchase of such artifacts and the involvement of museums and scholars with the display and discussion of such artifacts only serve to fund and encourage a practice that is stealing the past, the heritage of specific countries, peoples, and all humankind. Disturbing reports are now emerging of the systematic looting and destruction of the National Museum in Baghdad, the burning of the Ottoman, Royal, and State archives and the Ministry of Religious Endowments following the invasion by American and British forces. Such a loss of priceless artifacts, manuscripts, including Arabic, Turkish, and Persian manuscripts, along with illuminated Qur'ans, is little more than the erasure of historical memory. Iraq's history, and much of that of the region, has been systematically stolen and destroyed. In effect, it has been dehistoricized. The Jehoash inscription is a further example of the stealing of history. Disturbingly, the way in which it has been reported and interpreted is a similar case of the dehistoricization of Palestinian history.

The fact that the Jehoash inscription does not originate from a controlled excavation, with detailed information about its proper archaeological context, means that it is of little use to historians. Furthermore, it could not bear the weight of interpretation that reports and some experts have claimed for it, even if authentic. Of course, it would help to confirm that Jehoash carried out repairs to a temple in Jerusalem; this would add to our knowledge of the kingdom of Judah. But that is not the central issue in the current debates on the history of ancient Palestine. It is not that scholars deny the existence of a kingdom of Judah at this time, or of a similar kingdom in northern Israel, although this is frequently claimed by some. What is at issue in the discussions is the nature, size, and influence of such kingdoms in the region as well as the type of history that is being written. These kingdoms were important elements in the region, and worthy of study, but biblical scholarship and archeologists have tended to focus on these kingdoms and the royal elite to the exclusion of all else that goes to make up the history of ancient Palestine. The history of peasants and pastoralists on whose backs the history of Palestine, from antiquity to the present, has been carried, has until recently largely been ignored. It is this history, which is increasingly being explored, that offers a very different perspective on the history of ancient Palestine from that which has been constructed from the biblical traditions.

The frequently cited assertion that, if authentic, the inscription would vindicate the Jewish claim to the Temple Mount, the Haram al-Sharif, is a further expression of the dehistoricization of Palestinian history. As noted above, it is a claim that is advanced without question as though it is self-evident. Yet how could such an inscription come to be understood as a modern deed of title? It is a preposterous claim. In 1993, archeologists discovered a broken inscription at Tel Dan written in Aramaic that mentions the defeat of Israelite kings by a unknown king, thought to have been the ruler of Damascus. This inscription, which has caused a heated debate, is usually cited as primary evidence that scholars who question the traditional understanding of the period of David and Solomon are wrong, because of the inscription's mention of the house of David. Again, the inscription cannot be used to authenticate the whole of the biblical narrative about David. It provides proof of a monarchy that traces its origins to "the house of David," but it tells us nothing of the size or importance of the kingdom of its founder. Yet what is never mentioned by those who wish to use the Tel Dan inscription in such a way is that it reports the defeat of Israel and the loss of territory. Does this mean that this ancient artifact is also a modern title deed and that it justifies a contemporary Syrian claim to Tel Dan and northern Israel?

The reports of the finding of the Jehoash inscription draw upon the deeply ingrained historical memory that Jerusalem is the foundation of King David. A historical memory, based upon the importance of the biblical traditions in western imagination, which admits of no alternative claim to the land or of any alternative understanding of the history of Jerusalem and Palestine. The declaration of "Jerusalem 3000," and the many sites on the internet devoted to its celebrations, invoke and draw on a story and a past that has been central to western imagination. Crucially, the claims are an attempt to make real in the present an image of the city that is deeply rooted in the ways in which western tourists, travelers, and scholars have imagined Jerusalem. The idea that David captured and founded the city of Jerusalem is the prime example of dehistoricization. There is no mention that Jerusalem has a history stretching back centuries to the early Bronze Age (c. 3000 BCE), two millennia before the period when David is supposed to have made it his capital. The view of history projected in "Jerusalem 3000" celebrations and assumed in the reports on the Jehoash inscription leave no room for any counter-narrative, either in the past or the present. The loss of a modern Palestinian counter-narrative in the modern city is paralleled by the dehistoricization of the city prior to the period of the Israelite monarchy.

Such a manipulation of historical memory ignores the fact that any evidence for David's capital has eluded archeologists, despite the investment of vast amounts of time, money, and scholarly expertise. What little evidence there is suggests that Jerusalem in the 10th century BCE, rather than being the glorious capital of a major state in the region, was little more than a small isolated town. Herzog, in his now famous letter to *Ha'aretz* (October 29, 1999), says that despite excavations in Jerusalem over 150 years, while archeologists have unearthed impressive remains from the Middle Bronze Age and the Iron II periods, no remains of buildings from the time of David or Solomon have been found, only a few pottery shreds.

Nor does this ingrained historical memory admit that the story of David's capture of Jerusalem in the Bible is also an act of dispossession of the indigenous population. It is seen as a natural act of conquest that required no comment, just as the inscription of Jehoash is seen as a right of entitlement to the present city despite the counterclaims of the Palestinian population. In the same way, biblical scholarship until recently only emphasized the liberation themes of the Exodus traditions and ignored the dispossession and wholesale slaughter of the inhabitants of the land. Unfortunately, the reporting of the story of the "discovery" of the Jehoash inscription is not a harmless tale of intrigue in the cinema or in a novel, a piece of escapism in which we can shelter from the real world. The assumptions that underlie much of the reporting appeal to a historical memory and manipulate the past, however unwittingly in some cases, in favor of an exclusivist claim to Jerusalem, both in the past and the present.

THE ZIONIST CLAIMS TO AL-HARAM AL-SHARIF AND AL-AQSA MOSQUE: A BIBLICAL PERSPECTIVE

Michel Eddeh

With their bare hands and fresh blood, the Palestinians are continuing the struggle for their inalienable rights to their homeland. And as the Palestinian children, and old and young men and women sustain their intifada for al-Aqsa Mosque and al-Quds al-Sharif, they are not facing only the barbaric bullets, rockets, bulldozers, tanks and aircraft of the Israeli occupation forces. They are, in fact, defying a myth that has been successfully inculcated in the minds of westerners by the Zionist movement, with its potent influence on the media, its sturdy lobbies at the centers of political power, and alliance with the western colonial powers, old and new. They are also discrediting the main theses in this century-old myth. The myth rests on the assumption that a unified Jewish nation has maintained its presence since ancient history and lived in a Jewish state that emerged 3,000 years ago. This imagined nation has since taken what the Jews call "Yerushalaim" as its capital. The "Temple" has since been the pivotal focal point in the secular and spiritual life of the Jews.

The recent developments in the occupied Palestinian territories, and the massacres initiated by Israel following the defilement of the Islamic shrines, have prompted me to scrutinize these brazen Zionist claims to al-Quds and presumptions on the Temple by tracing their points of reference to the texts of the Old Testament.

Nearly two thousand years since its destruction in 70 CE, the Temple is still taking a larger-than-life space in the imagination and emotion of the Jews. The saga of the Temple has been repeatedly over-magnified, beautified, and glossed far beyond the historical reality of its status in the Jewish faith. It is still being often invoked as an epitome of a "paradise lost" and a symbol of a "golden age" of Judaism.

One cannot deny or underestimate the significance of the Wailing Wall as a principal holy site to which Jews have gravitated in great numbers throughout history. But the wall that dwells on the site is not related to the Temple or its reconstruction. The picture that emerges from historical documents as well as from texts and references cited by some prophets of the Bible provide direct rebuttal and refutation of the Zionist falsification and fraudulence.

Our biblical citations will highlight comments made by the Jewish prophets on the status and location of the Temple, and their often harsh criticism of the sacrificial rituals carried out therein.

We shall start with the stage when King David dominated Jerusalem and brought in the Ark of the Covenant, which contained the two plates of the Ten Commandments that had been hitherto moving with the Hebrew Masters. We read in 2 Samuel (7:1–7):

> And it came to pass,
> when the king sat in his house,
> and the Lord had given him rest round about from all his enemies;
> That the king said unto Nathan the prophet, See now, I dwell in an house of cedar,
> but the ark of God dwelleth within curtains.
> And Nathan said to the king,
> Go, do all that is in thine heart; for the Lord is with thee.
> And it came to pass that night, that the word of the Lord came unto Nathan, saying,
> Go and tell my servant David,
> Thus saith the Lord,
> Shalt thou build me an house for me to dwell in?
> Whereas I have not dwelt in any house
> since the time that I brought up the children of Israel out of Egypt,
> even to this day, but have walked in a tent and in a tabernacle.
> In all the places wherein I have walked with all the children of Israel
> spake I a word with any of the tribes of Israel,
> whom I commanded to feed my people Israel, saying,
> Why build ye not me a house of cedar?

Interpreters of these texts have concluded that King David refrained from building a temple to house the Ark of the Covenant, under the pretext that God could not be kept in a closed place. This means that the temple that was built at a later stage was not a fulfillment of a divine command and did not therefore assume the sacred nature that was subsequently given to it. However, the son and the successor of

King David, King Solomon, constructed a temple in Jerusalem that was described in elaborate detail in chapters 7 and 8 of 1 Kings as a magnificent, luxurious structure akin to the pagan altars of the Canaanites of the last stage of the Bronze Age, or the altar that had been built in Syria in the 9th century BCE.

According to some Jewish scholars of the Old Testament, Solomon's temple, which was huge and well-situated at the center of the fortified royal palace, maintained only a remote and thin connection and relevance to the purity of the religion that was brought by Moses' inspiration from God. A large number of Jewish purists expressed their vehement opposition to the idea of a royal central temple. In the region of the Israelites, the ten elders viewed the centralization of religion in the Jerusalem temple with suspicion and rejection since, they believed, it jeopardized the religious value of their temples in the north that were established in the times of Abraham, Isaac, and Jacob in such cities as Hebron, Beit Eil, and Bethlehem. In the eyes of the Israelites, King Solomon was therefore considered a spiritual exterminator and a secular prosecutor. Consequently the Israelites refused to endorse his son Rehoboam as a successor in Jerusalem and requested him to come to their city Schechem, where he arrived at a later stage requesting the people to give him the crown. According to 1 Kings (12:4–5), they told him:

> Thy father made our yoke grievous:
> now therefore make thou the grievous service of thy father,
> and his heavy yoke which he put upon us, lighter, and we
> will serve thee.
> And he said unto them,
> Depart yet for three days, then come again to me.
> And the people departed.

Rehoboam refused to accommodate the demands of the Israelites. The once unified kingdom survived only for 70 years—30 during King David's reign and 40 during King Solomon's. It then started to disintegrate. Contrary to Zionist pretensions of the continuity and permanence of Jewish statehood, this was virtually the only period of unity in the 3,000 years of Jewish history. The kingdom was then divided into two smaller kingdoms: the Kingdom of Israel that took Schechem then Samara as its capital; and the smaller Kingdom of Judea, which took Jerusalem as its capital for some time. Between the years 930 and 722 BCE—for a period of 210 years—the Kingdom of

Israel survived, until it was destroyed by the Assyrians. The smaller kingdom of Judea was swept away by the Babylonian king Nebuchadnezzar (r. 605–562 BCE) who destroyed Solomon's temple in 598 BCE and forced the Jewish population into exile in Babylon and Egypt. In the year 538 BCE the Persian king Cyrus conquered Babylonia and allowed the exiled Jews to return to Judea and build their temple there. During the period from 538 BCE to 135 CE the land of Judea did not enjoy any real independence but underwent a series of controls and conquests by the Persians, the Greeks, and finally the Romans. In 71 CE, after the Jewish revolt in 66 CE, the Roman general Titus demolished the Second Temple. The Temple has never been rebuilt. In the wake of another uprising in 132–135 CE by Simen Bar-Cochba (d. 135 CE), "Son of the Star," Emperor Hadrian (r. 117–138 CE) captured and razed the city to the ground. To annihilate forever all hopes of the restoration of a Jewish kingdom, a new city was founded on the site of Jerusalem and peopled by a colony of foreigners. The city received the name of Aelia Capitolina (later known to the Arabs as Ilya), and no Jew was allowed to reside in it or even approach its environs. The Jews were then expelled into diaspora for the following centuries.

This brief overview of the sporadic relationship of the Jews to Palestine provides a clear refutation of the Zionist claim to a sustained and solid material and spiritual connection to the area for the last 2,000 years. Such allegations deliberately overlook twenty centuries of the existence of Christianity and fourteen centuries of the presence of the Islamic and Arab civilization in the Holy Land. Furthermore, and even before the appearance of the Hebrew tribes in Palestine, the land was populated and developed by the Canaanites, who maintained their presence and their culture side by side with the Hebrews.

After the days of Solomon, the Old Testament texts were highly critical and deprecatory of the sacrificial rituals conducted by the Jews in the temple. We find such divine condemnation of the brutal and almost pagan feasts of sacrifice in the first chapter (1:11–14) of the Book of the Prophet Isaiah (who was later assassinated by extremists):

> What unto me is the multitude of your
> Sacrifices? saith Jehovah:
> I have had enough of the burnt-offerings of rams,
> and the fat of fed beasts;
> and I delight not in the blood of bullocks, or of lambs, or
> of he-goats.

When ye come to appear before me,
who hath required this at your hand, to trample my courts?
Bring no more vain oblations;
incense is an abomination unto me;
new moon and sabbath, the calling of assemblies,
I cannot away with iniquity and the solemn meeting.
Your new moons and your appointed feasts my soul hateth;
they are a trouble unto me;
I am weary of bearing them.

We find similar remarks on the function and the sacrificial carnivals at the altar in chapter seven (7:3–6) of the Book of the Prophet Jeremiah (who also suffered betrayals and was even stoned for his beliefs):

Thus saith Jehovah of hosts,
the God of Israel,
Amend your ways and your doings,
and I will cause you to dwell in this place.
Trust ye not in lying words, saying,
The temple of Jehovah,
the temple of Jehovah, the temple of Jehovah, are these.
For if ye thoroughly amend your ways and your doings;
if ye thoroughly execute justice between a man and his neighbor;
if ye oppress not the sojourner,
the fatherless, and the widow,
and shed not innocent blood in this place.

The Jewish Prophet Jeremiah adds, in the same chapter (7:21–23):

Thus saith the Lord of hosts, the God of Israel;
Put your burnt offerings unto your sacrifices, and eat flesh.
For I spake not unto your fathers,
nor commanded them in the day that I brought them out of the land of Egypt,
concerning burnt offerings or sacrifices:
But this thing commanded I them, saying,
Obey my voice, and I will be your God,
and ye shall be my people:
and walk ye in all the ways that I have commanded you,
that it may be well unto you.

Sometime before the destruction of the Second Temple, a Jewish pilgrim from Alexandria gives, with utmost disdain and disgust, his testimony of the rites he witnessed at the altar in Jerusalem:

> There were daily sacrifices: two lambs slain by 13 priests at dawn, and two other lambs at sunset.... For the visitors who witnessed these rituals, the scene was exceptionally weird, almost barbarian; most of the foreigners [the Jews of the diaspora] came to the place to attend the holiday celebrations, when the numbers of the slain sacrifices were outrageously large. There were appalling scenes inside the temple. In the midst of the noisy chaos, frightened animals were running amok, bleating sheep were bumping against bellowing cows. In this commotion of shrieking screams, boisterous incantations and howling horns, the temple turned into a slaughterhouse and blood was flowing everywhere.

The aim of our review of the Old Testament references to the issue of the Temple and our portrayal of the rough nature of the sacrificial rituals practiced in this altar in the antiquated past was to project the ultimate motive of the current Zionist offensive to impose control over al-Haram al-Sharif, which is now being redefined by Israeli extremists as standing on the Temple Mount. The Zionist scheme aims at rebuilding an altar whose rationale, nature, and particular sacrificial practices were criticized and often denounced by the prophets in biblical texts and by Jewish observers and historians over the last 2,500 years. These sacrifices were rightly taken as a violation of the Divine will and a distortion of the true message and faith of Moses.

The contortion of the Jewish faith had been affected amid complete silence of the so-called moderates in Israel and of the overwhelming majority, if not the entirety, of the diaspora Jews. The same silence has also blurred the vision of the countries that have been subjected to the undeterred and unchallenged intellectual nature of the propaganda disseminated by the Zionist-controlled media. This situation was regrettably aggravated by the apathy of some Arab and Islamic countries as well as the absence or the toning down of the official positions and the attitudes of the masses toward the grave and fatal dangers of the Zionist usurpation of Arab Jerusalem with a view to committing the most audacious plan of all, that is, the reconstruction of the temple, God forbid, on the ruins of al-Haram al-Sharif.

SPACE AND HOLINESS IN
MEDIEVAL JERUSALEM

Oleg Grabar

The usual way in which medieval Jerusalem is reconstructed and explained is both simple and logical. Leaving aside the imperial Roman paganism that ruled the city between 70 CE and the 4th century, three systems of religious beliefs and practices—Jewish, Christian, and Muslim, each one with ethnic, social, economic, political, ideological, and linguistic variables—were present and active in the city during the medieval millennium. One of them always dominated: the Christian one from Constantine to the early 7th century and in most of the 12th, the Muslim one the rest of the time. It is easy to demonstrate that the monumental infrastructure of the city—the Holy Sepulcher and the Nea during the so-called Byzantine Christian rule, the Holy Sepulcher and a host of other churches, few of which have remained, during Latin Christian times, the Haram al-Sharif and its immediate surroundings in Umayyad, Fatimid, or Mamluk guises, under Muslim rule—expressed religious and ideological values and ambitions characteristic of whatever system predominated. Significant Jewish monumental presence appears only in the 19th century, partly because Jews were not directly connected to political power since the 2nd century and partly because post-Temple Judaism did not need or require monumental expression until the modern era.

Domination was rarely total in medieval times, except perhaps in the Late Antique Christian town, and, as a result, it is reasonable and proper to posit, underneath the large constructions and shiny effects sponsored by princes, patriarchs, abbots, and civil or military governors, a daily life of multiple pieties and ethnicities. How these different communities lived and operated is often difficult to imagine for the first half of the Middle Ages, roughly before the Crusades, for the very interesting reason, still partly true of the Jerusalem of today, that the communities were (and are) closely connected to their correligionsists or compatriots elsewhere, but not to each other in Jerusalem itself. In most of the sources dealing with Jerusalem, other groups than one's own are hardly ever mentioned except for occasional complaints about some humiliation or levy imposed by whoever dominated.

Studies on Jerusalem in the Middle Ages have tended to concentrate on five neatly separated chronological segments—Late Antique or Byzantine, early Islamic, Latin, Ayyubid, Mamluk—or on the three ethno-religious communities and their subdivisions. This is so largely because of the linguistic competencies required to handle these fifteen academic boxes. Original sources on Jerusalem are in eight or nine languages and secondary literature in at least six additional ones. When one further adds the literary genres of written sources, matters become even more complicated. Inscriptions in Greek, Arabic, Syriac, or Armenian; Geniza fragments in Hebrew or Arabic written with Hebrew characters; travel books from many lands and endowed with varying degrees of imagination; court documents in Arabic; endless diplomas in Latin; grand chronicles from remote capitals like Cairo, Baghdad, Constantinople, Moscow, or Aachen; locally sponsored guidebooks, pious eschatological meditations and proclamations; all require awareness of specialized issues and vocabularies and of many other cultural milieus than strictly Palestinian ones. A similarly vast comparative baggage together with considerable linguistic skills is required to learn and understand the archaeological and visual data available for Jerusalem in unusually large and varied quantities.

It is indeed nearly impossible to handle all this information and, as a result, the vision we tend to have of medieval Jerusalem (when we actually do try to have one, for the period is remarkably telescoped in most surveys or guidebooks) is that of a relatively small number of discrete periods following each other. In each one, various kinds of Jews, Christians, and Muslims organized their lives and structured their behavior according to whatever constraints or opportunities affected each one of them. There were unusual moments involving all of the city's inhabitants, as when the emperor Julian (r. 360–363 CE) returned to paganism in the middle of the 4th century; when out of nowhere Persian invaders arrived around 614 CE and allegedly sacked the city; when Caliph al-Hakim (r. 386/996–411/1021) initiated measures against Christians and Jews that culminated in the looting and destruction of the Holy Sepulcher in 1009, or when Frederic II (r. 1198–1250 CE) set up his own peculiar arrangement in a presumably Ayyubid city. But, however interesting these episodes may be, the overwhelming picture offered of medieval Jerusalem is that of separate religious communities and the academic result is the ecumenical juxtaposition of the lives and activities of these communities. Compelled in part by the nature and accessibility of sources, this juxtaposition also corresponds to a very peculiar paradox of our own time, which is to cultivate differences without realizing compatibilities and to feel satisfied with an acknowledgment of variety while maintaining the indivisible uniqueness of one's own faith and nation. This paradox is deeply embedded in the very fabric of Jerusalem, medieval and probably contemporary.

Regardless of one's views about the ethics of a scholarship of juxtaposition, even when compelled by the sources and by the limitations of any one scholar, it is not the only way to look at the history of medieval Jerusalem. In fact the physical space of the city and the components of its holiness are constant features, partly independent of the faiths with which they are associated. They defined the city far more consistently than the changing mosaic of men and women, of authority and religion. These factors may in fact have shaped the ways of the faiths that came to them. Therein lies what seems to me to be the true originality of Jerusalem: that it, alone among all the holy cities or cities of God (whoever or whatever the divinity may be) known to me, is a holy city for three religions rather than for a single one and even can accommodate an unusual variety of subsets of these three religions.

I will first identify the key components of the space and holiness of Jerusalem and then give three examples of what could be called the "petrification" of the holiness, that is to say the transformation of a priori neutral spaces and stones into holy ones through the medium of stones, and to suggest something of the dialectic whereby hallowed spaces generate their own holiness, which, if evicted, must find a place elsewhere. My examples are medieval, but some of the remarks that follow may have implications for earlier times in the city. I suspect, although I have not studied the matter, that the very nature of Israeli and Palestinian nationalism has been modified by being associated with Jerusalem, as contemporary emotional allegiances are no less affected by the character of the city than were the old traditional religions.

The key event that created medieval Jerusalem was the destruction of the Herodian city after the two Jewish revolts of the first and second centuries and its transformation into Aelia Capitolina. The following two results ensued:

1. The Roman military establishment took over and transformed an enclosure hugging the ridges of sharply rising hills into a more or less square walled city with fixed gates, a backbone of regular main

streets, parts of which were excavated in the 1970s and successfully incorporated into the contemporary restoration of the Jewish quarter, and a number of water reservoirs. These walls, gates, reservoirs, and streets have remained as the main axes of the city's composition until today. This city included what is known as the western hill, a ridge with a succession of high points from Golgotha to the north to Mount Zion to the south, the upper and middle parts of the Tyropaeon valley, and the eastern hill strikingly modified by Herod the Great (r. 37–4 BCE), where the Temple had stood at the northern edge of the earliest city. A deep ravine on the eastern side, the Kedron valley, was used for centuries as a cemetery. Beyond it rose the steep slope of the Mount of Olives dominating the city and extending one's vision to the Mediterranean or to the Dead Sea. In ways for which there are parallels elsewhere (Montmartre and Montparnasse in Paris, seven hills in Rome, Istanbul, and San Francisco) but here on a strikingly small area, an east to west sequence of high ridges and narrow gulleys created a daunting setting for any sort of urban design. The genius of the Roman military establishment was to know how to form a coherent rectangular space with strong axes wherever it had to show its presence. It is fascinating to see how that presence has remained in the present configuration of the Old City, as well as in a Late Antique representation like the Madaba map, where an irrationally ovoid city totally focused on Christian buildings still identifies Roman imperial walls, gates, and main streets.

The Roman order highlighted for all times (or, at least, until Jerusalem became affected by the modernism of our own times) the physical shape of Jerusalem, both the key natural elements of the landscape, such as the high ridges and deep gulleys, and the artificial limbs forced on that landscape, such as the flattened Mount Moriah transformed into a huge platform. Since there are other imperial Roman examples, Jerash for instance, of adapting standard plans to terrains ill-suited for linear orders, there is no need to attribute a profound ideological significance to the design of Roman Jerusalem and one can consider it merely as a standard operational procedure. But a deeper purpose cannot be entirely excluded because of the second unique effect of the failed Jewish revolts of the 1st and 2nd centuries. Before turning to that, it is worthwhile to point out that, in our own times and under the effect of modernism in general and of tall buildings in particular, a new artificial and arbitrary pattern of planning and construction is being imposed on a much enlarged city. Romantic antiquarians and believers in history regret it, worshipers of the future and devotees of change love it. But, even if modern Jerusalem is not my concern in this article, the medieval city can either be incorporated into the language of modernism (or whatever follows post-modernism) or else swallowed and trivialized by it. For better or for worse, the Roman system of destroying and rebuilding is no longer morally viable.

2. The second major result of the fateful events of the 1st and 2nd century may be called the liberation of memory from space. The Roman city was provided with a number of monuments commemorating or expressing standard pagan and imperial themes— temples to Venus and Jupiter, statue of Hadrian, an ensemble which became known in later sources as a "capitol"—although the exact quality and character of these constructions may well have been exaggerated by later Christian writers.

Whatever may have been the case, the important points are that none of these buildings were in honor of anything that had been holy in Jerusalem and, thus, that memories were released from the spaces they had occupied. These memories were colored in Jewish and Christian terms, but I prefer, at this stage, to divide them into historical, sacred, pious, and eschatological, although the boundaries between categories are not always clear. Historical memories are those of clearly delineated events that are not necessarily transformed into places of holiness or worship; in Jerusalem, the most obvious examples are all the memories of David and Solomon, the real as well as mythical creators of the city's importance. Sacred memories also include events, but these events are associated with sacred figures. On the basis of evidence from later times, which can reasonably be used for earlier ones, Moses, Abraham, Adam, and, of course, Jesus were the principal agents of memory, but, over the centuries, many others will be added. Pious memories are memories requiring or inviting behavior, specific actions, or contact with hallowed places.

The main expression of pious behavior in Jerusalem was pilgrimage, and pilgrimage eventually became an activity independent of religious affiliation but demanding a religious allegiance. Thus, Islam, in the 7th and later centuries, developed pilgrimage to Jerusalem not because it was required by the faith itself, but because Islam became part of the city of Jerusalem. And a sociologist could well point out that tourism in Jerusalem has a pilgrimage-like aspect that is absent from tourism in Cairo or in Paris, but is partly present in Rome.

Finally, there is eschatology. It is, of course, not very logical to talk about a memory of something that has not happened yet, but, at some point of its history, Jerusalem became infused with the expectation of the end of time on the space of the city. Whether it is reasonable to assume this expectation as early as in the 2nd century is unclear to me, just as I am not certain about the ways in which and the times when the cemeteries and mausoleums or caves, and eventually the Garden of Gethsemane to the east of the city affected the emotions that became part of the city. But the presence of the dead, mighty or humble, in the hope of resurrection and eternal life became an essential psychological component of the city.

However one is to interpret the eschatological component need not affect the general point that, let us say around 200 CE, we can reconstruct and imagine a walled Roman garrison and administrative town with services associated with such functions artificially imposed on a rugged and waterless terrain and a host of displaced memories, some involving concrete events, others determining modes of behavior. The vast majority of these memories was Jewish, but a Christian differentiation had appeared and the southeastern corner of the Roman city with its presumed "capitol" was going to be the place where Jews sought (or were going to seek) traces of the ruined Temple, while Christians looked for the place of Jesus' preaching or of St. Stephen's martyrdom.

What is curious about the few accounts we have of these early times (the point even applies, I believe, to the "invention" of the Holy Sepulcher) is that there were searches based on memory, without a clear sense of where the searches would end. In theoretical terms, we could put it in the following way: the behavior of Christians and Jews who came to Jerusalem was focused on clear aims issued from collective or individual memories, without a knowledge of the spaces involved and without being as yet a liturgical search—in which the result of the search is known in advance, but the motions of the search are still required—nor was it a game-like search that remained open to success or to failure, something like Queen Helena's (d. 330 CE) activities or much of archaeology.

The Middle Ages were when the space of Jerusalem and the memories associated with the city were transformed by Christians and then by Muslims into monuments, into stones, what I called the "petrification" of the memories. Christians and Muslims could do that because they exercised political and financial power, but it is also possible to construe the relationship between the successive monotheistic versions of divine revelation in another way, which may become clearer after I sketch out reconstructions of the medieval city in three early medieval instances.

The Christian transformation was simple. The western hill was sanctified through the building of the Holy Sepulcher complex, the Zion complex, and, somewhat later, the Nea or New Church of the Virgin Mary as major monuments in the midst of many other, lesser constructions. The eastern hill was left in ruins as a sign of God's wrath with the Jews and as the fulfillment of the prediction in the Gospels that no stone shall remain upon another stone. Beyond the ruined Jewish space, the Mount of Olives, scene of the Ascension and location of the forthcoming Resurrection, rises beyond the valley of pain and of death. The whole city could become monumentally organized around foci of architectural or liturgical attention, because enough memories existed that became embodied in the space of the city. As one walked out of the Holy Sepulcher, one could see the destroyed Temple area with its pagan remains and the Nea's mighty substructures were facing Herod's tremendous western wall, which, at that time, was probably already associated with Solomon. The Greek account of the building of the Nea emphasizes primarily the engineering feats needed to carry stones into the building site and "forty oxen were specially selected by the emperor for their strength" to pull the carts that brought the stones. No one in Constantinople knew that carts were not used in Syria and Palestine at this time, but it is reasonable to assume that someone had persuaded the Byzantine emperor Justinian (r. 527–565 CE) to outdo Solomon's or Herod's work.

There was also a second level of "petrification" of memories. The Piacenza Pilgrim in 570 CE and other pilgrims around that time actually saw the fig-tree on which Judas hanged himself; the altar on which, according to Jewish and Christian beliefs, Abraham was meant to sacrifice Isaac, which is also Melchizedek's altar; the wood of the Cross; the sponge and the reed of the Passion; the onyx cup of the Last Supper; the Virgin's girdle and headband; the stones with which St. Stephen (in the 1st century CE) was killed; the ring of Solomon; the silver bowls with which Solomon ruled the demons; the horn with which David was anointed; and so on. In addition to an architecture organizing the space of the city, there was a reification of the memory of things, at times with movements from one place to the other, so that the same object could be seen in two different sanctuaries or in the treasury of two different churches.

The first Muslim transformation was that of the 7th century. Its key act was the resacralization of the area of the Herodian Temple. There are many reasons for this transformation and many different interpretations of it exist now, as they existed since the 9th century. From the point of view of this paper, the causes of the event are less important than its results.

Instead of the willfully ruined area of the Temple, the faithful Christians coming out of the Holy Sepulcher see now the shining and colorful Dome of the Rock. In stages which will probably never be known, Abraham, Moses, several Zacharias, Jesus, Jacob, and Joseph acquire their Muslim embodiment in the stones of what becomes the Haram al-Sharif. David and Solomon are also present, but in a different way because of their double quality in Islam of kings and prophets and because of a historical as well as mythical kernel to their association with Jerusalem.

The details of these changes are almost impossible to disentangle either chronologically or typologically, but two points are essential. One is that a space inherited by Islam required specifically Islamic meanings and within a century, beyond the early connection with the "*mihrab* of David" mentioned in the Qur'an (38:21) or with a place seen by the Prophet (there is much scholarly debate on both of these issues), the combined themes of the *isra* and of the *mi'raj*, the Night-Journey and the Ascension, of the Prophet became the main dominant theme of the Haram. The other point was the Muslim adoption of the general themes of resurrection, judgment, and eternal life. Themes of mystical visits and of ascension were already present in Jerusalem; they simply acquired a Muslim connotation.

The impact of this early Islamic transformation on the character of the physical city was, first of all, that the whole city became, so to speak, religiously charged rather than contrasted through an active western Christian pole and a negative, ruined, eastern one. It is, as far as I have been able to see, impossible to imagine the actual, physical presence of Jews in the city, which is unfortunate, as these must have been extraordinary decades—from circa 640 to 690—when very different and hardly homogeneous members of all three faiths were seeking or holding on to their place in Jerusalem and where there must have been a whole crowd of intermediaries ready to suggest where memories can find a place and which places needed memories. Let us just try to imagine in its actual places what a western pilgrim, Arculfus, described around 670, after he identifies the footprints of Christ before His Ascension:

> on the west of the round building [of the Ascension]
> described above there are eight upper windows paned with

glass. Inside the windows, and in corresponding positions, are eight lamps, positioned so that each one of them seems to hang neither above nor below the window, but just inside it. These lights shine out from their windows on the summit of the Mount of Olives with such brilliance that they light up not only the part of the Mount to the west.... but also the steps leading all the way up from the Valley of Jehosaphat to the city of Jerusalem, which are lighted, however dark the night. Most of the nearer part of the city is lighted as well. The remarkable brilliance of these eight lamps shining out by night from the holy Mount and the place of the Lord's Ascension brings to believing hearts a readiness for the love of God.[1]

Arculfus' emotions were affected by a spectacle of *lumière* heightened by liturgical singing, but which affected the whole part of the city, which by then was supposed to be Muslim and to contain a Jewish quarter.

The second important aspect of the early Islamic transformation of the city is, once again, difficult to explain, but easy to see. It was the building of the Dome of the Rock. Much is, has been, and will be written about the construction, iconography, history, patronage, and holiness of this most extraordinary and unique monument. But, for an understanding of the visual history of the city, it does not really matter why it was built, by whom, and for what Muslim purposes. The important point is that it was a truly unique work of art in its shape and in its decoration of shiny gold and mosaic on the outside, and with an extraordinary interior spatial order and marble as well as mosaic decoration. It was and still is a work of art, because its aesthetic magnetism and power kept it from destruction, since the abstract values by which it was (and is) perceived and judged could be adapted to the memories of Abraham or Solomon, to changing moods of Muslim piety, to a church, to a mosque, to Palestinian nationalism, or to Israeli tourist posters, to anything that required physical beauty and attraction. Urban planners see such buildings as challenges, if not even real problems, because they dominate space and constrict invention and innovation. They are also a problem for strict religious leaders, because they overwhelm the perception of space and lead one's emotions in other directions than strictly pious ones. It is possible that the building was built in this fashion because it is only by abstracting them into geometry and color that the Mediterranean and possibly even local builders and decorators could express the complex religious and ideological motivations of the building's patrons into terms understandable to all the inhabitants of Jerusalem.

My last vision of urban medieval Jerusalem is roughly that of the middle of the 11th century, when we have an important eye-witness account by the Persian traveler Nasir-i Khosrow (d. 453/1061) who, like a contemporary trained anthropologist, used field notes, measurements, and drawings to relate in remote northeastern Iran what he saw and did in Jerusalem (c. 439/1047). It is also the time of thousands of Geniza fragments with considerable information about Jews in the city, of Latin Christian pilgrims, and of the first *fada'il* or "praises" of the city for Muslims.

The main spatial changes were: shortening of the walls of the city to the south; reconstruction of the complex of the Holy Sepulcher after its destruction by order of al-Hakim; reconstruction of the al-Aqsa mosque and a new dome on the Dome of the Rock after an earthquake; abandonment and eventually closing of the southern gates of the Haram (the ones under al-Aqsa Mosque); a number of additions to the Haram itself, including a fancy new gate on the spot of the present Gate of the Chain, facing westward and dominating the city across the Tyropaeon valley, which was still very much a valley at that time. Most of these changes were the result of perfectly normal maintenance requirements. Some also reflected political decisions. The Holy Sepulcher was looted probably because it was alleged to be filled with expensive objects and Fatimid ideology was expressed through the dynasty's control of Jerusalem in particular and of Muslim piety in general, as is clear from the inscriptions found near the Holy Sepulcher, in the Dome of the Rock, and, most spectacularly, on the triumphal arch of the new al-Aqsa Mosque. In the latter the Qur'anic mention of the Masjid al-Aqsa (17:1) is the earliest remaining use of that important reference associated with Jerusalem and it is followed by the full titulature of the ruling caliph al-Zahir (r. 411/1021–427/1036) and with the names of his local representatives.

These spatial changes both reflected and affected holiness. They reflected it primarily in the Muslim sanctuary, with the full establishment through buildings and inscriptions of the two themes of the Prophet's Journey and of the Resurrection and Judgment as the dominant themes of Muslim piety. But it is also the time when the *fada'il*, these wonderful accounts of pious memories in Jerusalem, enshrine the prophet-kings, David and Solomon, in the Muslim stones of the city. These changes also reflected a new trend toward the withdrawal of religious systems into themselves. The new gate to the

Haram does dominate the city, but the Holy Sepulcher is closed unto itself and the probable completion of the colonnade on the north, west, and south of the Haram, as well as the building of parapets and formal gateways to its upper platform, are all features that emphasize the boundaries between spaces and, therefore, between groups. Two aspects of these changes remain unclear to me. One is why Mount Zion, the highest point in the city, with a church built or rebuilt in the late tenth century, was kept outside the walled city. The other one is whether there is evidence for Jewish holy spaces as opposed to religious or otherwise restricted institutions which existed, among other places, on the Mount of Olives.

If one excepts relatively minor modifications like the shifting of the names of gates from the south of the Haram to the north, the image suggested by this second definable moment in the history of Islamic Jerusalem is that of confessional communities acting out their lives and their beliefs separately from each other in their minds, if not necessarily in the streets they shared. They rarely talk about each other except at carefully staged moments when the Muslim Nasir-i Khosroaw is shown in the Holy Sepulcher paintings depicting the "Last Judgment" or the "Entry into Jerusalem," that is to say images that reflect shared beliefs or innocuous events in the life of Christ, not the "Crucifixion" or the "Resurrection" that must have existed in that sanctuary. A small group of 10th-century inscriptions do suggest something a bit different. They are epitaphs of Muslims and of Christians, which contain unusual curses on those who would deface the tombs or jump over them. They provide a curious glimpse of a time when relative peace in the living streets was possible because one could play one's antagonisms out in the cemeteries.

The time of the Crusades would see an explosion of Christian buildings and a partial eradication of Muslim memories. The latter would be revived in Ayyubid and Mamluk times. Under the less tolerant and more arbitrary late medieval domination of the latter, separate lives in separate quarters would become the lot of Jews, Christians, and Muslims. Their stories are better known, as they have been studied more frequently than the early medieval period that had been my primary concern.

Summary

What I have tried to show can be summed up in the following manner. An artificial Roman imperial space over ragged hills and valleys contained a rich trove of holy memories associated with the real and mythic history of Jews and of the first Christians, as well as with pious practices like pilgrimage or the deeper expectation of existence beyond time. Between 350 and 700 these memories (or most of them) found a space and spaces acquired holiness, a Christian holiness first and then a Muslim one. Over the centuries, memories changed location and even confessional allegiance—Abraham in particular, but also Jesus, Adam, and David—and spaces changed their holy names. But, sooner or later, sometimes as late as the 19th century, holy memories were still finding a space in Jerusalem and its surroundings and at times underdeveloped stones were suddenly given a meaning from the rich source of the Scriptures to please a wealthy visitor. At the same time large- or small-scale pilgrimage continued regardless of religious affiliation and the expectation of the end of time and beginning of eternity drew people, living or deceased, to the city as late as half a century ago. They still do so today.

The further uniqueness of Jerusalem was that most of its memories were Jewish, but that these Jewish memories became Christian, and Christian and Jewish memories became Muslim. Alone of all the holy cities of the world, the space of Jerusalem could accommodate all these pious expressions in every one of their confessional garbs. This was so in part because it is the same God who appeared differently to Jews, Christians, and Muslims. It is also so because Islam, which dominated the city during most of the Middle Ages, acknowledged and formalized the rights and beliefs of those who remained in the fold of older traditions. It was, finally, so because the Roman empire had freed the memories of the city from the places they had occupied and also freed the city from being a political capital. During 1,800 years or so, Jerusalem was an administrative and political *sous-préfecture* for all but one unsuccessful century. This, I submit, allowed for another set of values than those of power—values of belief and of piety—to define the purpose of the city. Yet, in a striking paradox, it is political and ideological power that, under Constantine (r. 306–337ce), Justinian (r. 527–565 ce), 'Abd al-Malik (r. 65/685–86/705), al-Walid (r. 86/705–96/715), al-Ma'mun (r. 198/813–218/833), al-Hakim (r. 386/996–411/1021), and al-Zahir (r. 411/1021–427/1036), created the monuments of the city that shaped the way we perceive it. And, as further paradox, it is the Dome of the Rock, the one building whose exact original function it still something of a mystery, that dominated the city in the past. In it the brilliant manipulation of space and of decoration restricted the certainty of holiness, but the aesthetic quality given to the holiness has made the space sacred.

Today that Old Roman City is a small part in a large metropolis with different expectations and different agendas. Whether the holiness of its spaces is still meaningful in other terms than those of contemporary ethnic and political passions, or whether it is destined to be transformed into the post-modernist spaces of contemporary architecture needed for international tourism and worldly taste will not be known for a while.

THE HEZEKIAH NARRATIVE AS A FOUNDATION MYTH FOR JERUSALEM'S RISE TO SOVEREIGNTY

Ingrið Hjelm

Introduction

It was not David's move of the ark to Jerusalem (2 Samuel 6) that gave the city and its temple their special status. The struggle for sovereignty had only begun. It was not until much later—half a century after Yahweh's election of the city during the reign of Hezekiah (c. 715–687 BCE) (2 Kings 18–20:6)—that competing cult places were finally destroyed and Jerusalem declared to be the only place fit for Yahweh worship (2 Kings 23). We are here dealing with a literary construction that, within the paradigm of "diversity" and "unity," writes "history" about a people in a constant move between these concepts.

Thus, the exodus narrative is the beginning of a dispersion of the people after the entrance into the promised land. Cooperation and commitment to one central leadership turn out to be almost disastrous. Because there was no king, "everyone did what he saw fit in his own eyes." However, the kingship did not solve this problem. The favoring position given to the tribe(s) of Judah (and Benjamin) increased the antagonism, and, although the narrative seeks to give the impression that the Davidic kingship (1000–961 BCE) finally united the tribes, this "unity" is not created by a removal of former disagreements. Solomon's peaceful reign (961–922 BCE) from Dan to Beer Sheba was one of exception (1 Kings 5:4–5) rather than normality. Everyday life did not secure Israel and Judah with shading branches of either fig or vine. Dispersion lay in wait. The rejection of Rehoboam (r. 922–c. 915 BCE) in Samaria (1 Kings 12:16) and the election of Jeroboam (r. 922–901 BCE), made clear that the house of David was supported primarily by the tribe of Judah, while the remaining ten (eleven)[1] tribes paid their allegiance elsewhere.[2] The judgment of the faithless Israel is demonstrably spelled out and made paradigmatic for the narrative as a whole. At the center of this narrative cycle (1 Kings 11:1–2 Kings 23:15)—thematically designed as "he walked in all the way of Jeroboam the son of Nebat and in the sins which he made Israel to sin, provoking the Lord the god of Israel to anger by their idols"—is the narrative about Ahab (King of Israel, 869–850 BCE) the son of Omri, or Humri (r. 876–869 BCE), who sinned even more by marrying the daughter of the Sidonian king Etba'al and raising an altar for Ba'al in Samaria (1 Kings 16:30–32).

The reiteration of this theme throughout the Books of Kings[3] relates the narratives to each other and forwards the fate of Israel, namely its disappearance as a kingdom and a people after the Assyrian king Shalmanezer's (Shalmanezer V, r. 727–722 BCE) conquest of Samaria and the deportation of its population around 722 BCE. It is contrasted with the elective salvation of Jerusalem from the Assyrians in 701 BCE and the reforms of the Judean king Josiah (c. 648–609 BCE), which, in a final reiteration of both Solomon's and Jeroboam's sins and the defilement of their cult places (2 Kings 23:13–20), marks every place outside the walls of Jerusalem as unclean.

Reiterating the Passover from the time of the Judges (2 Kings 23:22),[4] Israel's and Judaea's royal pasts are made parenthetical, and Judah has proved its sovereignty as the chosen tribe with Jerusalem as the chosen place. The intention of Josiah's reform is not unification but selection in a pre-monarchic past's hope for a new beginning. In the Josiah story's "transfer of the Law of Moses to Jerusalem," the reforms of Josiah not only signify that Israel's glorious past centered in the North is over, but also that Jerusalem has been chosen to bring it forward in a new beginning.[4]

This beginning, however, was doomed to fail before it had even begun in unfaithful pre-exilic Jerusalem (2 Kings 23:27). As argued by Provan, Josiah in 2 Kings 22–23 is portrayed rather as the figure of Moses than that of David, whom he "actually leaves behind (2 Kings 23:21–23)",[5] in his statement that "no such Passover was held from the days of the Judges… nor the days of the kings of Israel, nor the kings of Judah." Denigrating the rule of Solomon to a period of apostasy (2 Kings 23:13) and completely "forgetting" Hezekiah's faithfulness, Josiah is announced as the only king to have followed in the paths of Moses (2 Kings 23:25), without, however, benefiting much from it. It is not 2 Kings that informs us that, as Moses led the Israelites through the desert to enter the promised land, so Ezra (5th–4th century BCE) would reiterate this event in an inauguration of a New Jerusalem in post-exilic time, similarly threatened with failure because of "Solomon's sin" (Ezra 9 and Nehemiah 13).

In contrast to the Books of Kings, the Chronicler's portrayal of Josiah places him as a follower both of David and of Moses (2 Chronicles 34:3, 14; 35:3–6, 12–15). Reiterating the time of the prophet Samuel (11th century BCE) (2 Chronicles 35:18), the building of the Solomonic temple, the transfer of the ark and the directions for the temple service (2 Chronicles 35:3–5), the Chronicler "recreates" the foundation for a successful return to Israel's glorious past before the division of the kingdom.

In an imitation of Moses' and Samuel's mediating roles in Yahweh's rejection of the people in Jeremiah 15 and his forgiveness in Psalm 99's rejoicing of his exultation on Zion, the Chronicler's Josiah is given the role of delaying Yahweh's wrath (2 Chronicles 34:26–28). In a like manner, Hezekiah's Passover celebration (2 Chronicles 30) reiterates the time of the common monarchy. In a reconciliatory context Hezekiah celebrates the Passover twice. This suggests that he meets the calendar disagreements with the Northern tribes (those from Ephraim, Manasseh, Issachar, and Zebulon, cf. 2 Chronicles 30:18–20). The aim is the unity of the people, expressed in the statement that "since the time of Solomon, the son of David king of Israel, there had been nothing like this in Jerusalem" (2 Chronicles 30:26, cf. 1 Kings 8:65–66). Placing Hezekiah's reform before Sennacherib's invasion, with its demonstration of Jerusalem's inviolability, the author of 2 Chronicles creates the rationalistic basis for Jerusalem's election in a reconciliatory gesture towards the Northern tribes, which hereby are given reason to identify themselves with Jerusalem's surviving remnant. The initiative is received without much enthusiasm.

I

THE HEZEKIAH NARRATIVE AS A

FOUNDATION MYTH[6]

The Books of Kings' rendering of the saving of Jerusalem from the Assyrian attack by Sennacherib (r. 705–681 BCE) in 701 BCE is, in 2 Kings 17–19, contrasted with the fall of Samaria in 722 BCE at the hands of Sennacherib's predecessor Shalmanezer. Samaria fell and Israel[7] was brought into exile because "they did not obey the voice of Yahweh their God, but transgressed his covenant—all that Moses the servant of Yahweh had ordered" (2 Kings 18:10–12). 2 Kings 17 does not have this explicit reference to Moses. The transgression of laws and commandments is combined with a rejection of the prophets (2 Kings 17:14, 23) and of the House of David (2 Kings 17:21–22).

These theological explanations of the invasion and fall do not differ from the rationalistic "historical" one, that Hosea, king of Israel (732–724 BCE) had allied with the king of Egypt, had revolted against the king of Assur, and had not paid the tribute (2 Kings 17:3–5). At the core of both renderings lies a question of loyalty. The immigrants settled in Samaria by the Assyrian rulers are made paradigmatic for this theme of loyalty: they feared Yahweh, but they worshipped other gods from their homelands (2 Kings 17:33, 41), which means that they in fact did not fear Yahweh, since they did not follow the Law given to the sons of Jacob (v. 34).[8] Similarly, Hezekiah is described as having revolted against the king of Assur, as having refused to be his vassal (2 Kings 18:8). On a rationalistic level the political situations cannot be seen to differ, and yet that is exactly what is claimed in the narrative.

The threat against Jerusalem is set in perspective by Sennacherib's siege of Lachish, which leads Hezekiah to seek a peaceful solution. Not satisfied by the offer given—the trifling wealth of the temple as well as the palace, implicitly not only putting Hezekiah but also his patron Yahweh under siege[9]—Sennacherib sends his commander-in-chief to Hezekiah in Jerusalem in order to "persuade" him to submit. Here follows what I would call a biblical interpretation of events. Before we deal with this interpretation (2 Kings 18:17–19:37), we need to look briefly at some Assyrian sources.

In the Taylor inscription as well as in the Bull inscription,[10] Sennacherib's account of his third campaign is described as a campaign against "Hittiteland." Having taken all the coastal cities from Sidon to Ashkelon (whose King Sidka (c. 8th–7th century BCE) did not immediately submit to the king's yoke and was well punished for it), Sennacherib advanced to settle Judaean affairs. According to the Assyrian Annals, the cause of Sennacherib's campaign against the cities of the Shephelah and the southern coastal plain was their disloyalty.

Having revolted against Padî the king of Ekron (c. 8th–7th century BCE), who was an Assyrian vassal taken into captivity by Hezekiah, the nobles of Ekron, who had sided with Hezekiah in his revolt against the Assyrians, called upon Egyptian military forces, "the bowmen, chariots and horses of the king of Meluhha" (Ethiopia) to aid them in their struggle. They were finally defeated by Sennacherib in a fight that began in Eltekeh, north of Ekron, and which ended in the conquest of 46 of Hezekiah's strong walled cities as well as the small cities in their vicinity.

Two hundred thousand people were carried away as spoil, together with their belongings. What happened to Jerusalem and Hezekiah?

> Himself, like a caged bird, I shut up in Jerusalem, his royal city. Earthworks I threw up against him—the one coming out of his city gate I turned back to his misery. The cities of his, which I had despoiled, I cut off from his land and to Mitinti, king of Asdod (c. 8th–7th century BCE), Padî, king of Ekron, and Silli-bêl, king of Gaza (c. 8th–7th century BCE), I gave them. And thus I diminished his land. I added to the former tribute, and laid upon them as their yearly payment a tax (in the form of) gifts for my majesty. As for Hezekiah, the terrifying splendour of my majesty overcame him, and the Arabs and his mercenary troops which he had brought in to strengthen Jerusalem, his royal city, deserted him (lit., took leave).[11]

In addition to 30 talents of gold and 800 talents of silver, various treasures, as well as daughters, harems, and musicians, were brought after Sennacherib to Nineveh. Does this account imply a victory for Hezekiah? Or was Jerusalem spared or left because a "caged bird" is controlled already? According to Assyrian sources, the "cage" was not made by Assyrian troops laying siege to the city. It was formed by the conquered Judaean cities (of which Lachish posed a severe threat [cf. Assyrian reliefs in Sennacherib's palace in Nineveh]) as well as the conquered areas from Phoenicia in the north to Edom in the south, comprising all of the petty kingdoms on both sides of the Jordan. Seen in a more long-term historical perspective, the conquest of Palestine had begun half a century earlier. During the reign of Tiglat-pileser III (745–727 BCE), Azariah of Judaea (r. 791–739 BCE) sought to unite the coastal areas as far north as Hamath in an attempt to revolt against the Assyrians. Moving from north to south, waves of Assyrian armies suppressed the revolt and, over years, made the various regions subject to the Assyrian empire.[12] In this perspective, there is not much victory in the outcome of Hezekiah's unsuccessful revolt.

In the biblical text, the "cage" is interpreted as that which saves the remnant and gives them protection under Yahweh's power. In a "contest" with other Yahwist shrines Jerusalem is "proved" to have been the chosen one. Hezekiah's disloyalty is presented as a virtue: that he would not serve the Assyrian king and that he smote the Philistines as far as Gaza, from watchtower to fortified city (2 Kings 18:7–8). In the sermon put into the mouth of the Assyrian commander, the Rabshaqeh, Hezekiah is not said to have sided with the Egyptians, nor to have sought strength by establishing friendship with the people of Judah, whose altars and high places he had just destroyed. That lies implicit in the Rabshaqeh's mocking speech (2 Kings 18:20–25) and in the rumor that Tirha'kah, king of Ethiopia (r. 689–664 BCE), is advancing (2 Kings 19:9).[13] That Hezekiah should rely on such uncertain human powers is set in contrast to his trust in Yahweh as the only real power (2 Kings 18:22; 19:15–19).

With the Rabshaqeh's speech, the Bible sets the stage for the theological discussion intended, in a highly ironic play on the might of the Egyptian and Assyrian gods. The hubris of the Assyrian commander, who himself relies on the powers of this world—the gods made by men's hands, of wood and of stone—marks the Assyrian attack as a theological contest rather than a political issue. This is the message given in Isaiah's song (2 Kings 19:21–34). As in Psalm 2, Yahweh laughs at all the mighty Rabshaqeh of the world. In doing this, the story hides the fact that Hezekiah's historical revolt had failed. Following closely this narrative about the hubris of the Assyrian general, the story—anticipating Jerusalem's fall—finds Hezekiah himself falling victim to this same hubris. Relying on the powers of this world, he offers Babylonian envoys whatever they want from his treasure house. In this narrative (2 Kings 20:12–19), the critical voice is put in the mouth of the prophet Isaiah.

Second Chronicles is even more cautious in not mentioning any Egyptian connection. It shares the view with 2 Kings that it was Judah's king Ahaz (r. 735–715 BCE) that had first brought in the Assyrians (Tiglat-pileser III; 2 Chronicles 28:16–21, 2 Kings 16:7–9), and also that Hezekiah had separated himself from such worldly support. The weight given to the fall of Samaria, by the Books of Kings—that Shalmanezer conquered Samaria because Hosea had revolted, not paid tribute and had furthermore gone into a coalition with the Egyptian king (2 Kings 17:3–6)—is missing from Chronicles, which does not deal with the fall of Samaria at all. Contrasting with this biblical picture are the Assyrian inscriptions from Sargon II (r. 721–705 BCE), Sennacherib and Esarhaddon (r. 680–669 BCE). During the time of Sargon II, the kings of Philistea, Judah, Moab, and possibly Edom are claimed, trusting their own strength, to have revolted against the Assyrian king and to have tried to bribe the Egyptian king to become their ally.[14]

The Sennacherib case we have seen already. The Esarhaddon inscription concludes that Esarhaddon conquered the Egyptian-Ethiopian king Tirha'kah and his heir Ushanahuru in Egypt at Memphis, and that he had subdued Ba'lu, king of Tyre, who had put his trust in his friend Tirha'kah, king of Ethiopia.[15] According to these inscriptions, Egyptian presence in Palestine was a recurrent threat to the Assyrian Empire, also in Hezekiah's time.

So did Hezekiah rely on any of these powers, or did he have aspirations to establish a strong independent kingship in Judaea? Certainly in both narratives he challenged the patron–client system on which Assyrian policy was based, and, like Sidka, he was strongly rebuked for this. Petty kingdoms were not supposed to fight each other, or to rely on their own strength, if that conflicted with Assyrian interests. In the Bible's theological interpretation, with its constant critique of reliance on the great powers of the past, which the text knows all fell one after the other, we are placed at a good distance from the events implied in our texts. We are far from any historical event, referred to as an example of how Israel's fate turned disastrous every time it relied on one or another of the empires of the world.

In contrast to Hosea, king of Israel, who put his trust in the king of Egypt, from whom Yahweh had taken them away (*sic*; 2 Kings 17:4, 7), Hezekiah is presented as the just king, who trusts in none but Yahweh alone. Realizing that the gods of the nations are the works of humans, he is ready to pronounce Yahweh as the only God (2 Kings 19:19). This is what the fight is about. Although the narrative is presented as a narrative about Jerusalem against the empires of the world, its more specific purpose is related to the unsettled question about the fallen Samaria and the saved Jerusalem. In his saving of a remnant, Yahweh has affirmed his center.

The problem is not whether the gods of Hamat, Arpad, Sefarvayim, Hena, and Ivva saved their areas, but whether they saved Samaria (2 Kings 18:35)! Lacking any consideration for chronological consistency (these gods were first brought into the area after the fall of Samaria; cf. 2 Kings 17:24), the author of the narrative has revealed that his theological interest takes priority over historiographic truth.

The affirmation of Jerusalem becomes a constant conflict in Old Testament theology. Anticipating the fall of Jerusalem, Hezekiah is later placed in the role of the unjust king, who secures his own peace by making treaties with the Babylonians (2 Kings 20:12–19). Led to believe that Yahweh protects his city, we are immediately reminded that the city itself has no importance. When Yahweh's remnant is removed from the city, the city is cast into ruins. Using Manasseh as a connecting cue name,[16] Samaria's and Jerusalem's fate have been combined (2 Kings 21:12–15).

In Yahweh's doom of Jerusalem, references are not only given to the fall of Samaria in the mention of Ahab (2 Kings 21:13), but also to Israel's first sin from the time of the wandering in the desert: the making of the golden calf. In a fulfillment of the prophecy: "the day I punish, I will punish their sin upon them" (Exodus 32:34), Yahweh no longer worries about the judgment of the Egyptians (Exodus 32:12), but predicts that he will bring "such evil upon Jerusalem and Judah that the ears of every one who hears it will tingle" (2 Kings 21:12).

As the doom was pronounced over Samaria in 2 Kings 17, it is now pronounced also over Judah and Jerusalem, because they have "provoked me to anger since the day when their fathers came out of Egypt until this day" (2 Kings 21:15). In its didactic setting, the closure of the Josiah narrative, that Jerusalem too should become rejected, belongs to the narrative discourse of the Deuteronomistic history; however not to its perspective, which in the Hezekiah narrative pronounces a future for Jerusalem's remnant.

II

MOTIFS AND THEMES IN THE HEZEKIAH
NARRATIVE'S ZION IDEOLOGY

To speak about a Zion ideology in the Deuteronomistic history, or for that matter in the Chronistic history, is a kind of exegesis, which takes its content from Prophets and Psalms. The lack of any conscious Zion terminology in the historical books, which prefers the term "city of David" rather than "Zion" (of which the only occurrences are in the prophetic material of the Hezekiah story, and in the mention of the move of the ark from "the city of David, the same as Zion" to the temple in 2 Samuel 5:8; 1 Kings 8:1; 1 Chronicles 11:2 and 2 Chronicles 5:2) forms a sharp contrast to the term's numerous occurrences in, for example, the Book of Isaiah. This book, on the other hand, only mentions "city of David" once (Isaiah 22:9).

Not only does the specific term not occur often in the Deuteronomistic history, but neither does its associated terminology of trust (root: *ba'aḥ*)[17] and salvation (root: *na'aḥ*). The latter is a frequent term in Judges and the Books of Samuel. Almost half of its occurrences refer to Yahweh's acts as savior of his people or of David.[18] Childs' distinction between *ba'al* as Deuteronomistic rather than Isaianic, and *na'al* as Isaianic rather than Deuteronomistic,[19] cannot be confirmed, both terms clearly belonging to prophetic and psalmodic literature. Neither term occurs anywhere in the Books of Kings except in the Hezekiah story's testimony of whom to trust[20] and from whom to expect salvation.[21] The similar use of these terms in the Books of Chronicles' Hezekiah narrative[22] and their remarkably few occurrences outside this narrative, belonging to a similar theme, give reason to believe that we are dealing with a specific narrative stratum.

While the patronage motif of "my people–your god," such as expressed in the covenantal language of Deuteronomy 28, is a kind of presupposition for the Deuteronomistic history as a whole,[23] its adherence to the "threat–salvation" motif of prophetic and psalmodic literature is strikingly absent in Kings' part of the Deuteronomistic history. In the Books of Kings, Hezekiah is the only example of a king praying to Yahweh in the temple, in a critical situation that could not find its solution in paying off the oppressive foreign rulers. In similar narrative compositions, Hezekiah's predecessors gave away the treasures of temple and palace to avert the threat of neighboring rulers: Rehoboam to the Egyptian pharaoh Shishak (r. c. 946–913 BCE) (1 Kings 14:25–26); Asa (r. 914–874 BCE) to the Aramaean king Ben-Hadad (d.c. 841 BCE) (1 Kings 15:18–20); Jehoash (r. 799–784) to the Aramaean king Hazael (c. 844–800 BCE) (2 Kings 12:18–19) and Ahaz to the Assyrian king Tiglat-pileser (2 Kings 16:7–9). Both Asa and Ahaz bribed their future overlords to protect them against minor enemies: the Israelite king Basha (r. 910–887 BCE) in the Asa narrative (1 Kings 15:16–22); the Aramaean king Rezin (c. 740–732 BCE) together with the Israelite king Pekah (r. 741–730 BCE)—and perhaps also the king of Edom—in the Ahaz narrative (2 Kings 16.5–9). None of these four kings "cried to the Lord"; they paid their way out of the danger. The foreign rulers either went away (Shishak and Hazael) or they "listened to them," which means they accepted the bribe and conquered the minor enemies (Ben-Hadad [1 Kings 15.20] and Tiglat-pileser [2 Kings 16.9]).

In three of the narratives the threat is set against Jerusalem.[24] In an ABABA structure, we finally find Hezekiah not bribing but paying off the Assyrian king Sennacherib (2 Kings 18:14–16).[25] Moving a step further than in the previous stories, the Assyrian king does not accept the payment and there is no mighty king to bribe. Hezekiah is rather checkmated, and his belief in Yahweh is put to a test.[26] The test is not given in the voice of the prophet, but in that of the Assyrian commander. The language of this commander, however, is indistinguishable from the language of the biblical prophets.[27] Playing with the motifs of threat–salvation, the Rabshaqeh offers the Judaeans listening on the wall a patronage solution.

As Yahweh is said to have been with Hezekiah (2 Kings 18:7) because of his faithfulness towards Yahweh (2 Kings 18:5–6), the people are promised a future life in a land flowing with wine, olive, and honey if they will abandon their former patron (2 Kings 18:31–32) and "be with" the king of Assur. Using the covenantal language of the Pentateuch (especially Deuteronomy 28), the narrative is the sole example in the Books of Kings of a fulfillment of the "my people–your Lord" relationship expressed in Solomon's prayer in the temple inauguration narrative (1 Kings 8:23–53). Set in contrast to Yahweh's promise to his people—a land flowing with milk and honey, if they had the courage to go in and fight with giants (Numbers 14:8–9, 24)—the Rabshaqeh takes the role of trying to seduce the people into believing that they can have milk and honey without fighting. That they shall live and not die, in a land "as their own land, a land of grain and wine, of bread and vineyards, of olive trees and honey" (2 Kings 18.32).

While the Israelites in the desert did not have the courage to fight against giants, but cried, complained, rebelled[28] and died (!),[29] while only Kaleb and Joshua stood the test to become this story's surviving remnant,[30] the people on Jerusalem's wall remain silent to the Rabshaqeh's promise of survival. Obedient to the king's command, "do not answer him," they have demonstrated their allegiance (2 Kings 18:36). And good for them: it is not Assur's but Yahweh's vineyards which are prophesied a flourishing future in Isaiah's song (2 Kings 19:29–31). Demonstration of power belongs to the structure of patronage. Who is mightiest, the giants of the land flowing with milk and honey, or Yahweh, who had promised the people a secure future in that land? Mistrust in Yahweh's ability to fulfill his promise became disastrous. The language employed to express the range and consequence of such a mistake belongs to the realm of pride. With words like "despise" (2 Kings 19:3), "mock" (2 Kings 19:4, 16, 23) and "scorn"[31] (2 Kings 19:6, 21, 22), the Rabshaqeh is said to have despised the living god. As Yahweh did not allow the Israelites to enter the promised land, because of their contempt for him[32] (Numbers 14:11,

23), so Sennacherib shall not enter the city (2 Kings 19:28). The role of the giants—a play of comparables—is the role played by the mighty king of Assur. The argument implicit to the comparison is given in Hezekiah's prayer. Although the kings of Assur had fought against people, countries and gods, they nevertheless had not demonstrated superior power, since: "these were not gods, but the work of men's hands, wood and stone" (2 Kings 19:17–18).

The emptiness of such man-made gods is comparable to the emptiness of the all too feared giants whose "shadow has left them" (Numbers 14:9). Of all the possibilities for using this metaphor (cf. Psalms 102:12; 109:23 and 144:4), we find its only occurrence in the Books of Kings's Hezekiah illness narrative. His shadow did not leave him but was delayed for another fifteen years, because of his tears (2 Kings 20:5, 9–11). This life–death (emptiness) metaphor is given further expression in the designation of Yahweh's qualities: that he is a living God (2 Kings 19:4, 16) and the only one (2 Kings 19:19). In Numbers' rebellion story, Yahweh's anger is a consequence of the challenge to his sovereignty—"As I live, all the earth shall be filled with the glory of the Lord" (Numbers 14:21, 28): demonstration of his capacity to punish whom he wishes.[33] As with Israel's tears in the Josiah narrative, so the people's tears came much too late. Moses' plea for mercy, because of Egypt's embarrassing judgment—that Yahweh might not have had the power to lead the people into the promised land (Numbers 14:16)—forms a striking contrast to the Exodus narrative's demonstration of Yahweh's absolute power in the face of Pharaoh—"there is nobody like me in the whole world" (Exodus 9:13–16; 14:4)—and the Hezekiah narrative's demonstration of that power in the face of Sennacherib.

In biblical theology, salvation and punishment are problems both of narrative composition and of dogma. Obliteration is not total. Having been expelled twice, in the desert and in the exile tradition, hope is still awaiting the day of Yahweh's bringing home his scattered remnant as king of the whole world. The Hezekiah narrative's anticipation of this theme, which carries the weight of the whole world's submission to this god, connects it with the Zion ideology of the Prophets and Psalms. That the primary goal of the biblical authors was not to give an objective account of history's course should warn us that, because they used history as an interpretative matrix for a theological discussion, biblical scriptures must have been written later than the history implied.

Biblical narrative is not about Israel's history as such. It is not about any Israelite world of gods or religion. The narrative is about a people's, a community's, hope and expectations for an unknown future, projected as a consequence of what is understood to be history's course based on present and past experiences, whether written or not. Waiting within an interlude, the authors of the Old Testament's scriptures and prophets provide a theological "treatise," which discusses how its audience should understand itself and its God.

Recently, in a thorough study of the composition of the Book of Isaiah, Antti Laato[34] has demonstrated that the author behind the book cannot be earlier than the Persian (perhaps even Hellenistic) period; that the book was written with the purpose of establishing Jerusalem as a religious center for the whole world (Jews and non-Jews), and that the righteous of Jerusalem, following the preaching of Isaiah, considered themselves to be a saved remnant, who should bring about the fulfillment of these expectations. Using the ideology of Zion's inviolability in the 8th century BCE (Isaiah 36–39) in Isaiah 1–39 as a driving force, the audience is to be persuaded that "as Yahweh saved his city in the past, he can do it again." Utopian as Isaiah's message might be, it is not without its own realism. The validity of the argument relies on the purported election.

Voices of Jerusalem

FROM JEBU

Etal Adnan

... And the king and his men went to Jerusalem
unto the Jebusites, the inhabitants
of the land
... and David said on that day
Whosoever getteth up to the gutter and smiteth
the Jebusites, and the lame and the blind,
that are hated by David's soul,
he shall be chief and captain.

2 Samuel 5:6–8

The ignoble heart suffering from cold has vomited
our destiny on the asphalt of the foreign roads
and filled the sky with the mud of our hatred
      Jebu awoke
O tender eyes of Paris we have closed you
in the agony of the forgetting
found again the merciless compassion of
a faceless love which acts like an acid
on the roots of our vertebrae

Jebu sleeping   getting up
(they took advantage of his slowness)

He came to cry at the table of the
nations
(they will destroy him while he is
still young.)
he grew up under the shadow of the black palm tree.
Jebu presides over a procession of
angels   breaks the geraniums which cover
his tomb
     a smell of the Levant on the world!

Jebu shall return to distribute the land
to the land
to conquer the moon
with no armor
to pull the sun out
of its orbit
and transform the ecliptic
of the human race

Crawl on your belly
reach the well   drink   exhaust   swim in
the underground of petroleum and come back BLACK

Jebu
shaman   archetype   son   of animal bedu
inhabitant of the palm tree with a
thousand branches

O dead cities of the 21st century
Beirut and Tel Aviv

Jebu crawls underground like spring in love
with a woman   Jebu in love with Arabia   counts
the wild roses which journey to Palmyra

Jebu
your nocturnal sexual tenderness has
arisen   the desert shall bloom!
thunder of those who did not leave
loyalty of the people of Canaan who were
here before David who shall be here after Daniel

I came from a vertical land
my ancestors being born at the start
of great rivers

we are conquered by

falsifiers of History   thieves of
undergrounds   and we have in our own
councils a rottenness more dangerous
than the sea serpents surrounding Sinbad

There is a spring under the ground
the resurrection not of the dead
but of the living

O Palestine
O shipwreck
one hears at night the
moaning of your valleys
where even the dead have some tears

you shall drink a big measure of blood
and nauseated at heart
you are resurrecting
counting the inches of the land
with your nails
              the land of Canaan
              is a crown of thorns

Darkly our children are drowning
in our peaceful rivers   the people
were in a swamp and we called for liberation

now I do announce
              napalm
              hunger
              the cunning of the enemy
              the slow flying airplanes   the dynamite
              torture
              and more corpses than larvae in a rotten
              pond
              we are guilty of innocence

ༀ

the City covered by the wind   by tears   by ultraviolet
rays   is trembling

Palestine   mother of nations   is a glorified pestilence
with solar tumors on the face and repeated rapes in the
belly

Jerusalem is a city founded by the Jebusites
and its children packed under tents launch
blasphemies which blacken the air: Palestine is
sick of cancer
thirteen brothers in the UN
thirteen cowards castrated by
the smell of oil

O planet vomited by the Pleiades
O Palestine!

ༀ

nocturnal tenderness for those who eat
thorns   the eyes of the bedu-women are
tormented bottoms of craters. There are
women   bodies pounded by an enemy who is
still licking the boots of its former
executioners.   We could not do the same.
Palestine is a land planted by eyes
refusing to be closed.

Jerusalem is not the city of David
Jerusalem is the city of Jebu.

I LIVED IN JERUSALEM

Na'ila 'l-Wa'ri

I was born in this holy city, in our family house in one of the quarters of Old Jerusalem, a few yards away from the al-Aqsa Mosque. I lived my childhood years and part of my adolescence here. In its narrow streets and alleys, I played, cried, and sang. In its schools, I learned the alphabet and the philosophy of existence. I learned to be myself; I learned that the homeland belongs to us and we were ready to die for it.

This city has engulfed me with its warm sunshine, drenched me with its profuse rains, seared me with its intense cold. I loved it all, with a child's attachment to objects, with a young girl's clinging to hope and freedom, and, later, in exile, with a woman's yearning for her motherland, with estrangement and dispersion thrust like a dagger in the side.

I traveled to Jerusalem in an unexpected journey of return, a journey I dreamed about when the yearning for Jerusalem and the homeland kept nagging at me through the years. My hope for its liberation was a tattered motto. There I would find occupation and another people living in my homeland, while history remained hidden. The homeland moans now, but time is the only witness.

I returned as a tourist, I, who have been a tourist for many years in other people's lands, when I continued to look for a country similar to mine, for a Jerusalem that reminded me of my Jerusalem. I looked for it in Rome's old quarters and narrow streets; I searched for it in the Latin Quarter of Paris; in the piazzas of Milan and in its churches, but I never found what I sought. I have no doubt that even people living in places that are full and crowded, where life is not very easy, are equally attached to them. They would live and die for their homeland.

I returned today bearing all the love, loyalty, and devotion that thirty-three years of estrangement and yearning have kept intact, with the child inside me waking up. This city that has been present in my dreams is recalled to memory today, as I saw its face engulfed in gray smoke. I see it, touch its stones, and smell its soil. I returned today, a child with an aborted dream.

With a visa in hand, I stood at the border bridge entrance to my country, and remember crossing the same bridge in 1967 when the June war erupted and quickly turned us into refugees. We had left, my little sister and I, to join Father in Amman, walking over the partly destroyed bridge, my sister crying as she dropped her little doll into the water. I held and comforted her, pressing her against my breast for fear of losing her also, until a fellow traveler retrieved the doll and she was calm again. She has kept this doll with her to this day. Remembering, I closed my eyes trying to shake away the memory, and opened them to find that I was facing an occupier, on the other side of the bridge.

Eventually, I continued my journey towards Jerusalem. There it stood... with its cemeteries... its fortresses... its museums... its walls and gates... its tombs of the Romans and Crusaders... and the fragrant reminder of the Muslim leader, Salah al-Din al-Ayyubi, standing with his sword at its gates, defending it in the name of truth, religion, and honor. Now Jerusalem was draped in a black cape.

At the hotel, I looked out of the window, feeling the intense cold. I gazed at the city panorama, and realized that my heart has been here all the time, hiding in this part of the world. I had left my heart here when I left freedom, when destiny threw me from my homeland. Soon I realized I was soaked wet with the rain and closed my window.

Later, I retraced my footsteps over familiar parts of the old city inside the walls. I walked into the stone-paved alleys, through the crowded food and spice markets that greeted me with delicious smells... shopkeepers and peddlers intermingled with shoppers. I came to my grandfather's house, and paused to remember my grandmother's tales.

From these souqs, one reaches the Via Dolorosa, where Jesus Christ walked bearing his cross... From there I reached the Christian Quarter and the Holy Sepulcher. I went inside the church to be impressed again by its magnitude and beauty, and lit a candle asking Allah to end the Holy City's siege. From there I passed through the Jewish Quarter towards another of Jerusalem's gates, which opened onto West Jerusalem... I was anxious to see the family quarter in West Jerusalem, outside the city walls, and see the family homes I had only heard about, since I was born in East Jerusalem after the western part, with its many beautiful Arab houses, had been occupied in 1948 by the Jews. I gathered it would be very painful for me to see these places filled with strangers now. It was indeed painful when some relatives showed me around there later on.

Going past my old school, I walked around many familiar places, recalling details of my younger days. This experience left me with mixed emotions. My last day was left devoted to a visit to al-Haram al-Sharif: al-Aqsa Mosque and the Dome of the Rock. Open squares and wide stairways and terraces comprise al-Haram al-Sharif area. These were all green with grass intermingled with wild flowers. Fall fir trees and old pines surrounding al-Aqsa sheltered those who came to pray. I remembered how my mother held my hand once while I walked at her side, tripping all the time in my long white prayer robes. I was impressed with the beauty of its Islamic architecture, its Golden Dome, inside and outside, remembering how it was almost destroyed by burning in 1969, the act of a so-called madman. Now the Israelis are excavating, digging tunnels underneath and all around it, trying to locate, to no avail, what they claim to be Solomon's Temple, which they believe is buried there. They dig and dig, in spite of all the cries of protest of the Arab and Muslim world.

And on that visit, I learned of grievous experiences. To get to the Holy Mosque for prayers on Fridays, people have to go to all lengths of trouble, using alternate roads. Most of the time, the area is closed to certain categories of people: certain age groups and visitors from outside the city. More often, it is closed to West Bank citizens. Even praying now requires a permit from the Israelis. We are home but need to use permits and identity cards to reach our Mosque, while Jews from all over the world can visit the Wailing Wall anytime.

A massive cordon of Israeli settlements surrounds Jerusalem, built on land taken from its Arab owners by the power of occupation to make living quarters for Jews coming from far and wide. In the meantime life becomes difficult for those Arabs who remain, leaving most of us outside our country.

A few more hours, and I left my city. I leave again, dreaming and feeling the pain. I am now convinced that the road back is very long and the distance is very far for all of us. Yet, I must strive to return to Jerusalem, as a native and not as a tourist, because I am its legitimate daughter, with roots and a long and authentic history. There will come a day when I will re-enter not through a visitor's visa, but with the right to return and stay accompanied by family and children.

I had come filled with hope and expectations, but have left with a thorn in my throat and a pain in my heart. Writing this story has only made my pain greater.

I LIVED IN JERUSALEM

Subhi Ghosheh

During the forty-two years of my life that I spent in Jerusalem, I lived close to its streets, alleys, quarters, arches, mosques, churches, and stones. Every stone in Jerusalem speaks to you about the history of this city, its civilization, the holy messengers and prophets who walked its roads, about God's Messenger who made the night journey from the Ka'bah to the Aqsa mosque; it speaks to you about kings and princes, about invaders and conquerors, about those formidable heroes who made this city the flower of all cities and the graveyard of invaders.

From these stones the fragrance of holiness and spirituality emanates. You seem always, even now in your exile, to hear, yet again, the church bells ringing, and the voices of prayer and adhan, of local songs and children's rhymes, of the joyful music of weddings and the mournful exclamation when the national tragedy struck, of bereaved mothers, and of the invocations of the oppressed and the sick and needy. These images cannot leave you, even in your exile.

🙼

I opened my eyes at the family home in Shaykh Jarrah in Jerusalem. The house accommodated the grandfather, Haj Sa'id Ghosheh, his sons and daughters, and their spouses and children. My grandfather, with my grandmother, occupied a large room, and each of the other couples had a room for themselves and their children. This was a typical arrangement in homes at the time. Communal life imposed a kind of organized living, and the greatest authority was that of the grandparents, or of the grandmother if the grandfather was dead. They allotted the duties of cooking and cleaning and other household chores. Arab society in Jerusalem paid due respect to the grandparents—and we children observed all the duties imposed on us out of respect for them, anxious to avoid disturbing them, or even our aunts and uncles, in any way. We played in the large inner courtyards of those big houses, then spent the evenings listening to the stories and folk tales our grandmother or elderly visitors would tell us: tales of ghouls[1] and jinn, and stories of Aladdin and Clever Hassan. There were no radios or televisions at that time, and hardly any toys, so we had to invent everything. It was a settled life, well rooted in age-old traditions, in which people knew their particular place and how to enjoy what was available then.

After those days of early childhood, schooling began. My journey towards knowledge began in the kuttab[2] of Shaykh Wasfi al-Labadi, who taught me the alphabet and supervised my first memorizing of the short surahs of the Qur'an. It wasn't long, though, before my mother, insisting the kuttab wasn't enough, moved me to a regular school. So began a long period of learning during which my mother stood staunchly by my side. We used to think she was an educated woman, until we discovered that actually she only learned to read through supervising us. With the aid of my father, she succeeded in having all her twelve sons and daughters graduate with university degrees; and for her unstinting efforts she was, in 1964, given an award as "The Ideal Mother" by the Jerusalem broadcasting station. She was, in fact, an early and prime example of the Palestinian mother during the dark years of the Palestinian Diaspora following the tragedies of 1948 and 1967; of women who stood firmly by their children, urging them to acquire knowledge with which to fight the heavy hand of fate that had fallen on them so mercilessly and taken them from their towns and villages into the long night of forced exile and destitution.

Living as I did in the Jerusalem of the Mandate (which ended in 1948), I came to know the way the Jerusalem people took care of the needy families among them, especially on the occasions of the religious feasts. On 'Id days our mothers would send us, with food, sweets, and fruit, to some of those families whose undeclared poverty commanded the respect of their quarter—a custom that continues to this day in old Jerusalem. I also came to experience the ruthlessness of the mandatory system, whereby the British authorities, especially after the beginning of the 1936 Palestinian revolution, made constant searches of pedestrians and houses, destroying furniture and food, and arresting people without any basis or proof. It was during those years, in the thirties and forties, that I came to hate all forms of foreign rule and pledged a lifelong struggle against it. My experience in the Mutran or St. Georges school was equally painful. This was a Protestant missionary school connected to the Anglican Church and, being foreign, had remained open, while my Ibrahimiyyah Arab school had been closed by the British Police Authorities during the uprising. The headmaster of St. Georges would not allow Muslim students to be absent on their feast days, and once expelled the Muslim students of a whole class for having taken a holiday on the 'Id.

At the end of my secondary education, I expressed my wish to my parents to study medicine and they decided to send me to the American University of Beirut, despite their limited income. I went directly into the sophomore class.[3] In October 1947 I joined the pre-medic class, but the United Nations decision to partition Palestine led to very widespread political activity inside and outside the university. Later on we were among the volunteers helping the refugees who started pouring into Lebanon in the thousands. The troubled political situation led to severance of all contact with our families, and all financial help was stopped. We did, though, get some help from international organizations by selling our youthful blood for money and doing other work.

These were very hard experiences, but I managed to fulfill my academic requirements and left for Jerusalem, via Jordan, at the beginning of the summer. On arrival I learned that my family had left Shaykh Jarrah following its occupation by the Zionists and had taken refuge at one of the schools in the old city. My family of eleven were living in a single room, and there were many other families there, including some upper-class ones from the more affluent quarters of what came to be called West Jerusalem. This part—with its beautiful houses, often elegantly furnished, its personal libraries and the numerous personal effects left behind when the owners fled for their lives—was completely annexed by the Jews. Now these educated and once affluent people were only too happy to find a refuge in the old city, previously regarded by them as a place for workers and the poorer section of society. Water was scarce, full of impurities, and had to be boiled before drinking, while skin diseases reached epidemic proportions. People lived on rations: a family member would sometimes stand for hours to receive wheat or burghul[4] soup, along, sometimes, with a few pieces of meat. For poorer families, these rations were the only sustenance. Many men resorted to selling their womenfolk's golden bracelets and other precious items to meet daily needs. I began to think seriously of abandoning my education and taking a job to help the family, but the whole family rejected the idea, declaring themselves ready to sacrifice whatever they could to safeguard my continuing education.

I returned to the American University of Beirut in the autumn.

What Palestinian students, including myself, suffered in those years is beyond description. However, I graduated as a doctor in 1953, and, after the graduation ceremony, I packed and left for Jerusalem.

It was no longer the Jerusalem I had known. Arab Jerusalem had dwindled to the old city and some surrounding quarters, including our quarter of Shaykh Jarrah, which the Arabs had regained. What remained of Arab Jerusalem was surrounded by fences and barbed wire—a source of deep sorrow and frustration.

I found a part-time job as a doctor with the UNRWA, working for three hours a day. The rest of the time I practiced medicine at an office that my father, proud of my achievement, had rented for me. I helped poor people a great deal and made little money at this practice but was deeply happy to be in a position now to help my fellow countrymen. Arab Jerusalem, now ruled by the Jordanian authority, was full of refugees from evacuated villages living in abject conditions. It was also painful to discover, on my return to live in my home town, that most of my friends and colleagues had dispersed to numerous different parts of the world. At that time Jerusalem furnished no social life for bachelors; even the youth club had been closed for political reasons. We soon learned that, given the dire conditions facing people, frequenting bars and coffee houses was harmful to our reputations; and so we were restricted to socializing after hours in my office, or in that of a colleague. These regular meetings, though, aroused the suspicions of the Jordanian secret police, as all political parties were forbidden. It was easy to accuse any one of us of being a communist— which was the worst slur that could be hurled at anyone at the time. We became suspect, and I noted one or two men permanently outside my office, apparently intent on reading books. But, for all their persistent efforts to unearth any forbidden activity, they always came away empty-handed.

Eventually, I was convinced to joined the Arab Nationalist movement. I was quite happy with the services I could offer my country on the political, medical, and philanthropic levels. My family constantly urged me to get married and start a family, but I waited until 1961, when I met the girl I thought would make me happy and help me in my many-sided work.

We held our wedding at the Ambassador, and it was the second wedding in Jerusalem at which both men and women were present. Before that, people followed the traditional method: the marriage contract would be signed at the bridegroom's house in the sole presence of men, while a separate celebration would be held for the women, at which a number of hired dancers and singers would sing and attend to the bride, helping her change seven dresses. The bridegroom's sisters, aunts, and women cousins would dance, and people would give money as a gift to the bridegroom, to help him meet the expenses of the new life. My wedding, though, was different, and it was criticized not only by traditionalists but by the Arab Nationalist movement, which regarded it as bourgeois.

My choice of bride turned out to be a good one. My wife, Amal Dajani, proved to be an ideal mother to our three sons, the last of whom was born a few months after I entered the Israeli prison for the second time in 1969. Amal, in fact, stood by my side throughout all the crises and the other prison experiences that I suffered through my political career. I was imprisoned four times by the Jordanian authorities. Then, after the Israeli occupation of the city in 1967 and the immediate rise of resistance, I was twice imprisoned by the Israelis. During my second imprisonment, which was meant to be twelve years, I developed some heart trouble and consequently was released in 1971 and immediately deported. I went with my family to Kuwait and worked there as doctor until 1990, returning to Amman as a consequence of the Gulf War.

A LILY CALLED JERUSALEM

Nazik al-Mala'ika
translated by Patricia Alanah Burns with the help of the Editor

If the moaning of death's winds
Should pass
Obliterate the echo of our lives
.... and God reckons with us:
"Have I not given you a homeland?
Have I not let waters flow like mirrors
Decorated it with stars, embellished it with lovely maidens
Built trellises of vines and strewn fruits everywhere?
Colored even the stones?
Have I not raised in it summits and mountains
And laid down shades
covered its valleys with trees
burst open its fountains, crowned it with lilies?
Poured glowing light and greenery on its road bends
Made the earth fragrant and soft
Haven't I lit the slopes with starlight
And planted the moon in the darkness of your nights?
What have you done with all this rich harvest?"

God will ask us one day, what shall we say?
"Yes, we were granted the summits, the streams and the
glory of the hills,
the eyelashes of stars
the hair of the fields
But we did not protect them
Did not drive death away nor
the wayward winds
And it became like a lily in the
Midst of a roaring flood
Yes and we pushed our moons to extinction

Our ignoramuses gambled with the morning sun
   With the hills,
      With the plains
With a lily called Jerusalem that sleeps next to a stream
to a hill
A vine tree? Bends on it
The sky rains with reverence
The seasons pray
And its wheat stalks kneel, its fields keep night vigil
   to God,
And through its amber mosque the Prophet
   Went on his nocturnal journey
But what did we do with our white rose?

God, You know what we have done
with our rose,
We've plucked its petals and poured its
   Fragrance away
Gave its riches to the arms of an ogre
To the jaws of a hungry scorpion
So how can we reach it?
We fear that tomorrow, the fog shall arrive
And fog nights are long
and will stop our feet from arriving,
The age of fog might linger and our stars
Might perish and then the deluge will come
To drive away our seedlings
and the shadows of dark get longer,
We'll drown in our stupor
And the winds shall blow and wipe out our lost paradise
Our hopes shall fade away, with all their wide horizons
And our wheat stalks shall wilt. God, Your forgiveness!
What shall we say and on Your threshold how shall we stand?
You have granted us the free wing
   And we have invented the chains.

A ROOM

Nathalie Handal

a room hides
in the shadows of ancient believers
the old city breathes, breathes
leaving us hanging beneath its tongue,
deaf
    mute
cemetery after cemetery
haunting passers-by, hunchbacks, dry wells
gate after gate
Jaffa to St. Stephen's
    Damascus to Zion…

what is left between the rose petals
but wishes ablaze…
    weighing more than themselves, more
than the latecomers who know what everyone else
has missed—wild flutes in an empty history…

tell me, a room hides inside our childhood
tell me, the sea cups our origins, tell me, step after step
a room hides in the wailing of absence
veiling the sky of its shame, of ours
tell me, who is able to walk in the past
without coats or words,
    unable I tell you
to walk in a room that hides

in the windows of Jerusalem,
    Al-Quds
        Yerushalayim
the greatest illusion love crosses…

a room hides in the scars of our ancestral walls

through our days through our daze
through our nights through our maze
passed abandoned prayers, stoned faces...

now a silver blankness blinds us
but we sing continue to sing
as a sleeper remains caught in his own dreamless hours
and our whispers flee our hearts—
Al-Aqsa
Wailing
Holy
Sepulchre,
Redeeming
Golden Gate awaiting
the footprints of a secluded morning
reminiscing

as the room hides, hides behind us...

A JERUSALEMITE PAINTER REMEMBERS

Kamal Boullata

Visual expression is a language separate from verbal expression. One cannot give voice to the other nor can one be a substitute for the other. Painting proceeds from painting just as much as writing proceeds from reading.

As a child, the first contact I ever had with painted images came through Byzantine icons. A number of them were placed high up in a niche in the Jerusalem home in which I was born. One of them, probably belonging to the Jerusalem school of icon painting, had an Arabic inscription on it. Years later, I was able to decipher it to find that the man who had commissioned the icon was my paternal ancestor.

From the vaulted roof of our home within the walled city, one had a splendid view of domes and cupolas, belfries and minarets. The closest and most majestic dome in our neighborhood was that of the Basilica of the Holy Sepulcher with its adjacent rotunda of the Anastasis Chapel, which we used to call in Arabic *Nus iddiniya*, meaning "the nave of the world." The farthest in the distance was the tower of the Ascension Church nestled on the Mount of Olives. In between the two sites stood the exquisite Dome of the Rock.

All three sanctuaries were built on a site where a certain rock had been unearthed. Building on the Basilica of the Holy Sepulcher began in 327, soon after the rock of Golgotha was identified. Half a century later, the rock, believed to have been the one from which Christ ascended into heaven, became the center around which an octagonal ambulatory, the Church of the Ascension, was constructed. Between 688 and 691 the Dome of the Rock was elevated around the rock believed to have been the one upon which Abraham, according to Christian and Jewish belief, brought Isaac to be sacrificed and which was the site of the Prophet Muhammad's night journey into heaven. At the time, it never occurred to me that each of these three Jerusalem monuments sheltering a rock, the most elemental matter intrinsic to earth, had an identical building plan: one that was based on the rotation of two squares circumscribed within a circle and intersecting each other at an angle of 45 degrees.

🦚

"Geometry is to the plastic arts what grammar is to the art of the writer."
—Guilaume Apollinaire

During the early 1990s, I left the US, where I had been residing for the previous twenty-five years, to go to Morocco and Spain, where I wanted to pursue research in Islamic art. After years of working on the exploration of the square, the eight-pointed star generated by two squares intersecting at 45 degrees intrigued me. The octagonal star not only seemed to be at the center of every arabesque I examined, but its configuration, depending on the proportional subdivision of its module, indeed formed the master grid of endless patterns. From the tiniest ornamental detail adorning a personal object to the most complex structures found in a monument, it was the same octagonal constellation, its derivatives, or its double or triple rotation within the circle that formed the underlying grid of the most complex arabesques. What was the secret principle of this master grid? How is it capable of generating all these enigmatic complexities of pure abstraction that continue to create unspeakable pleasure for the eyes and mind?

I was soon to learn that since antiquity, the square and the circle had been fraught with symbolical and philosophical connotations. The earth was often symbolized by the square because of its four axes of spatial orientation, whereas the form of the circle represented the heavenly sphere. The rotation of the square within the circle was often referred to as the squaring of the circle. In it, the perimeter of the square is virtually equal to the circle's circumference. The geometric exercise sought to imply that the dimensions of the finite are able to express those of the infinite. It was through my research in Islamic art that I was finally able to retrace my earliest contact with image-making. By looking hard at the octagonal star made up of the intersection of two squares within the circle, I remembered Byzantine icons, whose motif embodied the meeting between earthly and heavenly bodies. This meeting was represented in the geometric shape of the mandorla surrounding the figure of Christ in the icons depicting the Transfiguration, Christ Pantocrator, or Christ on the Celestial Throne. In each one of those themes the mandorla had unfailingly taken the shape of two superposed quadrangles within a circular form.

Once I saw the link between the central motif in the icons of my childhood and the octagonal star that radiated with those mesmerizing arabesques evolved in Islamic art, I realized why all three monuments

I could see from our roof in Jerusalem shared a common building plan. By circumscribing the intersection of two squares within a circle, the ground plan of the Basilica of the Resurrection, the Church of the Ascension, and the Dome of the Rock sought to mark the divide between heaven and earth.

Only in the Dome of the Rock, however, was the architectural expression of the convergence between the physical and the metaphysical realms in itself a reflection of a historical meeting that made Jerusalem a city open for all its citizens and the rest of the world. This meeting, documented by different chroniclers, took place between Caliph 'Umar Ibn al-Khattab and Sophronius, the Byzantine patriarch of Jerusalem. It was Sophronius who demanded that the caliph come to Jerusalem in person for the signing of the treaty that handed over the city to the Muslim Arabs. We are told that he was the one who led the caliph through the city and who, legends claim, helped him unearth the debris from the sanctified rock under what has been considered for the last thirteen hundred years to be Jerusalem's central jewel. Is it any coincidence then that Islam's foremost monument continues to mirror the visual expression of a perfect architectural marriage between Byzantium and Islam?

Looking back at that meeting, which the world today no longer seems to remember, I cannot help but think that Sophronius may have been the first native of the city of my birth to realize that the road to Jerusalem is in the heart, and that only after one is capable of renouncing what one loves most can one hope to recreate it.

"Artistic creation is in fact fundamentally an act of generosity."
—Bridget Riley

Just below our roof, amidst our neighbor's houses in the Old City, we could also see a walled rectangular place that must have once served as a water reservoir. We used to call it Birket il-Khan (the pool of the inn). I don't know why, but I always thought that open space must have been the site referred to in the Gospel of St. John as Bethesda Pool. According to legend, the waters of Bethesda Pool had miraculous healing powers. People believed that an angel occasionally came down to stir its waters. The first person to dip in it afterwards was healed. For decades, a paralytic man had never succeeded in being first because he had no one to assist him. When Christ saw him lying there, he simply ordered him to stand up, carry his bed, and walk. The miracle believed to have taken place led to Jesus's condemnation by the city's Jews for having ordered the lame to take up his bed on a Sabbath.

The place I used to believe was Bethesda Pool was no more than a dry basin for most of the year. Our time, I was soon to realize, was not one of miracles. Refugee families from the 1948 war had swamped the houses surrounding the site. Today, it seems that the pool's basin has expanded beyond Palestine's borders to reach wherever the country's disinherited continue to live. All around, one sees the multitudes who have been maimed by the wars. Who could tell them to stop waiting for their miracle?

Here, on the shores of the Mediterranean, in this little town in southern France where one can practically walk to Italy, I am away from all that I have come to know in recent years and close to a place that reminds me of my earliest home. The bells of St. Michel's Chapel marking the day's passage do not sound like any of Jerusalem's bells, but painting continues to come from painting. Here, as I absorb the visual sensations around me, I recognize particular relationships with my colors that are made familiar in the light and air of the place. Outside one window, I see the silver green of an olive tree against the lavender of a bougainvillea. On our neighbor's side, Lily and I are inundated by a flowering laurel and a jasmine next to a cactus and a lemon tree, and below the window of my studio we can see the old city's houses assuming the colors of Giotto's dwellings as their rooftops descend among palm trees, black pines, and cypresses, towards the ever-changing blues of the ancient sea. On top of this hill in Menton, I am on the roof of the world.

Two particular French painters who escaped the worst wars this country had seen in our time found their solace in this region. I realize now, perhaps as they may have done then, that nothing remains after the wars except one's love for beauty. Matisse and Bonnard managed to be at home in this place. As for me, in the words of St. John Perse, here "I shall dwell in my name."

JERUSALEM SONG

Lisa Suhair Majaj

Your walls fold gently,
a wingspan
embracing the dreaming city.

Your air drifts with the odor of incense,
women's voices floating upwards,
a twist of prayer toward heaven's ear.

I hold your name beneath our tongue
like a seed
slipped into the mouth for safekeeping.

Jerusalem, fold me like a handkerchief
into your bosom. I am
one word in a lover's letter,

a chip of blue tile in your sky.
Even those who have never seen you
walk your streets at night.

We wipe your dust from our feet
each morning, rise from our beds wearied
by the long distances
we have traveled to reach you.

See how we save even the broken bits of pottery,
fitting fragments together
along jagged lines to remember you.
Jerusalem, we are fledglings
crying for a nest!

A MULTIPLE IDENTITY

Laila al-Atrash

I never realized how much Jerusalem was mine, how it had lived with me and within me, till I wrote my first novel, *The Sun Rises from the West*, in 1986. Then Jerusalem became a reality, a living pulse, stronger than all those years and deeper than all other feelings. Jerusalem became the core of my text, while Beit Aman—the city parallel to Jerusalem, the true city rooted in my depths—receded. Jerusalem occupied my text, and, in all its details, human, structural, and social, imposed itself upon me. My papers were redolent of its quarters and alleys. The water seller and his donkey would appear in the open square of al-Aqsa Mosque, or the Church of the Holy Sepulcher, or the Magdalene, or Salah al-Din Street, or the Khan al-Zait entrance, or the Via Dolorosa, or the Magarbeh Quarter, the Christian Quarter, the Mamuniyyah School, the Sahira Gate, the Hutta Gate, or Gethsemane.

Oh, how fascinating this old Jerusalem is; how beloved, how close to the heart, for all the great distance separating us! It's hard to write about a city that lives inside you, where its many aspects, all dear to your heart, mingle and intertwine as you imagine them. But I shall choose the beginning: my childhood in al-Quds.

I've felt, from my earliest consciousness, the weight of a question that's never ceased to perplex my heart: "Is it possible for Jerusalem, the city of peace, my city, the center of tolerance and the three monotheistic religions, truly to encompass the coexistence of Christians, Muslims, and Jews, after all the contention and dissent—ideological, political, social, and racial—that it's known? Can it permit these three to lie down together, to mingle within the calm shade of peace? Can all these different colors fuse together, blend with it and in it?"

This question remained a conundrum growing ever knottier with time. From early childhood on, I could recall something almost unconscious, something like a vision or a clouded dream, of a tree that time and again blazed with light and was then extinguished. Still it dominates my unconscious, even though it lies so remote and obscure.

Years passed, cloaking the secret of this blurred vision, till one day

I heard it spoken of. From the sad words of my uncle, and his distress each time he celebrated Christmas, I realized how he mourned the Christmas tree he and his wife would decorate each year in front of his house, now lost, in the Qatamon district of West Jerusalem. His wife was one of the first generation of education inspectors in Palestine, and he was the manager of Spinney's stores. They had an only daughter.

It was this daughter who, when I first woke to ideas, put many theories of knowledge to the test. For a long time, despite the age difference between us, her presence perplexed me; and the same puzzle occupied all the people of our town, despite the general heaviness and depression weighing on the place since the loss of Palestine. When, in 1948, she returned with her parents, as a refugee, to her father's birthplace, she was around ten years old. All I know of this I had from my mother, who described how my uncle and his family, along with his Muslim and Christian neighbors, took refuge in our house. This was a normal enough thing, with many parallels among people who left their homes in the face of the sudden Israeli occupation.

What was not normal—this I realized as I grew a little older—was that my so-called cousin was a Jewess. This was in fact the appellation always added to her name by strangers; and it was from this that the question stems. How could Jerusalem bring together Muslim and Christian neighbors, and a Jewish adopted daughter, then send them all out as refugees seeking shelter and the means of subsistence? How could Jerusalem contain all these three religions, in peace and freedom extending to actual brotherhood, then fail in the face of the State of Israel, expelling so many to live as refugees elsewhere?

After their exodus my uncle's family lived in our original town of Beit Sahour, near Bethlehem, just like thousands of other refugees; but my uncle still kept possession of the deeds to his house in the Qatamon district of West Jerusalem, and of its keys, waiting to return home. Death, though, proved closer. He soon passed away.

After a few months his Muslim neighbors left in search of income and education. Yet this girl of Arab nationality (but, as everyone claimed, of Jewish extraction) stayed on, living in anxiety and distress, almost destroying herself and others as she wandered in search of the real mother from whom she was now separated by wars, closed borders, and armies. Any approach outside would have been branded as treachery and espionage, giving rise to the gravest suspicion; it was quite unthinkable. Before his death, the father persistently denied all the rumors about her origins, asserting firmly that she was the daughter of himself and his wife. This he maintained in her presence and before others. The mother, though, stood weak and tearful in her knowledge of the truth, suffering through the girl's spiritual struggle and quest for the mirage of a faraway mother, a torment of her own beyond description.

The girl continued to bear my family name; but, whether consciously or not, she knew the truth, and strove to take revenge on this name, on what she regarded as my uncle's contribution to her tragedy. This drove her to opt out of all the well-entrenched Arab traditions, to trample on all the taboos binding the daughters of the family: she took it upon herself to lay down the limits of what was permissible and possible. Because of the way she behaved, the whole extended family became very cautious about the behavior of the rest of the family's daughters. We weren't allowed to mix with her or acknowledge her relationship to us. If, by chance, her name should be mentioned in front of strangers, our mothers would straight away relate her story in explanation of her wayward behavior.

People's feelings were divided, some siding with her, others standing against her. Many felt deep pity for her, unable to comprehend why she persisted in destroying herself. They told her to lead a normal life; but this was beyond the power of a woman who knew her roots were out there, behind the barbed wire, and the soldiers, and the animosities and wars—who knew her own kin had driven out her adopted family and closed all the doors against her own natural mother.

Could anything have been harsher than to be alone because you spring from two different, warring societies, something that makes you different from everyone else you know?

She married and produced two children, who later became two of the most famous engineers in Amman. One evening, when she paid a surprise visit to our town, I asked her: "Suppose, by some miracle, you found your mother. What would you want from her?" She answered impetuously, without a trace of hesitation: "I'd kiss her," she said, "and throw myself in her arms. No, I'd spit in her face and ask her why she did this to me. Or maybe I'd keep quiet, say nothing at all. I just want to see her!"

Then, since I'd chosen writing as a career, she asked me to write down her story. I'd never, to this day, dared do it; but now I'll set down here what I've managed to glean from those who knew the facts. The true, tragic story was told to me by my own mother, who heard it from my uncle's wife just a few days before she died. She admitted the truth, weeping bitterly and incessantly. Her Jewish neighbor, with whom she'd forged a close friendship, became pregnant in her husband's absence, and my aunt, who was childless, offered to adopt the baby so as to ward off the scandal. She pretended to be pregnant herself, imitating the normal stages of pregnancy along with her neighbor, till the baby was delivered. Then she adopted her, registering her in the family's name. She wanted to quench her own desire for a child, while, at the same time, the child herself would grow up near her natural mother. This arrangement was made at the end of the 1930s. Both anguished women believed that neighborhood and friendship between Arab and Jew, in Jerusalem, would be stronger than any political upheaval, that Jerusalem would be able to hide the truth from people's eyes. Then the 1948 disaster overtook the two families, and the tragedy began of a Jewish child with an Arab name and passport.

This stopped being such a great puzzle when I realized there were a number of Jewish women married to Christian or Muslim Arabs, who lived with their husbands till the end. I discovered, too, that some of the sons of these Jewish women had indeed joined the Palestinian resistance.

The behavior of my "cousin," though, led to further restrictions being imposed on us girls of the family. I mentioned how we weren't allowed, either as children or young women, to mix with her directly, because, in a conservative town, she'd opted out of all norms and traditional moral restrictions. The men of the family, who would never accept any behavior from their women that defied our code of honor and morality, let my cousin be so long as we weren't in direct contact with her. But they sharpened their vigilance, and none of us girls was allowed to go out unless chaperoned by her brother or father, or to stay out late, or to sit on the balcony for any length of time. Any such behavior would whip up a family storm, and the eyes of the men would glint with suspicion and fear for the family honor. They'd scrutinize everything, even the very skyline, for fear something male was moving there. We weren't even allowed to mix with the male members of our extended family.

Such was the beginning of Jerusalem for me: my uncle and his wife hiding the scandal of their Jewish neighbor, who entrusted her daughter to them in the hope the girl could be brought up close to her. No one could have predicted what was in store for the region. But, eventually, the greed for expansion and conquest separated two desperate neighbors: one woman unable to accommodate the child of her sin, and another eager to hold a child and love it.

This was the Jerusalem of my adolescence. I returned to it looking forward to a promising future as a writer, after my teachers had recognized my special aptitude and I'd published a number of short stories. Carrying my first novel, I went looking for a publisher, chaperoned by my sister's husband. During that particular trip, I fell in love; my heart throbbed with the pangs of first love, for all the chaperon's eagle eye. But I suppressed all expression of this love, hiding it even from the person concerned, blocking all attempts to be near him or let him discover my feelings towards him. To him, as to others, I had to remain the "good" Arab girl whose society proscribed love, whose traditions and upbringing decreed she behave like a virgin in heart and body, ready to offer both to her husband when fate and traditional arrangements brought him forth. I would suffer at night, react in lukewarm fashion when we met by chance or contrivance. The memory of that experience went on wounding me, even as I protected the family name untouched and won the happy approval of my family and society.

This was Jerusalem. She made my dream come true, like a sky opening with a miracle. In Jerusalem I became a well-known journalist, finding a place in this sphere faster than I'd ever dared expect. This happened after I'd whipped up a storm with an article entitled "Violence against Women."

And in Jerusalem, after a few years, I met a young poet and writer, a truly cultivated man. Our feelings for one another grew on a calm fire, to reveal a deep and serene love that ripened into marriage after the fall of Jerusalem.

The loss of Jerusalem came about when I was preparing for my university finals in Beirut. Suddenly, the road from Ras el-Amoud to the Jihad paper where I worked was filled with soldiers, road blocks, and death. A world we knew became split, taking away female friends brought together in Jerusalem's liberal ambience. Ah, the walks we'd take through its old streets, where we'd wander in the Via Dolorosa to visit the Holy Sepulcher, then go and pray in al-Aqsa Mosque. From them I learned where I could buy the less expensive clothes in the heart of the Old City, and the very expensive ones in Salah al-Din Street. One of them came from one of the remaining Moroccan families who had lived in Jerusalem for many decades; another was of Afghan extraction; others were from well-known Jerusalem families—all brought together through work or study in Beirut, Christians and

Muslims, who would go to light candles on the sacred grave of Jesus, or borrow scarves to cover their hair when visiting al-Aqsa Mosque.

And here the question poses itself: can you come to hate a city you've loved with profound passion? The pathways that bore your feet as you hurried in quest of your hopes and ambitions—can they turn dark and deny you? Can the faces you loved grow different, your city become a city you no longer know? Can she lose all trace of you, of the fragments of your soul you scattered so joyfully over her body?

You enter it now through a gate you didn't use before, the gates changing through time and space. Jerusalem's gate was the one next to the Mount of Olives and the Church of the Magdalene. How often I'd pray in the early days, as I returned home to Beit Sahour, that I'd meet the one I loved by chance, that he'd appear, suddenly, from the corner of the street. But my morning prayers were never answered; the one I loved worked in evening journalism. They say first love remains strongest of all in the memory. But I maintain its memory can be supplanted by a love stronger and more serene. Then the former becomes a mere recollection.

During the years of my first absence, when my city was taken captive as I sought knowledge at the university in Beirut, the walls grew old and decrepit. I came to the city looking to retrieve my identity, rejoin my family, carrying in my arms my first child, Dana, who was nine months old. I found my friends and colleagues had separated on the road of life. One had emigrated to America, another to Belgium, but most had been married in the traditional way, mostly to men less educated than themselves.

The deepest loss was our old intimacy and the ardor of life— replaced now by worries greater than the fact of alienation, too complex to be summed up in words. I found the working class that had built Israel's settlements had increased and flourished. Was this, I wondered, a matter of ignorance or need? But this working class had become, too, a weapon in the hands of Israel, one it used to threaten the livelihood of thousands of Arab families whenever it chose to slam the door in their faces. It was from this class that a number of my old friends had married.

Under occupation, concepts and attitudes changed profoundly! In quest of my identity card, lost between the Bethlehem and Jerusalem bureaus, I went to see the head of the Israeli Information Bureau. I later discovered the card had been withdrawn in response to an article I'd written, giving my view of the situation in Jerusalem after the occupation. It had been published in an Israeli paper, under the title

"How Can the Minister of Defense Allow an Antagonist Like Her to Return to Israel?" That was nothing to me. I'd returned to my own country and people. None of them was Israel, and they never would be.

Yet no words can encompass, can describe the feelings of a defeated person seeking to affirm identity in the face of a powerful occupier! All words are hollow, crippled in the face of such a situation. How can a stranger, who came to your city as an occupier, discuss your identity and grant you your citizenship?

JERUSALEM IN 1923: THE IMPRESSIONS OF
A YOUNG EUROPEAN[1]

Muhammad Asad (Leopold Weiss)
Translated by Elma Ruth Harder
Introduction by Muzaffar Iqbal

Introduction

"I was not happy," wrote Asad in his *The Road to Mecca*, first published
in 1954, "but my inability to share the diverse social, economic and
political hopes of those around me—of any group among them—grew
in time into a vague sense of not quite belonging to them,
accompanied, vaguely again, by a desire to belong—to whom?—to be
a part of something—of what? And then one day, in the spring of
1922, I received a letter from my uncle Dorian."[2]

Dorian, his mother's youngest brother, was then the head of a
mental hospital in Jerusalem. This letter from Uncle Dorian—who
"felt lonely and isolated in a world which had nothing to offer him but
work and income"—contained an invitation to the 22-year-old Asad
(then Leopold Weiss) to come and live for a few months in his
"delightful old Arab stone house." "I made up my mind," Asad wrote
years later, in the spiritual autobiography that would make him
famous, "with the promptness that has always characterized my major
decisions. Next morning I informed Dr. Dammert at the United
Telegraph that 'important business considerations' forced me to go to
the Near East, and that I would therefore have to quit the agency
within a week…"[3]

This trip was to become a turning point in his life. But at that
time he had no idea of its significance. "If anyone had told me that my
first acquaintance with the world of Islam would go far beyond a
holiday experience and indeed become a turning point in my life, I
would have laughed off the idea as utterly preposterous." Born in a
Jewish family in Lwów, eastern Galicia (now in Poland but then part
of the Austrian Empire) on July 2, 1900, Asad had grown up with a
"hazy, European bias against things Islamic." At birth he was called
Leopold Weiss, and he was the second of three children, descended

from a long line of rabbis, though his father had broken away from this tradition and become a barrister. During his early years (1900–1913) in Lwów, he had learned to read and speak Hebrew fluently. He also knew some Aramaic and had studied the Old Testament in the original, along with the Mishna and Gemara (the text and commentaries of the Talmud), and had become immersed in the intricacies of the Biblical exegesis called Targum. In 1914 his family moved to Vienna, where Leopold fled from school and tried to join the Austrian army under a false name, only to be recovered by his father after a week and taken home. In 1918 he was drafted into the army, but by then the Austrian empire was on the point of collapse, and the war ended a few weeks later. Leopold entered the University of Vienna to study history of art and philosophy.

The Vienna years (1918–20) were full of intellectual growth. At that time Vienna was the intellectual and cultural center of Europe, where the views of Freud, Alfred Adler, and Ludwig Wittgenstein filled the air. In the summer of 1920 Leopold traveled throughout Central Europe, doing "all manner of short-lived jobs." In 1920 he arrived in Berlin and found work for two months with the famous director F. W. Murnau as a temporary assistant. He also obtained a contract, with a friend, to write a film scenario. Then came a year of wandering in various cities of central Europe, before he finally found a job as a telephonist at the United Telegraph Press Service. It was at this time that he spotted Maxim Gorky's wife, who was on a secret mission to solicit aid from the West for a Brobdingnagian famine ravaging Soviet Russia, and succeeded in interviewing her. This "first-class scoop" led to his promotion to journalist—a job from which he resigned as soon as the letter from Uncle Dorian arrived. And so, on a foggy morning in the summer of 1922, he "stood on the planks of a ship on [his] way to the East." A few days later he arrived in Alexandria, and the same afternoon he went on to Palestine. "The train swept straight as an arrow through the afternoon and the soft, humid Delta landscape," Asad was to recall. "Nile canals, shaded by the sails of many barges, crossed our path." He changed trains at Kantara for a "lazy ferry" that carried him across the "silent waters" of the Suez Canal to the train station from where "the Palestinian train would take me to Jerusalem in about an hour."

But within that first hour he had a "mysterious experience." A railway worker had strolled towards him and invited him to come and see the big caravan that had just arrived from the Sinai Desert. He walked towards the caravan with the stranger and saw a great circle of crouching camels with heaps of pack-saddles and bags here and there, and among them the figures of men.

> The animal smell was sweet and heavy like wine. Sometimes one of the camels moved its body, which was smudged out of its shape by the darkness around it, lifted its neck and drew in the night air with a snorting sound, as if sighing: and thus I heard for the first time the sighing of camels. A sheep bleated softly; a dog growled; and everywhere outside the gorge the night was black and starless... It was already late; I had to get back to the station. But I walked very slowly, down the path by which we had come, dazed and strangely shaken, as if by a mysterious experience which had caught hold of a corner of my heart and would not let me go.[4]

On his way to Jerusalem, Asad experienced his first Arab encounters as if they were a "presentiment of coming upheavals" in his life. Not that he was then conscious of what the future held in store for him;

> it was, rather, as when you enter a strange house for the first time and an indefinable smell in the hallway gives you dimly a hint of things which will happen in this house, and will happen to you: and if they are to be joyful things, you feel a stab of rapture in your heart—and you will remember it much later, when all those happenings have long since taken place, and you will tell yourself: "All this I have sensed long ago, thus and in no other way, in that first moment in the hall."[5]

The Arab stone house of which Dorian had written was truly delightful. It stood on the fringe of the Old City near the Jaffa Gate. From the roof terrace he could see the sharply outlined area of the Old City, with its network of irregular streets and alleys carved in stone. There were Solomon's Temple, the al-Aqsa Mosque, and the Dome of the Rock. "Jerusalem was an entirely new world to me," he would write years later,

> ... although of Jewish origin myself, I conceived from the outset a strong objection to Zionism. Apart from my personal sympathy for the Arabs, I considered it immoral that immigrants, assisted by a foreign Great Power, should

come from abroad with the avowed intention of attaining to majority in the country and thus to dispossess the people whose country it had been since time immemorial.[6]

Those "fateful months" of his first stay among the Arabs set in motion

[a] whole train of impression and reflections; some inarticulate hopes of a personal nature demanded to be admitted to my consciousness… I had come face to face with a life-sense that was entirely new to me. A warm, human breath seemed to flow out of these people's blood into their thoughts and gestures… in time it became most important to me to grasp the spirit of these Muslim people; not because their religion attracted me (for at that time I knew very little about it), but because I recognized in them that organic coherence of the mind and the senses which we Europeans had lost.[7]

By the time Asad returned to Europe towards the end of 1923, after many trips into the Arab lands surrounding Jerusalem, he was a changed man. In 1922 he had already become a correspondent for the Frankfurter Zeitung, one of the most prestigious newspapers in Germany or anywhere in Europe. Back in Vienna, he was considered an expert on Arab and Middle Eastern affairs, and he signed a contract to write Unromantisches Morgenland (The Unromantic Orient)—an account of his first experiences in the Muslim world.

This first English translation of a long forgotten work, by one of the most significant Muslim converts of the 20th century, opens a way for us to relish the historic and the timeless aspects of a land full of spiritual and cultural riches. Written over 75 years ago, this is a work by a Jewish writer in his early twenties, a man who had yet to cross the boundary that would unite him for ever with his Arab brothers. This young Jew returned to Jerusalem late at night—the night of April 5, 1923—into a "threefold festival:… the Christian Easter and Jewish Passover and the Arab festival of the Prophet Musa."

It is a colorful world, and not merely because of the streets of Jerusalem; Asad himself seems to have been in that enchanting state of youthful exuberance that makes everything colorful. His descriptions of the city are vivid; the city resounds and pulsates. Asad had also walked into a city and a country undergoing a rapid transformation. Zionism was attracting Jews from all corners of the world to create a state that would eventually expel hundreds of thousands of Arabs from their ancestral land and unleash one of the most brutal conflicts of the century. Even at that time Asad seems to have grasped the terrible current of events. His political insights are amazingly clear, and his vivid description of a conflict in the making was borne out by events.

𐡀

JERUSALEM IN 1923: THE IMPRESSIONS OF A
YOUNG EUROPEAN

Sinai Desert, March 14, 1923

Jerusalem, this most amazing of all cities, goes far back. In recollection the dominant impression is of religious fanaticism, and streets smelling intensely of raw meat and leather, of masses of people recalling age-old images, of souks and noisy, voracious market alleyways. Nowhere else— not even in other parts of the East—is there a city so tightly ordered by its own code as Jerusalem. Existing vibrantly in the present, it is ahistorical in character, and its past serves as fodder for its ever-hungry will to live life to the fullest, to the very edge. This is the Arab Levant, the "eternal city." Jerusalem: eternal, because it's always in the present; at once eager and calm, and, to its very depths, utterly worldly, for all its ringing bells and wailing walls. You are fallen among the heathen, old city; your streets are sunken, steaming with forfeited life—which isn't a "life of God"; for before you ever drew breath you were a dark creature of this earthly side. On the upper surface, though, in its political aspect, Jerusalem (and Palestine) is the land of uneasy conflicts, which work their way into the lungs like a fine dust, stifling all breath; Zionism has bound itself irrevocably to outside, western powers; and, as such, is a wound in the body of the Near East. This is the reminiscing of one shaken by a moving train. We are racing through the Sinai desert now, and, in the midst of such an immense solitude, you are bound to yourself, the thoughts bouncing loosely around in your head....

Jerusalem, 5 April

I entered Jerusalem late at night. Jerusalem marks the crossing for a threefold festival: you sense, in all the streets, the Christian Easter and Jewish Passover, and even they are outdone by the color of the Arab festival of the Prophet Musa. The origins of this remarkable, ecstatic festival, famous for its power to move Arabs, are, it is said, political, and have nothing to do with the religious institution of Islam. Sultan Salah al-Din supposedly introduced it at the time of the Crusades, so as to have a Muslim counterpoise in Jerusalem during the annual Easter week gatherings of the Christians. The political significance came to be forgotten, but the festival kept its religious inspiration and today still throbs with national fervor. For these six festival days the Arabs flock to Jerusalem, from Nablus, Hebron, the Jordan Valley, and from the desert in the south. The city resounds and pulsates. Fantastic dance processions, in the colors of a thousand flowers. Kufiyyahs, white or brightly colored, the orange turbans of the country folk and the white of the clergy, the brown and brown-and-white striped robes of the Bedouin. Urban Arabs, fellahin and Bedouins are all one in the rhythmic sway to honor God. Simple instruments spur the ecstasy and drive it high—"There is no God but God." Dervishes dance to the sound of flutes, kettledrums and brass cymbals, foam at the mouth, eyes turned to an ungraspable eternity—"and Muhammad is God's messenger," always repeating this highest confession, "No God but God." Sword dances on the cobbled streets of the Old City. The Mufti rides on a white horse, surrounded by banners, leading the procession; the merrymakers go back and forth, dancing and proclaiming the articles of faith to the four corners of the earth. From time to time the shrill drawn-out ululation of women sounds, for minutes on end, from the half-dark streets. Just a few days, and the flocks of people will disperse back through the land. The squadrons of police will be able to unsaddle their horses once more, without fear of Jewish massacres. The British armored cars will once more be able to enter the barracks at dusk.

7 April

Here the strong hostilities between one person and another, the strained relations, are always apparent. Jews or Arabs? Always there is some invisible scale in the air, weighing the governing voice of the street. Everything that happens, every concern affecting more than ten people, has to sort itself out within this divisive hatred, which grows remorselessly by the day. The Balfour Declaration, and again the Balfour Declaration. It is—in a quite different sense—the key to the matter in both camps. The Jews base their Jewish homeland in Palestine on this official promise, and "don't want to suppress the Arabs." The Arabs will hear nothing of it, but point out, for their part, that they "don't want to suppress the Jews." All this in a free Palestine, where the overall population (of about 650,000 Arabs and 83,000 Jews) must be governed as a single entity.

8 April

Seat yourself on the wide stone parapet below David's fortress, where the porters, the hammals, squat or loiter, eat or wait for work. Watch the square in front of the Jaffa Gate—this is the focal point for commerce and traffic; this is the border between the Old City and the new city. And this is where they rub shoulders, where they jostle one another, Arab and Jew, all possible varieties of each; locally born Jews with tarboush and wide, colored coats, often indistinguishable in profile from the Arabs; Jews from Poland and Russia, from Persia and Bukhara, and the proud Magarbeh Jews from Morocco and Tunis in white 'abayahs; and alongside them the rootless urban Jews from all corners of Europe. Then the Arabs: city-dwellers, fellahin, Bedouins. With them the graduated differences of race are clear enough. Only the Bedouins can be spoken of as pure children of the Arabs—the pure Semitic type, with sharp, jutting features, the figure invariably lean (in large cloaks cut wide at the elbow, making it easier for them to place their hands on their hips and force others to give way). In the cities it's mostly foreign blood (Syrian). Yet it is in these very foreign folk that things Arab are most strongly evident; the plant that was splendid and unique for a thousand years, now planted in strange ground, has sprung up more vigorously than it ever did in its original home. Jew or Arab. Here they are brimming over with an intolerant hatred that leads them nowhere; for they will have nothing to do with each other. It is not a rebellion of weak against strong, or a conscious assertion of strong against weak, but the hatred of rivals. And when you take, on top of that, all the black priestly robes wandering through the streets, and the ringing of so many bells stressing yet another side to things, there is little air left to breathe in Jerusalem. Three voices cross continually, seem to tell one another: You shouldn't be here. The souks are an exception; there is scarcely room here for quarrelling or dissension. The East's profound zest for life is concentrated in their bustle, which wants only to take and encompass everything, without limit. Jerusalem's flavor is distinctive and quite remarkable; but for those coming from outside it is not a city one would wish to love.

10 April

Palestine finds itself in a state of total uncertainty—which isn't saying much in our time, when half the world lives in such a way. This state is a very particular one, even so; everything that happens is pressing, every event a mark of depreciation. The working class is embracing the

Zionists most of all. Their expectations, fervently directed towards a Jewish free state—"Jewish the way England's English and America's American"—have been dampened markedly with the gradual development of events. "No money, no money"; this is the daily litany of a capitalist country without capital. A deep insecurity reigns, every endeavor is provisional. People are somehow sickened—they are always "sickened" here—by this waiting for help from one side or another, from capitalists who, if they came, would shape the whole picture differently. Because initial support is needed from the rest of the world, the center of gravity (and, of course, the responsibility) for everything that happens with regard to Jewish Palestine is thrust towards the outside world. Everything that is morbid in Zionist politics finds its expression, I believe, in this unhealthy truism; revealing itself in terms of "uncomfortable" or stifling conflict. The Arab resistance has a quite different style. Born of immediate need, it doesn't aspire to, or attempt to, parallel Zionist strivings towards "cultural values"; at this moment—and perhaps for a long time to come—it is very young, and thus also honest; for actually nothing will be "realized" yet. It is a simple, defensive awakening of power in the face of obstacles to development, and because of that it's never reactionary and always free in spirit, in profound contrast to the spirit of European nationalism. The nationalism of the East is revolutionary, because it's fighting for undetermined things that lie in the future, rather than basing itself on symbols of the past.

In Palestine the Arab movement takes two forms: local, as the opposition force against Zionism; and, beyond that, as part of the greater Arab movement, which for practical purposes is about eight years old. The skillful, far-seeing British politicians knew enough to nurture the existing seeds to germination during the World War, and to extract huge profit from them. As with all large-scale English enterprises, everything started from the fostering of personal relations. Things began in 1915 through the mediation efforts of the Foreign Office—the High Commissioner in Egypt, Sir Henry McMahon, got in touch by letter with Hussein, the Grand Sharif in Makkah. Arab countries' dissatisfaction with Turkish domination was, of course, no secret, and Hussein himself, who traces his lineage directly back to the Prophet (he belongs to the Hashemite family), and who has very considerable influence with the Arabs of northwestern Arabia, Palestine, and Syria, dreams of tearing individual countries away from the Ottoman Empire and creating a unified national Arab state. In this historic, still not widely known exchange of letters, the Foreign Office promised that in the event of an Arab uprising against the Turks, it would establish an independent Arab empire from the Persian Gulf to the Red and Mediterranean Seas, including Palestine and Mesopotamia. The original author of the plan was Lord Kitchener, its keenest advocate the then powerful British military party.

Hussein was provisionally proclaimed King of Hijaz. Powerful propaganda went out from Makkah to the Arabs. Concern arose when the independent Emir of Najd, Ibn Saud, vigorously opposed Hussein, wanting to know nothing of this "high kingship" of a unified Arab Empire. And here the British contrived a diplomatic masterstroke: the whole gamut of problems of Greater Arabia under Makkah's hegemony was passed to the Foreign Office (supported by the military party), while the Colonial Office (obviously not in communication with the Foreign Office) began to work hand in hand with the Emir of Najd. This Arab split showed—fatally for the whole idea at this particular time—that the notion of a unified state was premature, perhaps even impossible; and this gave France as well as England the pretext for dismantling lands that properly belonged together. The French (who had adopted a hostile stance towards the Arab union right from the start) won the promise of a mandate over the territory of Lebanon, and in 1920, in the wake of fighting and intrigue, the rest of Syria and the Hauran followed. And in the same year the original promise given to the Arabs by the English was broken by the Balfour Declaration.

12 April

It grows more obvious by the day: while Arab opposition to Zionism and the British Mandate, by virtue of its organic unity, maintains a rigorous self control and a keen readiness for battle, always accomplishing everything that can be achieved at the particular moment and whatever England can allow without damage to its own prestige, the Zionists—the party actually loyal to the government— have no political power worth mentioning. Economically they have failed, and, by not fulfilling the relevant promises in this respect, they have given the British administration the chance it sought to pose a dangerous question: "Where is the capital your people promised to use to build up a Jewish homeland?" They can provide neither answer nor capital (the latter probably due, among other reasons, to a certain mistrust of English–Zionist politics in the outside Jewish world; American Jews, it is said, are not interested in spending their good dollars on an English colony…). And what does this lead to? Jewish immigration is kept to a minimum because there is no employment available in the country for immigrants (and foreign mistrust, with a side glance at London, rises a further notch). It seems to me that the unsuccessful (one can't yet say "failed") Zionist programs must be accounted for by factors beyond the economic and political tactics involved. A critical overview of economic possibilities is not in itself sufficient to judge this movement, for the sickness lies in the very foundations of Zionist thought.

To view the deep misfortune and longing of the Jewish people only in terms of a "homeland"—this is the sickness; to walk blindly past just this misfortune and just this longing, to establish pretexts without seeking the ultimate causes—this is the very sickness of Judaism! (They say, even so, that the misfortune springs from the alienated nature of Jewish life; that the longing is directed towards a lifting of this state of affairs and towards a free existence of their own. But the development of a nation is not just a series of random events; there has been a sense of homelessness, and, as long as this sense finds no remedy, it is merely senseless to strive after old forms without a new spirit.) What then is the Jewish tragedy—in truth? It is, briefly, the tragedy of a loss of ethical moorings. A mooring of this kind is, we should always remember, the prime goal for the healthy development of any nation, and only by its means can forces then be freed for productive progress; for it implies the giving up of every "if" and "but" (its content is pure symbol—and its value is determined solely by the intensity with which it is put into practice).

In the biblical concept of God, the young nation had established a mooring of the most exalted kind; the strength had attained form. It was forbidden them, a thousand times over, to worship idols, to pray to the works of their own hands, to pray to themselves: their advance was to remain pure and vigorous, not to be diverted. The nation was quite unique in this respect. Yet in biblical times it was precisely this intolerance towards "those of other faiths" that drove civilization on, for the precondition was the firm resolution of a nation to advance along the path recognized as the true one and to build up values from within their own selves. But their great faith in themselves entailed the peril of a boundless curse—in the event of turning away from "God," that is, of loosening the ethical moorings, despairing of their own strength and going along with their own destruction. For the strength they possessed had pledged itself, in "God," to great if as yet unrecognized goals, and now—as the curse struck home—it had become, inevitably, purposeless and self-destructive.

The deep sense of guilt, the sense of having betrayed "God" of their own volition, remained with the Jews; and when they scattered to the four winds, they automatically clutched at the concept of "God," clinging on to it as to a form, which became too demanding once the content had been lost. All the longing of the Jewish people gathered around the old symbol, as they thirsted for the new mooring they never found. God was very close—and at the same time so far away. And the earlier martial, domineering intolerance became the hating intolerance of the ghetto: the fearful sense of needing, constantly, to convince themselves of their own "true belief." From this, too, sprang the tragic contradiction within Jewish people: the knowledge of sacred things and the other, latent knowledge of being far from these things and far from pardon.

For two thousand years this longing and fear held the Jewish people in its grip, and made it dreadfully alone—far more alone than its strength had made it before—so that it became "hateful to the nations." And what of today? Even today there can be no "if" and "but" for the Jews. Their fate has been a heavy, quite extraordinary one, and this points equally to extraordinary paths for the future. Their need is to become quiet in themselves, to gather strength within—for a later mooring perhaps—to gather strength with no immediate goal, without wishing to "realize" at once. But Zionism seeks "realization" here and now, to begin building the house with a roof: a homeland for the Jews! Zionism raises the backdrop to the altar; longing for Palestine takes the place of the deepest human longings. It overlooks the fact that the creation of a homeland was actually the outcome of a nation's strength—never a hospice, a refuge in the face of suffering.

14 April

I live in the house of a Jewish friend, an old Arab stone house on the edge of the Old City. From the rooftop terrace one can see, ten meters away, the so-called Fortress of David, whose old grey walls, steep and somewhat weather-beaten, run on into the city walls. It is a typical Arab fortification from the Middle Ages, with a small minaret-like watchtower; but because David's fortress is said to have stood here on Mount Zion, the Jews leave it its resounding name. As I turn around, I can see over all the Old City.

Today is one of the last rainy days, with a misty atmosphere and heavy, overcast sky; but on such days, when the rain stops for a while and the warmth of the coming springtime air can already be felt, then Jerusalem appears clearer than ever before in its outer and inner contours: the sharply enclosed area of the Old City, the multiple broken lines of her streets can be seen like a carving in stone. Way over on the other side, yet because of its grandeur seeming quite close, lies the Temple Mount—and at its center the Dome of the Rock ('Umar's Mosque), the holiest mosque after the Makkan Ka'bah. Behind it, the city wall drops into the Kidron Valley; on the far side of the valley, the quiet, barren hills already climb upwards, their slopes sparsely dotted with olive trees. To the east, along the road to Jericho, there is a more luxurious growth, dark green, surrounded by a wall: the Garden of Gethsemane. It is set at an angle to the road; in its midst, from under olive and cypress trees, shines the Russian Orthodox Church with its golden onion domes.

15 April

Jerusalem. This can only be the name of a Jewish city, even though today it is a Jewish city no longer. It seems to me that the Jewish existence today is expressed very far from here, in the realm of longing for fulfillment; but what this existence wishes for is a step-by-step fulfillment springing from a recognition of its own life and rules, rather than some process of constructive "building." The Jews see themselves, perhaps without realizing it clearly, in terms of the same awareness and claim to moral conscience that Isaiah sought to instill in them. Then it was "God." But suppose they succeeded, today, in re-awakening the same values in terms of a new principle, where, in truth, would there be a cultural concept of comparable breadth? They had a mighty strength once: while, for all other nations, the "mooring" was based on myth, in terms of this or that force of nature, with differing moral standards established on the basis of these same natural forces, the Jews singly and independently developed the idea of a sole God, a principle of decisive justification that could be applied equally and without modification to everything in life, even down to the smallest issues. Their whole early life developed according to one criterion: righteous or unrighteous? Every other, debilitating option was gleaned away.

It wasn't suppressed, but simply didn't exist—just as there is no third option between straight and crooked. When will the Zionists grasp that they are turning one of civilization's fundamental endeavors to banality? That they evade suffering and lack the will to conquer it? And that the strongest representative of present-day Judaism is the Orthodox Jew from eastern Europe, who, in his faith in God, wants only to know of God and cares for nothing else; that this Jew will be next to tread the Jewish path—if imperfectly for some time yet—because at least his longing is directed towards Jewish strength and anguish?

19 April

I walk the old streets and observe your life, you traders in the stalls, as you send out your unsolicited calls to passers-by. It's the sweet longing to earn that imbues your day with excitement and experience, yet doesn't diminish your worth, as if here indeed were the fabled longing to "rest in idleness." Yes; for this longing quite lacks the frenzy that tries to snatch everything up. There is no haste in it. No envy. So much so that the owner of a shop, if he has to go off for a time, leaves it in the care of his neighbor and competitor. The Arab people rock gently in the unquestioned security of their existence—and seek to augment this existence through earning and acquisition? Why shouldn't they? Earning and acquisition have been viewed as contemptible in Europe, because they've arisen from a lie, a split existence; because the "soul" has thereby been betrayed and given over to "soulless material things." And so people have separated soul and materiality—and plunged into anguish. But here?

20 April

What do we in Europe know of the Arabs? We come here with various romantic, preconceived ideas—or, if we make an effort to come here in the best and noblest spirit, we come with no ideas at all. But, once here, we are made aware, more clearly and tangibly, that the Arab movement—this direct, straightforward movement of free humanity—really exists, is not just political fantasy. The legitimacy of such a new movement is, it is true, revealed by its success; but this is not the superficial "success" of momentary achievement, for already the movement's intrinsic presuppositions have served to bind its supporters in a firm unity. Where can such a thing be found so strikingly as among the Arabs? They see now that they must strive to keep their authenticity, if they don't want to be sucked into the European current and so made sterile. They don't ground themselves in any "historical memories," because the past is too far back; and this to some extent explains the homogeneous current now. (In Europe it's usually just the opposite: an appeal to the past is needed to engage the masses, given that present-day society is rarely convincing enough to arouse even a flicker.) Besides, what the Arabs are demanding is actually so simple that the adversary—which here in Palestine is England and Zionism—can't mobilize enough long-term opposition to silence the desires and forces involved. It's so simple it's spread from person to person with wondrous directness—so simple that no one, from child to elder, needs any reactionary incitement to support it and further it unchanged. I see no inner corruption in these instinctive people. It is hardly possible to stand still—every occasion rather serves to send the forces surging forward. What do you call people for whom everything in life only unifies them more?

You can surely call them blessed. The Arabs are blessed. But that, finally, is because they haven't fled from the blessings that are the due of all. No sins, be they ever so plentiful, can mount to the lofty plane of blessing.

22 April

There is an entrance into one side of the Old City through the short wide tower of David's fortress. A stone bridge with a number of steps arches over the ditch to the gate. Every day almost I see a motionless Bedouin up on the top of the bridge. It's always a different one. They seem to rendezvous here, when they've been out in the city for a time on some lone business. Today I saw one silhouetted, against the silver-grey sky, like a mythical apparition. He was tall and, like all Bedouins, strong-boned and lean. His face, with its jutting cheekbones and short red-blond beard, was filled with an accumulated gravity, sad and resigned, waiting yet expecting nothing. His 'abayah, that long brown and white striped robe, was threadbare, and, it seemed to me—I don't know why—worn out from some long flight. He was like one of David's generals, when David, with a small handful of men, fled before the mad hatred of his king Saul. Perhaps David was sleeping somewhere in the Judaean wilderness, and this man, this true and brave friend, had stolen here with a companion to sound out Saul's mood. Now he was waiting for that companion, evidently filled with a dark foreboding. He'll have no good news for David. Suddenly I realize: this man here is a Bedouin, and those other people—they were Jews! It seems to me—though I speak as a Jew myself—that the Jews of today (even the eastern ones) are much further from their own ancestral nature, from their nature in David's time, than the Bedouins are.

What a paradox Zionism is! Either the old Jewish nature lost its capacity to re-awaken in the Diaspora—and that certainly couldn't be done through the kind of European casuistry, new minted and pretty shallow, that modern Zionism represents—or else (the second possibility) we acknowledge the Jewish nature of today and yesterday, the Jewish social situation of today and yesterday, as that which is organic and given, and seek to construct from this a healthy Jewish reality. Then, though, every "historical claim," every sentimentally stressed "Palestine policy," simply falls by the wayside. Such an "alternative choice" is of course mere fantasy, for life actually concerns itself only with things that are organic and given.

26 April

A move. From the Arab house to a Jewish house. And this time they're Jews from Bukhara. There are many of their kind here in Jerusalem; they even have their own quarter in the northwest of the new city. (They wandered here more than twenty years ago, after Tsarist Russia's hatred for Jews was extended to Central Asia.) A large oil painting hangs in the family's living room—of an old man in a long robe of gold brocade and a red silk turban; at his breast he has a yellow rose. He is the father of the lady of the house, and was minister to the Bukhara Khans. Because Judaism was officially banned in the country, he made a pretence—like many other Jews—of being Muslim, attending the mosque on Fridays and drinking no wine. It was a similar situation to that of the Marranos in Spain, who became outwardly Christian under pressure from the Inquisition, while keeping an inner profession of their faith. The Khan of Bukhara was well aware of the true facts, but, not inquiring too closely into the conscience of his minister, valued him as a skillful human being. My hostess brought her father's state robes out from a cupboard. Plenty of other colorful clothes came out too, and so I saw, for the first time, the authentic old Bukhara textiles.

An age-old handicraft tradition. So perfectly executed it seemed to me impossible anything could match it. They weren't just flamboyant dress clothes; there were women's housedresses, men's holiday clothes, clothes for every purpose, for men and women and for every day. Cheerfully bright silk damask with entwined turquoise-blue flowers and golden leaves, scarlet silk stricken with stripes of bright red color, a woman's dress in chamois and cherry red, with vertical stripes as wide as a person's hand, a cream-colored stripe followed by a cherry one, and this last composed of tiny, innumerable tea roses that merged one into the next. A balance of unbroken, delicate tints. The kind of thing European professional art might gradually come to dream of—to dream of before it actually produced it. And here—everything in sovereign perfection and simplicity.

27 April

In front of the house is a large garden with tall fir trees. The walled and lockable openings to the cisterns are on a stone terrace, and they fill themselves with rainwater during the winter, then become the focus of survival itself in the warm dry season. Morning and evening, the women come out from the front part of the house—usually it is the lady of the house herself or her daughter—and draw water from the well in pails on long ropes. The woman potters about, disheveled, in her Bukharan housedress, which she lifts up on one side. Actually, the dress seems short enough; she does it just to lend her hands, which would prefer to be idle and enjoy a soft life, a certain hold on things. She has splendid dreamy eyes, black and laughing, that miss nothing.

There are so many differences among the Jews living here, but the ones from Bukhara, and especially the women, have something that might be singled out as "typically" eastern Jewish. In fact, it is simply that a pronounced distinctive quality is apparent among Bukharans and European eastern Jews alike, and this gives the impression of a collective archetype. The women of Bukhara, with their finely chiseled features, and their dark black hair and eyes, are beautiful in a striking and extraordinary way. They are lovely, because there is such great warmth and goodness spread over their strong, downy faces, because there is, in their movements, so much that is abiding, such inner peace, of the kind you sense at night sometimes in a barn full of sleeping animals. Today a Persian Jew came here too, a wandering cobbler. His eyes were like no others, smiling yet child-like (though children never smile like this—only men who are like children). From the midst of a burdened life, with no desire for leisure, he carried with him a quiet cheerfulness and a small, bright sphere of awareness. His piety was goodness, as if he spoke from God.

29 April

The priests are teeming in the streets of Jerusalem. Roman, Greek Orthodox, Armenian, Armenian Catholic, Protestant, Coptic, Syrian, Maronite. And apart from the brown habits of the Franciscans and Capuchins, everything is black, with a boundless, pointed pathos. Then there are the Hasidics and Sephardics, with turbans or fox fur hats, in black silk caftans and white stockings, or in white Tunisian robes and buckled shoes; old and young. From all these lives surges envy and voracious intolerance, like a poisonous breath; a longing for terror. They are, it seems to me, all on a chase, as if to murder the good Spirit in a hateful and suspicious cause. An insane city.

1 May

The Arab quarters, the Jewish quarters, the Greek and Armenian quarters in the Old City—this, for me, is Jerusalem. Above the steeply rising, stepped alleys the walls of the houses are locked together in a madcap tune; it takes its cue from life, from life alone. This life is still closed in on itself, not released and opened out to freedom; here there are too many clashing trends, inimical in their outer form. But as in political life the world over, as in art, as in revolution, the outer event (in art, the work; in revolution, the deed) has here a merely documentary sense, manifesting the condition of humankind, and of time, as against the Absolute Spirit. To arrive at the true value of an event, we should perhaps confine ourselves to tracing the "things between" that are imponderable and also sublime beyond the reach of skepticism; revealing as this does, at times, an irritable, wary tolerance within the framework of customary life. These things are elements of a second, mostly concealed conscious existence. Can one grasp them, take hold of them? Not really. And yet they are nothing less than the powerful spirit of life. An example comes to mind. In our purely human lives, it is not the formal "actions" of perfect spirits that have a positive effect, but rather the delicate, perfect way these spirits touch upon the world as a coherent whole; the "actions" are simply flung down, mere symbols for what is ineffable. And so "reality" will find its "real" exactly in these "things between."

6 May

Once more I make a discovery that had already emerged in Jerusalem, then fled away: here I am at the center of the world. Not because in this land Christ lived, preached, and was killed on the cross, nor because the story of my people, the Jewish people, had its beginning here, before maturing then crumbling, both in harsh circumstances. There is another reason. Here I am at the center of the world because in Arab life I hear the hum of the present as nowhere else. True it is that things acquire their worth mostly through the meaning they hold for a particular person. In the present fullness of this Arab people, and also in myself who perceives it—in this, now and for this one moment, lies the center of the world.

Jerusalem, 8 May

In my hands I held a container, an earthenware basin of unique festive design, large and circular, like a smooth flattened sphere. From the delicate rounding of its sides, two handles curved up into the air— molded by hand; in the clay I could still see the fingerprint of a primitive potter. Around the curved inward edge he had dug a fine-lined arabesque. And he had, I saw, made no effort to lay claim to this quite splendid simplicity. For it was a cooking pot. A pot of the kind the fellahin and Bedouin use everywhere. I know the Greeks achieved perfection before, very likely in cooking pots too. But we today, we know we shall never make such pots—as compensation, we refer to our "cultural level." Herein, of course, lies a misconception; for what European life accomplishes on a daily basis—that is not spoken of as "European culture." Awareness of our "cultural level" is based, commonly, on the heights of creative inspiration found in particular individuals, on a hundred selected peaks. Thus it may happen that our spiritual life fails to suffuse our daily life, and that we lose connection with ourselves and with one another. But they, the Arabs, have a common "level." It is the delightful grace that speaks from their blood and in their gestures, in word and inclination—in all the things in which reality lies. But true reality means to touch upon one another; which means, too, that our bitter solitude has stayed far from these people. Blessed is the people that cooks its daily food in pots like these.

9 May

Last night—all night long in fact—the Bukharan family held some kind of family worship, a memorial service for the father of the master or lady of the house—I'm not quite sure which. Many friends came by for it; all were Bukharan Jews, beautifully and festively dressed. The old women bore themselves like Asian queen mothers in their colorful robes, severe, serious, reserved, with white or brocade scarves wound around their heads like turbans. There was an old man, aged and shrunken, bent and supported by a cane, with a small blue cap embroidered with gold on his head. He wore a white satin robe with long, wide, rose-colored stripes, and on his feet were soft black leather slippers over yellow stockings.

They prayed and sang all night long, loudly, with hymns, but more wildly, in less restrained fashion, than other Jews. When it grew very late, the women went off to sleep. From the ground floor window in the yard I could see the whole room. It was laid only with carpets; on the floor in one corner stood a kerosene lamp, and close by a cooled-off copper samovar. The women slept in their clothes on the soft carpets, loosely stretched out close to one another, right and left, throughout the room in every direction. By the dim glow of the lamp I saw their colorful flowing garments, like a pond strewn with blossom, and the face of the eldest among them was bronzed with age, calm and peaceful. The white strands of hair flowing out from beneath the shifted headscarf gave her the look of the primal mother of an Indian race.

11 May

Ramadan. The holy fasting month of Ramadan will soon be at an end. What a happy thought, in a month of harsh discipline, to have the "night of power" in which Muhammad received the first revelation of the Qur'an. (The Prophet spoke thus: "The worship of limbs leads on to the worship of souls… "). From break of day till the fall of evening neither food nor drink can be consumed—for thirty whole days. They all walk around with glowing eyes; they have the elastic sense of being lifted up to the holy—for thirty whole days. You hear the firing of small mortar rounds, music, and joyful shouting in the thirty nights. During the days, the Arab streets of the Old City are thickly decorated with pepper tree branches and paper streamers.

12 May

(From a conversation with Musa Kasim Pasha, leader of the Arab movement in Palestine.) "Palestine is an Arab country. We shall never relinquish this right, or come to any agreement to divide it with other peoples. It is out of the question for a nation that has lived in, occupied, a land for hundreds of years to consider any historical claim from another nation that goes back thousands of years. We want to be free. Every Arab child grows up with one thought: freedom. We want to be neither a Jewish homeland nor an English colony—and attempts geared towards one or other of these (or indeed both together) will win no constructive cooperation from us. Our struggle is not against Judaism, but against political Zionism—and it is the fault of the Zionists if, today, the ordinary man sees Jews and Zionists as one and the same, and hatred is hurled against everything Jewish. Before the war, before political Zionism, there was no friction here in Palestine between Arab and Jewish elements. And for the future too our goal is a free Palestine, in which every race, every religion, enjoys equal rights. Even Jewish immigration will find no obstacles laid in its path, as long as this does not clash with the country's economic interests; permission or refusal for individual immigrants to take the rights of Palestinian citizenship will be subject to the pronouncement of a national assembly. Today, we know, we are still in the first stages of development. And we know too that we have to deal not just with the Zionists but with England. That makes things considerably harder for us, but doesn't, even so, rule out our prospects—for we believe in the intrinsic justice of our cause."

I come to this from another source. In the period straight after the announcement of the Balfour Declaration (up to about a year ago) the Zionists dispensed unheard-of sums in an attempt to win over at least part of the Arab population and so prevent the world from hearing the words: "Palestine is an Arab country!" This latter was the case anyway, for Arabs have no means of spreading propaganda in other countries and successfully combating the tendentious Zionist news services. But the first—Arab–Zionist co-operation—never succeeded. A then highly influential Zionist politician (formerly private secretary to Baron James Rothschild) did indeed found a "Muslim National Party," which was designed to show that large sections of the Arab population were ready to work positively on the basis of the Balfour Declaration. The party members (who were actually few in number) received payment from the Zionist treasury, in amounts that bore no relation whatever to the laughably meager success of the initiative as a whole. Now the Zionists have no more money to pay such sums to any newspapers and personalities that might approach them. And so these matters have gradually come to light.

13 May

(From a conversation with Lord Ussyskin, Chairman of the Zionist Action Committee in Palestine.) "How does Zionism, in the fulfillment of its programs, hope to overcome the political obstacles (i.e., the Arab counter-movement)? There is no Arab movement here that has its roots in the people. What appears as such can be traced back to the purely personal actions of a number of malcontent agitators; and this 'movement' will sooner or later collapse." It is marvelous how closely these words correspond to those of a British politician with whom I had a conversation, eight weeks ago in Cairo, about the Egyptian National Movement.

16 May

Now, however, the Arab Federation has come into being—provisionally, that is, on paper, in London. But being merely "on paper" is no hindrance to such a sound movement. We should not, even so, delude ourselves: the form in which this has occurred makes it still far distant from the realization of Arab wishes. It remains essentially a federation within the sphere of British influence and involving a particular royal family: for the father, Hussein (head of the projected Union) is King of Hijaz and Grand Sharif of Makkah; his younger, favorite son, Faisal, King of Iraq; and Abdullah, the older son,

Emir of Transjordan. We should probably not overestimate Hussein's influence among the Arabs; the agreement now finalized between him and England, and the union of the three territories—Hijaz, Iraq, and Transjordan (Kerak)—under Makkah's hegemony, will not for the foreseeable future be seen as a legally valid transaction between the Arabs and the west. It is untrustworthy—for people are all too aware of Hussein's friendly personal feelings towards England. But the first step has, nevertheless, been taken, and it is possible that the other Arab states—Asir, Yemen, perhaps even Najd—will join. The last-named will, though, only do so on certain conditions, which would necessarily rule out any "overlordship" on Hussein's part.

There are rumors circulating that Emir Abdullah is to become king of a united... Trans-Jordanian entity. Unlikely. The Zionists are naturally in the greatest agitation over any such notion—especially as Abdullah is now very much seen by Palestinian Arabs (the Muslims, that is, not the Christians) as the head of the national movement in Palestine.

18 May

Sometimes one sees black Bedouins in the street here: blacks who have, from time immemorial, been like free Bedouins in dress and custom, living among these latter as a separate race almost, but enjoying their full rights. It's remarkable: the proud B'dui despises the Europeans, despises the Turks (even though these are Muslims too)—and accepts the black, who, among Caucasian peoples, is mostly regarded as second-class. Racial confusion or democracy? These blacks, though, are free and proud.

21 May

As if from an alchemist's alembic, an oscillating mixture, clear, and yet of a thousand undefined colors, untouchable, indescribable—this is how you see the Jordan Valley and the Dead Sea from the Mount of Olives. Waves and waves of mountains, silhouettes, breathtaking and delicate, in an air filled with secrets. Far back the deep blue line of the Jordan and the rim of the Sea, and, beyond that, another world in itself, the dusky mountains of Moab. This landscape is made up of such unbelievable, multi-faceted beauty the mind cannot grasp it. It moves, celestially, over and away from you, troubling your soul....

23 May

... It's noon. I'm lying on a balcony overlooking the Old City and listening to the muffled blend of sounds in its streets. Before me, in the gallery of a minaret near the greenish dome of the Church of the Holy Sepulcher, a muezzin is singing his melancholy call to prayer, sensitive and inviting. I can see him clearly; he is bony and still young; and he sings well. Below in the yard, a camel calls—his call is like the roar of a legendary giant stag in the forest. It's noon, rest without haste. Someone is singing an Arabic song in the alleyways; I recognize the voice. I know this beggar, I love her old, broad Madonna's face, blind and painfully enraptured. As if bewitched, flocks of swallows wheel in great circles around the flat roofs and domes, flying in the midst of all these yellowish-white speckled buildings of stone, through the blinding light that shines around the gigantic courtyard of 'Umar's Mosque, flying over the hidden, humming alleys that rise in their steps, narrow as corridors.

The noon is quiet, even though bells are ringing. I said once that a person couldn't love this city. But maybe you could, if you could see it like this from above and think of its deepest, most living presence; there, where it isn't the "Holy City" but the precious Today. And as far as I'm concerned, that singing muezzin could belong to it, along with the Church of the Holy Sepulcher with its splendid bells; and so, even, could various others—as far as I'm concerned, the black-robed priests and the colorful rabbis too—if only the camel that's roaring down there, and that excellent water carrier in the street, weren't cheated of their rightful equality.

25 May

England's position vis-à-vis eastern socialism is clear to me now, and it doesn't surprise me. It's just the level of fear that's unusual. I spoke about it with a high-ranking English official, who'd taken me into his friendship and revealed various things that weren't supposed to be revealed. He told me, "in deepest confidence" (to break it appeared to me a self-evident responsibility), that the notion of latitude for socialism in England, but not in the colonies, has now become a "golden rule" throughout administrative offices in London. Confidential circulars urge that socialist tendencies should be combated by whatever means necessary; and carrying out these orders involves a whole separate espionage organization ("Intelligence"), which has its agents and informants at every level of the population, in Palestine and Egypt alike; any sixteen-year-old schoolboy showing "Bolshevik" inclinations is taken as a sign of some established tendency. And what's more, concern isn't just over hard-line communism but over any kind of trade union and party political labor organization.

With a view to paralyzing such initiatives, preferential treatment is given to the orthodox, religious-Zionist Mizrahi labor group. The perception reigns in Jerusalem government circles that the revolutionary currents of the Near East have their center in Moscow. This is a total misconception. There are scarcely any groups and committees here that receive money from foreign sources and use it to spread communist propaganda in the countryside; indeed, if you look closer at the size and distribution of these groups, it's clear they represent no "vital threat"—they're too unimportant and have no real impact. And yet, England's afraid. And maybe not without reason. For a curious parallel is emerging between the Arab and eastern national movements and the external political arms of the Russian revolution. It's not, as the English regularly claim, a question of influence from Moscow; rather the independent, not infrequently anti-communist Arab movements are visibly striving for the same aims as those of the Russian revolution—for this too implies no more than the will of the world to emerge somehow from the played-out, stifling power groupings, towards positive development—to find some way of taking control of the here and now. Taking control of the here and now. It's not so very far away for the Arabs. Perhaps they have to strive just a little more, and they'll grasp it....

27 May

I'm beginning, too, to understand how England's fears of "socialist," "disruptive" tendencies in the east, and the way it combats them, reflects a weakening of the old political instinct. The continuance of the British empire isn't threatened by some social revolution—which is too immature here, by far—but simply by the national revolution of the eastern peoples. It was the World War that stirred and awakened spirits in the East, showed them a way, and a tempo, to emerge from a maelstrom of present possibilities that were unthinkable only yesterday. The Arabs, with their keen, hard-headed, instinctive confidence, quickly learned to walk the new road; they had, from olden times, made an unambiguous maxim their own: "division of strength means surrender from the start." All they want is what lies straight ahead: independence. And that requires all available strength.

By and large the English occupation policy in Palestine is moderate and not at all party political: it simply involves playing Zionism off against the Arab movement, and vice versa. Since there has to date been no incidence of English violence, and since England, for its part, repeatedly insists it is merely here to fulfill the terms of its League of

Nations mandate, the "Tommies" are nowhere near as hated as they are in Egypt. (And in any case these are mostly Indian troops, with English and Irish units carrying out police duties.) Finally the Arabs of this country have, over the years, had no such experiences of the English as the Egyptians have. Moreover, in the north, in Syria, they see the harsh French "bayonet-terror" and are indirectly grateful (if one can use the word) to the English for the "tolerance" they see in contrast to matters there. Nevertheless, the knowledge that England fostered the Balfour Declaration releases a much sharper opposition than a straightforward English colonial policy could ever have done. Zionism appears to the Arabs as a symbol of the western will for power.

31 May

Will Zionism die soon? Whatever the answer may be, one thing is certain: it is not alive today. Not here. It has not died indeed; no violent end—from without or within—has been put to the living organism. But the organism lacks the essential breath, which instills life and is life itself. In a kind of oppressive, dusty atmosphere, one minute slides into the next, one hour into the next, one day into the next—this is the sad drama of Jewish Palestine today. Nothing fulfills, everything disappoints. The fiction that "new life blossoms from the ruins" will preserve its resonance only outside the country; here it represents, at best, hope for an uncertain future. And it is hard to feel any pity for this striving, which seems now to have sunk into terminal disillusion; so strongly does the realization crowd in that something false has been unleashed here, on the basis of false suppositions.

Will Zionism die soon? The Arabs fervently wish it so; they will never pardon it for handing English policy the pretext for making Palestine a de facto colony of the British Crown. On the other hand, the leaders of the Zionist movement know well enough how they are basically serving a foreign power in order to subjugate a third nation; and in the light of this they willingly renounce their own nation's sovereignty for the foreseeable future; herein lies the fiasco, the self-condemnation of the movement. And yet the English are slowly dropping Zionism. Not explicitly, for there is the League of Nations to consider, and the Mandate, and the Balfour Declaration—an ethical mantle of such international importance isn't relinquished just like that. Still, you can note, right here in Jerusalem, a change in the British tactical attitude vis-à-vis the Zionist problem, a kind of lukewarm, undeclared, latent refusal—accompanied by a veering (equally lukewarm and equally undeclared) towards an Arab realpolitik. Not indeed with any thought of Arab rights; rather, England will be for the Arabs, so that, should things turn dangerous, they will not have to be against them.

But the Balfour Declaration—the promise to the Jewish nation—will this promise be thrown over too? Impossible. The Balfour Declaration will never be revoked. Even if one day it were to be tossed out of the sphere of practical politics, it would still find a quiet de jure existence in the midst of so many other obsolete statutes and programs, for in England laws are not easily revoked. And this international gesture, this Declaration for a "human civilization," will reveal its advantages. It will be on hand when, one day, it is worthwhile to play a trump card against the Palestinian Arabs. The need for this will be frequent over the coming years. For Palestine—this is the be all and end all—represents the eastern bank of the Suez Canal. (And herein lies the rationale for an Arab Confederation under the auspices of Downing Street—for Arab lands do, after all, lie to the east of the Suez Canal...)

6 June
The part around the Damascus Gate is the most Arab of all Jerusalem. While the Levant shows its unmistakable colors in the other parts of the Old City, here life is thoroughly Arab. Sometimes I sit on one of the tiny stools by the wall of an Arab café and watch the purity and grace of this life. Fellahin from the country pass, strong-boned and with heavy step, with their loaded donkeys and mules. The train of a long Bedouin robe trails majestically through the dust of the street; and at times one sees these proud men accompanied by an exquisitely beautiful woman, who, showing her slender-featured face (for only in the city women are required to wear the veil), passes a cold glance over you as a foreigner. A food seller offers me his pilaf, the Arab-Turkish rice dish. I eat without concern from his common dishes, common for all the world, and don't feel any of the disgust which, in a similar situation in Europe (in Leipzig, say), would overwhelm me; for the grace of these Arab people is evident in everything they do—and grace is never dirty.

[After his time in Jerusalem, Leopold Weiss traveled on to other parts of the Middle East, which he recorded in detail in his travelogue.]

DIASPORA, STEP BY STEP

Ibtisam Barakat

A man from Palestine,
Who has lived for forty years
Away from his home, tells me:

I used to be able
To close my eyes
And count the steps
Of any street
In the old city of Jerusalem.

They were the wrinkles
On the face of my old city,
Inside of which I had a place.

I used to be able
To clench my eyes
And visit my old household
Inside the old city of Jerusalem.

Now, my eyes are failing.
My memories are fainting.
And the roads are blocked;
I do not dare.

But his last word about daring
Suddenly breathed defiance
Into his face.

He locked his hands;
Looked up at me,
And his eyes blinked rapidly
And brushed my face.

Perhaps I can return
One more time
To that beloved place.

Remember Salah Eddin street?
The vendors with round sesame cake and
Falafel?[1]
The semi terrace
Facing the entrance to Bab al-'Amoud?[2]

Hurry up! let us go
Sit on the steps,
And see who's there.

Now looking at Bab al-'Amoud
Through his words,
Our eyes entered a square
A frame of a living picture
Where all things
Could oddly melt
And pass through with grace.

I see them now
In October, he says.
My grand-mom
And the village women
Wearing embroidered dresses,
Sitting on the ground
Selling figs and pears.

The shoeless boys
Selling combs, key chains, and chewing gum
In and out of the frame.
The money changers
Speaking tens of tongues
That only money
Could readily translate.

And priests, in ink-like garments
And processions

And high-horsed soldiers
On their daily crusades.

They all pass through the gate
With a kiss on their fingertips
As they turn the page
And take their turn
In the torn-up book of history
Of my old city of Jerusalem.

I used to close my eyes
And be able to count its steps
Even on rainy days.

But now my heart
Cannot hold its history
And its beat
Cannot knock at the gates.

And my hands
Cannot reach my chest
And enter the purse
In which I'd stored
The number of the steps
In each street
Of my old Jerusalem

And the feel of wrinkles
Of its old face
Inside which
I had a place.

JERUSALEM SUNFLOWER

Saleh Abudayyeh

Her land was occupied
Roots were exposed
Name demonized
Mouth gagged
Dreams
Were jailed
But she countered
    With one brilliant smile.

Smile—the secret of her might
And when the oppressor
Came with a bulldozer,
And a compressor
To crush,
Her seeds
Source of power,
And her prayer beads,
She continued to shine—
Her right.
    Will he see the light?

CITY OF OLIVE BRANCHES

Nizar Qabbani

I wept
Until every tear had dried

I prayed
Until every candle had melted

I asked
About Muhammad within your walls

I begged news
Of Jesus in your street

O Jerusalem!
Swiftest path between heaven and earth

O Jerusalem

City of sorrow
Swollen teardrop brimming in the eyes

Who can prevent
Atrocities at your holy gates?

Jerusalem
My city!

Tomorrow
Orange blossoms will flower again

Tomorrow
Wheat will fatten, olives will fruit

Tomorrow
Laughter will ring out once more

Tomorrow
Doves will return to the blessed rooftops

Tomorrow
Children will take up their games

Tomorrow
Fathers and sons will meet again

Jerusalem
City of olive branches

Jerusalem
City of peace!

ISLAMIC ARCHITECTURAL CHARACTER OF JERUSALEM: WITH SPECIAL DESCRIPTION OF THE AL-AQSA AND THE DOME OF THE ROCK

Ra'ef Najm

> *Let my heart burn*
> *A candle of love*
> *At al-Aqsa Gate.*
> —Hydar Mahmoud

There are general basic principles that govern the construction of the Islamic city, irrespective of time and place. There are also special technical, social, and environmental characteristics that are liable to vary according to time and locality. In the holy city of Jerusalem these latter characteristics seem prevalent, and the fundamental link with its religious identity, with the Mosque at the core, is predominant. The al-Aqsa Mosque was in fact the principal focus in planning the enlargement of the city following the Muslim rule in Jerusalem. To this must be added harmony with the environment, a general spirituality, and a simplicity of planning suggesting tranquility and architectural beauty. It has been said that Almighty God divided beauty into ten equal parts, nine of which He bestowed on Jerusalem, leaving the remaining tenth to the rest of the world.

One of the essential features of the character and identity of Jerusalem is the way it maintains its constituent parts, which are inextricably linked with the mores, traditions, and culture of its Arab inhabitants. These parts comprise, *inter alia*, the compact residential quarters and the major conveniences and facilities, such as markets, mosques, schools, sports grounds, and health services, which are inseparably tied to the residential quarters themselves. Moreover, Jerusalem's cultural, environmental, and architectural heritage is established in such a way as to ensure that no alien element can infiltrate or intrude into its harmony, and no parts of the heritage can be removed without leaving a gaping hole. This legacy is subject to a continuous process of repair and restoration.

When speaking of the al-Aqsa Mosque as a main focal point of the city of Jerusalem, we mean specifically the Holy Haram (sanctuary) with its two main components: the al-Aqsa Mosque and the Dome of the Rock, both of which lie within the area inside the walls of the Haram. The city is surrounded by a high stone wall with seven open gates: Herod's Gate, St. Stephen's Gate, the Damascus Gate, the New Gate, the Jaffa Gate, the Zion Gate, and the Maghareba Gate. There are four further closed gates: the Single Gate, the Double Gate, the Triple Gate, and the Golden Gate.

The Holy Haram, for its part, is encircled by a stone wall with three gates opening to the north: the Lion's Gate, the Faysal or al-'Item Gate, and the Huttah or Remission Gate. Seven gates open to the west: the Ghawanmeh Gate, the Nazer Gate, the Iron Gate, the Qattanin Gate, the Silsilah Gate, the Magarbeh Gate and the Matharah (ablution) Gate. The Haram is connected to the rest of the city by streets branching out from its ten gates and extending throughout the various parts, which have different functions to perform. It should be noted, in this context, that the different topographic levels within the city have not deterred the city's planners and designers. The obstacle has been surmounted through the use of broad and convenient flights of steps taking people from one level to another. The roads of the Holy City, characterized by their narrowness, were designed for pedestrian use only. Some, but not all, are roofed with beautiful stone vaults dating back to the medieval Islamic eras. Schools, residential homes, *zawiyah*s, and drinking fountains were built on both sides of the roads. The stone vaults have stone buildings overlooking the road, with windows and small, latticed oriels or *mashrabiyyah*s. This method of utilizing narrow roads provides pedestrians with comfortable shade, alleviates heat, and protects walkers from the sun, especially in summer. This is in fact a distinctive feature of historical Islamic cities.

The roads allocated as trading centers form an open expanse to facilitate interconnection between these centers and the markets. In contrast, some residential quarters end in cul-de-sacs, giving the quarter a sense of individuality and independence. One can traverse all the roads of Holy Jerusalem in a short time, meeting one's needs and performing all errands on foot, without becoming tired or bored. This is due to sound city planning, applying the correct methods of Islamic architecture and abiding by human scales. All the buildings of Jerusalem are of stone. Lime mortar was used in the construction, cement being unknown. Stone, mortar, and lime were used in the construction of domes and vaults. The windows were small and cut into thick walls to secure ventilation and lighting, while keeping out direct sunlight. Some buildings overlook the road through beautifully wrought wooden latticed oriels that help ventilate the houses. They also enable people to sit and watch the road without being exposed to the gaze of passers-by. The buildings are set compactly together, which gives Jerusalem the appearance of a single, interlinked building—and this, in turn, forms the tightly interlaced, serene, and beautiful texture of the city. The simplicity of house design is manifest in the open inner courtyard, which is the most important and distinctive quality of Islamic architecture. One may add here that the wholeness of engineering design, its simplicity and functionality, and the use of local construction materials, effective ventilation, and uniformity of building in the Holy City are all important basics of Islamic architecture. Jerusalem enjoyed this tranquil architectural character until the Israeli occupation of the city, when the Israelis embarked on a transformation of its beautiful architectural image and texture. They have dealt irreversible blows and traumatic wounds to the city's fine structure; more especially, they have constructed ugly high-rise buildings adjacent to the Holy Haram, higher than the Haram and overlooking it, whereas before the Haram had overlooked everything around it.

The Blessed al-Aqsa Mosque

"Mounts are saddled to three mosques only: the Holy Mosque of Makkah, this Mosque of mine [the Prophet's Mosque in Madinah] and the al-Aqsa Mosque," said Prophet Muhammad (peace be on him).[1]

The first builder of the Blessed al-Aqsa Mosque was Caliph 'Umar ibn al-Khattab (r. 13–23/634–644), when the keys of Jerusalem were handed over to him in 15/636. It was erected at the front of the place from which Prophet Muhammad (peace be on him) had made his miraculous night journey from Makkah to Jerusalem (the event known as the Isra'). The original al-Aqsa could accommodate three thousand worshippers, but within a few decades it had been destroyed by earthquakes. It was then rebuilt by the Umayyad Caliph 'Abd al-Malik ibn Marwan (r. 65–85/685–704) in 73/692, and completed by his son and successor al-Walid (r. 85–96/704–715) in 86/705, on the same site of the Mosque of Caliph 'Umar ibn al-Khattab. The Mosque is about 80 meters (263 ft) long and nearly 55 meters (181 ft) in width, and is erected on 53 marble columns and 49 square stone pillars. When they occupied Jerusalem, the Crusaders converted part

of the al-Aqsa into a church, making the other part a residence for
their Knights Templar and a store for their munitions. Salah al-Din (r.
564–589/ 1168–1193), however, repaired the Mosque, renovated the
mihrab (prayer niche), covered the dome with mosaic, and brought
from Aleppo the wooden *minbar* (pulpit) made of cedar and ebony
wood and inlaid with ivory. This he placed in the Mosque as a symbol
of victory.

The al-Aqsa Mosque highlights the beauty of Islamic decoration,
as represented by the internal wooden dome, which is covered with
relief plant drawings made of gypsum, by beautiful gilded coloring,
and by windows made of wood and gypsum engraved in slanted lines
on a base of colored glass to keep out direct sunlight. These windows
bestow splendor and beauty upon the place, and are suggestive of
sanctity and spirituality. The Mosque consists of seven longitudinal
porticoes extending from north to south. On the left wall one finds the
Mosque of 'Umar, the Niche of Zakariyya and the Shrine of the Forty.
The main gate is installed at the entrance of the middle portico from
the north. The ceilings are decorated with colored gypsum. The Surah
al-Isra', inlaid with mosaic, is superimposed over the niche to a length
of 23 meters (76 ft).

The Holy Dome of the Rock
Date of Construction
The Holy Dome of the Rock was built by the Umayyad Caliph 'Abd
al-Malik ibn Marwan, who entrusted two of his men with the task:
one was Raja' ibn Hayat ibn Jud al-Kindi, the other Yazid ibn Salam,
a freedman of the Caliph. Building began in 66/685 and was
completed in 72/691. First they constructed the Silsilah Dome to the
east of the Holy Dome of the Rock; then they built the Dome of the
Rock itself. The Silsilah Dome is said to be a model for the Holy
Dome of the Rock; but this is at variance with the facts, for the Silsilah
Dome is hexagonal, the Dome of the Rock octagonal.

Why Was the Holy Dome of the Rock Built?
Whatever may be said of 'Abd al-Malik ibn Marwan's aim in erecting
this edifice, there is no doubt that he consulted Muslims before
embarking on the project. Accounts of historians conflict, however, as
to the responses he received. It is said that when he decided to build
the Dome of the Rock he came from Damascus to Jerusalem and sent
letters to his viceroys in the provinces, writing that he wished to build

a Dome above the Rock to shelter Muslims from heat and cold, but that, before doing so, he preferred to know the viewpoints and attitudes of his subjects. Replies came to him as follows: The Prince of the Faithful [the Caliph] is right in wishing to do this. We wish him all success, and beseech Almighty God to enable him to erect His House and Mosque, and earnestly entreat Him to make this edifice a grace bestowed upon the Caliph and a memorial to his predecessors. Certain philosophical trends were reflected in building this Dome, as in setting the geographical location over the Mi'raj (ascension to heaven) Rock. Further artistic trends were taken into account, namely the choice of the octagonal shape and the double central dome.

Dimensions of the Holy Rock

According to Mr. K. A. C. Creswell, in his book *The Dome of the Rock*, those who built the Holy Dome of the Rock benefited from the measurements of the Church of the Holy Sepulcher. The internal diameter of the Dome of the Rock is 20.3 meters (66.6 ft) and its height 20.48 meters (67.2 ft), while the internal diameter of the Church of the Holy Sepulcher is 20.9 meters (68.6 ft) and its height 21.05 meters (69.1 ft). The octagonal shape of the Dome of the Rock is also similar to that of certain significant Byzantine buildings. It is superimposed by a cylinder with 16 windows, while the cylinder itself is supported by four props and twelve pillars arranged in circular fashion around the Mi'raj Rock. The external side of the octagon is 20.6 meters (67.6 ft) long, paralleled on the inside by another octagonal structure, each side of which is 14.45 meters (47.4 ft) long. There are 40 columns total inside the building, and it has four outer gates. This architectural device reflects a design unmatched in Islamic architecture; it has symmetry, homogeneity, and engineering fineness, and of course the study of light that filters down on the Mi'raj Rock from the upper windows. In this context, we read in *Al-Uns al-Jalil bi Ta'rikh al-Quds wa'l-Khalil by Mujir al-Din al-Hanbali* (10th century AH/16th century CE) that Jerusalem had three jewels: the al-Aqsa Mosque, the Dome of the Rock, and the Ashrafiyyah school. Thus the Holy Dome of the Rock is the second jewel of Jerusalem. According to historians and archeologists, the Holy Dome of the Rock is one of the finest buildings ever built by man, its beauty and splendor being beyond description. Creswell follows his profound study of the building's architecture by noting that the Dome of the Rock is of distinctive importance in the history of Islamic architecture; its structure, glamour, grandeur, magic, symmetry, exactitude, and precision of proportion have dazzled all the scientists and researchers who have attempted to study it.

Internal and External Decoration

The internal decoration of this historic monument is distinguished by its mosaic works, which reflect the most beautiful decors of the Umayyad period, notably the strip extending along the upper internal part of the eight walls to a length of 240 meters (788 ft). The strip comprises Umayyad Kufic calligraphy in gilt mosaic on a dark blue background. As for external decoration, this used to include parts made of marble and mosaic. In 960/1552 Sultan Sulayman al-Qanuni (r. 926–974/1520–1566) replaced the mosaic with glazed earthenware superimposed by Qur'anic writings. The four outer gates were formerly decorated with mosaic, but only small remnants of this have survived at the eastern entrance. The original dome, which collapsed in the 4th/11th century, was covered with lead sheets over which 10,210 gilded copper sheets were fixed. The total area of the mosaic covering different parts inside the Holy Dome of the Rock amounts to 1,200 square meters (12,900 sq ft) and is regarded as globally unique, not only for its outstanding beauty but also on account of its Umayyad origin, which endows it with a significance all the greater in that only a limited part of this art now survives. The surviving example at the Holy Dome of the Rock has been conserved and restored throughout the ages. The predominant colors in the decoration of the Holy Dome are green, blue, and gold. The green is variegated into eight shades and the blue into six. Other colors, such as silver, were used in small areas. Mosaic decoration in the Dome of the Rock is regarded as reflecting the Syrian school of art of that time. This school was completely independent of Byzantine art, just as the Syrian architectural school was independent of the Byzantine and had roots traceable to Greek origins.

JERUSALEM AND I: A PERSONAL RECORD

Hala Sakakini

Jerusalem is my hometown. Both my parents were born in that great city, so were my grandparents on both sides, and so were seven of my great-grandparents. (My father's paternal grandmother was a Greek woman born in Istanbul.) Although I myself spent only the first twenty-four years of my life as a resident of Jerusalem, I rightly feel bound to that great city by centuries of family history. Wherever I may live, I will always remain a Jerusalemite.

My father, Khalil Sakakini, was born on January 23, 1878, of Arab parents. My mother, Sultaneh Abdo, was born on December 19, 1888, also of Arab parents. Both the Sakakinis and the Abdos lived in the Christian Quarter in the Old City and were what we call "stone neighbors" in Arabic; that is, they lived in adjacent houses. The two families were the owners of the houses they lived in, not tenants, and they had been neighbors for generations.

A major festive event was the Muslim al-Nabi Musa feast, which always coincided with the Easter Holy Week. Peasants from all over Palestine took part in it and made it most colorful. From the early morning on Palm Sunday young peasants wearing their beautiful festive attires started streaming into Jerusalem from all directions. The people from Nablus and the villages around it would enter the Old City through Damascus Gate, and those from Hebron and the villages around it would enter through Jaffa Gate, which in Arabic is called Bab al-Khalil (Hebron Gate) because of this long-standing tradition. A great procession made up of groups from the various regions of Palestine would move slowly through the streets of the city towards St. Stephen's Gate on their way to al-Nabi Musa,[1] which lies northwest of Jerusalem. On the following Thursday, the same multitudinous procession would wind its way up the hills towards Jerusalem on its way back from al-Nabi Musa. At the head of the procession would be the Mufti of Jerusalem riding a horse and carrying the banner of al-Nabi Musa. A huge crowd would have gathered just outside St. Stephen's Gate to welcome them back.

Only once in my life did I attend this exciting pageant. Again it was in the company of Aunt Melia, who had many Muslim friends.

We sat on a high spot on the slope north of St. Stephen's Gate. The place was densely crowded. Everywhere you could see the Arab flag with its green, red, white, and black colors fluttering high above the heads. The scene filled us with enthusiasm and national pride. Every now and then strong young men would link their arms together and, forming circles, would start dancing the *dabkeh* and singing. It was thrilling to watch and wonderful for the spirit. Although the Nabi Musa feast was supposed to be a religious occasion, it was in fact a national day in which all the Arabs of Palestine, Christians and Muslims alike, shared.

The new [pre-1948] residential areas in the southern part of the city[2]—Talbieh, Namamra, Katamon, Lower Baq'a were the fashionable Arab quarters. Together they formed a garden city, as they consisted mainly of villas surrounded by gardens. All houses, almost without exception, were built of stone, and the largest were two-story four-apartment buildings. A simple, modern architectural style was prevalent in the residential areas, yet every house had individuality; somehow it was marked by the personality of its owner.

The majority of the houses were built of beige or greyish stone, but among them there were quite a number of beautiful pink stone. Differences in the stone work were apparent. Some home-owners liked to have the walls of their houses finely chiselled and smooth; others preferred a more rustic effect and so their houses had rough-hewn, irregular surfaces. Skillful masonry was often manifest in the way the stones were arranged around the windows and doors and over the verandas.

Many of the one-story villas had red-tiled sloping roofs. The color of the iron shutters at the windows provided a pleasant variety; the greyish houses usually had dark green shutters, the beige houses creamish ones, and the pink houses black ones. Individual taste was also shown in the iron bars at the windows and in the banisters. In general these were simple, but here and there one could notice intricate, beautifully wrought designs, something like lattice work.

The Arab Jerusalemite has always been known as a proud person, perhaps even an arrogant person. As regards his appearance he is in general clean, neat, well-groomed, but never over-dressed or ostentatious. Just as his general looks express his personality, so also does the house he lives in. He never allows his house to dilapidate (if he can help it). Since all houses in those Arab quarters of ("West" Jerusalem) were privately owned, they were in general well looked after.

How sadly changed these Arab quarters are now! Everywhere you can see signs of neglect—the iron of the shutters, the windows and the banisters has been allowed to rust; ugly wooden or tin shacks have been put up on the balconies and the verandas to provide more living space for the new dwellers; the gardens are dry and covered with litter—all of which goes to prove that the people now occupying the houses have no sentimental attachment to them.

And what ugly, huge tenant houses have sprung up in what used to be open countryside to the south of Jerusalem. Those rolling hills once strewn with olive trees, where we used to picnic as children, have become congested areas. Immense, featureless cement structures fill the wide valley where we used to roam in spring picking red anemones. Everything now looks so disorderly, so utilitarian, so impersonal, so shabby. By putting up these houses, Israel has failed to create new neighborhoods; it has only provided new immigrants with places to dwell in.

MY CITY DENIED TO ME

'Atallah Kuttab

A few months ago I was informed by the Israeli occupation authority that my right to live in Jerusalem was to be denied. The decision was based on the premise that, since I now had a German passport and had been living for a few years outside Palestine, I was only a temporary guest in my city of birth and family history. The Israelis have unilaterally deemed that my life must be centered elsewhere, and the privilege of being considered a Jerusalemite should be withdrawn accordingly. This came after many months of writing letters, making telephone calls, and paying visits in my ongoing efforts to obtain the necessary re-entry permits, make the requisite appearances, and keep my papers in order. Try as I might, they are now attempting to deny me my city.

Yet the situation has, paradoxically, benefited, in one respect: I have more freedom to move around the whole of Palestine now, on my German passport, than I ever did as a Jerusalem resident. On a three-month tourist visa in my own country, I can go to Haifa and Nazareth and Gaza, anywhere indeed in historic Palestine, without the humiliation of waiting for days for permits to do the simplest things. I can drive anywhere and visit anyone. As a German, protected by the German state, I have more privileges in my Palestinian Jerusalem than as a Palestinian.

It is a painful dilemma to be caught between my present legal identity and my real, personal one; to have freedom, or else to give it up for the right to Jerusalem. I could never understand why it was impossible for me to have both. I shall probably never understand it, nor can I ever give up either. Such is my dilemma as a Jerusalemite.

I was born in Jerusalem in 1954, and grew up in the Christian Quarter of the Old City, just inside the New Gate, which had been sealed off since the 1948 War. I grew up amidst its corners and alleys, looking over the walls onto that strip of no-man's-land that divided the City after 1948. Mine is one of the oldest Christian families in the Old City; we have our own space in the Church of the Holy Sepulcher and our own *sanjaq* or church standard. Generation after generation we bore that *sanjaq* through all the religious holidays, all the processions, and all the dramatic events affecting the Holy City. My mother's family, the Shama's, still have their traditional compound inside the Old City walls, between the New Gate and the Jaffa Gate. We were, and still are, part of the core of the Old City's Christian Arabs. We have always felt that we were, indeed, the Old City.

During the war of 1948, the family was living in the Musrara quarter, a short distance from the Old City wall. When a Jewish barrel-bomb exploded, killing an aunt of mine, we and many others fled back into the shelter of the Old City. By virtue of making the two-hundred-meter walk from the Musrara back through the New Gate, my family became card-carrying refugees, registered with the United Nations Relief and Works Agency for Palestinian Refugees (UNRWA) and thereby eligible for rations and relief assistance. This relief proved invaluable as the economic situation steadily worsened in the ten years immediately following the war, and especially for our community, trapped as it was in the corner of the Old City Christian Quarter, far from its commercial traffic and cut off from the outside world by the sealed New Gate. It was a working class community: eight or so carpenters and woodworkers, a blacksmith, two framing shops, a print shop, and several shoemakers. Survival depended on mutual support and assistance, which came easily because of a strong sense of community that lingers in my mind to this day like innocence lost. I still hold heartfelt memories of people, places, and events, of smells and sounds, of help mutually and gladly offered and received. The community took care of its own, in sickness and health, applying its own traditional methods when modern means were unavailable. Although we were dependent on UNRWA rations for some time, it was not unusual for us to have as many as 30 people at dinner, especially when my uncle's family moved in with us for a time. Our immediate family of seven was of modest means. We lived in three rooms opening on to a courtyard. We, along with many of our neighbors, could not even afford electricity, let alone television and telephones. Night lighting was provided by kerosene lanterns and candles. A water carrier used to bring water around, and we also used to buy it from a surly neighbor with a tap that gave out water once a week. This we used to store in twenty-liter canisters for our daily needs and weekly baths.

My father owned a small traditional coffee shop and tea-house just inside the New Gate; he had inherited it from his own father. Everyone in our tight-knit community knew my father's coffee shop, Qahwat

Abu 'Ata', just as we knew everyone in the neighborhood. It was a small center of a small communal universe, a meeting place for political and other kinds of gossip, and for playing backgammon and chess and *dhama*. Like most boys of my generation, I spent my whole childhood, from the age of four onwards, working in my father's shop. I would go there straight after school, spend my afternoons making cups of coffee and tea and taking them to customers, setting up water pipes, and studying in between. I remember Sundays with particular distaste, as I had to wake up at five in the morning to help give the coffee shop a thorough clean before going to church. It was a constant struggle to make ends meet, and I remember only too well pulling heavy loads of watermelon, in my homemade cart, from the Lion's Gate to the New Gate to sell. I also sold hot corn, and used to collect orange peel, to sell for making marmalade. UNRWA continued to distribute oil, bread, and milk as food supplements, and it was a competition in cleverness as to who would be the early bird. At seven or eight years of age I would stand in line for hours to get my family's share. The difficult economic conditions forced many of the businesses in the Old City to close down and move to Amman.

With financial assistance I was able to study at the Frere School in our neighborhood, and we attended along with children of the more well-to-do who could afford to pay the tuition. Many of my friends had to drop out over the years in order to work, eventually taking over their fathers' businesses, according to the usual tradition. I was lucky to be able to stay at school through graduation. I could never have done it, though, without the community. Everyone had some contribution to make; everyone was somehow responsible for everyone else.

My childhood, like that of most boys in our neighborhood, consisted of work and study, and we had to steal time for play between the two. The Old City streets and its Ottoman wall were our playground, the streets our football pitches, ancient broken-down walls our jungle dens. We would leap around, here and there, and sneak out into no-man's-land to pick flowers and Indian figs, to the annoyance of the Jordanian soldiers now guarding the walls, who had to be appeased with free cups of tea from our coffee shop. That microcosmos, a small, cut-off corner of the Old City, was our own magical kingdom filled with corners and alleys, caves and secret hiding places. We were always discovering new spaces, jumping across the roofs of houses to visit one another, and sometimes falling through crevices and holes in the ground.

The immediacy of daily work and study in our pre-teen years also precluded any understanding of the larger political picture; this came much later. Even when East Jerusalem fell to the Israelis in 1967, I still knew only that the Jordanians were on the wall, and that the Israelis were out there on the other side. On that fateful June day in 1967, I was carrying an order of hummus[1] for a customer when violent shooting flared up all around me. I can still see the hummus flying through the air, and myself flying home, where we remained stuck for a week because of all the shooting. The radios that had once hummed with Um Kulthum's[2] songs on the first Thursday of every month now carried war propaganda, making us believe that the Israelis were Iraqi soldiers coming to liberate us. The Israelis blew up their way into the New Gate, causing damage to several old buildings. Later, when they broke into my father's shop and robbed it, I sensed at once that we were in for different kinds of trouble.

The real political sea-change came a year later, when news began filtering through of the existence of Palestinian Fidayeen, who were driving the Israelis crazy, and were on the verge of liberating Jerusalem; it was only a matter of time. One day our teacher, Mr. Abu Sa'da from Beit Sahour near Bethlehem, stopped the lesson: "I can't continue," he said, "I must hear the news." The battle of al-Karama between the Fidayeen and the Israeli army was being fought near the Jordanian border, where the Israelis were suffering heavy losses. This created a new kind of excitement. Older students began talking of running off to join them, to fight for the liberation of the homeland, and some actually did so.

I graduated from high school in 1971, and became the first of my family to go on to college, to Bir Zeit University. The process of political self-discovery began through voluntary work committees and other types of involvement, but my real political education came during the difficult years at the American University in Beirut. The AUB offered only one scholarship to Bir Zeit students and I received it. All I needed was documentation and money, and the first proved much more difficult than the second. Since I could not study in Beirut with an Israeli-issued *Laissez Passer*, a Jordanian passport was necessary. This was extremely difficult, but finally I managed it. The unexpected problem was that my father, who had never left Jerusalem, had never had a passport issued. What saved the day, and opened up the world for me, was an aunt's miraculous retrieval of an UNRWA ration card from 1949 or 1950 with our names and address on it.

This was, of course, the first of many battles to prove my right in

Jerusalem, and to hold on to that right. My quest for education took me to Beirut, then to the US and the UK. To complete my studies, and take advantage of scholarships, I had to endure many humiliations: to line up, time and again, at the Israeli Ministry of Interior to get the necessary re-entry permits, to get a new *Laissez Passer*, to make sure I returned within specified periods, to make sure I did not violate their laws. After a short employment in the Gulf, I returned to teach at Bir Zeit University, and to endure periodic closures of Jerusalem—the inability to leave the Old City one day or enter it on another. I recall, with a still simmering anger, the frustrations of dealing with checkpoints, the blanket prohibitions against going to the Galilee and other parts of Palestine. Like most of my generation, I was also arrested a few times. Then, of course, in the late 80s came the first intifada, about which much has been written.

When my first child was born, I made certain to register the birth and get my child his own resident ID number. However, by the time I went to register my second child, the laws had changed once again, and the attempt failed. My wife and younger son have no IDs, while my older son and myself have them—and now I'm informed that the Israelis don't actually think I have mine any more.

Through this, I have maintained my contact with home, returning regularly to the Christian Quarter, to my old neighborhood. My family still lives there; and it continues to have a standard and still has a mausoleum in a corner of the Church of the Holy Sepulcher. My mother insists on keeping up the old community spirit, even though a community hardly remains. On one visit, when I was teaching engineering at Bir Zeit, my mother woke me up in the middle of the night to take a neighbor, who was in labor, to hospital. We didn't make it, and I helped deliver twins that night.

THE MOSQUE OF OMAR

Nikos Kazantzakis

The two great Annunciations, the Christian and the Greek, sparkle in my mind and unite in a mystic synthesis: In the one, the ethereal, vigorous Angel swoops down from heaven with a lily in its hand; and the Virgin, fascinated and trembling, turns with her whole body toward the door that has just opened. In the other Annunciation, the Swan, a dazzling creature, rises from the muddy waters and anchors itself intimately in the age-old custom on the female body. And the woman bends with abandon and horror over the long swaying neck, the palms of her hands raised beseechingly, like a creature in pain and ashamed, but unable and unwilling to resist the animal.

Today I saw a third Annunciation: the angel does not descend from heaven nor does the animal rise from the muddy waters; upon this earth, ardently and humanly, man brings the "good news" to woman. I walk around the Mosque of Omar and my heart beats carefree, like a kid on the cliffs. I don't stretch my body toward heaven—this earth looks good to me. This country of mine is made especially for my soul and my body. I am reminded of another day when I was wandering, tired and restless, in Kurd-besieged Eriban, in the heart of Armenia. The doors were bolted, the streets deserted, the women and children wailing behind the heavy shutters. I wandered alone, full of agony and exasperation. And suddenly, in the midday heat of the burning sun, another sacred mosque unexpectedly rose before me, covered from the foundation to its cupolas with green and blue porcelain and coral flowers. My blood at once grew calm, my mind rejoiced, and as I sat beneath the pointed Arabic arch in the cool shade all seemed good and right to me and death but a cool shadow after a blistering march. Similarly today, after upholding the Christian ideal to scorn the earth and leave it behind, this Mosque of Omar comforts and reconciles my heart with the soil. It gleams brilliantly in the sun, sparkling, joyful, multicolored, like a gigantic male peacock.

I stride hurriedly across the great square over the ancient quays of Jerusalem. I walk around the magnificent Mosque for hours, delaying as long as possible entering the dark door and plunging into the refreshing cool marvel. I look through the embrasures at the surrounding vision of Jerusalem. Beyond, the Moab Mountains steam gently, they sway slightly and shimmeringly disappear in the sun. The Mount of Olives is before me, parched, thirsty, covered with dust; and below lies the city, eroded by the burning sun, its bald houses with their black window holes resembling skulls. Camels pass, one behind the other, swaying rhythmically, indestructible, as though they had set out thousands of years ago.

This is the peak, I reflected, upon which Jehovah stood with distended nostrils, accepting the sacrifices and smelling the blood. Here is where the great Temple of Solomon rose, impenetrable fortress of the stiff-necked God; and I relived all its bloody, hate-filled, polemic history. The hard, sunburned heads, the hawk nose, the narrow unrelenting forehead, the rigid neck, the burning rapacious eye of the Hebrew race.

But as I was wandering through this bloody cesspool of Israel, I turned. The Mosque of Omar was rising in the sun, like a fountain of sculpted precious stones, climbing, playing a little in the air, circling, giving way and coming back to earth. It did not want to leave. I approached fascinated. The Arabic letters, plaited like flowers, were turning into maxims of the Qur'an, intertwining like creeping vines on the columns, blooming, grasping the dome. Thus they embraced and captivated God in the blooming, wild vineyard of earth. My eyes were refreshed as I crossed the threshold and plunged into the multicolored, mysterious shade of the temple. At first, as I came in from the raw light, I could not distinguish anything. Only a sweetness spilled over me and relieved me, like a bath; first my body and, immediately after, my mind. I walked on, trembling with joy and anticipation. This is how the faithful Muslims must walk in the dark, after death, in the cool paradise of righteous recompense.

I moved ahead with arms outstretched and little by little my eyes became adjusted. The windows rose before me like constellations, the dome, all gold and emerald, softly filled with light; the details began to appear, dancing ahead in the azure shadow—the lines, the decorations, the quotations from the Qur'an that were lying in ambush like insatiable, amorous eyes, behind profusely flowering branches and ethereal animals. A believer, kneeling on a straw mat with his face turned toward Makkah, was praying. He remained for a long while with his forehead touching the ground, trustingly, like an infant on its mother's bosom. Then slowly he lifted his head, sat up and gazed high into the golden green strip of the dome. His eyes ecstatically pursue the hidden, slippery quotation of Mohammed in the midst of the intricate lines and patterns. As though in a dream pursuing the mysterious doe. And what joy when he finally understands that all these narrow, intertwining lines are not an idle game of fantasy but a high, austere commandment of the Prophet! Only the believer can distinguish and fit together the unmatched difficult outlines, integrating the great message into a mystical synthesis in his heart. He does not scorn the apparent, nor does he seek the essence beyond the apparent; nor does he restrict himself only to the visible palpable world, without yearning for anything more. The phenomena are what create the essence. All this life—water, bread, woman, mountains, and animals—are "outlines and games"; and joy to the heart that can fit them together and find the phrase to grasp the meaning.

Christ commands: "Scorn the earth and its riches. Beyond the phenomena is the essence, beyond this transient life shines immortality." Apollo stands firm on the marble and commands: "Harmonize your heart with the earth, calmly rejoice in the ephemeral, solid order of things; outside the harmony of your mind is chaos." And Buddha, with his deep, seductive, serpentine eye, looks at us smilingly, finger in mouth, and drags us into chaos.

Today, inside the Mosque of Omar, wanting to discipline the anxieties of my heart, I struggle to harmonize whatever I love deeply in this world: the sober mind and burning imagination, geometric solidity and precision, and at the same time, not beyond, but within, the mystical flame of anxious yearning. I gaze at the dome of the Mosque for hours, like a believer: the Arabic capers transform the animals and plants into decorations, the decorations into letters, and they uncover God— and we see him as we see a lord through the thick foliage of his garden. I sit in a corner of the Mosque, on the straw mat, overcome by an indescribable sweetness. The rigid, austere outline of the Parthenon suddenly looms in my mind. Similarly, the pure divine countenance of Beatrice must have risen in the mind of Dante at the moment he was surrendering, exhausted, to the warm, earthly embrace.

I know you have always served as a lesson in balance, hardness, and discipline in a rhythm superior to me. You set limits to my desires, you set a barrier around the disorderly energies of my youth. You found concise words without tenderness, commanding, like orders to an athlete in order to open a path for me. In the beginning you seemed to me the rigid achievement of abstract thought, and my heart did not want to follow you. But little by little, in time, with love, I understood. You revealed yourself to me like an airy ripple, subordinated to the straight line; a violent passion which from its abundant strength binds itself to a superior health, a geometry pulsating like music. And slowly I understood, sitting at your feet, O Parthenon, that serenity is the resultant of all storms. That the highest mission of man is in faithfully continuing the formless struggle of matter, to liberate it by subordinating it to solid human form.

For the first time on this earth, it seemed to me the chaos of the heart subordinated itself with such grace, and without renouncing its riches, to the austere outline of the mind. The victorious mind, assembling infinity on a dry, sun-baked skull-like cliff, gave it a broader kingdom to rule. Just as, when in the midst of chaos, man finds the law that governs a series of phenomena and strictly encloses it in the word and the world becomes calm and the contradictory forces are regulated, similarly in the anarchy of natural forces, the Parthenon rises soberly and legislates the chaos.

But today, recalling this victory of logic, constriction and rage beleaguer my soul. My heart is not pure, my mind has shattered the old equilibrium. Today, whatever balance holds the rebellious forces in divine serenity seems foreign to me, narrow and false, and I do not understand it. Great concerns have been born, Lucifers have risen from the earth with arms full of dangerous gifts, with lips that twitch from smiles that are inscrutable, mocking, perplexing. The helmet of Athena has shattered and no longer can hold the head of the world. An irresistible instinct urges me to dig under the foundations of the serene temple. I know this unsparing marble syllogism has its foundations in the passionate Caryatids, with the high, agitated breasts, the painted lips and dark, dangerous eyes.

With difficulty I struggle to make clear my emotions. The contemporary Caryatids who convulse our souls do not have the enchanting visage of this ancient harem. They look more like the Furies and the Fates. One is called Hunger and she walks ahead and countless men follow her. Aphrodite never had so many lovers as this sallow, flat-chested, unsmiling, unconquered Amazon. The others are called Revenge, Rage, Freedom.

What Parthenon, what mosque, will be built upon these Caryatids? I sit in this cool corner of the Mosque and realize that all my joy has left me. Life has become oppressively heavy. Today, every moment that passes cannot satisfy us, either with its joy or with its sorrow. We push it aside roughly, in haste to see the next moment. In another age, man would surely be happy to continue to remain in the austere certainty of the Parthenon; or to sit cross-legged and glorify

God in the cheerful Mosque of Omar that exudes a faith of flesh and aroma. Today, the heart beats impatiently, it cannot be contained, it fights to make distinctions—and more important, to participate in building the future temple of its as yet faceless, fermenting God.

THE THRICE-LOVED LAND

Isma'il Ibrahim Nawwab

There's husbandry in heaven;
Their candles are all out.
Peace finds no nourishment in the thrice-loved land,
Olive orchards lie blighted,
Orange groves wither away.

In the City,
Transplanted Sharons and Shamirs—
Fed on the milk of myths,
Floating on the foam of invincibility—
Go on the rampage.

Uzis.
Rat-a-tat! Rat-a-tat!
Lazarus is dead.
He shall not rise again.

Turning their backs on the quotidian scene,
Samson and Delilah, arm in arm,
Comb their hair, walk the street,
And swagger into a neon-lit, gyrating discotheque.

Here rests the head upon the lap of Earth.
Lazarus is dead.
He shall not rise again.
How the Galilean loved him!

Bygone footsteps
Indelibly imprinted in the corridors of time:
The Son of Mary
And the Meccan Messenger on a nocturnal journey
Trod this holy ground.
Now their footprints fill with blood.

Leafless Jerusalem laments.
The City awaits
The second coming of
A sandalled savior knight.

I RETURNED TO JERUSALEM

Liyana Badr

I was born in the Holy City and spent my childhood and early youth there, only to be forced to leave it, returning, in 1994, after a full 27 years. And what a return it was! I came back only to find my identity card from the West Bank no longer allowed me to live in Jerusalem. Since that first moment of realization, the constant Israeli closure imposed on the city, and the permits Israel has imposed on us Palestinians since it occupied our city in 1967, has allowed me only brief, stolen visits, made in secret, as though I were not a daughter of this city, which witnessed my first steps in life.

The Israeli occupation has willed that Jerusalem become a city where life and living were forbidden. It doesn't realize how, for all the rattle of weapons and clatter of arms, the spirit never relinquishes its first secure abode.

I was born in the last house in the area that divides the city in two, near the Mandelbaum Gate. There I spent my whole childhood and a good part of my early youth. After leaving it I was forced, while still in the prime of youth and still unseasoned in the ways of the world, to live a life of destitution in various exiles. Since that time I have seen all other cities as mirrors returning me, in one way or another, to my own city—until at last I returned and saw it once more after 27 years of exile. In 1994 I returned, and it was as though I had never left. The air redolent with ripe pine cones, the evening with its magic hues. The special sound of the lone black crow, which seemed to have been sauntering on the asphalt since the days of my childhood, when the street was a forbidden place. The demure almond trees and the branches of *eski dunya* in the family garden, the stone steps leading to the wide veranda, the fifth of which took me to my childhood home. And, all around, those tiny needle-like arrows of the *sarw* trees filling the entrance, all reminding me, so sharply, of the afternoons I spent hiding under the branches of those trees in the endless game of hide and seek.

My aunt appeared, bearing with her the memory of my mother. She embraced me. Her hair was silver now, and many wrinkles of worry had been engraved on her face since those bitter years began: of diaspora for us and occupation for her.

Yet all was still as before. It was as though I'd never left; or as though I'd gone off on a mere school excursion or scholarship abroad, for a time only. It was as though I'd never been in a diaspora stretching over 27 years and many long exiles, over several continents. It was as though the other cities I'd lived in were mere black holes where the spirit was stifled. But not here. No, not here.

I felt for the things in my handbag, to assure myself I'd really returned. That at last I was here. That the devils wouldn't contrive to find new exiles for me. And yet I was entering Jerusalem only to leave it again; here just for the few hours of my visit. I'm denied identity here, like so many thousands of Jerusalemites, all denied entry to the city of their birth. It was one dusk in July 1994 that I entered the family enclave, half expecting to hear the barks of Lucky, with his lilac-grey color and the woolly curls falling gracefully over his well-fed body. I'd loved him so much when I was four years old; then, after he bit my mother and she had to go to the hospital for injections, I grew afraid of him.

A peal of laughter rose from deep inside me. Years had passed since that happened. So why was I hesitating so fearfully in front of the steps, my feet dragging, as though not moving at all? I retraced my first childhood footsteps. I climbed these steps, feeling the black railings, rough but warm, reassured to find the old stone column, with its lotus-like crown, still there in the middle of the veranda. I gazed at the white and black etchings on the old tiles, and I noticed the change in the main gate, where there was less colored glass now—the change of an alien time. I rushed to embrace the children, the progeny of the family. My aunt embraced me, and I was comforted in her arms, where the intimacy of life itself was to be found; those same arms had borne me, in one of the rooms of this house, in the moments I first entered life. The house was the same house, even if the hand of time had worked long upon it, stripping it of its old gloss. Whenever I went there, I'd look for the two striped seats of white and red satin—very comfortable seats they were, brought here in 1948 from my grandfather's house in Katamon [in West Jerusalem, completely taken over by the Jews]. They were irrevocably linked with two pieces from brass missiles that had fallen on my grandfather's house during the 1948 war; these were always kept near the chairs. The treasures were there no more. Yet I still seemed to smell the odor of brass mixed with lemons, which I smelled so often during my childhood, when the grown-ups would polish all the brass with Brasso, along with lemon peels, to impart a special gleam. What troubled me now was the great number of seats cluttering up the entrance, limiting the space there. I didn't like, either, a piece of furniture placed just where it blocked the entrance to the bedrooms. If only I could, I would have rolled up my sleeves and begun re-arranging the furniture, piece by piece, back to the way it was before the Six Day War. It was as though I'd expected familiar things to stay the same. As though the inner miracle that had raised me above the clutch of time, and let me leap over so many places to return to my first place, had the power to breathe a magical energy into the furniture, imbuing it with its old shine and color, the power to re-shape the space in the rooms in the old way, as it had been during that far-off time.

The very air bore the memory of family members, those still living and those who had passed away. I saw them all: the grandmothers, the aunts from both sides, my own father's aunts beckoning to me, congratulating me on my return. I saluted all those who'd gone far from our world. I conveyed to my mother, the fount of goodness and joy, my sense that the message had reached me. But can we bring back any luster to hope, any authority to the good now past; can our capacity to tap into the universal secret be reborn? Was I deluding myself as I followed the paths of the city, seeing for myself the destruction brought on by occupation? Houses demolished, houses abandoned or ready to crumble in ruins—these were everywhere in the city, showing all too clearly how the Israeli municipality denied Palestinians permits to build or repair; how it was bent on seizing the houses of the Arab quarters, systematically, one by one. Wherever I walk now, in the alleys of the Old City, I find the houses have been taken over, or are about to be. I see notices to vacate hung like swords over the heads of inhabitants, on the pretext that these houses are Jewish-owned! This acquisition of Arab houses reflects the very basis on which the Israeli state has been founded: the boundless greed, the confiscation of history and the collective memory of others, all others, without distinction. This aggressive, usurping power sees nothing before it but itself. The city's old, entrancing plurality is going to rack and ruin, because of the constant pressure on its people, all the various sects, religions, races, languages, customs, and cultures: a mosaic pattern that had found its own perfect harmony—before the city was occupied by the Jews.

The seizure of identity cards from Jerusalemites who'd lived in the suburbs of the city or a few kilometers from its walls has been carried

out now. And all proofs of citizenship have been wiped out. The city
authority gives Jews possession and ownership of parts of the Old City.
Palestinian merchants endure grave hardship as they cross the bridges
and borders; they face vast, constant economic pressures, while those
on the Jewish merchants are light.

As I walk in any part of the city, memories flow in my mind and
things become real once more. The Hallaq family house before the old
post office, where I lived from the ages of two to four; the Zananiri
shop for household utensils and children's toys, facing the Sahira Gate;
the post office, marked out in Hebrew letters now; the Jaffa Gate; the
small gate of the Ma'muniyyah school, where I began my secondary
education; the Hashim grocery where I bought the chocolate I loved,
before my memories of things began even to form; Zahra street where
the Quds cinema was, become a deserted ruin since those days when
its screen was a way to the paradise of tales and lovely song; the
National Hotel, closed now in the face of worsening times since the
intifada began, the street in front becoming a dump for rubbish. I
recalled so vividly how my mother would take us there, again and
again, to eat the restaurant's celebrated lentil soup. She brought us still
even when she was barely mobile, when the accursed illness took away
her power to walk upright except in a special corset. I recalled the
Armenian cobbler who, when I was fourteen, gave me a beautiful pair
of shoes because the name of his place was like my own.

I feel how every corner, every hole, every bend in a street or scratch
on a wall, has a place in my heart. Whenever I can come here, I take
refuge in the family home, sensing clearly how we Jerusalemites,
deprived of the right to live in our city, feel for it a unique love that
tears at our hearts and will embrace it forever in the hope of stopping
the bulldozers from demolishing our homes and plundering our
property, of defying this indifference the Israelis show towards our
right to Jerusalem and to life within its boundaries.

The time will surely come when the major powers abandon their
blind support for the most racist state in the world.

THIS CITY

Aida Hasan Damuni

Grandfather loved Jerusalem
Oh how he loved Jerusalem
He knew
that there is something about
this city
where past and present touch
A loftiness
a simpleness, a truth
a pride and love
of every Palestinian

I want to breathe in its history
let my soul drink in
the serenity of my faith
in this city
where the heavens feel so near

"Please, she came all the way from America"
our host pleads with the soldier
"she simply wants to pray"
Eyes cold reveal
a selfishness, a hate
that does not belong
in this holy city

Reluctance, arrogance
rudeness
pause
He lets us pass

Tell me your secrets, old city
Teach me the ancient wisdom
that fortifies your walls

I want to unshackle you
from your silence and sorrow
dust off the evil
that covers you
Feel the calm
of wind
free
Shine light on you once more

One city, three prayers

This city
occupation, oppression
prayers muffled
How long?

After the dawn, morning comes
This city
a pride and love
of every Palestinian
Grandfather loved Jerusalem

FROM SHEPHERD TO PAINTER

Mahmoud Shahin

What a store of memories I have of Jerusalem, starting with childhood and early youth, then moving on to my young manhood. I was born into a family of Bedouin shepherds, and, when young, I took many jobs in Jerusalem: as a builder, a house painter, and as a waiter too, working in numerous hotels. I learned to cook in the W.M.C.A. Hotel before going on to work at the Saint George Hotel and others.

It was in Jerusalem that I watched my very first film, an Indian film, at the Nuzha Cinema. It was in Jerusalem that I knew my first love, a platonic love that happened after the Israeli occupation. And it was to Jerusalem that I returned after some years as a *fida'i* (freedom fighter), hiding in various places, in extremely difficult circumstances, in the course of my work as a resistance fighter.

When I became a writer, I wrote a good deal about Jerusalem. No work of mine, I think, lacks some description of experiences there; indeed, all the experiences involved may well have taken place in Jerusalem and its environs. It's no longer possible to relate all of these, now that the occupation weighs down on the city's breast.

In the suburbs of Jerusalem I tended my parents' sheep as a lad, and I learned to play the flute and the *urghul* and the *majwiz*. I retain many memories of people from those early days, and many memories of the flocks, all of this being reflected in my later writings. And recently, when, in addition to literature and journalism, I decided to take up painting, the image of the Holy Rock hanging between earth and heaven figured largely in my work as a symbol of Jerusalem. I don't know whether the small shepherd boy from Jerusalem—who would go to the Holy Haram to contemplate that Dome of the Rock, his eyes filled with wonder—will take up other disciplines in the service of the Rock and of Jerusalem; but the notion of writing poetry has filled my mind for some years now, and I've composed a number of poems.

A Meeting with the Land

When the June War broke out, I was working as a waiter at a Spanish restaurant in Amman, the Villa Rosa, where the royal family were regular guests. They used to call me the Jerusalemite. I have delightful memories of some of the family members, and in particular of Princess Alya, who was then a small girl.

After a few months, I joined the Palestinian revolution, choosing the al-Fath group. I was given my military training in Iraq, at the Rashid camp and became skilled in the use of arms. At the end of 1969 I entered Palestine at night, crossing the Dead Sea along with fifteen other freedom fighters. We stumbled on an Israeli ambush and lost touch with one another. I spent about a week looking for my comrades, by night, in the mountains of Bethlehem—but quite fruitlessly. I was unfamiliar with these mountains; I'd walk in them by night, cautious and fearful as though in a minefield, ever alert, my hand constantly on my rifle. At last I decided to move back to the Jerusalem mountains, of which I knew every inch.

I'd hide during the day, venturing out at night. Even so, it wasn't easy to find a way through that mountain terrain. When I reached what I thought must be the Jerusalem mountains, the moon hadn't yet risen, and I couldn't be sure whether I was climbing one of its mountains or not. I was, wasn't I, climbing the southern slopes of the Muntar mountain, on which I'd so often tended our flocks—close by the St. Saba Convent that stood alone there in the wilderness, raising so many questions in my mind and stirring such wonder in my heart?

It took me about an hour to climb the slope. When I reached the peak, I saw the lights of scores of villages and towns, a few kilometers away to the west. For a while I stood perplexed, not knowing where exactly I was, unable to identify those villages and towns. The outline of the lighting had changed a good deal, or so I felt—I wasn't sure whether or not those lights were from Jerusalem. I couldn't believe what was happening to me. Where else could I have been but in the Jerusalem district? Yet how could I possibly fail to recognize the place where I was standing? Concentrating hard, I fixed my gaze on the place, striving to recall how, once, I'd known the lights from those other mountaintops. Weren't those the lights of the Mukabber Mountain? And those others, weren't they the Aizariyya lights—and weren't those the lights of Abu Dis? I couldn't tell. I wasn't sure of anything.

I began gazing towards places closer at hand, seeing scattered lights here and there, and hearing the howling of dogs from afar. I looked hard, contemplating the chain of hills on which I stood; but darkness blocked the view around me, and I couldn't make them out. Unable to wait for the moon to rise and help me recognize the terrain, I walked slowly on, feeling utterly bewildered. Then I stopped, took out a cigarette and lit it. Before the match was spent, the idea came to me to look down at my feet. Might I see something I recognized? The match was out soon enough, yet I felt I knew that patch of land. Wanting to be sure, I lit another match and gazed hard; and this time, before the match was spent, recognition was certain. This was a spot on which I'd so often sat, slept, played my flute, frolicked with the other shepherds, or read a book. I held on to the match, gazing down at the place, till the fire burned my finger. A moment later I found myself throwing down my rifle, shaking the cartridge pouch from my back and lying down on the earth, my arms outstretched, striving to embrace just as much of the land as I could. I embraced it passionately. I don't know just how long I rolled about in that place, now on my back, now on my stomach, filled with matchless peace and utter delight.

The place was a continuation of the chain of mountains sloping from the Mintar summits. I started recalling all the different spots, all the valleys and hills, all the slopes and dales surrounding me. Near me, on the slope, was a well of which I had many memories. I'd go to it now, I thought, in the hope of finding a pail, for I was parched and famished. Now that I was here, I'd never, I knew, lose my way again; I'd no longer have to be constantly on the alert, my hand on the trigger. I knew of many huts where I could hide during the day, proof against the searches of any occupation army.

I went over to the well, and there, sure enough, was a pail. I drew some water, drank my fill, then took out a tin of sardines and a loaf of bread and ate. I began thinking of going to see my family, and of other young men that I could recruit for the revolution and train in military skills, and planned exploits for the near future. I plunged deep in reflection, feeling myself a Guevara in the mountains of Jerusalem.

Meeting My Mother

I left the well and walked on, feeling totally secure. The moon had risen, which made my progress easier.

My family spent the winters, with their sheep usually, at a farmstead not far from where I was, and I decided to go to them. As I approached the place, though, I heard no sound of barking, and realized my father couldn't have settled there that year. I reached the old place to find the gate open. Then, entering, I found the sheep's feeding rack flung down in front of the farm, and their fold closed by a wooden door fortified with iron, which I knew well enough. They'd be coming during the day, I felt sure, to feed the sheep, before returning to the place where they'd settled that year. I was tired and very sleepy, and thought of sheltering and sleeping in a cave, putting off my search for my family till the next night.

There was a cave just beneath our farmstead. The winter rains had blocked most of its opening with mud, making it more like a burrow. I crawled down towards it, lay flat on my stomach, then crawled inside, my rifle in front of me. Then I lit a match and peered around the cave to make sure there were no animals there, hyena, wolf, fox, or whatever. The place was quite empty, but the stench of dung was overpowering—we'd always let our flock sleep in there when the nights were very cold.

Lighting another match and gazing hard at the ground, I looked for a spot to lie down. The place was swarming with bugs, ticks, and other insects. What was I to do? My only practical course was to scuff away the surface dust and make myself a place to sleep. I laid my jacket down and stretched out on it, hoping this would make it harder for the bugs to find me. But my efforts were fruitless. These creatures sensed rich pickings in the cave and swarmed towards me, sucking my blood all through the night and the next day. I spent my time scratching my body, which was already inflamed from bites in the Bethlehem mountains. I don't think I slept a wink. My legs became puffed up, and so did my arms, hands, neck, and face, and all the other parts the bugs could reach. Spots the size of chickpeas sprang up all over my body, leaving me sick for a whole week.

Before dusk next day, I heard the feet of the flock above the cave. They were butting one another and jostling round the rack. They were our sheep, I was sure of that. What was the best thing to do? If I came out from the cave, someone might see me, and the consequent gossip might lead the occupation authority to me. So, I elected to stay put till the flock had finished eating. Sitting there behind the blocked entrance to the cave, peering out through the crack, I watched and waited for the flock to leave the farmstead. The shepherd, I thought, would either be my father, or my brother, or else a hired hand.

The sheep stopped fighting and began moving slowly forward past the hut. After a brief while I saw some of them leave the farm and scatter over the side of the valley opposite. Up to that point I hadn't heard the shepherd's voice, or seen him. Then, unable to believe my ears, I heard my mother's voice crying out to the flock, trying to move it westward towards the village.

Oh God! It was my mother shepherding the flock! What had happened? Was my father dead? And my brother.—where was my brother?

For a few seconds I was powerless to act, unable even to think of what to do. I hadn't seen my mother for about five years. As far as she knew, I was working in Jordan. How was I to meet her now, so suddenly, in this fearfully shabby state?

The sheep weren't obeying her call. I saw her hurry towards them to stop them straying further. It was drizzling, and my mother had donned a sack she'd made into a mask and placed on her head. Now she was calling out to the sheep once more, to bring them back.

I couldn't decide whether or not it was lucky my mother was with the flock. Of course I was happier to see her than anyone else. But what was I to do? Should I hail her from where I was? Wouldn't she think I was some giant, or a jinni calling to her from the depths of the earth? She'd be petrified. But there was nothing else for it. She was already moving further off, about forty meters away now. I waited till she was right opposite me on the slope, then called out, in a low voice: "Yamma!"

Not hearing me, she went on talking to the flock. I repeated my call, a little more loudly this time: "Yam–ma!" She stopped dead for a few seconds, then, apparently supposing she'd misheard, went on calling to the flock. A third time I called, louder still: "Yam–maa!" She stopped dead and started looking about her, repeating her invocations to God: "Bismillah al-Rahman al-Rahim!" Still she stood there, gazing around in utter bewilderment. How could someone be calling out to her, "Yamma"? I called her for a fourth time, making sure, this time, to raise my voice even higher: "Yam–maaa–h!" But, before I could pronounce the last sound, she'd heard me well enough, and looked in amazement towards the source of the voice, to see my face filling the opening of the cave. For a few seconds she gazed at me without a word. Then she came rushing down, still, in her fear, repeating her *basmalah*, to which she added: "You there, what are you? Are you human or jinni?" But her motherhood was spurring her on towards me. She was repeating her words, without a pause, in the Bedouin dialect, while I was repeating: "Mother, don't be afraid. It's me, Mahmoud!" She didn't hear me. She repeated her invocations swiftly, never stopping, till she reached the cave and was standing there in front of me. She gazed for a few moments at my puffed-up face, then exclaimed: "Hungry! And thirsty! I'll fetch some water and food."

With that she went off. Yes, she left me, without kissing my cheeks or asking how I was. She didn't even lean towards me, not at all—still thinking maybe that I was a jinni. Or perhaps she hadn't woken yet from the terrifying shock.

After some minutes, though, she returned to ask: "Did I greet you, son?" "No, Mother," I answered. My eyes filled with tears, while she was crawling on her stomach now, to approach me, and clutch my head to her breast, and kiss me warmly, asking God to keep the oppressors' eyes turned from me, to open a path for me along every difficult road, and to grant me victory against all my enemies.

I described this meeting, subsequently, in my novel *The Usurped Land.* My mother died sixteen years after that meeting. We didn't see one another, and I couldn't walk at her funeral and bury her with my own hands. All this was a result of the Israeli occupation. She died in 1985, when I was in Damascus. I got the news, a few days after she'd died, by phone from Amman, and I began weeping and lamenting. All I had from my mother was a handkerchief she'd sent me in Damascus. One evening, I took it out in the house of my friend Mustafa al-Hallaj, took my flute and began playing and weeping. The tune I composed that evening became my friends' favorite. One evening I played it in the presence of a number of poets and writers, including Mahmoud Darwish. They loved it.

HAMZA AWEIWI, A SHOEMAKER

Hayan Charara

The taps have not been running
Since July seventeenth,
His wedding day.
Now it's twenty-nine days
Without clean water.

He has tanks on the roof.
Some days he manages to shave,
Or his wife prepares the tea kettle.
But he knows the price of water.
It's holy, hard to come by.

Outside the shop, fat and bald,
An electrician with seven children
Admits he does not wash his clothes.
A young girl, a yellow ribbon
In her hair, is laughing.
She knows grown men
Should not smell this way.

He yanks a nail from a shoe
That needs to be resoled.
He knows he wouldn't need to fix them
To walk as far as where people live differently.
There, boys are washing cars,
Housewives water lawns.

He seems troubled, hesitant,
Looking for something in the distance,
But a cluster of trees
Blocks the view.
He still daydreams
About taking long showers,

Or even two a day.
But it's almost noon,
The temperature unbearable.
And the shoes are piling up!

JERUSALEM REMINISCENCES

Mureed Barghouthy

All that the world knows of Jerusalem is the power of the symbol. The Dome of the Rock is what the eye sees, and so it sees Jerusalem and is satisfied.

The Jerusalem of religions, the Jerusalem of politics, the Jerusalem of conflict is the Jerusalem of the world. But the world does not care for our Jerusalem, the Jerusalem of the people. The Jerusalem of houses and cobbled streets and spice markets, the Jerusalem of the Arab college, the Rashidiyyah school, and the 'Umariyyah school. The Jerusalem of the porters and the tourist guides who know just enough of every language to guarantee them three reasonable meals a day. The oil market and the sellers of the antiques and mother-of-pearl and of sesame cakes. The library, the doctor, the lawyer, the engineer, and the dressers of brides with high dowries. The terminals of the buses that trundle in every morning from all the villages with peasants come to buy and to sell. The Jerusalem of white cheese, of oil and olives and thyme, of baskets of figs and necklaces and leather and Salah al-Din Street. Our neighbor the nun, and her neighbor, the muezzin who was always in a hurry. The palm frond in all the streets on Palm Sunday, the Jerusalem of houseplants, cobbled alleys, and narrow covered lanes. The Jerusalem of clotheslines. This is the city of our senses, our bodies, and our childhood. The Jerusalem that we walk in without much noticing its "sacredness," because we are in it, because it is us. We loiter or hurry in our sandals or our brown or black shoes, bargaining with the shopkeepers and buying new clothes for the 'Id. We shop for Ramadan and pretend to fast and feel that secret pleasure when our adolescent bodies touch the bodies of the European girls on Easter Saturday. We share with them the darkness of the church of the Holy Sepulcher and raise with them the white candles that they light. This is the ordinary Jerusalem. The city of our little moments that we forget quickly because we will not need to remember, and because they are ordinary like water is water and lightning is lightning. And as it slips from our hands it is elevated to a symbol, up there in the sky.

All conflicts prefer symbols. Jerusalem now is the Jerusalem of theology. The world is concerned with the "status" of Jerusalem, the idea and the myth of Jerusalem, but our lives in Jerusalem and the Jerusalem of our lives do not concern it. The Jerusalem of the sky will live forever, but our life in it is threatened with extinction. They limit the number of Palestinians in the city, the number of Palestinian houses, the windows, balconies, schools, and nurseries, the number of people praying on Friday and Sunday. They tell the tourists where to buy their gifts, which lanes to walk in, which bazaars to enter. Now we cannot enter the city as tourists or students or old people. We cannot live there or leave there, we cannot get bored with Jerusalem and leave it for Nablus or Damascus or Baghdad or Cairo or America. We cannot desert it because of the high rents. We cannot grumble about it as people grumble about their tiresome capitals. Perhaps the worst thing about occupied cities is that their children cannot make fun of them. Who could make fun of Jerusalem! Now, letters to our addresses there will not reach us. They took the addresses of our homes and the dust of our drawers. They took the city's throngs and its doors and its lanes; they took even that secret brothel that stimulated our adolescent imaginations in Bab Huttah Alley, with its courtesans as fat as Indian statues. They took the St. Augusta Victoria Hospital and Jebel al-Tur, where Khali [uncle] 'Ata lived, and the Shaykh Jarrah district, where we lived once upon a time. They took the yawning of the pupils at their desks and their boredom in Tuesday's last lesson. They took the footsteps of my grandmother on her way to visit Hajjah Hafizah and her daughter Hajjah Rashidah. They took those two women's prayers and their small room in the old city and the straw mat on which they used to play cards: *barjis* and *basra.* They took that shop I traveled to specially from Ramallah to buy a pair of quality leather shoes, to return to my family with cakes from Zalatimo and *kunafa* from Ja'far's: after sixteen kilometers in the Bamyeh bus for five piasters I went back to our house in Ramallah, proud and boastful—for I was returning from Jerusalem.

Now, I will not see either Jerusalem of the sky or Jerusalem of the clotheslines. Israel, with the excuse of the sky, has occupied the land.

WE ARE ICARUS

Patricia B. Cosentino

for Jerusalem's fallen children

Mortals, wax wings and feathers.
Why, what's wrong with real feathers?
We, not less than gods know.

The war goes on, eye-balling the
universe of myths, fables, folklore.
Mortals, wax wings and feathers.

Moons wax and wane daring
encounters, lawlessness,
we, not less than gods know.

Brachial warning, do not fly too near
the sun, don't eat apples, don't cry.
Mortals, wax wings and feathers.

Beyond gravity, stolen scenes play out,
unrequited. Son challenges fate, fails because
we, not less than gods, know.

Usurping destiny, father survives.
No safety net, a catch phrase for
mortals, wax wings and feathers.
We not less than gods know.

THE DEBRIS OF MEMORY

Ruanne Abou-Rahme

The debris of memory
    engulfs us
like a shadowless night,
    we step into the remains
of our history
    our cold feet
    touching the traces
of the forgotten
    the displaced,
the ruins of a house,
    the bare skin of youth unraveled

And they spoke of you, Jerusalem,
as though you were a vacuous symbol

'In that holy place
    The golden dome
has been sealed,
    The blood of young men
still fresh beneath the soldiers' boots
and outside, under the blistering sun
    they pray on a crammed street'

Scorched by the sun
    our blistered feet
       step
on the belly of the past,
    and I sleep in drunken memory
       to forget
a boy with a marble,
    a boy with a stone,
       the remains of a homeland,
       a boy
with a bullet in his head

And they wrote of you, Jerusalem,
as though you were a myth

'Here is your promised land
  here is the checkpoint
    the guard tower,
      the sniper who sneers
        at his victims,
          the soldier
            who laughs
as he lines my father up on the wall
        pushes his steel on to my brothers' face,
Here is the promised land
    where
      pregnant women
        bare out
          the youth
  of their wombs
    waiting
for the break of curfew
    Where
      youth bleed out
        their childhood
          waiting at a checkpoint.'

The debris rises
    our breath is
caught in its residue
    as the story unfolds
and refolds
    back
      into a cloud of dust,
and we walk across
    another crossing,
        an imagined boundary,
    an erected checkpoint

And they spoke to me, Jerusalem
as though I had lost and forgotten you

'Yet you were
the place I had marked my own
a hot summer hush of refuge
the fountain of a childhood
too quickly overshadowed
And you were the spring of my voice
the place of belonging
the unanswered question
the long night of laughter
the sigh of memory'

In the dusk
in that quiet ending
they have marked us
    to disappear,
  rewritten our names in numbers,
    drawn the limits
    and now
        What is left to come?
among the rubble,
   among the stone and cactus
       through the barbed wire
and the dirt filled roads

'Jerusalem they have asked
me to remember you
as though you were only
shrine and stone,
When you are
the valley where I ran
the fig that I picked
the shade of vine leaves,
You are
The woman who sold
grapes on her back
The man who packed
Rukab ice cream

The neighborhood
  children
    who played late into the night
  with marbles in one hand
  and stones in the other'

After all
  what is left
but for our feet
  to return

JERUSALEM

Izzat Khattab

Thou three-suitors' bride
The prize of the holiest last.
Whose ascension was a domed rock.
A rock: the very word calls
For the deepest of meditations:
Encompassing thrice-connected stories:
The Dome, and Peter's in Rome,
And Moses gushing life
To the unslaked Israelites.
The dowry is immeasurable:
It's not in Moloch's war drums,
Nor in Peter's ever slanted vision,
It's in the Arabian's holy suras.
The rock of justice and blissful law.

"CHECKPOTHT"

Azmi Bishara
translated by May Jayyusi

It was in those days that my daughter mastered language in a manner that aroused our wonder. The first childhood words and sentences have a magical effect, making the things named seem beautiful. The words of children are like a magic wand that for a few moments scatters golden stars in the expanse of our burdened lives. So begins our anticipation of a new word—if we wait too long we start insisting, then begging, "What's this?" We repeat the question with the hope that words will fly out to breathe new life in old things, transforming ordinary things into singular ones, and providing a new topic of conversation: "Tell them what you told me yesterday." As though she realizes our new addiction to this magic, she tortures us with looks that elicit more pleading, followed by a smile that turns the pleadings into hugs and kisses, and then wild running throughout the house, "Baba, what's all this laughter about?" Excited by the clamor, our son, who has not yet mastered words, follows us, crawling. I pick him up, running, panting, and cursing cigarettes. Her words distance us from politics, for the parents' conversation is full of astonishment at the source of words, the distinctions made between past and present and between qualities. They are full of excitement at their daughter's smartness: Is it something ordinary that parental love exaggerates, or something exceptional that our excitement does not allow us to realize fully?

No sooner was I convinced that my daughter had mastered words, having only to master prose, poetry, *fiqh*, and linguistics, then she came to me from the nursery. "Baba," I asked, "Where have you been?" "I was at the *mahthoum.*" I paused a moment: *mahthoum*, or "checkpotht," was a magical childish pronunciation of the Hebrew word *mahsoum*. Its linguistic root was *husam*, meaning to block the road; this is the word for checkpoint, meaning the checkpoints that the occupation forces set up and that block people's pathways of life in occupied Palestine. Our people in the West Bank and Gaza insist on retaining the Hebrew word *mahsoum* in the singular, but using the Arabic form for the plural: *mahasim*. Every day my daughter spends enough time at the checkpoint to make her forget her time at the nursery. She goes in the morning to the nursery talking about her teachers, Miss So-and-so, but she returns talking of the *mahthoum*/checkpotht. "Baba, what did you do at the *mahsoum*?" "I sang." "What did you sing?" Immediately she begins singing, "Happy birthday to you," a sign that the nursery today had celebrated some child's birthday, with the sweet tones of her voice that melts the hardest things into tender streams, which surround us as we stand on our particular piece of heaven, among the checkpoints.

Four months later, equal in length but unequal in breadth, the checkpoint was no longer simply expected or familiar; since the invasion it has become an overpowering declaration of the presence of those who placed it. The checkpoint is that which separates but also that which connects the two worlds. It is the border and the crossing point. It is both the pain and the hope of exit. The checkpoint began to take itself seriously, the amount of iron and hard materials increased, as did the numbers of soldiers and their scowls. It developed a structure. It was no longer made up of army remnants: barrels, concrete cubes, and different rocks. Pre-fabricated rooms of concrete or iron spread around it. Even the color was now a monotonous brown-gray. It lost its haphazard and unkempt appearance and became impassive.

Waiting time at the checkpoint increased, while the complaints of those waiting decreased. Their suffering increased, as did their patience at their suffering. Their forbearance increased, not because their skins had hardened, but because the checkpoint was now volatile, unable to bear any complaint, while fear left no room for complaints. In the period after the invasion the checkpoint cannot be joked with because its finger, trembling, is light on the trigger, and because it too is afraid.

Yet the balance of terror at the checkpoint cannot conceal the identity of the oppressor or the oppressed, the identity of the dominant or the dominated; the identity of he who permits and he who begs for permission. Reality boils down to a checkpoint, and in reality, there is no balance of terror. There exists two terrors with no balance between them, two fears unequal.

The checkpoint is no longer satisfied except if it absorbs all your time, all your effort, all your nerves. Even the day spends its time waiting at the checkpoint; time itself waited in its turn. Ramallah is now a whole day's journey away. The day of travel is one thing and the day at the flourmill is another, as they used to say. Except that now, you could end up with dust all over your clothes but with no flour.

People live in the shadow of the checkpoint, whether they travel or not, leave or not. Its presence overwhelms everything else; it permeates into the details of life, coloring everything with its own palette. Peoples' moods are linked to news coming from there—their plans and projects, their livelihood, the decision on where to live, where to work, where to send the kids to school. All such considerations begin at the checkpoint, and all purposes have to explain themselves, justify themselves to it.

In the last few months my daughter had become neat and tidy to the extent that she chooses her clothes with care, asking, "Is what I'm wearing pretty or not?" and, without waiting for an answer, "Do you know who brought me this?" She had recently became accustomed to performing her natural functions in a place that we had creatively named "al-pota" from the English word pot, then we had moved on to the French *toilette*. It was a great achievement when she was elevated to sit on the toilet seat, and she teased her brother that he could only sit at that throne when he grew up.

Nursery was out and my daughter and son were on their way home across the checkpoint. I had called two hours before and I had heard her singing, while her brother, without meaning to disturb, was making sounds that bore no relation to her song. He too was singing; one singing with words and the other without.

After two hours, I called again. They were still at the checkpoint, but the singing was now replaced by crying. The melody had turned into intermittent, rasping nervous screams followed by repeated whinings of "Oh, Oh, Oh," followed by, "I want to go home," repeated dozens of times and, "Where is the house?"

"Wajd wants to talk with you," her mother said, not hoping that a telephone call would solve anything, but only to break the monotony of the whining, to catch her breath and relieve her hearing for a while. The whining stopped and Wajd began talking and crying, like an adult who all of a sudden collapses: "Daddy, I have peepee, I want to go home." She proudly refused to relieve herself in her clothing and the checkpoint was a barrier between her and her home. Our pleadings that she do the job in the car and in any manner she liked were of no avail—she was already in pain but could not bring herself to do that. I began to follow up, calling every five minutes, "How many cars are left in front of you? Are they searching each car?" until Wajd arrived home. As soon as the car entered the doorway, she relieved herself in the car, perhaps because she suddenly relaxed and could not hold it in any longer. The barrier was no longer there.

It is not difficult to imagine what sick people or pregnant women in labor go through at the checkpoint. We have no need of imagination for that; lately poetry itself is unable to illuminate us on this point. Creativity and art picture the reality only to reap benefit from it, not to change it. It has been some time since we have abandoned art; reality has overtaken it in creativity and truth. The apparitions of suffering have themselves come to haunt the checkpoint. They are always there. In every car, there is a man, a woman, children, and a story, a thousand stories and tales. Some of them call out asking for help from the passers-by and from the soldiers, imploring; others vent their anger at the car in front, or at the wife sitting beside them, or the children in the back seat, in a display of the honor and manhood that had retreated in the face of the soldiers, was crushed at the checkpoint, or had been voluntarily repressed before arriving. Some whisper; some suffer in silence; others tell of the brawls and quarrels that they pick at the checkpoint. The more important and tragic story is the loss of feeling that takes place, the degradation of sensitivity.

The following day at the breakfast table Wajd suddenly said, "There is peepee!" "Good, fine, what do we do when there is peepee?" She stood up and peed in her clothes. Thank God, she was still in her underclothes. "The house is far," she said, and laughed. Did she laugh to make up to us before we could scold her or did she laugh at us? Or maybe she laughed at something she genuinely found funny—the astonished expressions on our faces, for example.

Checkpoint Neighborhoods

With the passage of time, in the orbit of the city, neighborhoods have sprung up that only increase the brittleness of the city core, now suffering under the repulsive power that emanates from its center. The city has become a passageway for the inhabitants of these neighborhoods that, arbitrarily, have been counted as part of Jerusalem and so become nonnegotiable. Everything touched with the name of Jerusalem—even if unconnected to it—becomes, in the hands of the powerful and through their deployment of religion in politics, sacred. Among these are neighborhoods planned with care, wide roads, sidewalks, gardens, houses built of white Jerusalem stone and capped with red bricks... It is only in Jerusalem that the stone hewn out of its mountains seems alien to the mountains themselves. These resemble "facts on the ground," as they are termed in the discourse of the politicians of that state, more than actual neighborhoods. It is not often that one can see politics embodied in three-dimensional concrete, as one sees in these lands. It seems that when politics is embodied, in a rush to fulfill itself and the wishes of its masters, it produces a body ugly in the extreme.

In contrast to these planned neighborhoods, there arose—or rather, there amassed, spontaneously and arbitrarily—neighborhoods constituting the negation of planning. "Pirate constructions": that was the name given to this Arab phenomenon in Hebrew. It was unplanned construction in a country in which the only plans made for the Arabs were for their departure, a country in which the continued existence of the indigenous inhabitants was counter to all planning. In these neighborhoods, the roads were not paved; the infrastructure not dug in, to be followed by gardens and then houses, as the public engendered the private. Here, along the main road that connected two cities, houses were built, which then gradually began to retreat, as the masters of the checkpoint demolished them. Here, buildings sprang up and only later did the spaces in between turn into roads. There is no neighborhood, no public space, only a collection of buildings connected solely by the need for housing. A string of housing structures on both sides of a road between two cities, leaving no space for crossing or distinguishing marks, except where the checkpoint arbitrarily broke the continuity. At the base of each building stand shops, mouths gaping at passers-by whenever their bellies were empty.

The secondary roads were not blessed with names or numbers. No committee met to bestow a name on them, unlike in those neighborhoods planned by the masters of the checkpoints, where the act of inventing a history was inevitably mixed with derision for the indigenous people. A street is named after one of the leaders of the Zionist movement, or the name or date of one of the battles of the masters of the checkpoints, especially those that were raged to liberate the city from its natives.

The new neighborhood has no focal point, no center, and no public space to knit relations between people. It is a road that stretches for seven kilometers. Cars race through it as though it were a highway between two cities, and crossing to the other side could be lethal. The road links neighborhoods together, but divides its sides into two distinct neighborhoods. The road generates not a public space but a public danger. The foremost feature of the road is the grocery shops—the answer to people's primary needs in the shadow of the checkpoints, shops that welcome onto their bit of pavement cars arriving to stock up with food in the same way they fill up at gas stations. Shops are also useful for giving directions to the place of habitation: "After so and so supermarket there is a sharp turn to the right. Take care not to approach it fast because you may miss it. After the supermarket slow down and then after a hundred meters turn right at the burned garbage dumpster (it is black and green) and at the first grocery called Paradise take another right, be careful of the first road track, be careful! Some of them are flooded with polluted water. You will see four apartment blocks right next to each other, each four stories high. Inquire at the exhibition store called Granada or Venezi—no, it is called Arizona because the owner's son studies there and, God willing, will turn out a success like his father—ask there for so and so building..." and so on. Mail does not arrive here, for buildings are places to reside in but not an address; there are no municipal services here and no police. Here the jeeps of the border guards incessantly shuttle back and forth, looking for those who, circumventing the checkpoints, managed to infiltrate through back ways between the houses into Jerusalem, in order to beat and arrest them, or simply beat them. Arrests with no beatings are seldom. A simple arrest is a matter of law, but the land in between the checkpoints is a land without law, or perhaps law here yields itself to the inventive interpretation of the soldiers, in their forays between the houses and into their dark backyards.

In these neighborhoods, no civic communities emerged on the ruins of the villages they replaced, no stable neighborly relations developed between those who rented from the original villagers and their landlords, those whose villages had become neighborhoods in the city and who were now proprietors in Jerusalem. At the best of times, relationships here resembled encounters at the supermarket; at the worst of times, encounters at the checkpoint. Like those brief encounters at airports or central train stations; a fleeting interaction of people passing through on their way to another place. Even when people are united by a previous acquaintance, the encounter is less intimate since its time span is limited, accompanied by the anxious anticipation of the plane or train or bus, and the continuation of the journey after the conversation is ended. The moment escapes because it is the moment after that which is the goal.

As in all the land, checkpoints were erected on all the main roads connecting the city, north to Ramallah, and south to Bethlehem along the axis called "*kaf ha tever.*" In the language of that country this means the seam line, a term borrowed from the thread that mends a rent in a piece of cloth and at the same time signifies the tear, repairing the fissure while asserting its existence. It is the fastening between two pieces of cloth or the scab of human skin where a wound is sutured.

The checkpoint was erected with the help of big empty metal containers of food used in wholesale trade; stones were put in some and others had a fire lit in them at night. With the passage of time, barrels filled with cement took their place, only to be replaced by white and red plastic barriers, normally used in that country by the department of public works to divert traffic away from road repairs. Soon enough, cement barriers replaced them, and blocks with iron dividers and rocks of all sizes split the road into two passages for searching.

In the beginning the soldiers stood out in the open. Then an iron tower rose beside them, bearing a black plastic water container, a field tent at its base, soon replaced by a pre-fabricated room, protected from the street by bare and ugly concrete blocks. Every now and then, rocks or large garbage containers would be used creatively to block off pathways on both sides of the road that the soldiers could not easily see. These had another function: to stop cars from making U-turns and beating a retreat. If you got stuck at the checkpoint, you could not turn back out of boredom or anger except after getting checked. Along the length of the road cement barrels, metal sheets, and rocks prevented you from changing your mind and returning whence you came. The long wait, that there was no way back, no way out, turned waiting at the checkpoint into a state of nervous irritability, silent and pent up, and the only point of release was through the checkpoint itself.

At the beginning, the formation of the checkpoint was haphazard just like the surrounding neighborhoods, lacking order, cleanliness, and the solemnity of borders. For that reason, it had to impose the awe that it structurally lacked through the cruelty of human behavior. The checkpoint checks movement and divides space into "before the checkpoint" and "after the checkpoint." There is no need to divide time—what came before the checkpoint is just memory. Along that same extended road, people now live either before or after the checkpoint; there are of course those who pride themselves and insist that they live in Jerusalem because they are before the checkpoint, while their neighbors live in Ramallah because they are after the checkpoint:

"Hey man, are you Jerusalem or Ramallah?"

"No, we're Jerusalem, the car plates are yellow."

"No, the car plates are not important. I mean, do you live before or after the checkpoint—if you live after the checkpoint they won't let you keep the yellow car plates. You will also lose the Jerusalem identity card. In other words this means in Hebrew that 'you have moved the center of your life outside Jerusalem,' and that means you don't have a right to permanent residence in Jerusalem, which is what the ID is all about."

"Did I move the center of my life or did they move it? After all who was it that decided to set up the checkpoint? Did I set it up? If they had just set it up two meters down, I would now be Jerusalem. Anyway, is this really Jerusalem? These areas are the villages around

Jerusalem… Israel decided to incorporate them into Jerusalem and they became its neighborhoods, like Beit Hanina, Shu'fat, Abu Dis, al-'Izzariyyeh [Bethany], Az'ayyam, at-Turi, al-Mukabber. Are you all better than me because you are Jerusalem while I'm not, simply because the checkpoint decided this?"

"Oh, if you want to argue like this, that's not important, after all they've occupied the whole country; the important thing is that you're no longer Jerusalem. Nevertheless, you demand Jerusalem rents. It doesn't make sense, your rents should be lower because this house is in the West Bank and not in Jerusalem."

"If you want to talk like this then no one has to rent to you, since the foreigners are standing in line to rent houses in Jerusalem, and they pay, are not demanding, have no children, have no clans or family… They won't be sending me their men every time we have a disagreement, nobody is carrying their cause, and they don't want compensation every time someone shouts at one of their kids."

"Well, it's the foreigners who should have no problems with the checkpoint—what can anyone do to them at the checkpoint? The landlords should have solidarity with us and allow us to rent in Jerusalem."

"What do you mean have solidarity? I don't understand!"

"It seems you really are not a foreigner, otherwise you would have solidarity, but the cause is your cause just like the house is your house. How can you have solidarity when the cause is yours? You should make gains from the cause not have solidarity… Yes, by God, that is the truth, by God, how did I forget, why did I forget? I don't want to live in this country. Does a sane person chose to live in a country where every stone considers itself holy, because there are mad men in America who want to buy it, and that attracts the crackpots of the whole world."

Before the checkpoint acquired an overwhelming or totalitarian existence (in the periods called "*seger*," or closure, in the language of its masters, siege in Arabic) many years passed of intermittent closures followed by an easing, in the primitive manner of Pavlov's or Skinner's behavioral response experiments on dogs and other animals. That is why there was time to develop a way of life and a culture of the checkpoint in this period, for the checkpoint became a fixture, distinguishing it from the flying checkpoints that are set up for a few hours or a day, and are considered an unpleasant surprise in an unusual place for passersby. The latter, however, soon disappear, leaving behind painful knees and joints from the forced squat waiting for the checking of the numbers of the IDs via wireless, as well as cursing drivers, forced to unscrew the reserve tire and everything on top it for the meticulous search. University students recall how a flying checkpoint left behind two student martyrs and six months of closure, before the so-called first intifada. By its very nature, the flying checkpoint inspires spontaneous reactions: angry, sudden, and not thought out. Because a person stumbles across it when he is not psychologically ready, has not calculated his behavior in advance, his responses and behavior constrain him.

The checkpoint represents a turning point in public space. It is not a place but an edge, a borderline, a crossing point. It is a beginning and an end at the same point. It is the brink of passing through, and if a person does not walk in a balanced manner, then it can become the brink of the abyss, for instead of arriving at his destination, the person can arrive to be arrested or suffer physical humiliation. At the point of the checkpoint one public space ends and another begins. Theoretically then, the checkpoint is not a place but a point in space. Yet, the actual checkpoint is a place; it is a place that constantly expands to become itself a public space. The checkpoint reconstructs the place in its own image. This is how the intersections of the neighborhoods next to the checkpoint turn into its surrounding, into a periphery that bears its stamp. There, people await each other and wait for their turn. There, parking lots are set up; merchandise is traded and transferred from one truck to another. Here, luggage is unloaded and carts are pulled. Here are passenger terminals, and falafel stands spring up as an authentic Palestinian testimony to the existence of crowds. In the lands of the checkpoints, the crowd carries the smell of cigarettes, falafel, grilled kebab, and the sound of empty soda cans rolling between feet. It is a stop for the cars that transport workers who cross on foot to their workplaces before the sun rises, the only sign of their existence the parking spots of some—while others, not so lucky, are still waiting at the checkpoint for someone with influence who can take them to work. There are places for a quick hideout from the soldiers, and secluded places where soldiers can drag people for searching and beatings far from people's eyes.

The checkpoint is the expression of the situation; it is the order of things. Even for the soldiers, the checkpoint is not a place. It is a site where they are positioned because of their relation to the state; they are installed there, appointed and sent there. It is a zone of control and despotism. It is a site and a fortification. The fortification that oversees the checkpoint can only be seen from outside. You can see it but you are forbidden to enter or touch it. It is not a public space but the site that controls public space.

JERUSALEM IS THE DOOR TO MY LOVE.

Lena Jayyusi

Swallow of the heart
  rising towards minaret and spire
    across a half-moon evening
  winging to your brown eyes
    behind the backs of soldiers
You, carried on the generous palms
  of cousins
    battle expatriates
    who know freedom in a prison cell
    measure its space by the blocked passageways
    of the city
      and of our lives
  who blink away the ancient questions
    to open
      gates
        for our embrace.

POEM TO JERUSALEM

Jinan May Coulter

Imagining—you ask
I
Imagined
My grandmother's house
perched above the roots of time
undisturbed
olive green vistas
hung gently
under crescent moon
the silhouette of promise
lingering
warm in the night

Dreaming—you wonder
I
Dreamt
of wild blushing groves
my city rolling free with the valley

Yet I dreamt
of the arched window
time frozen
etched on a weeping tile
the shadow of memory
flung across
these walls

an opening
a passage
history's forgotten witness

DEATH IN JERUSALEM

Jinan May Coulter

On the evening of March 19, 2004, George Ilyas Khouri, 19, went jogging in Jerusalem where he lived, treading the hazy space between the city's east and west, or, in other words, between Arab and Jewish Jerusalem. A sniper in a fleeting car shot two bullets, and George lay dead on the pavement. Whether he was an Arab or Jewish boy, the tragedy holds equally. Gratuitous death in this holy city—and because its holiness is claimed by so many—lies at the very heart of the tragic existence of its citizens.

Jinan May Coulter was Khouri's schoolmate and friend at the Anglican School in Jerusalem.

Night curls round the edges
A yellow smoke moon sags low and lazy
above the East side
A *muezzin's** echo pervades the hollow divide
Up in the slim folding alleys
on a heaving olive hill
a black heel shuffle begins

Across the valley
hot air stirs on asphalt
the silhouette of knife-edged wire
glistens along a vanishing road
and there you are
your car murmurs
snakes round the blind bend
peddling towards the faint cusp of time

Yes
there you are
my friend
treading the quietly sinking terrain
easing into rhythmic stride

moon swelling
preparing to betray you

Then the wind turns
and fans the burning ember
the eye flinches
as the cruel shadow of terror
is cast upon pale stone.

---

*Muslim call to prayer.

THE *MUKHTAR* AND I:
MY VERY LAST SUMMER IN JERUSALEM

Michel Moushabeck

The morning my grandfather and I took a walk together—after feasting on a breakfast of *ka'ak* (over-sized sesame bagels) and *bayd hammeem* (oven-baked eggs) that my grandmother bought from a street vendor by yelling and dropping a basket-on-a-rope from the dining room bay window that overlooked the market in the Christian Quarter—he turned to me and said, "Today you get to spend the day with Sido (Arabic for grandfather); you are now old enough to come help me at the *qahwe* (café)."

The year was 1966 and I was barely eleven years old. At that time, we were living in Beirut. Often during the summertime, my mother would take me, together with my younger brother and my sister, to visit Tata and Sido in the Old City of Jerusalem. It was a summer holiday I often resisted and fought against, for I preferred to spend my time on the beach in Beirut with my best friends Munir and Imad instead of visiting my grandfather—a stern-looking, *tarboosh*-wearing (fez-wearing), *za'oot*-sniffing (snuff), *nargileh*-puffing, mustachioed man who to me looked more like an Ottoman Pasha than a grandfather, a man almost feared by everyone around him (at least that was my perception at the time), someone who had never shown the slightest interest in me or any affection towards me.

I not only feared my grandfather, but I was petrified by the sight of all the ugly, bearded monks who occupied the Greek Orthodox Convent where my grandparents lived after their forced exile from their home in the Katamon Quarter. The intoxicating smell of incense and burning candles, the spooky, narrow, cobble-stoned alleyways of the convent grounds, the robed priests roaming around in the dark (they gave me the creeps every time they looked me in the eye and whispered *kalimera* and *kalispera*, which I didn't know at the time meant good morning and good evening in Greek)—all contributed to a feeling of anxiety and discomfort I could do without.

My grandfather Issa Toubbeh, known to everyone as Abu Michel (father of Michael), was the *Mukhtar* (literally, the chosen), the head of the Eastern Orthodox Christian Arab community in Jerusalem, whom he dutifully served, as his father had done before him and his eldest son after him, for over 50 years. As *Mukhtar*, he was given a residence inside the Convent, which consisted of several large, high-ceilinged rooms abutting the walls of Mar Ya'coub (St. Jacob's Orthodox Church) and the Holy Sepulcher, located on the Convent grounds. Two rows of sweet-smelling potted plants and flowers, including gardenias and jasmine, lovingly tended to by my grandmother Tata Maria, graced the front entrance of the house and provided a welcome antidote to the unpleasant and overpowering (at least to a child) holy scents one encountered along the way. From the rooftop—the makeshift playground my cousins and I often frequented—the view of the Mount of Olives, the Dome of the Rock, the al-Aqsa Mosque and the Church of the Holy Sepulcher entrance overwhelmed my 11-year-old eyes every time I gazed in the distance.

Everyone spoke highly of my grandfather, the *Mukhtar*, and his important role in Palestinian society. Abu Michel was quite erudite and always commanded people's attention and respect. He spoke fluent Arabic, Turkish, Greek, Armenian, and Russian. And he could even swear in English—with a posh British accent, nonetheless—something he picked up during his numerous dealings with the "cursed" British before their departure from Palestine in 1948. He survived the rule of the Ottomans, the English, Hashemite Transjordan, and the Jewish state, and was considered a shrewd and highly experienced problem-solver—a necessary prerequisite for the job of *Mukhtar* or community leader. His reputation as a successful mediator spread beyond his flock in the Eastern Orthodox Christian Arab community and his services were highly sought after by people in the Muslim as well as the Jewish communities in Jerusalem. "Abused women rushed to our house for protection while their abusers waited patiently outside for the arrival of my father, the mediator," my uncle Jamil once told me. It was also rumored that whenever my grandfather accompanied an entourage of men assembled for the purpose of asking for a girl's hand in marriage, it was guaranteed that their request would be granted.

Such was the importance of *my* grandfather, the *Mukhtar*. But no matter what people said about him, no matter how much praise was bestowed on his position in the society, it never really impressed me much. My older cousin Basima once came up to me and proudly told me that she saw Sido's picture in the newspaper. It showed him walking next to the Greek Orthodox Patriarch of Jerusalem at the head of the procession on Easter Sunday. Big deal, I thought. My aunt Widad, the sweetest of my six aunts, bragged that no marriage in the community could take place without the official stamp of the *Mukhtar* on the marriage certificate; no birth could be legalized without his seal; no divorce approved without his counsel; no death authenticated without his presence. The more stories I heard about him the less affection I felt towards him. There is someone, I said to myself, who is doing good deeds all over town but has never said a kind word to me, let alone given me a grandfatherly hug. I was puzzled. How could a person have so much power over a community? Many more questions crossed my 11-year-old mind: Do I really have to get his approval before I get married? Will he stand in my way if I choose to marry the belly dancer I saw in the restaurant in Beirut a month ago? Will I have to steal the round, brass seal with the Arabic calligraphy he keeps chained to his vest in order to do so? And so on.

The side I saw of Sido was in stark contrast to his reputation on the street. The verbal abuse he often unleashed on my aunts (mind you, never on my uncles) was shocking. The time he yelled at my mother for her disrespectful act of lighting a cigarette in his presence, and his refusal to speak to her for several days afterwards, was quite upsetting for me to witness. The way he treated my Tata (the world's kindest grandmother) was also painful to watch – especially the daily, evening ritual of her taking off his shoes and socks and messaging his feet in a bowl of hot water for hours on end after his return from work. As if her days were easy when compared to his, I used to complain to my mother. I remember my mother scolding me one day for asking why it was that he never messaged her feet as payback or reward for taking her away from her family at age thirteen and impregnating her ten times (not counting the several miscarriages she had to go through) without a break in between.

Spending time at home with my grandmother and watching her slave away in the house all day made me very resentful of my grandfather's behavior. Maybe I felt this way because I grew up in cosmopolitan Beirut. Or maybe it was because I never saw my father treat my mother in this manner. I was too young to understand the role customs played on his attitudes, too naïve to fathom how deep-rooted in tradition people are. But despite all this, I was not too young to understand that being "the grandson of the *Mukhtar*" had its benefits too. And I shamefully admit that I exploited them to the maximum. I wasn't about to let these brief, unpleasant family episodes stand in the way of my having fun on my summer vacation in

Jerusalem. Everybody in the community knew the *Mukhtar* and, in very short time after my arrival, wherever I went people would say: "Ah, you must be the *Mukhtar*'s grandson." The local grocer would give me free sugar-covered chickpeas, the juice vendor, free lemonade. I got free ice cream, free falafel sandwiches, free bicycle rentals, free olive wood crosses (which I later sold to tourists a few blocks away) and—most important of all—free donkey rides. The *Mukhtar* connection opened so many doors for me that the Old City was soon transformed into one big amusement park. I would spend my days roaming the streets, going from quarter to quarter, hanging out with Hassan and Ahmad in the courtyard of the al-Aqsa Mosque while they waited for their father to come out of Friday prayer services, playing in and around the Church of the Holy Sepulcher with Charlie and George, sons of a souvenir store owner, and watching the mini-skirt clad *ajnabiyyat* (foreign women)— some pretty, I thought, but no match to the love of my life, the dark-haired belly dancer in the Beirut restaurant.

I had the freedom to go anywhere I wanted in the Old City—no worries there, since I was the *Mukhtar*'s grandson and the *entire* community would look after me (be held responsible for my safety is more like it). My only condition was that I return to the Convent before the 8:00 PM closing time of the little, studded, metal door carved in the center-bottom of the monstrous iron door that sealed off and protected the fortress known as the Greek Orthodox Convent. I was constantly warned about this by my mother and always allowed ample time for the walk back home—except once. It was Sunday evening and I was having so much fun flying Salim's kite that I lost track of time. When I got to the Convent, the dreaded metal door was shut. And that was a lesson to remember. The street was almost deserted and the amplified sound of occasional hurried footsteps on the cobble-stoned sidewalk did little to ease my fears. Alone, I stood outside the Convent door sobbing for what seemed like eternity (it couldn't have been more than ten minutes) until a nice, elegantly-dressed lady came up to me and uttered the magic words: "You must be the *Mukhtar*'s grandson." She gently held my hand and let me rest my head on her chest (later I thought of marrying her too) until someone sent a message to the monk inside who unhappily came and opened the door. After I thanked and bade my savior goodbye, the monk with the foot-long keys hanging from his belt slammed shut the squeaky metal door behind us, and I quickly ran to the house—totally ignoring the angry Greek words he spewed in my direction.

The "walk" with my grandfather took place the morning after

this incident. And I dreaded it. My time of scolding has come, I said to myself, especially after his total silence on the matter the evening before. But to my surprise, there was no mention of it. Instead, he extended his hand to me and gave me a warm and loving look—something I was not accustomed to seeing. As we passed the frowning monk at the Convent entrance, the one whose prayer I disrupted the night before, Sido looked at me and gave me a wink and a smile. That moment was the start of a day I will remember and cherish for the rest of my life.

The first order of the day was a visit to the *Batrak*, the grand old Patriarch of the Greek Orthodox Church in Jerusalem—a real treat and a privilege very few people get, Sido told me. I was not only special but also the oldest son of his youngest daughter, he went on to say (a reason only a real smoothie would think about). Our audience with the *Batrak* was very brief. I remember feeling dazzled by the opulence of his quarters, but had very little time to absorb any details except for the long baton with the round, golden head the *Batrak* held in his right hand. I was not too thrilled at having to kiss the wrinkled old man's hand. And I had to do it twice—once at the beginning and another time after he placed around my neck a gold chain with a black and gold cross. This gift was special and would protect me from future evil, Sido quietly whispered in my ear, since the gold cross I was just given had inside it a wood splinter that came directly from the cross of Jesus Christ. (This valuable piece of information came in handy when I later sold the cross to my Lebanese Maronite schoolmate who paid me the desperately needed Lebanese pounds I wanted to shower on the love of my life, the belly dancer, the next time I saw her.)

My memories of that day are as vivid and as bright as a silver coin in the sun. Sido and I, hand in hand, walked through the streets of Jerusalem, stopping every few paces to greet people he knew and those who knew of him. Along the way we passed the market, a bustling collection of colorful fruit and vegetable vendors. I could instantly feel the flow of musical energy emanating from the place and its people. Music was simply all around: from the unforgettable melodic chanting of the *muezzin's* call to prayer—often juxtaposed against the ringing of church bells—to fruit and vegetable vendors in the market singing praises about pickling cucumbers (as small as babies' fingers) or prickly pears (so delicious they melt in your mouth); from the cheerful foot-thumping sounds of children practicing *dabkeh* dancing to the powerful emotional songs of Um Kulthum blasting from transistor radios on window sills. To this day I am still able to close my eyes and transport myself back to my Jerusalem days. I am still able to smell the delicious food sold by street vendors, especially the wonderfully rich and evocative scent of roasted chestnuts and, of course, the sumptuous sweets drenched in *ater* (sugar syrup) sold at Zalatimo's; I am still able to see the old street photographer with the wooden camera whose head often disappeared underneath its black cloth; still able to touch the olive oil soap stacked in the long cylindrical towers at the corner store.

But the one thing that intrigued me most of all, the one person that had a profound influence on me, was the juice vendor who walked with his body leaning forward and his Bordeaux fez with the black tassels tipped back. Not only did he carry a big tank filled with *sous*, *jellab*, and lemonade on his back as he traveled by foot from neighborhood to neighborhood, but he was a percussionist of the highest degree. I was fascinated by how he announced his arrival, and mesmerized by how he played beautiful, intricate rhythmic patterns, using brass cups and saucers, to entertain customers and alert them of his presence—rhythms that were very similar to the ones the belly dancer in the Beirut restaurant moved her hips to. From that moment on I was hooked. I would sit on the sidewalk with my eyes fixed on the juice vendor's hands so I could learn his art. Back at the house later on, to my grandmother's horror, I would practice the same rhythms using her china, which produced disastrous results and, it goes without saying, a spanking. This marked the beginning of what was to become later a life-long passion for Arabic music and rhythms.

Adjacent to Jaffa Gate was my grandfather's long-established café. Known to family and friends as al-Mahal (The Place) and to others as Qahwet Abu Michel (Father of Michael's Café) or Qahwet *al-Mukhtar*, the café was a renowned Jerusalem institution frequented in its heyday by the Palestinian literati, nicknamed *al-sa'aleek* (the vagabonds). According to my uncle Jamil, it was Palestinian author and educator Khalil Sakakini "who bestowed the title of *sa'aleek* on the group of intellectuals who met at al-Mahal. Members of the *sa'aleek* included Yusef el-Issa, publisher/editor of the daily *Alef Ba*, and Issa el Issa, publisher/editor of the daily *Filistine*, as well as Anistas Hanania, Adel Jaber, Ahmad Zaki Pasha, Khalil Mutran, Yacoub Farraj and others." Poets, musicians, historians, storytellers, folks who wanted to be seen in their company, young Palestinians who aspired to be like them, or simply those who just wanted to listen to the exchange of ideas taking place, gathered at *al-Mukhtar*'s café.

The café was buzzing with people when my grandfather and I arrived from the market. As we walked in the door, we were greeted by my uncle Mitri, who gave me a kiss on each cheek before going back behind the counter to prepare an order of *mezze* for one of the customers. I was immediately put to work cutting cucumbers, chopping parsley, and preparing plates of olives and pickled turnips for the busy lunch crowd. *Arak* (a Lebanese alcoholic drink made of distilled grape juice flavored with anis) and *nargileh* were present at almost every table, which accounted for the lively, albeit smoky, atmosphere of the place. For the next hour or so Sido attended to the business of recording births, deaths, and marriages in his oversized leather book, giving advice in between to visitors and stamping official documents that required his seal. When he was done, he signaled to me with his walking stick to follow him to the café backyard, a large paved area with rows of plants on each side, a round tiled fountain in the middle surrounded by tables and chairs, and a massive cage that housed chickens and over a hundred pigeons.

As we sat in the sun and snacked on watermelon and *Nabulsiyyeh* cheese, he told me funny stories and answered the many questions I had stored up over the years. His answers to silly questions like "Why do you wear a *tarboosh* (fez)?" and "What's that stuff you sniff and makes you sneeze all the time?" and more serious ones like "Why did you leave Katamon?" and "Why did you not fight the *Yahood* (the Jews) when they took your home?" kept me enthralled the whole afternoon. He told me about the bombing that demolished the Samiramis hotel down the road from their house in Katamon in January 1948 and how the blast that Menachem Begin masterminded at the King David Hotel, close to my uncle Michel's office, instilled fear in the community and was the catalyst that drove many Katamonians to flee their homes. I laughed when he described how one morning, on orders of Haj Amin Al-Husseini, the *mufti* of Palestine, he received a delivery of antiquated guns and ammunition loaded on five donkeys to be distributed to the men in the community at a time when the *Yahood* were parading the streets with tanks and cannons. I cried when he told me the story of the massacre that took place at the village of Deir Yassin. A quick change of subject to the art of pigeon flying restored my smile. And before we headed back home, he gave me an impressive demonstration by releasing all the pigeons and showing me how to fly them in a circle and then guide them back to their cage—all with only the help of a black piece of cloth tied to the end of a long stick. What he failed to tell me at the time was that this exercise is done to attract other flying pigeons to the flock and ultimately back to the cage so that my uncle Mitri could later serve them to the customers.

Back at the house that evening, while my grandfather rested his feet on a chair in the living room, Tata asked me to run over to the neighbor's to borrow a bowl of rice. Along the way, I met another neighbor who asked, "Where are you headed, son?" I told him about my mission to which he inquired, "Why? What's going down at *beit al-Mukhtar* (the *Mukhtar's* house)?" I shrugged and kept on going. My guess was that he told another in the neighborhood, and another told another, and in no time more than twenty or so family and friends descended on my grandparents' house, which sent my grandmother—and a dozen or so female helpers—scrambling to the kitchen to prepare food for the guests. The feast and the festive atmosphere that ensued were like nothing I'd encountered before. Suddenly musical instruments appeared from nowhere, and poetry became the flavor of the day. While the men sang and played music in the living room, the women danced in the kitchen, and the children shuttled back and forth between the two. In between solo improvisations on the *oud* (a fretless lute), the *qanoun* (a zither-like, plucked instrument), and the *nay* (a reed flute), that brought sighs of appreciation, the singer sang soulful *mawwals* (vocal improvisations in dialect) and made up new lyrics to familiar tunes. I recognized many of the rhythms the juice vendor played and I was encouraged to join the musicians on the tambourine. The fun was interrupted when Tata ordered everyone to the dining room table. And what a table that was! There were *keftas* and *kababs, hashwet jaaj* (chicken with rice and pine nuts) and *koosa mahshi* (stuffed zucchini), and *mezze* plates as far as the eye could see: Hummus (chickpea dip), *babghannouj* (eggplant dip), stuffed vine leaves, glistening black olives, braided white cheese, glossy vegetables, plump nuts and lush juicy fruits. It was like magic: Where did it all come from? I wondered.

After stuffing ourselves to the chin (an Arabic expression often used by my mother), we all retired to the living room and the music resumed. This time the men and women danced together to the soothing and hypnotic compositions of Zakaria Ahmad and Sayyid Darweesh, Mohammad Abd el-Wahab and Fareed el-Atrash. And I, naturally exhausted by the events of day, fell asleep on my grandfather's lap.

Early the next morning, a crowd of family and friends lined up at the entrance of the Convent door to bid us farewell as we got into the *service* (taxi) that drove us to Amman and from there back home to Beirut. From the car window I waved goodbye to my teary-eyed Tata and Sido and yelled *kalimera* to the bearded monk with foot-long keys.

That was the last time I saw my grandparents; the last time I saw Jerusalem.

THE MUSLIM QUARTER

Sarah Maguire

The Old City unspools behind me
    as I slip down the Suq Khan ez-Zeit
    close as a shadow to a hand.

Sallow lamps pool on the ceiling
    threading me down
        to the bottom of light.

The markets have been closed for the night;
    the stalls' rusted doors
        belted and padlocked,

the cabinets of objects concertinaed
    and concealed.
        Cheek by jowl

sleep dustpans and dresses
    and dolls that blink,
        crockery, suitcases,

razorblades and prayer mats,
    oil, olive oil, and olive-oil soap.
        Tucked up, packed up,

mouths stitched shut.
    The vaulted roof gives way
        to a canopy of milky glass,

fine wrought iron finishing the panes.
    Through a crack the stars fall in,
        the heedless stars

dazzling in their freezing orbits.
     I feel my way
          down a corridor of silence

trying to imagine these are buildings
     ordinary, useful and at rest
          as eighteen soldiers

watch me cross the Via Dolorosa
     The Day of Atonement is finished.
          Even as I turn

and walk back to the East
     the Tunnel is dug out
          under my feet.

CONTRIBUTORS

Ruanne Abou-Rahme is an Arab-Israeli born in the US and an avid poet. As an undergraduate at the University of London, she participated in the making of the film *Fragile*, which received an award for best student film in 2004. She intends to pursue her higher studies in new, interactive, and digital media.

Saleh Abudayyeh was born in Amman and now lives in the Minnesota, where he is an accomplished poet, a teacher of mathematics, and co-founder with Kathryn Haddad of *Mizna*, a journal featuring poetry, prose, and art that explore Arab America.

Etal Adnan, a writer, poet, and visual artist, is the author of over a dozen volumes of poetry and prose. Her work has been translated into many languages, including Greek, German, Italian, Dutch, and Urdu. Her recent works include *There: In the Light and the Darkness of the Self and the Other* and *In/somnia*. Born in Lebanon, Adnan moved to the US in 1955, and now divides her time between California, Paris, and Beirut.

M. Modassir Ali is research associate in the Islamic Research Institute, International Islamic University, Islamabad.

Zafar Ishaq Ansari has been director general of the Islamic Research Institute, International Islamic University, Islamabad since 1988, and holds a Ph.D. in Islamic Studies from McGill University. He has taught at universities around the world, and has been editing *Islamic Studies*, a quarterly journal, since 1989. His publications include *Muslims and the West: Encounter and Dialogue* (2001), which he co-edited with J. L. Esposito.

Muhammad Asad was born in 1900 in the city of Lvov (Lemberg), Galicia, now in Poland, as Leopold Weiss. He embraced Islam in the mid-1920s and wrote several works, including *The Road to Mecca* and *Islam at the Crossroads*. He died in 1992 in Spain.

Laila al-Atrash is a Palestinian novelist, journalist, and prominent media figure. Her novels include *The Sun Rises from the West* (1988); the acclaimed *A Woman of Five Seasons* (Interlink Books, 2001), translated by PROTA; *A Day Like Any Other* (1991); *The Neighing of Distances* (1999); and *Illusive Anchors*, forthcoming. She currently lives in Amman, Jordan.

Abd al-Fattah el-Awaisi is the principal and vice-chancellor of Al-Maktoum Institute for Arabic and Islamic Studies in Dundee, United Kingdom. He is the first chair in Islamic Jerusalem Studies, the editor-in-chief of the *Journal of Islamic Jerusalem Studies*, and the director of the Center of Islamic Jerusalem Studies.

Liyana Badr is a Palestinian writer, born in Jerusalem, whose works include *A Balcony Over the Fakihani* (Interlink Books, 1993), as well as short stories, children's books, and a study of Fadwa Tuqan. She runs the cinema department at the Palestinian Ministry of Culture in Ramallah.

Ibtisam Barakat is an educator, poet, and writer, born in Ramallah and now residing in the US; her acclaimed poems and short stories have been included in numerous anthologies. She leads the "Write Your Life" workshops, which use writing personal narrative as a means of social healing.

Mureed Barghouthy is a prominent Palestinian poet who lives in Cairo and Ramallah. Among his collections are *Poems of the Pavement* (1980) and *Endless Estrangement* (1987). *I Saw Ramallah*, his account of his return to Ramallah, Palestine, after years of forced exile in the Palestinian diaspora, has won great acclaim in both its Arabic original and its English translation.

Azmi Bishara is a prominent Palestinian intellectual and a leading Arab-Israeli political activist. A member of the Israeli Knesset, he has defended the cause of the Israeli Arabs with great strength and effectiveness. He is also a founding member of the National Democratic Assembly (NDA), which represents the Arab minority in Israel.

Kamal Boullata, a well-known Palestinian-American painter, was born in Jerusalem and now lives in France. His work has been exhibited in the US, Europe, and the Middle East, and he completed a Fulbright Senior Scholar Fellowship studying Islamic art in

Morocco. He has also edited several anthologies and is the author of *Faithful Witnesses: Palestinian Children Recreate Their World.*

Hayan Charara is an Arab-American poet and teacher. His published works include *The Alchemist's Diary* (Hanging Loose Press, 2001); since 1994, he has edited the annual literary anthology *Graffiti Rag.*

Anthony Coon is senior research fellow, department of environmental planning, University of Strathclyde, Glasgow, Scotland.

Patricia B. Cosentino has written three books of poetry, including *Always Being Born* (2003). She is the second translator of Arabic poetry for PROTA/Nexus. She teaches writing and poetry in the LIFE program at Mount Wachusett Community College in Gardner, Massachusetts, and is the editor of *Tapestries: An Anthology.*

Eugene Cotran is serving the British judiciary and is a visiting professor of law and chairman of the Center of Islamic and Middle Eastern Law at the School of Oriental and African Studies, University of London.

Jinan May Coulter is half Palestinian, half English, and an American citizen; her diverse talents include poetry, painting, film, and music. She has co-directed and co-produced three films, including *To Whom It May Concern* (2004), which won the Best First Short Film award at the Greenwich Film Festival. She is pursuing a masters in documentary film.

Aida Hasan Damuni is a Palestinian-American poet. She edits a website on Arab culture and experience.

Michel Eddeh is a former minister of information and education of Lebanon.

Muhammad Husain al-Farra was ambassador of Jordan to the United Nations during the June 1967 Arab–Israeli War.

Subhi Ghosheh practices medicine in Amman and works for the cause of his native city, Jerusalem. He is the chairman of Al-Quds Day Committee in Jordan.

Oleg Grabar, author of eighteen books, is one of the best known specialists on Islamic monuments, and has written extensively on the al-Aqsa Mosque. He is professor emeritus of the Institute for Advanced Study in the School of Historical Studies at Princeton. At Harvard University, where he taught from 1968–1990, he was the first Aga Khan Professor of Islamic Art and Architecture.

Nathalie Handal is a Palestinian-American writer who has lived around the world and now teaches at Columbia University. Her work includes the award-winning anthology *The Poetry of Arab Women* (Interlink Books, 2000), as well as the collections *The Neverfield* and *The Lives of Rain* (both Interlink, 2004). *The Lives of Rain* was shortlisted for the Agnes Starret Lynch Poetry Prize/Pitt Poetry Series.

Elma Ruth Harder is a Canadian educationist and writer who lives in Alberta, Canada.

Ingrid Hjelm is a Danish scholar of the Bible associated with the department of biblical studies, University of Copenhagen, Denmark.

Adnan al-Sayyid Hussein is professor of international relations in the faculty of law and political science at the Lebanese University, Beirut.

Bayan Nuwaihed al-Hut is professor in the faculty of law and political science at the Lebanese University, Beirut, and a member of the Pan-National Islamic Conference.

Muzaffar Iqbal is the president of the Center for Islam and Science in Canada, and the regional director for the Muslim World at the Center for Theology and the Natural Sciences, Berkeley, California. He lives in Sherwood Park, Alberta, Canada.

Lena Jayyusi is professor of communication studies at Zayid University in Dubai, the United Arab Emirates. She also specializes in sociology, particularly the ethno-methodological approach to social studies, on which she has written extensively, including in her book *Categorization and the Moral Order* (1984).

Salma Khadra Jayyusi is one of the Arab world's most distinguished literary personalities. She is the founder and director of PROTA (Project of Translation from Arabic), and East–West Nexus, Amman,

Jordan. She is widely known for her poetry and literary criticism; her books include *Trends and Movements in Modern Arabic Poetry*, 2 volumes, her edited work, *The Legacy of Muslim Spain*, and *Short Arabic Plays: An Anthology* (Interlink Books, 2003).

Nikos Kazantzakis (1883–1956) was a Greek novelist who worked as a journalist in his youth. Among his acclaimed novels are *The Last Temptation of Christ* and *Zorba the Greek*.

Izzat Khattab is professor emeritus of english at King Saud University, Riyadh, Saudi Arabia.

'Atallah Kuttab is an engineer and is director of the Save the Children field office in Cairo.

Sarah Maguire is an English poet and translator. Her interest in contemporary Palestinian poetry has led her to translate selections from several poets in the West Bank; her lucid and lively style reflects fervor and warmth of feeling. Her poetry collections include *Spilt Milk* and *The Invisible Mends*.

Haydar Mahmoud is a poet of Palestinian origin; he once worked as a Jordanian diplomat and for a short period was minister of culture in Jordan.

Lisa Suhair Majaj is a Palestinian-American poet, writer, and one of the leading scholars of Arab-American literature. Her books include *Etel Adnan: Critical Essays on the Arab-American Writer and Artist* (2002), which she co-edited, and *Intersections: Gender, Nation and Community in Arab Women's Novels* (2002), also co-edited.

Nazik al-Mala'ika is one of the Arab world's most prominent poets, critics, and writers. She was a pioneer in the establishment of the free verse movement in Arabic, which radically changed the age-old two hemistich form in Arabic poetry; her influence has been irreplaceable.

Michel S. Moushabeck is an essayist, editor, publisher, and musician. He is the founder of Interlink Publishing, a Massachusetts-based independent publishing house. His books include *Beyond the Storm: A Gulf Crisis Reader* (with Phyllis Bennis) and *Altered States: A Reader in the New World Order*. He is a founding member of Layaali Arabic

Music Ensemble, and his recording credits include two albums: *Lost Songs of Palestine* and *Folk Songs and Dance Music from Turkey and the Arab World.*

Ra'ef Najm is an engineer and a specialist on the architecture and town planning of Jerusalem.

Isma'il Ibrahim Nawwab has taught in the University of Edinburgh, Scotland, and the University of Malaya at Kuala Lumpur, Malaysia, and was a general manager of Aramco, Dhahran, Saudi Arabia.

Naomi Shihab Nye is a celebrated American poet of Palestinian descent. Her newest work is the forthcoming *You and Yours* (2005); she is also the author/editor of a number of acclaimed books and poetry collections for children. Her *19 Varieties of Gazelle: Poems from the Middle East* was a finalist for the National Book Award; she has, among other honors, been a Guggenheim Fellow and a three-time winner of the Pushcart Prize.

Michael Prior (1942–2004) was a principal lecturer at St. Mary's College, Strawberry Hill, University of Surrey, UK, and co-founder of the group *Living Stones,* which aims to connect Christian communities in Britain with those in the Middle East. His works include *The Bible and Colonialism* and *Speaking the Truth: Zionism, Israel, and Occupation* (Interlink Books, 2004).

Nizar Qabbani (1923–1998), one of the modern Arab world's leading poets, was also a Syrian diplomat. His major themes were the political malaise of the present-day Arab world, love, and the condition of women; he became one of the most endeared voices advocating for the liberation of Arab women everywhere.

Yasser Ibrahim Rajjal is assistant professor of architectural engineering at Petra University in Amman; his specialty is the Islamic city.

André Raymond is professor emeritus of Islamic architecture and art at the University of Aix en Provence. He has written extensively in his field, and his major specialization is the city of Cairo.

Hala Sakakini is a well-known Palestinian educator and memoirist. Her writing concentrates mainly on Jerusalem, her birthplace, where her family lived until their house was seized in 1948. She moved to Ramallah, where she lived until her death with her sister Dumia. Her books include *Jerusalem and I* (1990).

Mahmoud Shahin is a Palestinian novelist, short story writer, and painter. He comes from a Bedouin background and presently lives in Damascus, Syria. His short story collections include *The Visitors* (1979) and *Ordeal by Fire* (1979), and his novels include *Forbidden Land* (1983), *Migration to Hell* (1984), *Crossing Over to the Homeland* (1985), and *Usurped Land* (1989).

Thomas L. Thompson is currently professor of Old Testament studies at the University of Copenhagen, Denmark. Among his best known works are *The Historicity of the Patriarchal Narratives* (1974), *The Early History of Israelite People* (1992), and *The Bible in History: How Writers Create A Past* (2000).

Fadwa Tuqan, 1917–2003, was a pre-eminent Palestinian poet and noted voice of the Palestinian resistance. Her many collections include *I Found It* (1958), *In Front of the Closed Door* (1967), and *Alone on the Summit of the World* (1973), as well as a two-volume autobiography, *A Mountainous Journey* (1985) and *The Journey More Difficult* (1976). During her lifetime she received prizes from Greece, Italy, and Jordan, the Uweis literary prize of the United Arab Emirates in 1990, as well as the Jerusalem Award for Culture and Art in 1990.

Na'ila 'l-Wa'ri is a Jerusalemite social activist living in Bahrain, currently working towards a Ph.D. in history. Her social work revolves around her country's plight, to which she dedicates extensive time and energy.

Keith W. Whitelam is professor of biblical studies at the University of Sheffield, UK.

NOTES

Foreword

[1] For the text of the covenant in English, see p. 113–114.

[2] It would be pertinent to mention an incident during 'Umar's visit to Jerusalem: Escorted by the Patriarch Sophronius, 'Umar was looking around at the religious sites of Jerusalem when it was time for him to pray and he needed a place to do so. Sophronius suggested to 'Umar to pray in the church. He, however, declined on grounds that if he would pray in the church, Muslims would follow his example, and in time they would virtually turn the Christians out of it in total contravention of the terms of the Covenant. (See Muhammad Husayn Haykal, *al-Faruq 'Umar* (Cairo: Maktabat Misr, 1346 AH, 1:258).

The Arabs, Islam, and Jerusalem

[1] André Raymond is professor emeritus of the University of Provence. He states as follows:

> The following text, solicited by the Paris Mairie for the "Essays" section of the catalogue for the exhibition Voir Jérusalem, was accepted and set as it stood. It failed to meet the approval of Mme B. Philippe, who withdrew it from the catalogue without informingme. It was replaced in the form of an addendum.

Jerusalem as the Key Issue

[1] Martin Gilbert, "Jerusalem—Whose City?," 2, http://www.cdn-friends-icej.ca, visited November 23, 1999.

[2] Reuters (News agency), July 28, 1998.

[3] George To'meh, ed., *Qararat al-Umam al-Mutahidah wa al-Sira al-'Arabi al-Isra'ili 1947–1974* (Beirut: Palestine Studies Institute, 1975), 4–16.

[4] Usamah Halabi, *al-Wad'al-Qanuni li Madinat al-Quds wa Muwatiniha al-'Arab* (Beirut: Palestine Studies Institute, 1997), 9–19. Text in Arabic.

[5] Ibid., 23–24.

[6] Wafa, *I'lan Mabadi Hawla Tartibat al-Hukumah al-Dhatiyyah al-Intiqaliyyah* (Wafa Palestine News Agency); as distributed by Wafa to members of the Palestinian National Council on October 10, 1993.

[7] "The Stage of Legislation and Colonization," part 5, in *Jerusalem: History and Present*, 1–3, http://www.palestine-info.net, visited October 25, 1999.

[8] "Israel to End Ethnic Cleansing Policy," in *Law: The Palestinian Society for the Protection of Human Rights and the Environment*, 1–2, http://www.lawsociety.org, visited October 25, 1999.

[9] Dan Leon, "Who is a Jerusalemite?," http://www.al-bushra.org, visited November 6, 1999.

[10] The Palestine Day Committee, *Jerusalem: A Trust for the Conscience of Every Muslim* (Amman: Committee Publications, 1996), 21–26.

[11] Rochelle Davis, "Ottoman Jerusalem: The Growth of the City Outside the Walls" in Salim Tamari, ed., *Jerusalem 1948: The Arab Neighbourhoods and Their Fate in the War* (Jerusalem: Institute of Jerusalem Studies; Bethlehem: Badil Resource Centre for Palestinian Residency and Refugee Rights, 1999), 21–24.

[12] Samir Jiryes, *al-Quds: al-Mukhattatat al-Sayhuniyyah: al-Ihtilal, al-Tahwid* (Beirut: Palestine Studies Institute, 1981), 23.

[13] Ibid., 25.

[14] Rochelle Davis, "The Growth of the Western Communities," in Tamari, *Jerusalem 1948*, 50–51.

[15] Salim Tamari, "The City and its Rural Hinterland" in his *Jerusalem 1948*, 78.

[16] 'Abd Allah al-Tall, *Mukhtarat 'Abd Allah al-Tall: Karithat Filastin* (Cairo: Dar al-Qalam, 1959), 199–206.

[17] A *dunum* equals 0.23 acres.

[18] "The Achievement of Demographical Superiority (1917–1947)," part 3, in *Jerusalem: History and Present*, 4–9, http://www.palestine-info.net, visited October 25, 1999.

[19] "Terrorism and Deportation Stage (1947–1949)," part 4, in ibid., 2–3.

[20] "The Stage of Legislation and Colonization (1949–1967)," part 5, in ibid., 5.

[21] Rawhi al-Khatib, "A Statement to the Security Council–United Nations, on 3/5/1968," as cited in *al-Mu'amrah al-Yahudiyyah al-Ijramiyah 'ala Salamat Masjid al-Aqsa wa Bayt al-Maqdis* (A Memorandum from the Islamic World Conference to All Muslims, c. 1968), 17.

[22] Ibid.

[23] "Expanding Jewish Presence in the Old City of Jerusalem," in *The Old City of Jerusalem*, 3–4, http://www.arij.org, visited November 5, 1999.

[24] "Annexation and Occupation Stage (1967–1997)," part 6, in *Jerusalem: History and Present*, 1, http://www.palestine-info.net, visited October 25, 1999.

[25] Ibid., 2–3, 5.

[26] "Jerusalem in 2000," in *Mehanei* [military magazine], (19/9/1991) as cited in ibid., 5.

[27] "Plans for a 'Greater Jerusalem': The Illegal Israeli Annexation of Jerusalem Continues" in *Law: The Palestinian Society for the Protection of Human Rights and the Environment*, http://www.lawsociety.org, visited October 25, 1999.

[28] Ibid., 2–4.

[29] Ghada Karmi, "Jerusalem: A City of All Its Citizens," paper presented at "Arab Jerusalem, 1996," Symposium held by the Center for Contemporary Arab Studies in Georgetown University, Washington, DC, US, 2.

[30] Shaykh 'Akramah Sabri (Mufti of Jerusalem and Palestine), interview on al-Jazeera TV, October 21, 1999.

[31] Walid al-Khalidi, "Jerusalem is the Key to Peace," keynote address at the "Jerusalem Now Conference," Beirut, November 8, 1999.

[32] Karmi, "Jerusalem: A City of All Its Citizens," 3–4.

[33] Sabri, interview on al-Jazeera TV, October 21, 1999.

[34] "Israel to End Ethnic Cleansing Policy," 1–2.

[35] Michel Eddeh, "The Zionist Scheme to Judaize Bayt al-Maqdis," a lecture at the Bayt al-Maqdis Seminar, Beirut, January 4, 1999.

[36] Sabri, interview on al-Jazeera TV, October 21, 1999.

[37] "House Demolitions since the Oslo Agreement," in *Law: The Palestinian Society for the Protection of Human Rights and the Environment*, 1–2, http://www.lawsociety.org, visited October 25, 1999.

[38] Halabi, The Legal Status of Jerusalem, 32–37.

[39] "Israel to End Ethnic Cleansing Policy," 1–2.

[40] Nina Pinto (*Ha'aretz* correspondent), October 26, 1999, as quoted from "American Moslems for Jerusalem."

[41] "Expanding Jewish Presence in the Old City of Jerusalem," 4–5.

[42] "Annexation and Occupation Stage (1967–1997)," 6–7.

[43] Eddeh, "Zionist Scheme…," lecture.

[44] Kaye Corbett, "Covenant of Jerusalem——Key to 25th Anniversary," in *Whose Jerusalem?*, 1, http://www.cdn-friends-icej.ca.

[45] Ibid.

[46] Halabi, *The Legal Status of Jerusalem*, 32–37.

[47] Eddeh, "Zionist Scheme."

[48] Ibid.

[49] Sabri, interview on al-Jazeera TV.

[50] Ibid.

[51] Ibid.

Jerusalem: Occupation and Challenges to Urban Identity

[1] For the constituents of urban identity formation, see Christian Norberg-Sochulz, *Genius Loci: Toward a Phenomenology of Architecture* (New York: Preager, 1979), 5–15.

[2] See, for example, Edmund Bacon, *Design of Cities* (New York: Thames and Hudson, 1982), 23–27. See also Vincent Scully, *Architecture, the Natural and the Manmade* (London: Harvill, 1991).

[3] Norberg-Sochulz, *Genius Loci: Towards a Phenomenology of Architecture*, 5–15.

[4] Khalil Tafakji, "al-Istitan al-Jughrafi wa al-Dimugrafi wa Akhtaruhu fi Qadiyyat al-Quds," paper presented to the International Symposium for Jerusalem Affairs, General Islamic Conference for Jerusalem (Amman: 2000), 3.

[5] Ibid., 1–2.

[6] Lajnat al-Quds, *Wathiqat al-Quds* (Rabat: Munazzamat al-Mu'tamar al-Islami, 1984), 79.

[7] Ibid., 75.

[8] Tafakji, "al-Istitan al-Jughrafi wa al-Dimugrafi wa Akhtaruhu fi Qadiyyat al-Quds," 8.

[9] Ibid., 1–2.

[10] See Khalil Tafakji, *al-Tahwid al-Mubarmaj li al-Baldah al-Qadimah li Madinat al-Quds*, a bulletin review at the Orient House (Jerusalem: Department of Maps and Surveying, 1999).

[11] Samih el-Abed, "Master Plan of Greater Jerusalem: The Israeli and Palestinian Perspectives" in Essam Salam, ed., *Jerusalem Today: City and People: Continuing Challenges* (Beirut: Association of Arab Architects, 2000), 118–21.

[12] Tafakji, "al-Istitan al-Jughrafi wa al-Dimugrafi wa Akhtaruhu fi Qadiyyat al-Quds," 7.

[13] Ibid.

[14] This planning model was presented in Ariel Sharon, *Planning Jerusalem: The Master Plan for the Old City of Jerusalem and its Environs* (New York: McGraw Hill, 1974). See also the discussion of this in Arthur Kutcher, *The New Jerusalem: Planning and Politics* (London: Thames and Hudson, 1993), 51–55 and 88–108.

[15] Lajnat al-Quds, *Wathiqat al-Quds*, 82.

[16] Ibid., 75.

[17] Tafakji, *al-Tahwid al-Mubarmaj li al-Baldah al-Qadimah li Madinat al-Quds*, 2–4.

[18] Tafakji, "al-Istitan al-Jughrafi wa al-Dimugrafi wa Akhtarufu fi Qadiyyat al-Quds," 12–13.

[19] Lajnat al-Quds, *Wathiqat al-Quds*, 82–83.

[20] See, for example, Anthony Coon, *Town Planning under Military Occupation* (Aldershot: Dartmouth Publishing Co., 1992).

[21] Ra'ef Najm, "Muslim and Christian *Waqf* Properties in Jerusalem," in Essam Salam, ed., *Jerusalem Today*, 130–132.

[22] 'Abd Allah 'Asim Gosheh, "al-Akhtar al-'Imraniyyah 'ala Madinat al-Quds" in *al-Muhandis al-*

Urdani, 34: 67 (August 1999), 47–49.

[23] Ra'ef Yousef Najm, "al-Haram al-Sharif khilal Fatrat al-Ihtilal al-Isra'ali" in Isma'il Siraj al-Din and Samir al-Sadiq, eds., *Abhath Nadwat al-Madinah al-'Arabiyyah* (Riyadh: al-Ma'had al-'Arabi li Inma' al-Mudun, 1981), 151–161.

[24] See, for example, Shadia Touqan, "Adaptive Re-Use of Historic Buildings in Old Jerusalem" in Essam Salam, ed., *Jerusalem Today,* 133–7. See also the documentary studies proceedings carried out by Mickle Hamilton Borgoune in *Mamluk Jerusalem: An Architectural Study* (London: World of Islamic Festival Trust, 1987); and Archie G. Walls, *Geometry and Architecture in Islamic Jerusalem* (London: World of Islamic Festival Trust, 1990), 41–43.

The Urban Transformation of Jerusalem After 1967

[1] Walid Mustafa, *Jerusalem Population and Urbanisation from 1850 to 2000* (Jerusalem: Jerusalem Media and Communications Centre, 2000), 69.

[2] I.e., the area designated following the 1995 Interim Agreement, in which the Palestinian Authority would have responsibility for civil affairs.

[3] Henry Kendall, *Jerusalem City Plan: Preservation of the Old City and Planning of the New* (London: His Majesty's Stationery Office, 1948), especially 6, 30.

[4] Law of Planning for Cities, Villages and Buildings, No. 31, 1955.

[5] As indicated on the diagram on p. 126 of Elisha Efrat, *Physical Planning Prospects of Israel during 50 Years of Statehood* (Berlin: Galda und Wilch, 1998).

[6] The Hague Convention, 43 4G 64.

[7] Sarah Kaminker, "East Jerusalem: A Case Study," in *Palestine–Israel Journal,* 2: 2, 65.

[8] Anthony Coon, *Town Planning under Military Occupation: An Examination of the Law and Practice of Town Planning in the Occupied West Bank* (Aldershot: Dartmouth, 1992), chapter 4.

[9] *Abd al Rahman Yousef Afiq v. High Planning Council for Judea and Samaria* (case ref. 676/89), August 28, 1989. (Israeli) High Court.

[10] I.e., the areas (outside annexed East Jerusalem) designated under the "Interim Agreement" of 1995 that remain under Israeli administration.

[11] Eitan Felner, *A Policy of Discrimination: Land Expropriation, Planning and Building in East Jerusalem* (Jerusalem: B'tselem, 1997).

[12] Amnesty International, *Israel and the Occupied Territories. Demolition and Dispossession: The Destruction of Palestinian Homes* (London: Amnesty International, 1999), 31.

[13] Hamoked and B'tselem, *The Quiet Deportation Continues* (Jerusalem: B'tselem, 1998), 11.

[14] Yael Hurwitz, *East Jerusalem—The Current Planning Situation: A Survey of Municipal Plans and Planning Policy* (Jerusalem: Ir Shalem, 1999), 6.

[15] Land Ordinance: Expropriation for Public Purposes.

[16] Meron Benvenisti, *City of Stone* (Berkeley: University of California Press, 1996), 155.

[17] Raja Shehadeh, *The Law of the Land: Settlements and Land Issues Under Israeli Military Occupation* (Jerusalem: Passia, 1993).

[18] Israeli Settlements and International Law, (Israeli) Ministry of Foreign Affairs website, visited May, 2001.

[19] Sources: (1) site visit June 2, 1999; (2) Alison B. Hodgkins, *Israeli Settlement Policy in Jerusalem: Facts on the Ground* (Jerusalem: Passia, 1998), 46; (3) Al-Haq report, September 14, 2000.

[20] Population data from *Statistical Year Book of Jerusalem,* 1998, and relate to 1997.

[21] In the case of land outside annexed East Jerusalem the agency is the "Government Custodian of Abandoned and State Land; Civil Administration of Judea and Samaria." This is a branch of the ILA, and the procedures are identical.

[22] Law of Return, sections 1 and 4b (1950). "Jew" means a person who was born of a Jewish mother, or who has converted to Judaism and is not a member of another religion.

[23] Hodgkins, *Israeli Settlement Policy in Jerusalem*, 27.

[24] Hurwitz, 48.

[25] Benvenisti, *City of Stone*, 159.

[26] Kaminker, "East Jerusalem: A Case Study", 14.

[27] Amnesty International, *Israel and the Occupied Territories. Demolition and Dispossession: The Destruction of Palestinian Homes*, 33. This relates to annexed East Jerusalem, in which the population has increased by some 110,000 during this period.

[28] The average number of persons per room in the Palestinian sector is twice as high as the figure for Jews in annexed East Jerusalem.

[29] Amnesty International, *Israel and the Occupied Territories*, 34.

[30] e.g., "Amnesty Report Misleading," in *Planning* (August 4, 2000), 13.

The Jerusalem Question in International Law: The Way to a Solution

[1] General Assembly Resolution 181. Official Records, 2nd Session, Resolutions, pt. 3, UN Document A/519 (1947), 131. The Resolution was reaffirmed by Resolution 194 of December 11, 1948 and 303 of December 9, 1949.

[2] See Raja Shehadeh, *Occupiers Law: Israel and the West Bank*, revised ed. (Washington DC: Institute of Palestine Studies, 1988); Raja Shehadah, *From Occupation to Interim Accords: Israel and the Palestinian Territories*, CIMEL Book Series No 4 (London: Kluwer Law International, 1997).

[3] "Basic Law: Jerusalem Capital of Israel," in *Laws of the State of Israel*, Vol. 34 (1980), 209.

[4] Henry Cattan, *The Palestine Question* (London: Croom Helm, 1988).

[5] Ibid., 257–259.

[6] See my articles in *al-Sharq al-Awsat*, No. 5417 (September 27, 1993) and in *Middle East International*, No 461 (October 24, 1993); and "Some Legal Aspects of the Declaration of Principles: A Palestinian View," in Eugene Cotran and Chibil Mallet, eds., *The Arab–Israeli Accords: Legal Perspectives*, CIMEL Book Series No. 1 (London: Kluwer International, 1996), 67–77.

[7] Declaration of Principles (A, XV) and Interim Agreement (AXXI).

[8] See *Palestinian Human Rights in Jerusalem: 30 Years after Occupation* (London: Lawyers for Palestinian Human Rights, June 1997); *A Policy of Discrimination: Land Expropiation, Planning and Building in East Jerusalem* (Jerusalem: B'tselem, June 1997); and *The Quiet Deportation: Revocation of Residency of East Jerusalem Palestinians*, (Jerusalem: B'tselem and Hamokedi, April 1997).

[9] Haim Baram, "A Society Gone Mad," in *Middle East International*, No. 537 (November 8, 1996), 6.

[10] UN Convention against Torture and other Cruel, Inhuman, Degrading Forms of Punishment.

[11] See *Legitimising Torture: The Israeli High Court of Justice Rulings in the Bilbesi, Hamdan and Mubarak Cases: An Annotated Source Book* (Jerusalem: B'tselem, January 1997).

[12] The second resolution was adopted at the 10th Emergency Special Session on May 5, 1997 (ES 10/2) (see below).

[13] Ibid. ES 10/2. Illegal Israeli actions in Occupied East Jerusalem and rest of the Occupied Palestinian Territory.

[14] United Nations, Treaty Series, Vol. 75, No. 973.

[15] See Carnegie Endowment for International Peace, *The Hague Conventions and Declarations of 1899 and 1907* (New York: Oxford University Press, 1915).

[16] Adnan Abu Odeh, "The Ownership of Jerusalem: A Jordanian View," in Ghada Karmi, Ed., *Jerusalem Today: What Future for the Peace Process?* (Reading: Ithaca Press, 1997), 64.

[17] John V. Whitbeck, "The Road to Peace Starts in Jerusalem: The 'Condominium' Solution," in *Middle East International*, No. 538 (November 22, 1996), 19.

[18] See Gershon Baskin, Ed., "New Thinking on the Future of Jerusalem: A Model for the Future of Jerusalem: Sovereignty, the IPCRI Plan," in *IPCRI*, 111: 2 (June 1994).

Holy Places, Unholy Domination: The Scramble for Jerusalem

[1] For a comprehensive treatment of the imperial imperative in Zionism see Nur Masalha, *Imperial Israel and the Palestinians: The Politics of Expansion, 1967–2000* (London: Pluto, 2000).

[2] The option of Jews settling in Uganda, rather than Palestine was hotly debated at the Sixth Zionist Congress at Basle (August 22–28, 1903). However, Theodor Herzl emphasised that Uganda would only be a staging post to the ultimate goal of Palestine, but fearing that the issue might split the Zionist movement, lifting his right hand, he cried out, "*Im Yeshkakhekh Yerushalayim...*" ("If I forget you, O Jerusalem, may my right hand wither"), quoting Psalm 137:5. [Walter Laqueur, *History of Zionism* (New York: Holt, Rinehart and Winston, 1972), 129]. The Seventh Congress (1905), at which Herzl was not present—he died the previous year—officially buried the Uganda scheme. Later, in August 1946, the Zionist leadership in Palestine proposed a plan which envisaged partition. It proposed a Jewish state consisting of all of Galilee, the Negev, and the Golan Heights, with a corridor to the sea at Jaffa for the Arab state. Significantly, the Zionists awarded Jerusalem to the Arab state [see J.C. Hurewitz, *Diplomacy in the Near and Middle East* (Princeton, NJ: D. Van Nostrand, 1956), 2:260], or envisaged a special status for it.

[3] Although the terms are used interchangeably in common parlance, one ought to distinguish between the Holy See and the Vatican. The Holy See is the juridical personification of the more than one billion Christians who are in communion with the Church of Rome (Catholics), and, while not a state, enjoys the rights to make international agreements and receive and dispatch representatives. The Vatican, on the other hand, is a state, albeit of less than 1 sq km, and of only some 1,000 inhabitants.

[4] See Robert L. Wilken, *The Land Called Holy: Palestine in Christian History and Thought* (New York and London: Yale University Press, 1992), 119.

[5] For a systematic treatment of each of the New Testament witnesses to Jerusalem, see Peter W. L. Walker, *Jesus and the Holy City: New Testament Perspectives on Jerusalem* (Grand Rapids, MI and Cambridge, UK: Eerdmans, 1996).

[6] See further my *Jesus the Liberator: Nazareth Liberation Theology (Luke 4.16–30)* (Sheffield: Sheffield Academic Press, 1995), 24–25, 52–60.

[7] Mircea Eliade, *Patterns in Comparative Religion* (London/New York: Sheed and Ward, 1958), 375.

[8] Ibid., 383.

[9] Gregory's context in this second extract was different from the earlier one. Here he was reacting against the uncompromising intellectualism of a fellow bishop, Eunomius, for whom the dogmatic exactness of Christianity, couched in the language of a philosophical system, was prized above all else. Gregory insisted in this second context that Christianity was not a matter of the mind only, but invited participation in sacramental practices and symbols. The terrain of the holy places "received the footprints of Life itself," and served to remind one that God once walked the earth. See further my "Pilgrimage to the Holy Land, Yesterday and Today," in Michael Prior and William Taylor, eds., *Christians in the Holy Land* (London: WIFT/Scorpion Press, 1994), 169–75.

[10] See further my "Pilgrimage to the Holy Land, Yesterday and Today," 169–199, and "A Perspective on Pilgrimage to the Holy Land," in Naim Ateek, Cedar Duaybis and Marla Schrader, *Jerusalem: What Makes for Peace?* (London: Melisende, 1997), 114–131, and "Christian Pilgrimage to the Holy Land," in Duncan Macpherson, ed., *A Millennium Guide to Christian*

Pilgrimage to the Holy Land (London: Melisende, 2000), 25–39.

[11] Melito of Sardis visited the Holy Land in the middle of the 2nd century, so as to establish accurately the books of the Old Testament, and to examine the relevant places. He, the earliest known Christian pilgrim, was in search of the biblical past. Alexander, a future bishop of Jerusalem, traveled from Cappadocia in the reign of Caracalla, with the stated purpose of prayer and investigation of the sites. Origen traveled around Palestine seeking out the location of events recorded in the Scriptures. Firmilianus, a Cappadocian bishop, visited Origen, and was in the Holy Land for the sake of the holy places. Pionius, a contemporary of Origen, also visited the Holy Land.

[12] Wilken, *The Land Called Holy*, 119.

[13] Louise Riley-Smith and Jonathan Riley-Smith, *The Crusades: Idea and Reality, 1095–1274* (London: Edward Arnold, 1981), 1.

[14] Ibid., 43.

[15] Ibid., 44.

[16] Daniela Fabrizio provides a detailed discussion of the interplay between religious, cultural and political interests in the question of the Holy Places and the political arrangements for Palestine, *La Questione dei Luoghi Santi e l'Assetto della Palestina 1914–1992* (Milano: FrancoAngeli, 2000).

[17] Sergio I. Minerbi, *The Vatican and Zionism: Conflict in the Holy Land, 1895–1925* (New York/Oxford: Oxford University Press, 1990), xiii.

[18] In Andrej Kreutz, "The Vatican and the Palestinians: A Historical Overview," in *Islamochristiana* 18 (1992): 109–125, 115.

[19] Perowne to Burrows, January 19, 1948 – FO 371/68500, in Ibid., 116.

[20] Elia Zureik surveys the estimates of those expelled, showing that they fall within the range, 700–800,000. See, "Palestinian Refugees and Peace," in *Journal of Palestine Studies* 93 (1994): 5–17, Table 3, 11. But more recently Salman H. Abu-Sitta argues for a total figure of 935,000. See his *The Palestinian Nakba 1948: The Register of Depopulated Localities in Palestine* [with accompanying Map, *Palestine 1948 50 Years after Al Nakba. The Towns and Villages Depopulated by the Zionist Invasion of 1948*] (London: The Palestine Return Centre, 1998), 14.

[21] See the encyclicals of John XXIII, *Mater et Magistra, Pacem in Terris*, of Paul VI, *Populorum Progressio, Evangelii Nuntiandi*, and more recently of John Paul II, *Redemptoris Hominis*, and *Laborem Exercens*.

[22] Apostolic Exhortation, "Concerning the Increased Needs of the Church in the Holy Land," 1974.

[23] *Acta Apostolicae Sedis* (January–March 1976), 134.

[24] According to Fr Giovanni Caprile, the problems were: a just solution to the Palestinian problem, and the establishment of a Palestinian homeland; an internationally guaranteed special status for Jerusalem, with access to, and equality for Christians, Jews, and Muslims, making Jerusalem a real center of spiritual and fraternal development; and, finally, an improvement in the legal rights and social situations of the Christian communities living under Israeli control. See "La Santa Sede e lo Stato d'Israele" in *La Civiltà Cattolica* (February 16, 1991), 357–358.

[25] *La Documentation Catholique 73* (October 17, 1982), 921 and 947.

[26] "Secretariatus pro non-Christianis," in *Bulletin 57* (1984), XIX(3), 254.

[27] See Bernard Sabella, "Socio-Economic Characteristics and the Challenges to Palestinian Christians in the Holy Land" and Sami Geraisy, "Socio-Demographic Characteristics: Reality, Problems and Aspirations within Israel" in Prior and Taylor, *Christians in the Holy Land*, 31–44, 45–55. Palestinian Christians worldwide number some 400,000, constituting some 6.7 percent of some six million Palestinians. Abu-Sitta's estimate of 8,415,930 for the number of Palestinians worldwide in 1998 alters the percentages somewhat (*The Palestinian Nakba 1948*, 15).

[28] *MECC News Report* (January 1992), 2.

[29] See Sabella, "Socio-Economic Characteristics…" and Geraisy, "Socio-Demographic

Characteristics…"

[30] *Impressions of Intifada: Report of a British Council of Churches Delegation to Israel and the Occupied Territories*, March 1989 (London: BCC, Inter-Church House, 1989).

[31] E.g., Elias Chacour, *Blood Brothers* (Eastbourne: Kingsway, 1985) and *We Belong to the Land* (San Francisco: Harper, 1992); Naim Stifan Ateek, *Justice and Only Justice: A Palestinian Theology of Liberation* (Maryknoll, New York: Orbis, 1989); Audeh Rantisi, *Blessed are the Peacemakers: The Story of a Palestinian Christian* (Guildford: Eagle, 1990); Mitri Raheb, *I am a Palestinian Christian* (Minneapolis: Fortress Press, 1995); and, most recently, Riah Abu El-Assal, *Caught in Between* (London: SPCK, 1999).

[32] E.g., Rosemary R. Ruether and M.H. Ellis, eds., *Beyond Occupation* (Boston: Beacon Press, 1990); Donald E. Wagner, *Anxious for Armageddon: A Call to Partnership for Middle Eastern and Western Christians* (Scottdale: Herald Press, 1995); Kenneth Cragg, *The Arab Christian: A History of the Middle East* (London: Mowbray, 1992), and *Palestine: The Prize and Price of Zion* (London and Washington: Cassell, 1997); and Michael Prior, *The Bible and Colonialism: A Moral Critique* (Sheffield: Sheffield Academic Press, 1997), *A Land Flowing with Milk, Honey, and People*, The Lattey Lecture 1997 (St. Edmund's College, Von Hügel Institute, Cambridge University, 1998), *Western Scholarship and the History of Palestine* (London: Melisende, 1998), and *Zionism and the State of Israel: A Moral Inquiry* (London: Routledge, 1999). See also Anthony O'Mahony, ed., *Palestinian Christians: Religion, Politics and Society in the Holy Land* (London: Melisende, 1999).

[33] The most significant of these are the three international conferences convened by *Sabeel*. The first was held in March 1990 in Tantur Ecumenical Institute, Jerusalem, and the papers were edited by Naim Stifan Ateek, M. H. Ellis, and R. R. Ruether, and published: *Faith and the Intifada: Palestinian Christian Voices* (Maryknoll, New York: Orbis, 1992). Selected papers of the 1996 Conference, "The Significance of Jerusalem for Christians and of Christians for Jerusalem" were edited by Naim Ateek, Cedar Duaybis, and Marla Schrader and published: *Jerusalem: What Makes for Peace? A Palestinian Christian Contribution to Peacemaking* (London: Melisende, 1997). Selected papers of the 1998 Conference, "The Challenge of Jubilee," were edited by Naim Ateek and Michael Prior and published: *Holy Land—Hollow Jubilee: God, Justice and the Palestinians* (London: Melisende, 1999). Another major international conference was held in Jerusalem in 1994, whose proceedings were edited by Anthony O'Mahony, with G. Gunner and K. Hintlian, *The Christian Heritage in the Holy Land* (London: Scorpion Cavendish, 1995).

[34] In Britain alone, there have been several conferences on Christians in the Holy Land. In addition to the Cumberland Lodge 1993 Conference (see Prior and Taylor, *Christians in the Holy Land*), major conferences were held in London University (1991 and 1993), Cambridge University (1992), and in Warwick University (1993—the December 1993 special edition of *The Month* 26 [2nd. n.s.] contains a number of these papers).

[35] Michael Prior, *They Came and They Saw: Western Christian Experiences of the Holy Land* (London: Melisende, 2000).

[36] It was issued in Jerusalem, with the authority of the Greek Orthodox Patriarch, the Latin Patriarch, the Armenian Patriarch, the Custos of the Holy Land, the Coptic Archbishop, the Syriac Archbishop, the Ethiopian Archbishop, the Anglican Bishop, the Greek-Catholic Patriarchal Vicar, the Lutheran Bishop, the Maronite Patriarchal Vicar, and the Catholic Syriac Patriarchal Vicar. The text is reproduced in *Documents on Jerusalem* (Jerusalem: PASSIA, 1996), 28–31, and in my article, "'You will be my witnesses in Jerusalem, in all Judaea and Samaria, and to the ends of the earth': Christian Perspectives on Jerusalem," in O'Mahony, ed., *Palestinian Christians: Religion, Politics and Society in the Holy Land*, 96–140. This invaluable PASSIA resource contains also other Christian documents on Jerusalem, plus documents reflecting Muslim and Jewish religious positions, as well as a range of documents portraying their political perspectives.

[37] Other contributions were made by the late Faisal Husseini, and by Hayim Ramon, Harry Hagopian and Fr Majdi al-Siryani.

[38] Archbishop Tauran's paper is published in *Bulletin Associated Christian Press*, no. 403 (Jerusalem: Christian Information Centre, November-December 1998), 2–7.

[39] Ibid., 7–8.

[40] See my Zionism and the State of Israel: A Moral Inquiry, 112–123.

[41] For my own attempts at such a critique, see my *Zionism and the State of Israel: A Moral Inquiry*.

Jerusalem and the Forgotten Documents

[1] Security Council Document No. S/8426, also issued under No. A/7057.

[2] On January 14, 1930, the Council of the League of Nations passed the following resolution:

> The Council,
>
> Being anxious to place the mandatory Power, in accordance with its request, in a position to carry out the responsibilities laid upon it in Article 13 of the Mandate for Palestine under the most favourable conditions for safeguarding the material and moral interests of the population placed under its mandate;
>
> Wishing not to prejudice, in any way, the solution of the problems relating to the question of the holy places of Palestine, which may have to be settled in the future;
>
> Considering, however, that the question of the rights and claims of the Jews and Moslems with regard to the Wailing Wall urgently calls for final settlement;
>
> Decides that,
>
> (1) A Commission shall be entrusted with this settlement,
>
> (2) The Commission shall consist of three members who shall not be of British nationality and at least one of whom shall be a person eminently qualified for the purpose by the judicial functions he has performed;
>
> (3) The names of the persons whom the mandatory Power intends to appoint as members of the Commission shall be submitted for approval to the Council whose members shall be consulted by the President if the Council is no longer in session;
>
> (4) The duties of the Commission shall cease as soon as it has pronounced on the rights and claims mentioned above.

For more extensive details on this, see "The Rights and Claims of Moslems and Jews in Connection with the Wailing Wall at Jerusalem," *Special Report of the Palestine Yearbook of International Law*, IX (1996–1997), 375–416. For the above mentioned text see ibid., 411. Ed.

[3] It is pertinent to note here that Muslims were fully aware, at least as early as the beginning of formal British-sponsored Jewish immigration, of the basic aims of the Zionists regarding the area they took to be the original site of the Temple. In the section on "Moslem Contentions" before the Shaw Commission, the Muslim representatives mentioned above expressed their views as to the true intentions of the Jews. As summarized in the *Special Report of the Palestine Yearbook of International Law*, Vol. IX (1996–7), the Muslims expressed their reservations, and their fears concerning Jewish intentions, in the following terms:

> The aim of the Jewish agitation is not merely to obtain seats for the aged and invalids to rest on. In reality, what we have to deal with here is a Zionist movement that has in view the securing of advantages for the Jews to which they have no right. In spite of all their statements to the contrary, the real aim of the Zionists is to obtain possession of the Haram-esh-Sherif. (p. 389.)

"The Shaw Commission itself," the summary continues, "admitted [in its report, p. 73] that the fears of the Arabs in this respect were reasonable" (Ibid.).

Muslim representatives, as the summary explains, insisted as follows:

Even if they [the Zionists] allege, before the Commission, that they do not claim the property right to the Wall [as in fact they did allege: see p. 384, which confirms how Jewish representatives stated before the Commission that "the Jewish Side do not claim any proprietary rights to the Wall"], they do in reality aim at this. The fundamental aspiration of Zionism is to take possession of the Mosque of Omar and the whole Temple area, and to drive the Arabs out of Palestine, where they [the Zionists] would then install themselves in their place. (Ibid., 389)

[4] The Muslim lawyers, in their defense, stressed that the Wall and the surrounding area, including the Magharibah Quarter, were Waqf property, and hence not subject to controversy on any legal grounds. Another argument propounded by them was that the Arabs conquered Palestine, "not from the Jews, who had been driven out of Palestine several centuries before, but from the Byzantines. It was not a Jewish kingdom that the Arabs occupied in the seventh century, but a country to which the Jews had no right whatever" (Ibid., 386.)

A third potent point put forward by the Muslim side was that Jews had been permitted, over centuries of Islamic rule (including the long Ottoman period), to pray and lament at the Wall on account of "the toleration shown towards them by the Moslems… The Jews cannot build upon this toleration to put forward claims to positive rights as they are trying to do." Ibid. Ed.

[5] The exact wording of the Commission is as follows:

> To the Moslems belong the sole ownership of, and the sole proprietary right to, the Western Wall, seeing that it forms an integral part of the Haram-esh-Sherif area, which is Waqf property.

To the Moslems there also belongs the ownership of the Pavement in front of the Wall and of the adjacent so-called Moghrabi (Moroccan) Quarter opposite the Wall [completely demolished straight after the 1967 War], inasmuch as the last-mentioned property was made Waqf under Moslem Sharia Law, it being dedicated to charitable purposes. (Ibid., 408. Ed.)

[6] Security Council Resolution No. 242, dated November 22, 1967. Security Council Session 1382.

[7] Security Council Meeting 1426, May 21, 1968.

'Umar's Assurance of Safety to the People of Aelia (Jerusalem)

[1] Zakariyya al-Quda "Mu'ahadat Fatih Bayt al-Maqdis: al-'Uhda al-'Umariyya" in Muhammad 'Adnan al-Bakhit and Ihsan 'Abass (edes.), Bilad al-Sham fi Sadir al-Islam, (University of Jordan and University of Yarmuk, Jordan, 1987), vol. 2, 279–283.

[2] 'Ali 'Ajin "Al-'Uhda al-'Umariyya." Al-Hikma Journal (no. 10, 1417 AH), 75–87.

[3] Daniel J. Sahas "Patriarch Sophronius, Umar Ibn al-Khattab and the Conquest of Jerusalem", in Hadia Dajani-Shakeel and Burhan Dajani, Al-Sira' al-Islami al-Faranji 'ala Filastin fi al-Qurun al-Wasta (The Islamic–Frankish [Ifranj] Conflict over Palestine During the Middle Ages) (The Institute of Palestine Studies, Beirut, 1994), 54

[4] Muhammad Ibn 'Umar al-Waqidi, Futuh al-Sham (Cairo, 1954), part 1, 214, 242.

[5] Muhammad al-Baladhuri, Futuh al-Buldan (Cairo, 1936), part 1, 114–145. It is interesting to note that the narrations of al-Baladhuri and Abu 'Ubayd (died 224 AH)—in his book Al-Amwal from 'Abdullah Ibn Salih from al-Layth Ibn Sa'id from Yazid Ibn Abi Habib—concur that it was agreed that everything within the city walls should remain in the hands of the inhabitants as long as they paid the Jizya tax. The areas outside the city walls would be in the hands of the conquering Muslims. Abu 'Ubayed al-Qassim Ibn Salam, Al-Amwal, (Beirut, 1986), 168. This historical event undoubtedly ties in with our forthcoming discussion of Islam's attitude toward plurality, conflict, and justice. It also supports the hypothesis of Haitham al-Ratrout, a post-graduate student at Al-Maktoum Institute for Arabic and Islamic Studies, Dundee, UK, in his doctoral thesis on the status of al-Aqsa Mosque in Jerusalem's early Islamic architecture. From his

study of the historical sources, archaeological and architectural studies and reports on excavations in Jerusalem, al-Ratrout attempts to ascertain whether the area on which the Muslims built Aqsa mosque after the conquest fell outside or within the city walls. I am indebted to al-Ratrout for providing this information and for introducing him to the narration of Abu 'Ubayd in his book *Al-Amwal.*

[6] Sa'id Ibn al-Batriq (Eutychius), *Al-Tarikh al-Majmu'* (Beirut, 1905), part 2, 16.

[7] AI-Ya'qubi, *Tarikh al-Ya'qubi* (Beirut, 1960), part 2, 46, 167

[8] Daniel J. Sahas, "Patriarch Sophronius, Umar Ibn al-Khattab and the Conquest of Jerusalem," 65.

[9] Al-Tabari, *Tarikh al-Rusul wa al-Muluk* (Cairo, 1960), part 1, 2399, 2405–2406.

[10] Ibn al-Jawzi, *Fada 'il al-Quds* (Beirut, 1980), 123–124.

[11] Some investigation needs to be done about the identity of that person and whether he had any links with Shi'ite Islam before concluding that it was an intentional mistake.

[12] Al-Waqidi, *Futuh al-Sham,* 236.

[13] 'Abd al-Rahman al-Azaw'i, *Al-Tabari* (Baghdad, 1989), 134.

[14] 'Ali 'Ajin, "Al-'Uhda al-'Umariyya," 71.

[15] Welhausen, *Skizzen und Vorarbeiten Heft IV,* cited by Israel Ben Zeev (Abu Zuaib), *Ka'b al-Ahbar: Jews and Judaism in the Islamic Tradition* (Jerusalem, 1976), 37.

[16] Shlomo D. Goitein "Jerusalem in the Arab Period: 638–1099," *The Jerusalem Cathedra,* 2 (1982), p. 171. However, Moshe Gil argues that "there seems to be little justification for this very stringent attitude (of Goitein) towards a source that has been preserved for more than a thousand years." Moshe Gil, *A History of Palestine: 634–1099* (Cambridge University Press, 1992), 73.

[17] Goitein, "Jerusalem in the Arab Period: 638–1099," 169.

[18] Hussain 'Atwan, al-Riwiya al-Tarikhia fi Bilad al-Sham fi al-'Asr al-Umawi (Amman, 1986), pp. 231–232.

[19] Sahas, 70–71. For the attitude of Heraclitus towards the Jews in Aelia, see Karen Armstrong, *A History of Jerusalem: One City, Three Faiths* (HarperCollins Publishers, London, 1996), 215, 233.

[20] 'Abdul 'Aziz Duri, "Jerusalem in the Early Islamic Period: 7th–11th Centuries AD" in K.J. Asali (ed.), *Jerusalem in History,* (Northampton, MA: Olive Branch Press, 1999), 107.

[21] Ibid., 107; see also Moshe Gil, *A History of Palestine: 634–1099,* 56. Gil argues that as "one might anticipate, the subject of Jews appeared important to almost all the Christian chroniclers."

[22] Duri, 107.

[23] Sahas, 67. Moshe Gil, *A History of Palestine: 634–1099,* 70

[24] Israel Ben Zeev (Abu Zuaib), *Ka'b al-Ahbar,* 35.

[25] Ibid, 36–37; see also Armstrong, *A History of Jerusalem: One City, Three Faiths,* 230.

[26] Gil, *A History of Palestine: 634–1099,* 71.

[27] Patricia Crone and Michael Cook, *Hagarism: the Making of the Islamic World* (Cambridge University Press, 1977), 156.

[28] Goitein, 171–172. Karen Armstrong, in her report on this article, commented on Goitein's claim "that the Jews had acted as guides around the City" by saying that "I have never seen this argued." She argues that

> Jews certainly helped the Muslim army as scouts in the countryside of Palestine, but it was the Christian patriarch who showed Umar around Aelia. But the story that Umar brought rabbis with him from Tiberias may have some historical relevance, even if not literally true. These rabbis were not brought to show the Muslims around the *Bayt al-Maqdis,* the city, but to act as consultants about the reconsecration of the Holy Place...

[29] John Wilkinson "Jerusalem under Rome and Byzantium: 63 BC–637 AD," in Asali, 75.

[30] Ibid, 88.

[31] The area of Aelia Capitolina (40 square miles) contained the districts of Gophna, Herodium, and the area west of Jerusalem, which was called Oreine or "Hill Country." See figure 5 in Ibid, 89; see also Muhammad al-Maqdisi, *Ahsan al-Taqasim fi Ma'rifat al-Aqalim*, (Baghdad, 1977), 173. John Wilkinson argues that "the area called Jerusalem in Aelia Capitolina was thus a very small city," see 90.

[32] Karen Armstrong, "Sacred Space: the Holiness of Islamic Jerusalem," *Journal of Islamic Jerusalem Studies* 1.1, (Winter 1997), 5.

[33] See the manuscript in Israel Ben Zeev (Abu Zuaib), *Ka'b al- Ahbar*, 39; see also Karen Armstrong, *A History of Jerusalem: One City, Three Faiths*, 233. Moshe Gil stated that "Cairo Geniza documents occupy first place among Jewish sources, for these were written by contemporaries of the period." Moshe Gil, *A History of Palestine: 634–1099*, 70.

[34] Mustafa A. Hiyari, "Crusader Jerusalem: 1099–1187 AD," in Asali, 131–132. As a result of Fatimid-Byzantium's conflict, al-Hakim in 1009 CE, for example, ordered his governor of Palestine to destroy the Church of the Holy Sepulcher in Jerusalem.

[35] Fred McGraw Donner, *The Early Islamic Conquests* (Princeton University Press, New Jersey, 1981), pp. 322, 287–289; see also Gil, 71.

[36] Neubauer, *Aus der Peterburger Bibliothek*, 109 VII, 12 cited by Israel Ben Zeev (Abu Zuaib), *Ka'b al-Ahbar*, 40.

[37] J. Mann, *The Jews in Egypt and Palestine under the Fatimid Caliphs*, 43–47: Muir, *Annals of the Early Califate*, 212; Dubnow, *Geschichte des judischen Volkes*, III, 410 cited by Israel Ben Zeev (Abu Zuaib), *Ka'b al-Ahbar*, 37–38; see also Moshe Gil, 71.

[38] Schwabe's "Al-yahud wa al-Haram ba'd al-Fath al-'Umari," *Zion Journal* (vol. 2), 102 cited by Israel Ben Zeev (Abu Zuaib), *Ka'b al- Ahbar*, 38.

[39] Arculf, *Eines Pilgers Reise nach dem Heiligen Land um 670 aus dem lateinischen ubersetzt und erklart von Paul Mickley* (Leipzig, 1917), 29–31 cited by Israel Ben Zeev (Abu Zuaib), *Ka'b al-Ahbar*, 38.

[40] Israel Ben Zeev (Abu Zuaib), *Ka'b al-Ahbar*, 40.

[41] Shafiq Jasir, "Al-Taghayrat al-Diymughrafiyya fi al-Quds 'Abra Tarikhiha," in Shafiq Jasir (ed.), *Jerusalem fi al-Khitab al-Mu'asir* (Jordan, 1999), 337–338; see also Gil, 71–72; see also Armstrong, *A History of Jerusalem*, 233.

[42] Mustafa A. Hiyari, "Crusader Jerusalem: 1099–1187 AD," 170. During the Latin period only a few Jews lived in Jerusalem near the Citadel. Saladin's tolerant policy allowed the Jews to return to the City. Accordingly, they gradually began to constitute a community. According to J. Prawer, three groups settled this time in Jerusalem, two of them Jewish groups: the Jews from Morocco who fled to the East around 1198–1199, and the Jews from France—some three hundred families—who migrated in two groups in 1210. When Jerusalem was handed over to Frederick II in 1229, anti-Jewish legislation of the Crusaders was re-established and all Jews were prohibited again from living in the City. J. Prawer "Minorities in the Crusader states" in *A History of the Crusades* (New York, 1964), 97; Steven Runciman, *A History of the Crusades* (London, 1965), 467; Armstrong, *A History of Jerusalem*, 298–299.

[43] Donald P. Little, "Jerusalem under the Ayyubids and Mamluks," in Asali, 195.

[44] Joseph Drory, "Jerusalem During the Mamluk period: 1250–1517," *The Jerusalem Cathedra* (1981), 213.

[45] Donald Little, "Haram Documents related to the Jews of Late 14th-Century Jerusalem," *Journal of Semitic Studies* 30.2 (1985), 227–264.

[46] Yusuf al-Qaradawi, "Al-Quds fi al-Wa'y al-Islami," *Journal of Islamic Jerusalem Studies* 1.1 (Winter 1997), 13–14.

[47] Baha' al-Din Ibn Shaddad, *Al-Nawadir al-Sultaniyya wa al- Mahasin al-Yusufiyya* (Cairo,

1964), III, 265; see also Donald P. Little, "Jerusalem under the Ayyubids and Mamluks," 179.

[48] Ahmad al-Sharif, *Dirasat fi al-Hadara al-Islamiyya* (Cairo, 1976), 123.

[49] Muhammad Sa'id al-Buti, "Mu'amalat al-Dawla al-Islamiyya li ghayr al-Muslimin: al-Quds Namudhajan," *Journal of Islamic Jerusalem Studies* 1.3 (Winter 1999), 3-4.

[50] Ibid, 10.

[51] Zakariyya al-Quda, "Mu'ahadat Fatih Bayt al-Maqdis: al-'Uhda al-'Umariyya," 276.

[52] Mujir al-Din al-'Alimi, *Al-Uns al-Jalil bi tarikh al-Quds wa al-Khalil* (Amman, 1977), part 1, 253–254.

[53] Zakariyya al-Quda, "Mu'ahadat Fatih Bayt al-Maqdis: al-'Uhda al-'Umariyya," 276.

[54] Asad Rustum, *Mustalah al-Tarikh* (Beirut, 1939), 13–20.

[55] 'Abd Allah al-Bakiri al-Andalusi, *Mu'jam ma Istu'jim* (Cairo, 1947), part 1, 217; see also Shafiq Jasir, *Tarikh al-Quds*, (Amman, 1989), 19.

[56] Ibn Kathir, *Al-Bidaya wa al-Nihayya* (Beirut, 1978), part 7, 55.

[57] K.J. Asali, "Jerusalem under the Ottomans: 1516–1831 AD," in Asali, 206, 210, 221.

[58] Moshe Gil added that the "language" of it and "its details appear authentic and reliable and in keeping with what is known of Jerusalem at that time." Gil, 56.

[59] Philip Hitti, *Tarikh al-'Arab* (Beirut, 1957), part 3, 19–20.

[60] A.S. Tritton, *The Caliphs and their non-Muslim Subjects* (Oxford, 1930), 12.

[61] Goitein, 171.

[62] Ibid., 171.

[63] Ibn 'Asakir, *Tarikh al-Sham* (Damascus, 1329–1332 AH), part 1, 563–564, 566–567.

[64] Mujir al-Din al-'Alimi, *Al-Uns al-Jalil bi tarikh al-Quds wa al-Khalil*, part 1, 253–254.

[65] For example, Haroun al-Rashid ordered in 191 AH that non-Muslims in areas near the Byzantine frontiers should have a different form of address from those of Muslims for security reasons. See Ibn al-Athir, *Al-Kamil fi al-Tarikh* (Beirut, 1982), part 6, 206.

[66] Duri, 107

[67] Sahas, 54.

[68] Sahas, 60. Karen Armstrong argues that "societies that have lasted the longest in the holy city have, generally, been the ones that were prepared for some kind of tolerance and co-existence in the holy city"; and "the Muslims got their City back because the Crusaders became trapped in a dream of hatred and intolerance." Armstrong, *A History of Jerusalem*, 426–427.

[69] Karen Armstrong "Sacred Space," 14, 18–19. Armstrong argues that "the Muslims had established a system that enabled Jews, Christians, and Muslims to live in Jerusalem together for the first time." See Karen Armstrong, *A History of Jerusalem*. 246 and 233.

[70] Karen Armstrong argues that "on two occasions in the past, it was an Islamic conquest of Jerusalem that made it possible for Jews to return to their holy City. Umar and Saladin both invited Jews to settle in Jerusalem when they replaced Christian rulers there." See Armstrong, *A History of Jerusalem*, 420; for the same view, see Amnon Cohen, *Jewish Life under Islam: Jerusalem in the 16th Century* (Cambridge, MA: Harvard University Press, 1984), 14.

Jerusalem as the City of God's Kingdom: Common Tropes in the Bible and the Ancient Near East

[1] See Job 42:5.

[2] See the classical studies of B. Albrektson, *History and the Gods* (Lund: 1967); H. W. F. Saggs, *Encounter with the Divine in Mesopotamia and Israel* (London: 1978); *idem*, "Assyrian Prisoners of War and the Right to Live," in *Archiv für Orientforschung*, 19 (1982), 85–93 and M. Liverani, *Prestige and Interest: International Relations in the Near East, ca. 1600–1100 BC*, History of the

Ancient Near East Studies 1 (Sargon srl: Padua, 1990), 126–150. Unfortunately, the dominant historicizing tendency of Sa-Moon Kang's Hebrew University dissertation, *Divine War in the Old Testament and in the Ancient Near East, BZAW* 177 (Berlin: de Gruyter, 1989) limits this ambitious work's usefulness in either literary or religio-historical analysis of the "divine war" theme, in spite of its numerous useful references to relevant ancient Near Eastern texts. Similarly tendentious problems plague the studies of P. D. Miller, *The Divine Warrior in Early Israel, HSM* 5 (Cambridge, MA: Harvard University Press, 1973) and of P. D. Miller and J. J. M. Roberts, *The Hand of the Lord: A Reassessment of the Ark Narrative* (Baltimore: 1977). Less problematic in this respect is F. M. Cross, *Canaanite Myth and Hebrew Epic* (Cambridge, MA: Harvard University Press, 1973).

[3] Thomas. L. Thompson, "Historiography in the Pentateuch: 25 Years after Historicity" in *Scandinavian Journal of the Old Testament,* 13 (1999), 258–283; *idem,* "Kingship and the Wrath of God: Or Teaching Humility" in *Revue Biblique,* 2001.

[4] Thompson, "Historiography," 258–283; *idem,* "Kingship."

[5] Ibid.

[6] Th. L. Thompson, *The Bible in History: How Writers Create a Past* (London: Cape, 1999/2000), 359–361; 372–374.

[7] Ibid., See, also, H. Niehr, *Der Höchste Gott, BZAW* 190 (Berlin: de Gruyter, 1990).

[8] N. P. Lemche, "Salme 2-midt mellem fortid og fremtid" in *Det gamle Testamente i jødedom og kristendom, Forum for Bibelsk Eksegese* 4 (København: Museum Tusculanum, 1993), 57–78; *idem,* "Indledningen til Davids Salmer: Nye betragtninger vedrørende Salme 2" in *Tro og historie, Forum for Bibelsk Eksegese* 7 (København: Museum Tusculanum, 1996), 142–151; see most recently, Thompson, "Kingship." For a discussion of the various stories about sons of God in the Bible, see, *idem, The Bible in History,* 323–374.

[9] Marduk is considered to be the supreme God in Babylonian religion.

[10] Tiamat is considered to be a goddess personifying the primal salt-water ocean, according to the creation myth of Babylonian religion.

[11] Th. L. Thompson, "….. : 25 Years after Historicity".

[12] Ishtar, considered as chief goddess by the Babylonians and the Assyrians.

[13] L.W. King, *Chronicles Concerning Early Babylonian Kings* (1907), II: 87–96; James Bennett Pritchard, ed., *Ancient Near Eastern Texts relating to the Old Testament* [Henceforth *ANET*] (Princeton, NJ: Princeton University Press, 1950), 119; see also P. Jensen, "Aussetzungsgeschichten" in *Reallexikon der Assyriologie,* I (1928), 22–324.

[14] See Isa. 40:3–4; 41:15, and 45:2.

[15] Psalter 2; 110; cf. also Isa 41:8–9; 42:1–7; 44:1–5 and 45:1 for similar figures.

[16] Psalm 115:16.

[17] For a fuller discussion, see Thompson, "The Wrath of God", *passim.* The role of Yahweh as king in the Book of Psalms is found particularly in Ps. 5, 10, 29, 44, 47, 95, and 145.

[18] The Gilgamesh epic is an important Middle Eastern literary work, written in cuneiform on twelve clay tablets around 2000 BCE. Gilgamesh is a tyrannical Babylonian king.

[19] According to the Sumerian version of the story of the Flood, Umapishtim is the man who built the Ark and the survived the great flood.

[20] J. B. Pritchard, ed., *ANET* 94: tablet XI, ll.136–138.

[21] See my discussion in the "The Wrath of God" and, further, below.

[22] Pritchard, *ANET,* 6 n.11; 8 n.6; 11 n.6 and 366 n.17.

[23] See Th. L. Thompson, "On Baby's Crying and Psalm 8:3."

[24] Jeremiah 29:12–13; on the theme of exile, cf. Thompson, *The Bible in History,* 217–225.

[25] Cf. Genesis 1.26; 9.2.

[26] Psalm 2.1.

[27] James Henry Breasted, tr. and ed., *Ancient Records of Egypt* (Urbana, IL: University of Illinois Press, 2001), 3:16–22; especially §§ 26, 30, 38 and 44; see further Ingrid Hjelm and Th. L. Thompson, "The Victory Song of Merneptah: Israel and the People of Palestine" in *Journal for the Study of the Old Testament*, 2002.

[28] Enuma Elish, Babylonian mythological poem of creation.

[29] See, for example, the reiterated motif of twelve enemy kings in the inscriptions from the reigns of Shalmaneser II (r. c. 10th century BCE) and Shalmaneser III (858–824 BCE) in Pritchard, *ANET*, 276–281, but also the allusions to the plant of life and cosmic battle that is engaged in the description of Adadnirari III's (r. 810–783 BCE) campaign against Palestine (*ANET*, 281), as well as the nearly ubiquitous self-description of Assyrian kings as usum. gal, "the Great Dragon," a description that first appears on the Hammurabi stele (*ANET*, 276); further, Thompson, "The Wrath of God."

[30] Joshua 24:19.

[31] For translation, see Pritchard, *ANET*, 320–321.

[32] A comparable story is found in the Bible in 1 Sam 15.

[33] Pritchard, *ANET*, 378.

[34] Ibid., 373–375.

[35] Cf. Genesis 15 and 2 Sam 7 with the last paragraph of Thutmosis song: Pritchard, *ANET*, 375.

[36] Such a view of patronage, of course, is the social basis for the biblical command to love your enemies; for they too are properly clients of the divine (2 Sam 26:17–25).

[37] These stereotypical oppositions are, in fact, often descriptions of the single change in status from enemy to client. See further, B. Oded, *Mass Deportation and Deportees in the Neo-Assyrian Empire* (Wiesbaden: Harrassowitz, 1979), 19:28–30; for the impact of such policies on Israel and Judah, see Th. L. Thompson, *The Early History of the Israelite People* (Leiden: Brill, 1992/ 2000), 339–351.

[38] Jeremiah 5:1–17.

[39] Similarly Isa 42:5.

[40] Pritchard, *ANET*, 376–378.

[41] Such as those of Esarhaddon [r. 681–669 BC] (Pritchard, *ANET*, 534–541), especially clauses 37–106, where the king plays the role of determining the destiny of the vassal and the prosperity of his land.

[42] As in the epilogue of Hammurabi's code, Pritchard, *ANET*, 177–180.

[43] For a discussion of this aspect of divine patronage as expressed in the Psalter, see Th. L. Thompson, "Salmernes Bogs 'enten-eller' spørgsmål" in T. Joergensen and P. K. Westergaard, eds., *Teologien i samfundet: Festskrift til Jens Glebe Möller* (Frederiksberg: ANIS, 1998), 289–308.

[44] I. Hjelm and Th. L. Thompson, "The Victory Song of Merneptah".

[45] In the epilogue of Hammurabi's code "giving justice to the oppressed" epitomizes the function of the good king (Pritchard, *ANET*, 177). The utopian character of this element of song is particularly clear in the Hittite prayers and hymns (Keilschrifturkunden aus Boghazköi, xxiv, 1–4) translated in Pritchard, *ANET*, 396–97. It is the signal mark of the king's role as patron in the Kalamuwa inscription (W.W. Hallo, *The Context of Scripture* (Leiden: Brill, 2000), II: 147–148) and it is used to announce the good news of Ramses IV's accession to the throne [r. 1166–1160 BCE] (See further, "The Wrath of God"; I. Hjelm and Th. L. Thompson, "The Victory Song of Merneptah").

[46] A song at the accession of Ramses IV, 1166 BCE, Pritchard, *ANET*, 379.

[47] 1 Samuel 2, 4–9.

[48] Luke 7:18–23. Cf. Matthew 11:2–6. Psalms 107:33–38; 113:7–9. Isaiah 29:18–20; 35:5–7; 41:18–20; 61:1–3. Matthew 5:3–12. Luke 4:18–19; 6:20–26.

[49] 1 Samuel 1–2 and 7; 2 Samuel 22–23.

[50] Joshua 23–24; Deuteronomy 32–33; cf. e.g., Joshua 23:1 with 2 Samuel 22:1.

[51] Isaiah 40:2.

[52] Isaiah 40:3–5; cf. Malachi 3:1–7.

[53] Cf. 3 Moses 4:1–21.

[54] Pritchard, *ANET,* 367.

[55] Psalm 2, 7.

[56] Pritchard, *ANET,* 373.

[57] Cf. Psalms 65:4; 89:2–9.

[58] Cf. Psalms 89:23–24, 29–30.

[59] Cf. Psalms, 89:28–37.

[60] Cf. Psalms 89:38–45.

[61] Jeremiah 4:23.

[62] 2 Samuel 22.

Reporting the Jehoash Inscription: An Exclusivist Claim to Israel

[1] Professor Joseph Naveh, one of the leading authorities on the development of the alphabet, revealed that he had been approached in 2001 to look at the inscription. Nadav Shagrai, writting in *Ha'aretz,* says that Naveh was asked to meet agents of the collector in a hotel room in Jerusalem. He was introduced to a man named Tzur and "an Arab youth who never opened his mouth the entire time." Naveh was made to promise not to mention the meeting or inscription because "the life of the Palestinian who found it and sold it would be endangered." He only revealed the meeting once the news of the inscription's existence had been revealed. It is reported that Professor Naveh plans to publish his own study of the inscription, which he believes is a forgery.

[2] It is noticeable that Gabriel Barkay's comments here, which are taken as an endorsement of the authenticity of the inscription, are separated from his more cautious comments, which only appear at the end of the article. There he notes that the fact that the circumstances of the find are not clear is a major problem and that it needs to be investigated carefully. He is reported on the Middle East Information Center site, on April 10, 2003, as saying that "if it is authentic, then we're talking of a major discovery—maybe the most significant ever made in Israeli archaeology." However, the article notes that Barkai also said that "At this point in time, it is simply impossible to say for sure where of [*sic*] not the stone is the genuine item."

[3] A similar, abbreviated report by Ostling appeared on News-Star.com on March 29, 2003.

[4] Said to be by "Bible Network News Staff, with files from Associated Press, *Ha'aretz,* Arutz Sheva IsraelNationalNews.com. Datelined Jerusalem, Israel, January 14, 2003."

[5] Its own description of its activities are:

> The International Christian Embassy Jerusalem was founded in 1980 as an evangelical Christian response to the need to comfort Zion according to the command of scripture found in Isaiah 40:1–2: "Comfort, comfort my people, says your God. Speak tenderly to Jerusalem, and proclaim to her that her hard service has been completed, that her sin has been paid for, that she has received from the Lord's hand double for all her sins."

See the International Christian Embassy's Jerusalem website at www.icej.org/news/specials/special10.html.

[6] See www.templemountfaithful.org/News/20030113.htm.

[7] Ibid.

[8] Ibid.

[9] http://laputan.blogspot.com/2003_03_16_laputan_archive.html.

Space and Holiness in Medieval Jerusalem

[1] J. Wilkinson, *Jerusalem Pilgrims before the Crusades* (Warminster: 1977), 107.

The Hezekiah Narrative as a Foundation Myth for Jerusalem's Rise to Sovereignty

[1] The tribe of Benjamin, placed on the border between the Northern and Southern Kingdoms, plays an ambiguous role in the biblical narratives. In 1 Kings 11:35–36, Yahweh promises Jeroboam ten tribes, while David's son shall be given one tribe, that of Judah. However, paradigmatically, the full number should be twelve, such as expressed in Rehoboam's war with Jeroboam, in which situation, Rehoboam numbers Benjamin together with Judah (1 Kings 12:21). Just above this verse, it is said that only the tribe of Judah was loyal to the House of David (1 Kings 12:20).

[2] It should not go unnoticed that the division of the tribes follows the division and antagonism played out in the return narrative of Ezra 1:5; 2:1; 4:1, 12, 23; 5:1, 5; 6:7–8, 14 and of Neh. 3:34; 4:6 and 13:23.

[3] 1 Kings 15:34; 16:19, 26, 31; 22:53 and 2 Kgs 3:3; 10:29, 31; 13:2, 11; 14:24; 15:9, 18, 24, 28; 17:22; 23:15.

[4] Might even exclude that time, since no Passover is mentioned in the Book of Judges.

[5] It hardly is coincidental that the term "Lord, God of Israel" disappears in the Judaean parts of Kings' narrative after Solomon's reign, not to be taken up again before the Northern Kingdom has been removed from the scene (2 Kings 18:5; 19:15, 20; 21:12; 22:15, 18).

[6] I. W. Provan, *Hezekiah and the Books of Kings: A Contribution to the Debate about the Composition of the Deuteronomistic History* (Berlin: Walter de Gruyter, 1988), 116.

[7] See Isaiah 36:1–39:8 parr. 2 Kings 18:13–20:19. For the sake of rhetorical clarity, we take our departure in Kings' version and not in Isaiah's. Scholars have for centuries discussed the provenance of the narrative.

[8] The Septuagint (=LXX): "Samaria" in 18:11, but "Israel" in the variant account in 17:6. The distinction might be well founded, since only 17:5 (both the LXX and the Masoretic Tradition [= MT] mentions that the Assyrian king went against the whole country.

[9] According to Assyrian inscriptions it was Sargon II (r. 721–705 BCE), who took the city in the first year of his reign (721 BCE), removed its population (27,290 people), rebuilt the city "more splendid than before," repopulated it with people of his conquered lands and placed one of his officials as governor there. Samaria had thus become the capital of the Assyrian province Samarina. See, D. D. Luckenbill, *Ancient Records of Assyria and Babylonia* (Chicago: Chicago Press, 1927; reprint: New York: Greenwood Press, 1968), II: §§ 4. 92. 99. See, however, the discussion of the chronological problems in B. Becking, *The Fall of Samaria: An Historical and Archaeological Study* (Leiden: E.J. Brill, 1992), ch. 3, and of the number of deportees and re-population, chapters 4 and 5.

[10] The parallel story in 2 Chron 32, 1–19 does not mention this act, but rather portrays Hezekiah as a vigorous king who from the time of the threat mobilizes the army and takes measures to counter the siege.

[11] D. D. Luckenbill, *Ancient Records of Assyria and Babylonia*, II: §§ 239–240, 309–312.

[12] Luckenbill, *Ancient Records*, II: § 240.

[13] Luckenbill, I: § 770; N. Na'aman, "The Kingdom of Judah under Josiah," in *Tel Aviv* 18 (1991), 3–71 [3–4]; J. Strange, *Bibelatlas* (København: Det Danske Bibelselskab, 1998), maps 17, 42 and 43.

[14] That 2 Kings here mentions Tirha'kah, who did not become king before at least 699 BC, should not lead to the assumption that the narrative (2 Kgs 18.17–19.37) reflects two campaigns instead of one. A view recently revived by J. Bright, *The History of Israel*, 2nd ed. (London: SCM Press, 1972), 298–308; W. H. Shea, "Sennacherib's Second Palestinian Campaign" in *JBL* 104 (1985),

401–418; reasserted in *idem*, "Jerusalem Under Siege. Did Sennacherib Attack Twice?" in *BAR* 25/6 (1999), 36–44, 64. The theory has been refuted by several scholars because of lack of "evidence" [cf. the discussion in H. H. Rowley, *Men of God: Studies in Old Testament History and Prophecy* (London: Thomas Nelson and Sons, 1963), 120–122; Fr. J. Goncalves, *L'expédition de Sennachérib en Palestine dans la littérature hébraïque ancienne* (Paris: J. Gabalda, 1986), 129–131; B. Becking, "Chronology: A Skeleton Without Flesh? Sennacherib's Campaign as a Case–Study" in forthcoming *ESHM*, 5 (2001)]. Assyrian inscriptions do not give any name to the Egyptian king nor mention the siege of Lachish in the "accounts" of Sennacherib's campaign against Judaea. In 2 Kings these "names" set the stage for the threat against Hezekiah: the fall of mighty Lachish and the *absence* of the Kushite king, who is advancing only (2 Kgs 19.8–9).

[15] Luckenbill, II: § 195.

[16] Ibid., II: § 556.

[17] Ingrid Hjelm, *The Samaritans and Early Judaism: A Literary Analysis*. JSOT Supp. 303, CIS 7. (Sheffield: Sheffield Academic Press, 2000), 193, 227, 254.

[18] Deut. 28:52; Judg. 9:26; 18:7, 10, 27.

[19] Judg. 6:9; 8:34; 1 Sam. 7:3; 10:18; 12:11; 17:37; 2 Sam. 12:7; 22:1; 22:49.

[20] B. S. Childs, *Isaiah and the Assyrian Crisis*. SBT, 2/3. (London: SCM Press, 1967), 84–85.

[21] 2 Kings 18:5, 19, 20, 21, 22, 24, 30; 19:10.

[22] 2 Kings 18:29, 30. 32, 33, 34, 35; 19. 11, 12; 20:6.

[23] 1 Kings 5:5, 2 Kings 17:39; 1 Chron 5:20; 11:14; 16:35; 25:15

[24] R. E. Friedman, "From Egypt to Egypt: Dtr 1 and Dtr 2," in B. Halpern and J. D. Levenson, eds., *Traditions in Transformation: Turning Points in Biblical Faith* (Winona Lake, Indiana: Eisenbrauns, 1981), 167–192.

[25] Israel's king Basha's rebuilding of Ramah in the Asa narrative is in order to prevent people from going to Asa of Judah and does not explicitly mention Jerusalem.

[26] The verses are missing in Isa. 36:1–2.

[27] Fr. Goncalves, "2 Rois 18.13–20.19 par. Isaïe 36–39: Encore une fois, lequel des deux livres fut le premier?" in J. M. Auwers and A. Wénin, eds., *Lectures et relectures de la Bible*. Festschrift P.-M. Bogaert; BETL, 144 (Leuven: Leuven University Press, 1999) 27–55 [31]: "En rapportant la conquête de toutes les villes de Juda, ce verset souligne la gravité de la situation supposée par 2 R 18.17–19.37 par. Is 36.2–37.38 et, du fait même, met en lumiére la grandeur de la confiance d'Ézéchias en Yahvé." The possibility of reading 2 Kings 18:13a, 14–16 together with 2 Kings 20; 2 Chronicles 32 and Isaiah 22 and based on the Azekah inscription as an account reflecting Sargon II's retributive action against Hezekiah's conquests of Philistine areas before 712 BCE might be historically justified. Cf. J. Goldberg, "Two Assyrian Campaigns against Hezekiah and Later Eight Century Biblical Chronology," in *Biblica*, 80: 3 [1999], 360–390. Reading 2 Kings 18:14–16 as reflecting Sennacherib's Campaign in 701 BCE and 2 Kings 18:17–19:37 as reflecting Sargon II's *possible* campaign against Judah (and Jerusalem) in 715 BCE (not to be confused with his campaign against Asdod in 712 BCE), as B. Becking, "Chronology: A Skeleton Without Flesh?," 2001, has recently argued, partly following A. K. Jenkins, "Hezekiah's Fourteenth Year," in *VT* 26 (1976), 296, is equally possible, although both proposals raise considerable problems. The author of 2 Kings' Hezekiah narrative, however, had no intention of rhetorically separating events and thereby diminish the treath faced by Hezekiah, a matter Bob Becking is well aware of. The repetitive "and he sent" (2 Kings 18:14 and 17) together with a repetition of "the king of Assur" (vv. 16 and 17) indicates the continuity of the paragraphs.

[28] K. A. D. Smelik, "Distortion of Old Testament Prophecy: The Purpose of Isaiah 36 and 37" in *OTS*, 24 (1986), 70–93 [86]: "Rabshakeh is a literary figure who plays the opposite to Isaiah and has to speak in a similar way." E. Ben Zvi, "Who Wrote the Speech of Rabshakeh and When?" in *JBL*, 109 (1990), 79–92; Burke O. Long, *2 Kings*, The Forms of Old Testament Literature, 10 (Grand Rapids, MI: Wm. B. Eerdmans, 1991), 219–220, following the argument of Childs, *Isaiah and the Assyrian Crisis*, 84–85, but without accepting Child's argument for historical veracity based on comparative studies and redaction criticism: "At best we may assert

that the biblical writer's presentation of the Rabshakeh's disputation accords with literary convention found in other types of contemporary historiography (e.g., royal inscriptions) and historical materials (e.g., letters). The scene may or may not have been fictionalized in ways familiar to us from a few Greek and Roman historians, who invented credible speeches for their literary personages see, James A. Montgomery, *A Critical and Exegetical Commentary On the Books of Kings* (Edinburg: Edinburg University Press, 1951), 487. See also, G. H. Jones, *1 and 2 Kings,* 2 vols. (Grand Rapids, MI Wm. B. Eerdmans, 1984) 2: 570; D. Rudman, "Is Rabshakeh also Among the Prophets? A Rhetorical Study of 2 Kings XVIII 17–35" in *VTQ,* 50: 1 (2000), 100–110.

[29] Kaleb's admonition to the people not to rebel against Yahweh, further confirms the relationship between these narratives, as the word's rare occurrences in Kings are found in Hezekiah's rebellion against Assyria (2 Kings 18:7, 20) and in Jehoiakim's and Zedekiah's rebellion against the Babylonians (2 Kings 24:1, 20). While only Hezekiah's rebellion is judged positively, Israel's rebellion against Yahweh and Judah's rebellion against the Babylonians is doomed to fail. In this light the author's judgement of Hezekiah's cooperation with the Babylonians (2 Kings 20:12–19) seems ambiguous.

[30] Num 14:1–12, 21–24, 28–30; 16:12–15; 26.64; Deut 1:26.

[31] Num. 14:24, 30; 26:65; Deut. 1:36; Josh.14:6–14.

[32] The Hebrew term is found only here in the Books of Kings; it belongs to Psalms and Prophets.

[33] Same Hebrew term as in 2 Kings 19:3.

[34] The thematic reiteration of Moses' plea for mercy and God's steadfast anger in the Pentateuch (Exod. 32:30–34; Num. 14:11–45; Deut. 28–30) forms a contrast to Solomon's confidence in Yahweh's mercy, "since there is no man who does not sin" (1 Kings 8:31–40, [46]–51).

[35] Attin Laato, *About Zion I Will Not Be Silent: The Book of Isaiah as an Ideological Unity.* CB OTS, 44 (Stockholm: Almquist & Wiksell Int., 1998).

I Lived in Jerusalem (Ghosheh)

[1] Ogre.

[2] The *kuttab* is a traditional elementary school where the Qur'an is taught with a simple introduction to writing and Arabic. It used to be found all over the Arab world but has been now replaced by regular schooling.

[3] Palestinian students who succeeded in the Palestinian matriculation at the end of their secondary education were admitted to the sophomore instead of the freshman class at the American University of Beirut and other American colleges.

[4] Crushed wheat.

Jerusalem in 1923: The Impressions of a Young European

[1] These are excerpts from Muhammad Asad's (then Leopold Weiss) *Unromantisches Morgenland* (Frankfurt: Societäts-Druckerei, 1924); which has recently been published in translation, also by Elma Ruth Harder, as *The Unromantic Orient* (Al-Qalam Publishing, 2004). For more details about Muhammad Asad's life and thought see *Islamic Studies,* 39.2 (Summer 2000). It features two extensive articles: "A Matter of Love: Muhammad Asad and Islam" by Isma'il Ibrahim Nawwab and "Muhammad Asad: Europe's Gift to Islam" by Murad Hofmann. ed.

[2] Muhammad Asad, *The Road to Mecca* (London: Max Reinhardt, 1954), 74.

[3] Ibid.

[4] Ibid., 81–82.

[5] Ibid., 84–5.

[6] Ibid., 93.

[7] Ibid., 100.

Diaspora: Step by Step

[1] Falafel is a savory cake made of chickpeas and condiments and then fried.

[2] Bab al-'Amoud is Damascus Gate, one of the seven main gates of the Old City.

Islamic Architechtural Character of Jerusalem: With Special Description of Al-Aqsa and the Dome of the Rock

[1] Muhammad ibn Isma'il Bukhari, *Sahih al-Bukhari,* Kitab al-Hajj, Bab Hajj al-Nisa'.

Jerusalem and I: A Personal Record

[1] The author remembers as a little girl the Nabi Musa feast or Mawsim al-Nabi Musa, as it was referred to in Arabic.

[2] That is, Jerusalem. Ed.

My City Denied to Me

[1] *Hummus* is an Arab dish now become internationally acclaimed. It is made of chickpeas paste with *tahinah* (from sesame oil), and mixed with lemon juice, some crushed garlic, and salt.

[2] Um Kulthum: she is the renowned Egyptian singer, the foremost woman singer of the 20th-century Arab world, and one of the two greatest of any period.

WITHDRAWN